SEVEN SEAS ENTERTAINMENT PRESENTS

Masamune-k
REVENG

story by **HAZUKI TAKEOKA** ▼ art by

D1435527

TRANSLATION
Andrew Cunningham

ADAPTATION
Bambi Eloriaga-Amago

LETTERING AND LAYOUT
Jennifer Skarupa

LOGO DESIGN
Karis Page

COVER DESIGN
KC Fabellon

PROOFREADER
Stephanie Cohen
Shanti Whitesides

EDITOR
Shannon Fay

PRODUCTION ASSISTANT
CK Russell

PRODUCTION MANAGER
Lissa Pattillo

EDITOR-IN-CHIEF
Adam Arnold

PUBLISHER
Jason DeAngelis

MASAMUNE-KUN'S REVENGE VOL. 9
©HAZUKI TAKEOKA · TIV 2018
First published in Japan in 2018 by ICHIJINSHA Inc., Tokyo.
English translation rights arranged with ICHIJINSHA Inc., Tokyo.

No portion of this book may be reproduced or transmitted in any form without
written permission from the copyright holders. This is a work of fiction. Names,
characters, places, and incidents are the products of the author's imagination
or are used fictitiously. Any resemblance to actual events, locales, or persons,
living or dead, is entirely coincidental.

Seven Seas books may be purchased in bulk for promotional, educational, or
business use. Please contact your local bookseller or the Macmillan Corporate
and Premium Sales Department at 1-800-221-7945, extension 5442, or by
e-mail at MacmillanSpecialMarkets@macmillan.com.

Seven Seas and the Seven Seas logo are trademarks of
Seven Seas Entertainment, LLC. All rights reserved.

ISBN: 978-1-626929-44-9

Printed in Canada

First Printing: March 2019

10 9 8 7 6 5 4 3 2 1

LLOW US ONLINE: *www.sevenseasentertainment.com*

READING DIRECTIONS

This book reads from *right to left*, Japanese style.
If this is your first time reading manga, you start
reading from the top right panel on each page and
take it from there. If you get lost, just follow the
numbered diagram here. It may seem backwards at
first, but you'll get the hang of it! Have fun!!

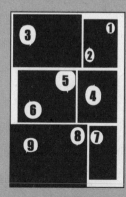

9

Masamune-kun's REVENGE

Presented by Hazuki Takeoka & TIV

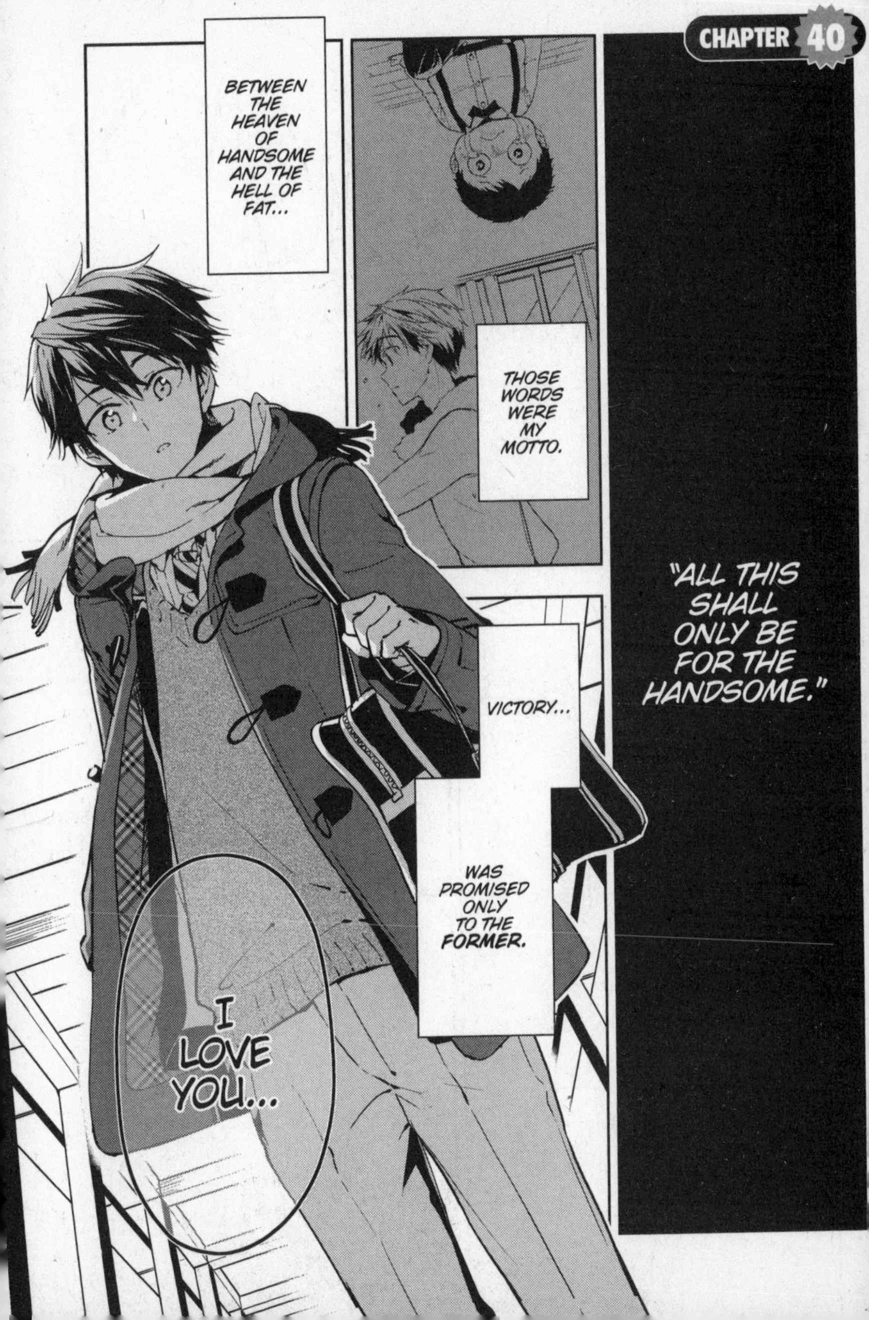
CHAPTER 40
"ALL THIS SHALL ONLY BE FOR THE HANDSOME."
BETWEEN THE HEAVEN OF HANDSOME AND THE HELL OF FAT...
THOSE WORDS WERE MY MOTTO.
VICTORY...
WAS PROMISED ONLY TO THE FORMER.
I LOVE YOU...

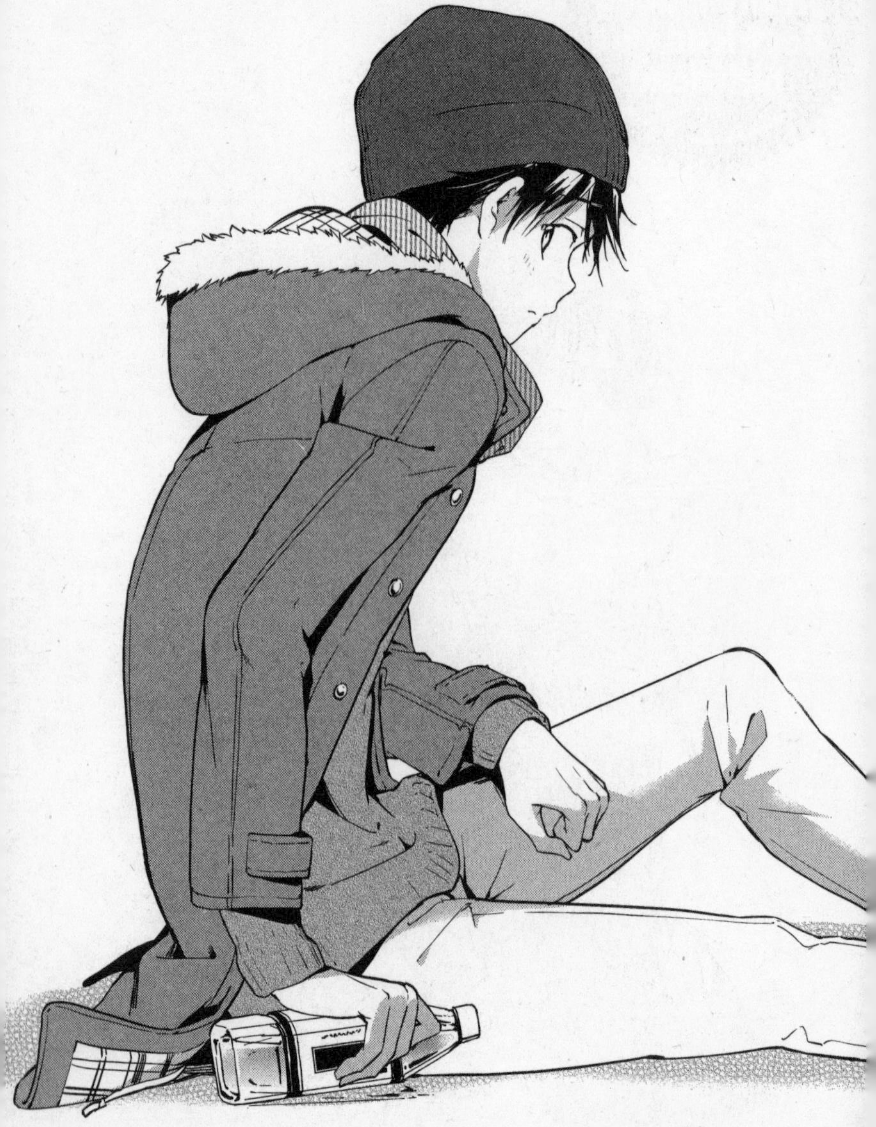

CHAPTER 40
Newly Minted Boyfriend and Girlfriend

Masamune-kun's Revenge

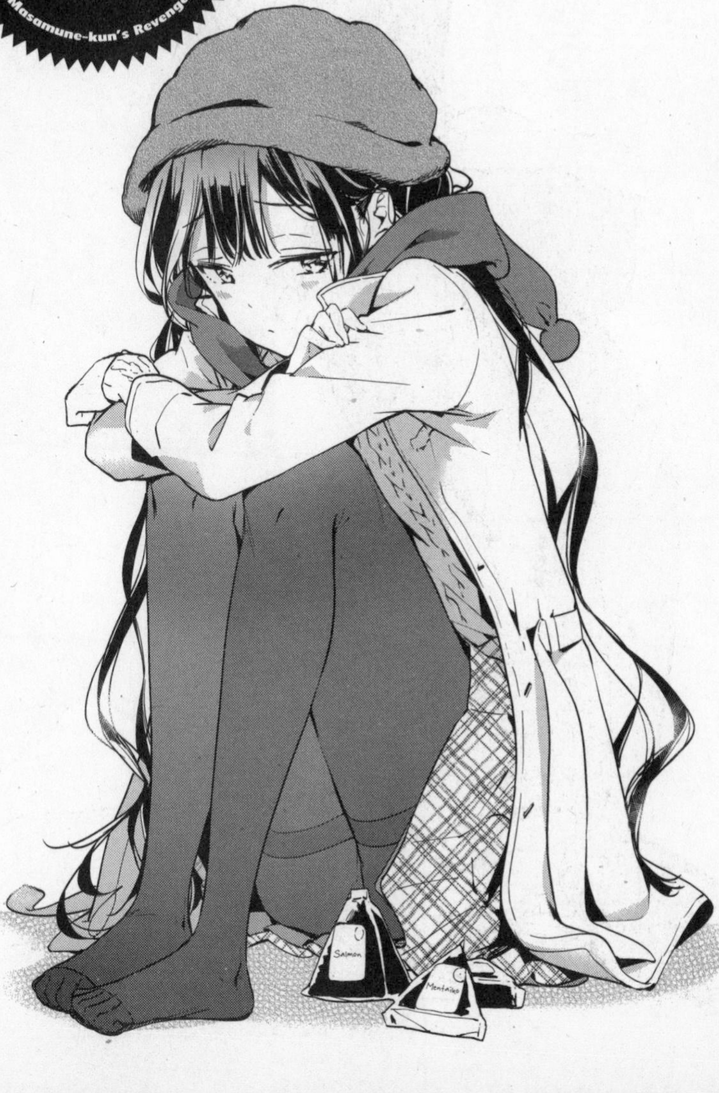

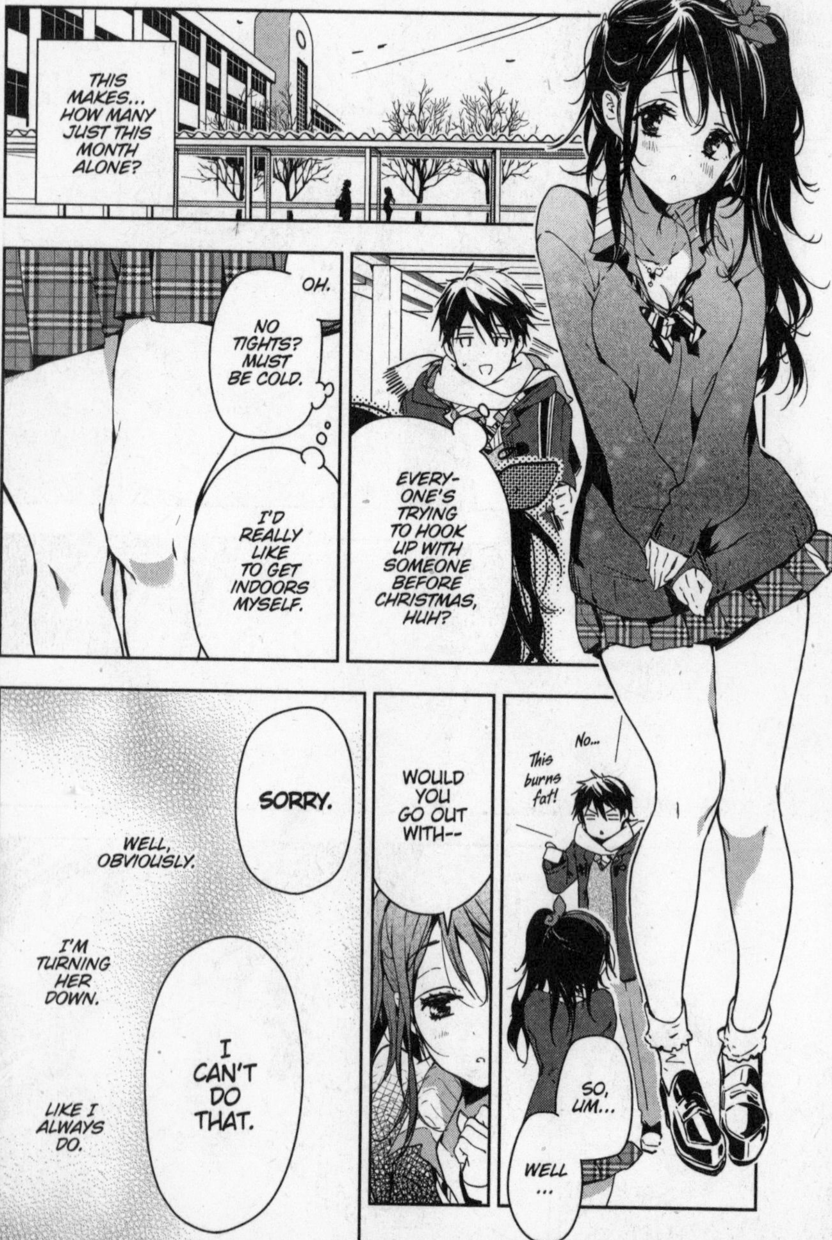
THIS MAKES... HOW MANY JUST THIS MONTH ALONE?
EVERY-ONE'S TRYING TO HOOK UP WITH SOMEONE BEFORE CHRISTMAS, HUH?
OH.
NO TIGHTS? MUST BE COLD.
I'D REALLY LIKE TO GET INDOORS MYSELF.
No...
This burns fat!
SO, UM...
WELL...
WOULD YOU GO OUT WITH--
SORRY.
I CAN'T DO THAT.
WELL, OBVIOUSLY.
I'M TURNING HER DOWN.
LIKE I ALWAYS DO.

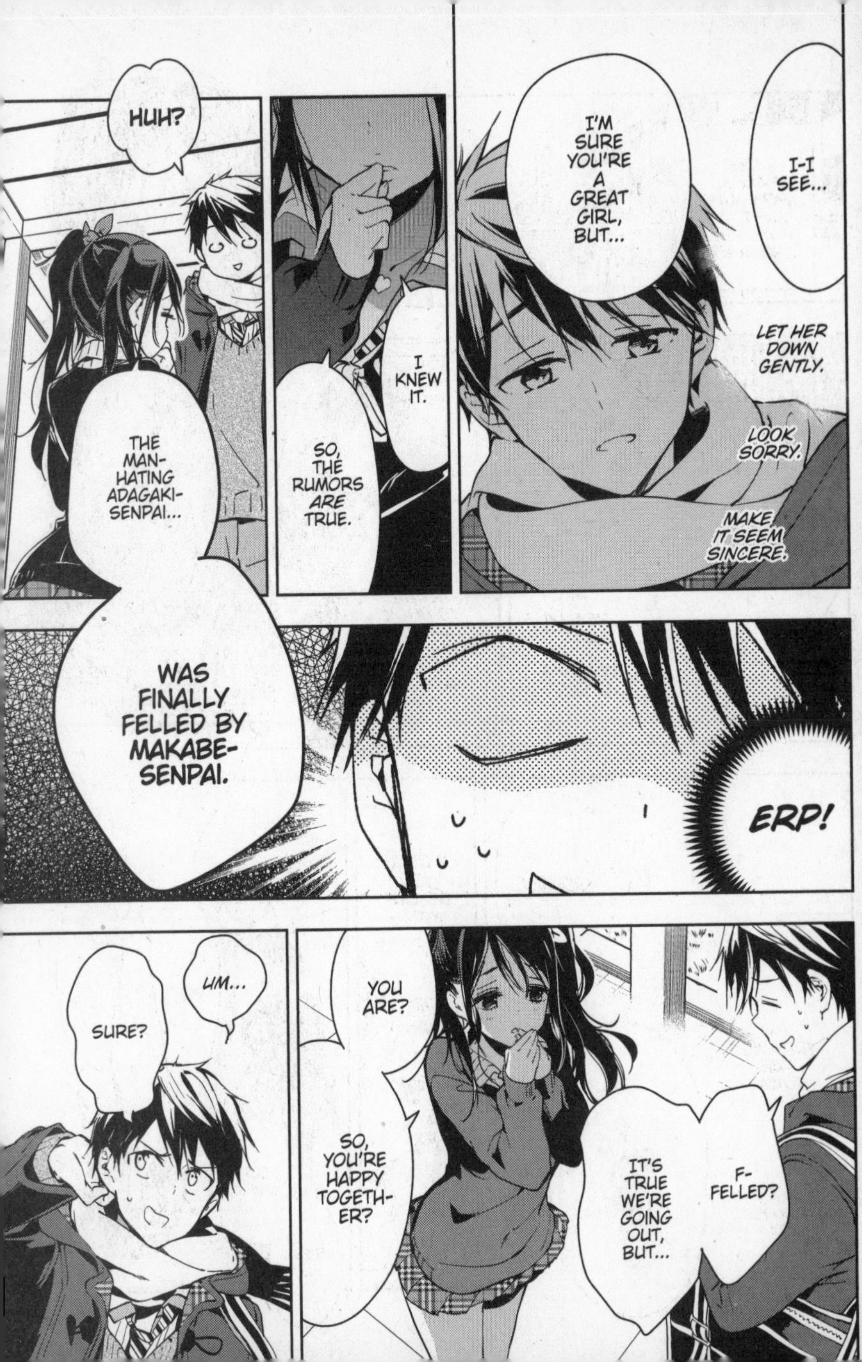
I-I SEE...
I'M SURE YOU'RE A GREAT GIRL, BUT...
LET HER DOWN GENTLY.
LOOK SORRY.
MAKE IT SEEM SINCERE.
I KNEW IT.
SO, THE RUMORS ARE TRUE.
HUH?
THE MAN-HATING ADAGAKI-SENPAI...
WAS FINALLY FELLED BY MAKABE-SENPAI.
ERP!
F-FELLED?
IT'S TRUE WE'RE GOING OUT, BUT...
YOU ARE?
SO, YOU'RE HAPPY TOGETHER?
UM...
SURE?

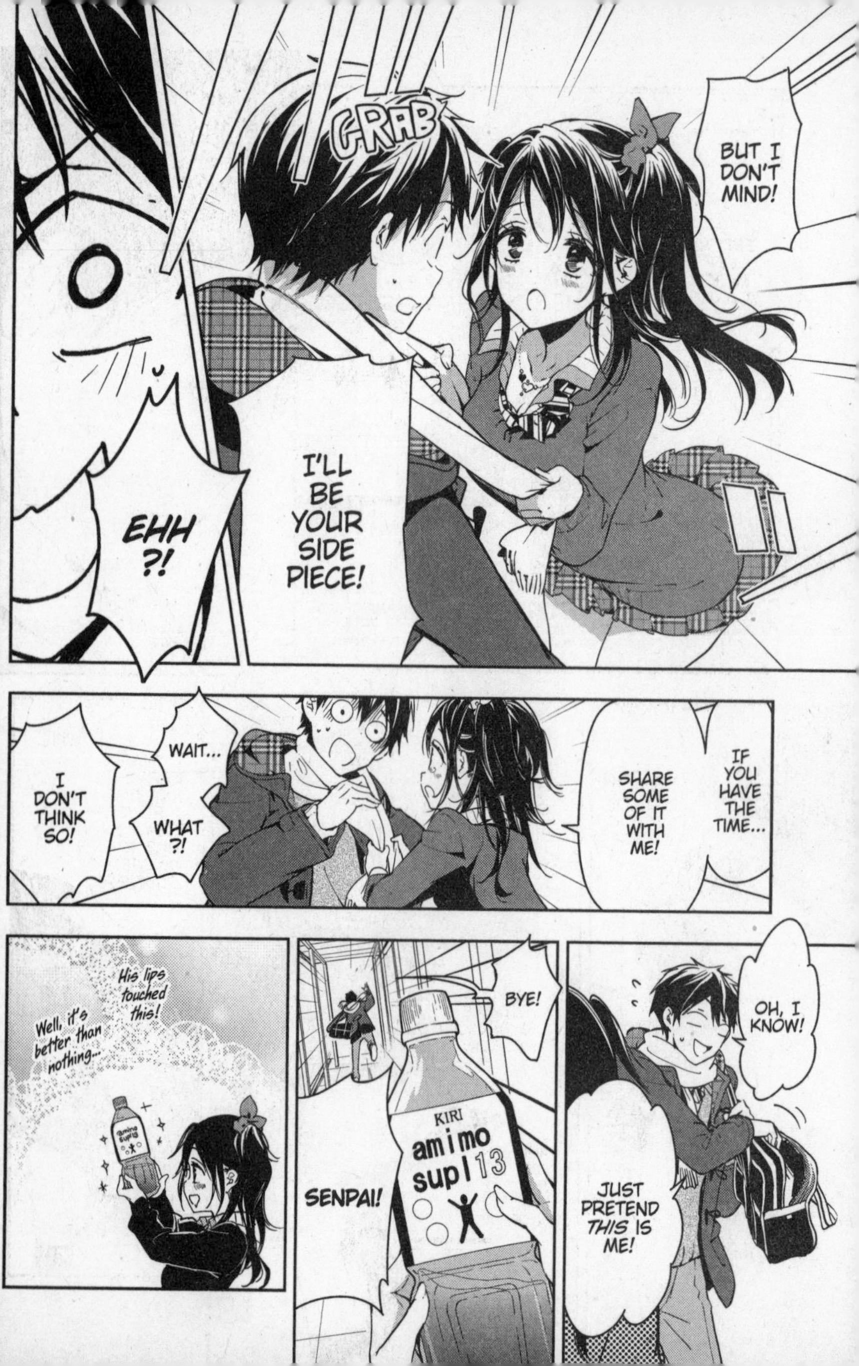
GRAB
BUT I DON'T MIND!
I'LL BE YOUR SIDE PIECE!
EHH ?!
IF YOU HAVE THE TIME...
SHARE SOME OF IT WITH ME!
WAIT...
WHAT ?!
I DON'T THINK SO!
OH, I KNOW!
JUST PRETEND THIS IS ME!
BYE!
SENPAI!
KIRI
am i mo sup l 13
His lips touched this!
Well, it's better than nothing...

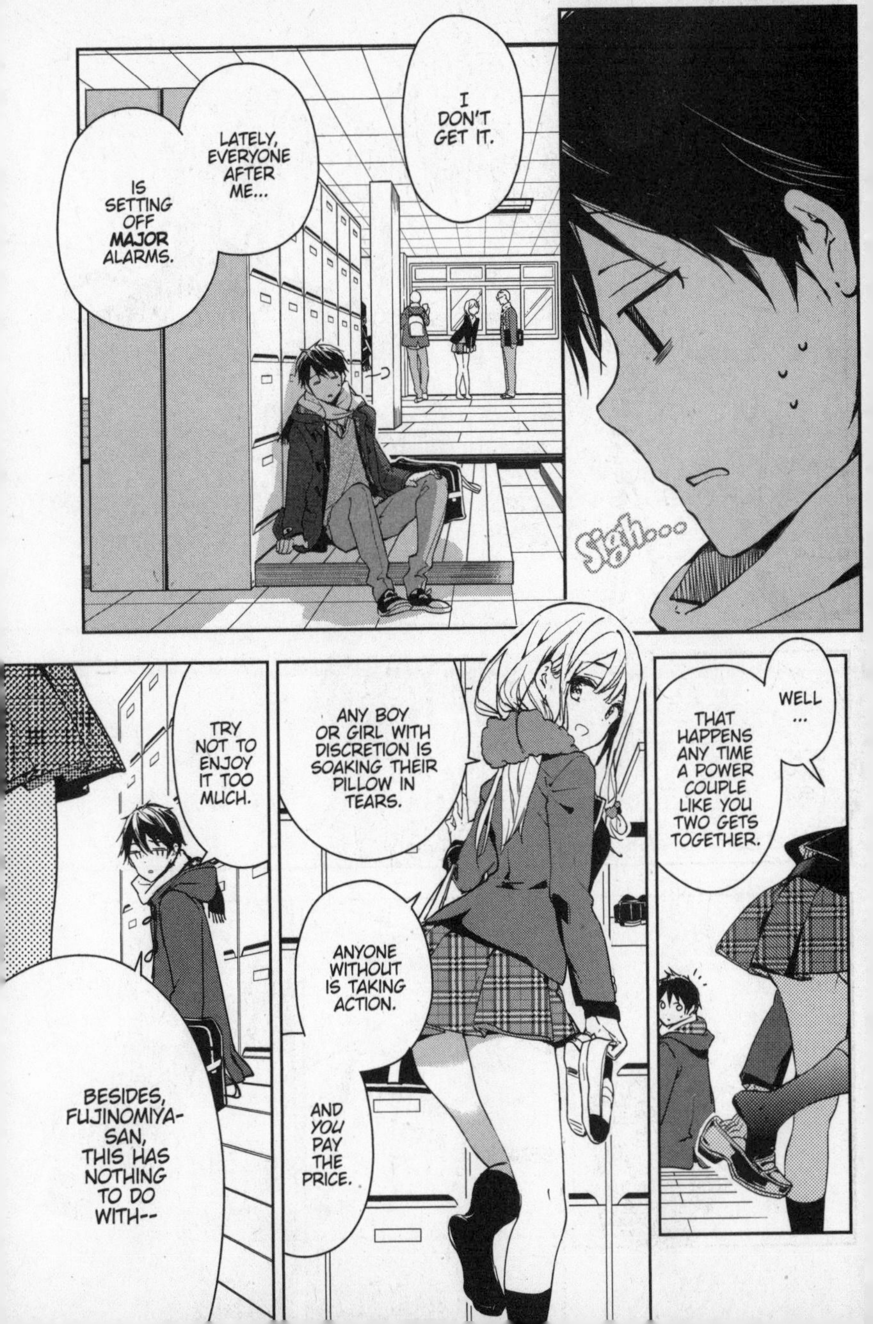
Sigh...
I DON'T GET IT.
LATELY, EVERYONE AFTER ME...
IS SETTING OFF **MAJOR** ALARMS.
WELL...
THAT HAPPENS ANY TIME A POWER COUPLE LIKE YOU TWO GETS TOGETHER.
ANY BOY OR GIRL WITH DISCRETION IS SOAKING THEIR PILLOW IN TEARS.
ANYONE WITHOUT IS TAKING ACTION.
AND *YOU* PAY THE PRICE.
TRY NOT TO ENJOY IT TOO MUCH.
BESIDES, FUJINOMIYA-SAN, THIS HAS NOTHING TO DO WITH--

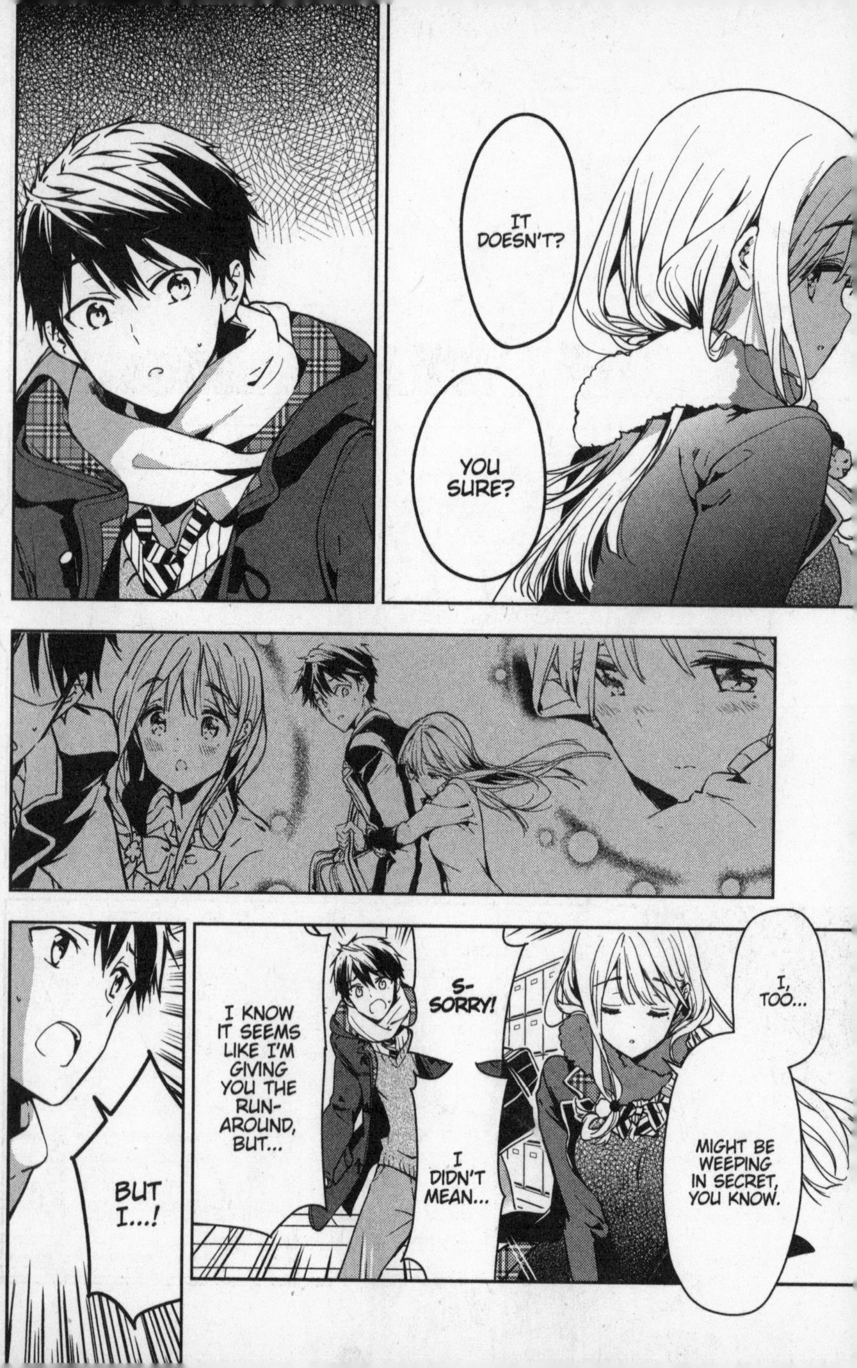
IT DOESN'T?
YOU SURE?
I, TOO...
MIGHT BE WEEPING IN SECRET, YOU KNOW.
S-SORRY!
I DIDN'T MEAN...
I KNOW IT SEEMS LIKE I'M GIVING YOU THE RUN-AROUND, BUT...
BUT I...!

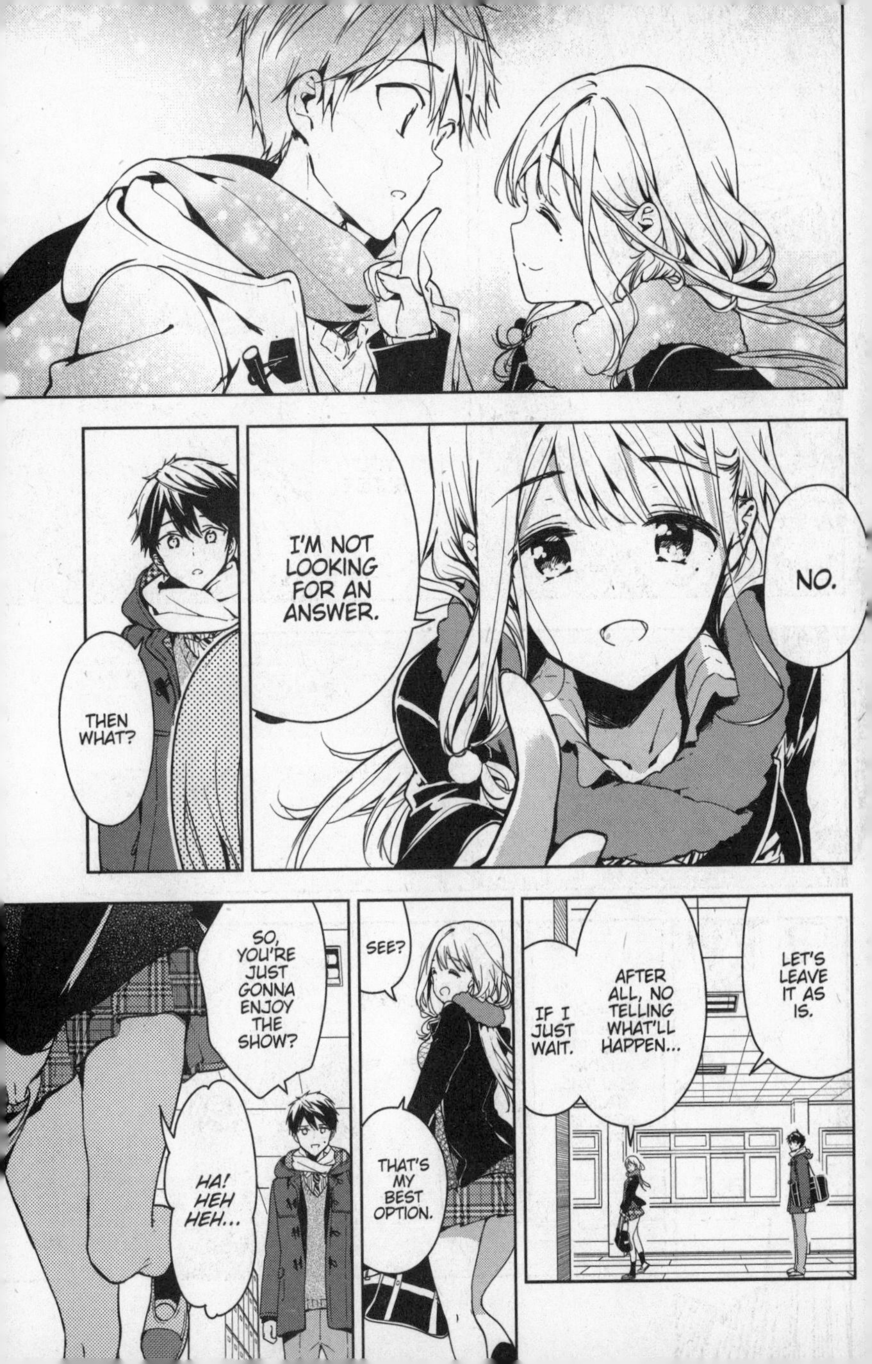
NO.
I'M NOT LOOKING FOR AN ANSWER.
THEN WHAT?
LET'S LEAVE IT AS IS.
AFTER ALL, NO TELLING WHAT'LL HAPPEN...
IF I JUST WAIT.
SEE?
THAT'S MY BEST OPTION.
SO, YOU'RE JUST GONNA ENJOY THE SHOW?
HA! HEH HEH...

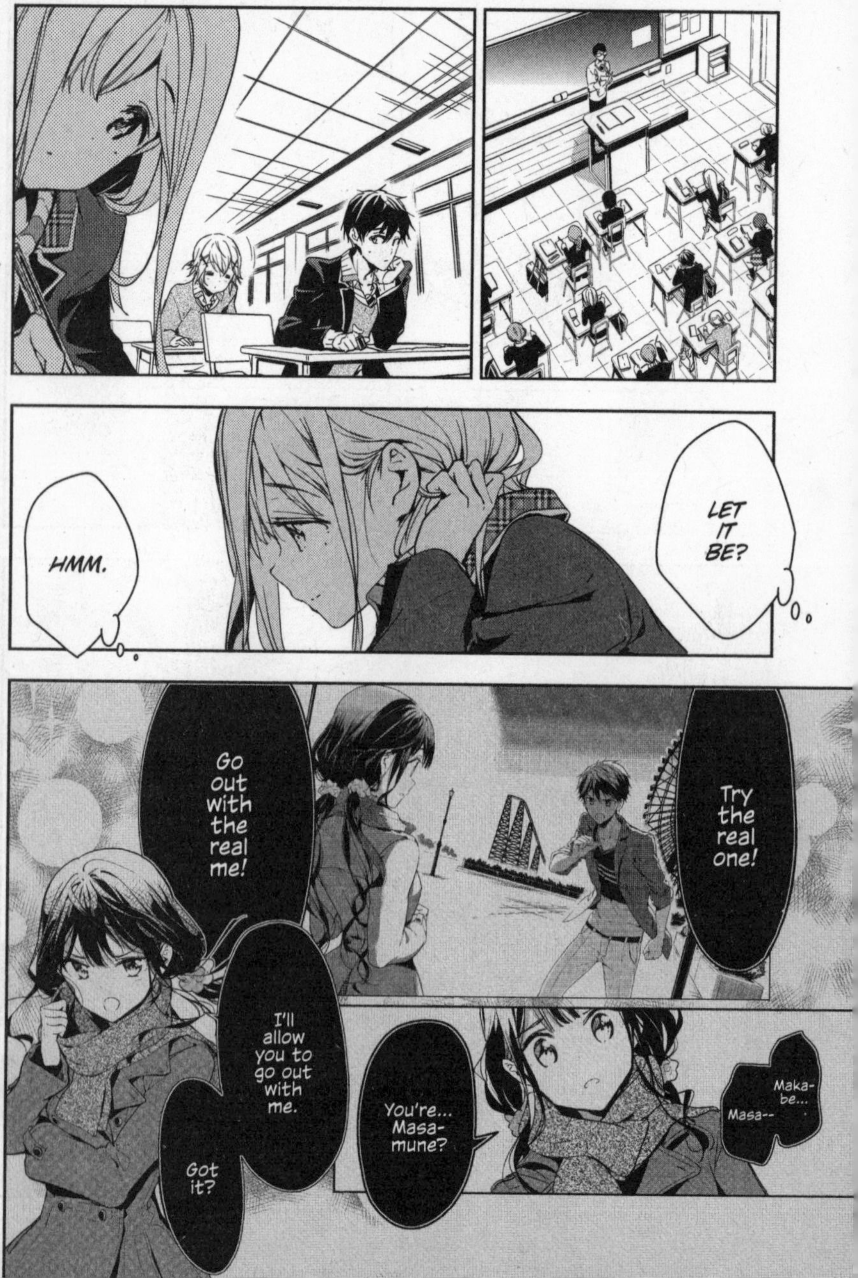
LET IT BE?
HMM.
Try the real one!
Go out with the real me!
Maka-be... Masa--
You're... Masa-mune?
I'll allow you to go out with me.
Got it?

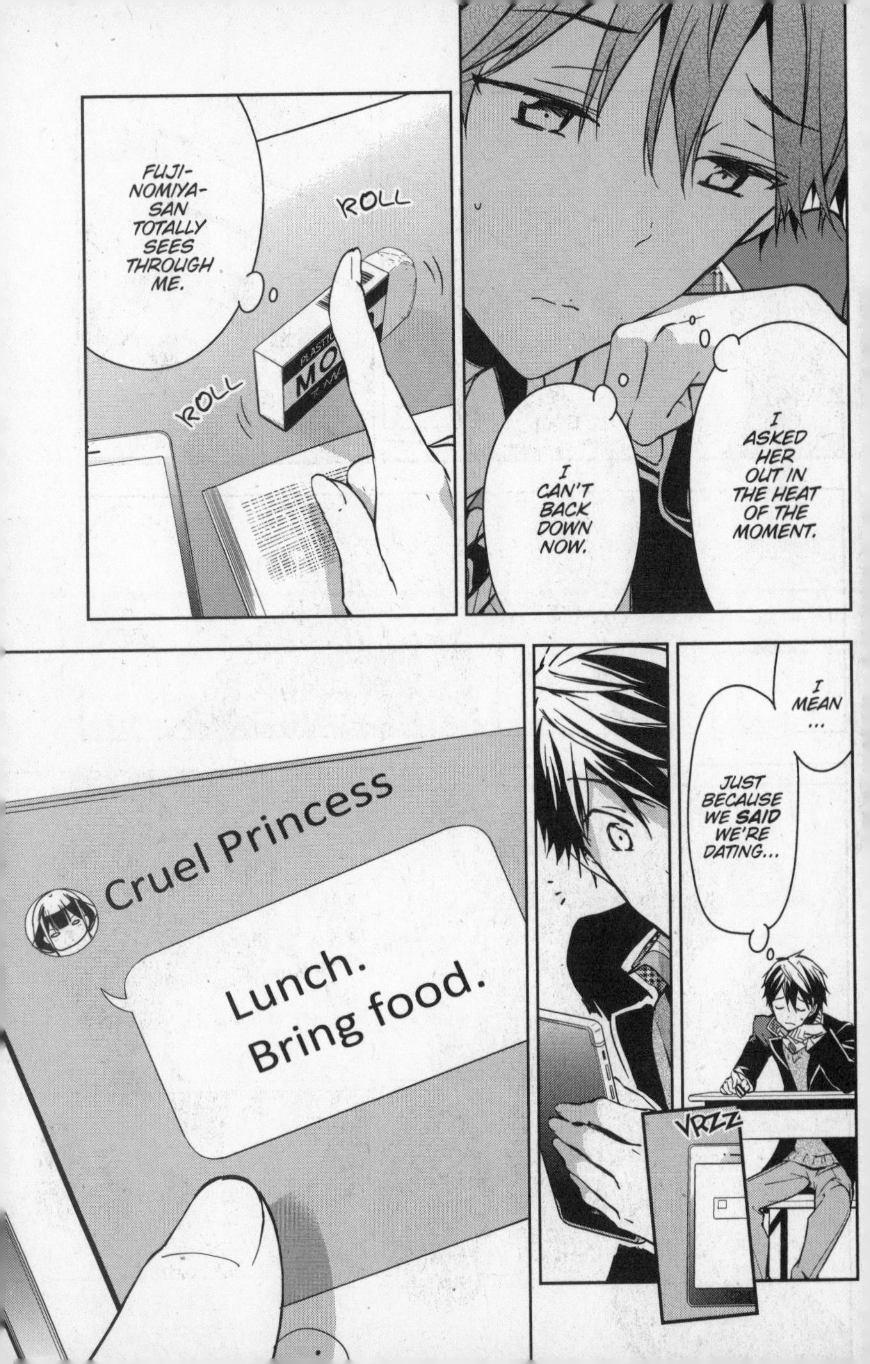
I ASKED HER OUT IN THE HEAT OF THE MOMENT.
I CAN'T BACK DOWN NOW.
FUJI-NOMIYA-SAN TOTALLY SEES THROUGH ME.
ROLL
ROLL
I MEAN ...
JUST BECAUSE WE SAID WE'RE DATING...
VRZZ
Cruel Princess
Lunch. Bring food.

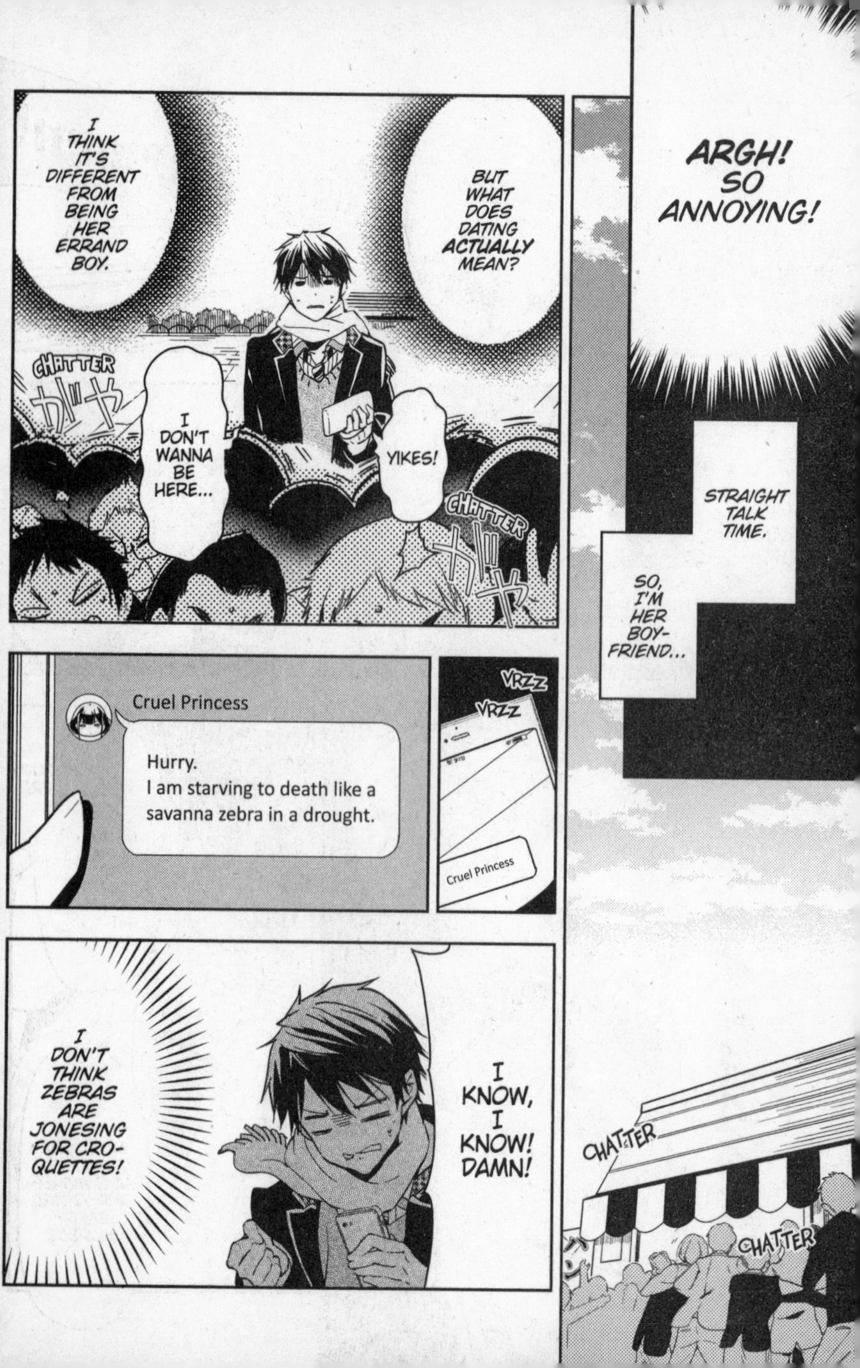
ARGH! SO ANNOYING!
STRAIGHT TALK TIME.
SO, I'M HER BOYFRIEND...
CHATTER
CHATTER
BUT WHAT DOES DATING ACTUALLY MEAN?
I THINK IT'S DIFFERENT FROM BEING HER ERRAND BOY.
YIKES!
CHATTER
I DON'T WANNA BE HERE...
CHATTER
VRZZ
VRZZ
Cruel Princess
Cruel Princess
Hurry.
I am starving to death like a savanna zebra in a drought.
I KNOW, I KNOW! DAMN!
I DON'T THINK ZEBRAS ARE JONESING FOR CRO-QUETTES!

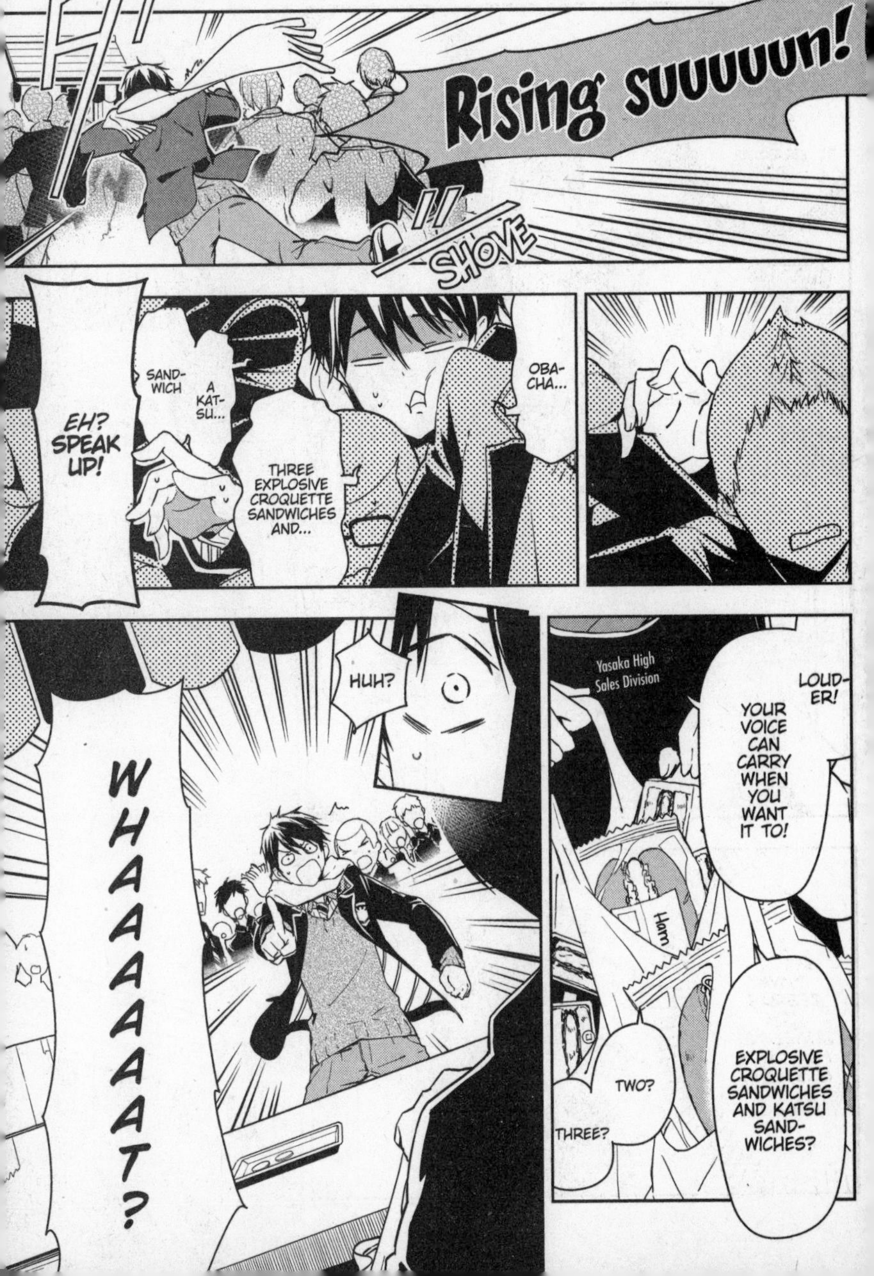
Rising suuuuuun!
SHOVE
OBA-CHA...
THREE EXPLOSIVE CROQUETTE SANDWICHES AND...
A KAT-SU... SAND-WICH
EH? SPEAK UP!
Yasaka High Sales Division
LOUD-ER!
YOUR VOICE CAN CARRY WHEN YOU WANT IT TO!
EXPLOSIVE CROQUETTE SANDWICHES AND KATSU SAND-WICHES?
TWO?
THREE?
Ham
HUH?
WHAAAAAAAT?

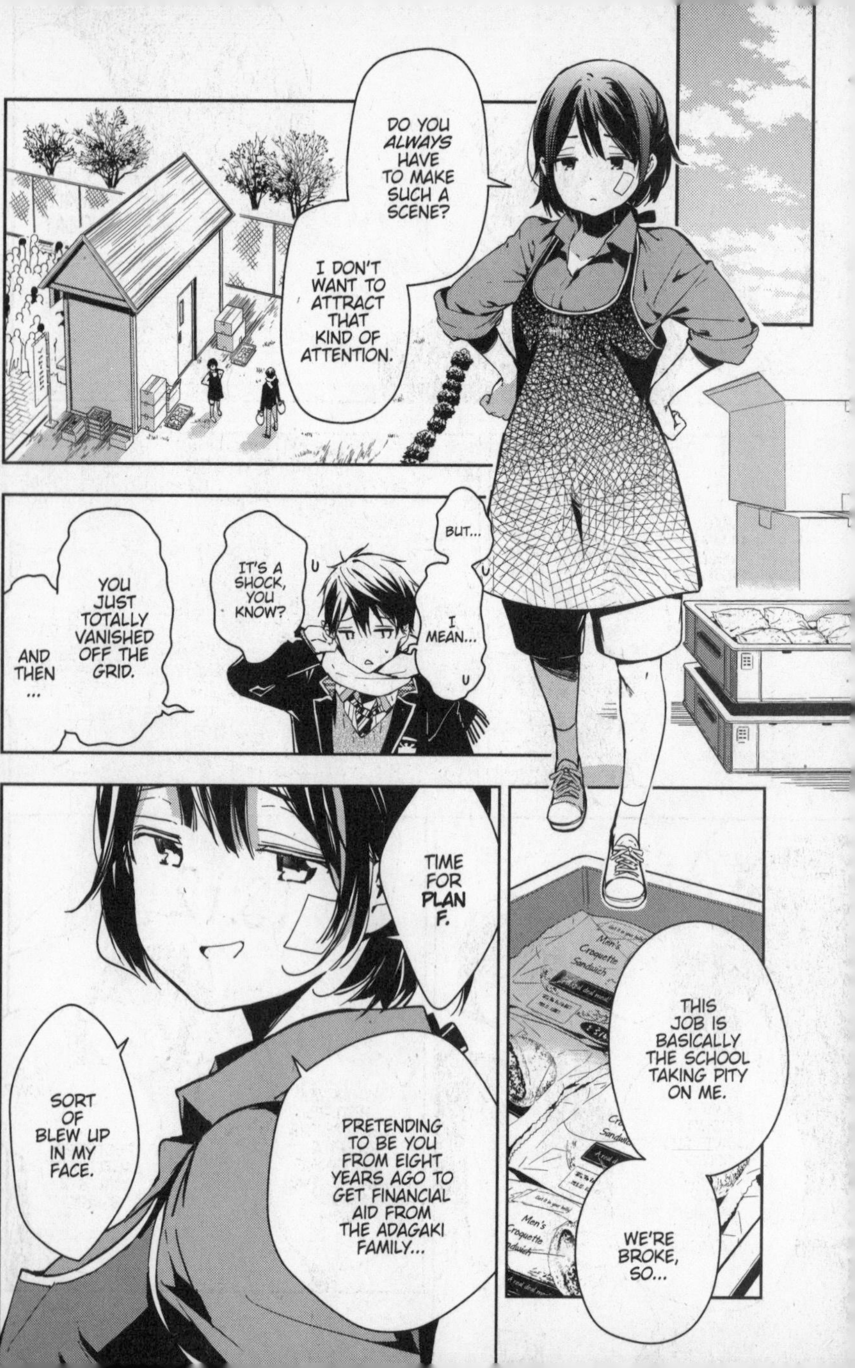
DO YOU *ALWAYS* HAVE TO MAKE SUCH A SCENE?
I DON'T WANT TO ATTRACT THAT KIND OF ATTENTION.
BUT...
I MEAN...
IT'S A SHOCK, YOU KNOW?
YOU JUST TOTALLY VANISHED OFF THE GRID.
AND THEN ...
THIS JOB IS BASICALLY THE SCHOOL TAKING PITY ON ME.
Men's Croquette Sandwich
WE'RE BROKE, SO...
TIME FOR **PLAN F.**
PRETENDING TO BE YOU FROM EIGHT YEARS AGO TO GET FINANCIAL AID FROM THE ADAGAKI FAMILY...
SORT OF BLEW UP IN MY FACE.

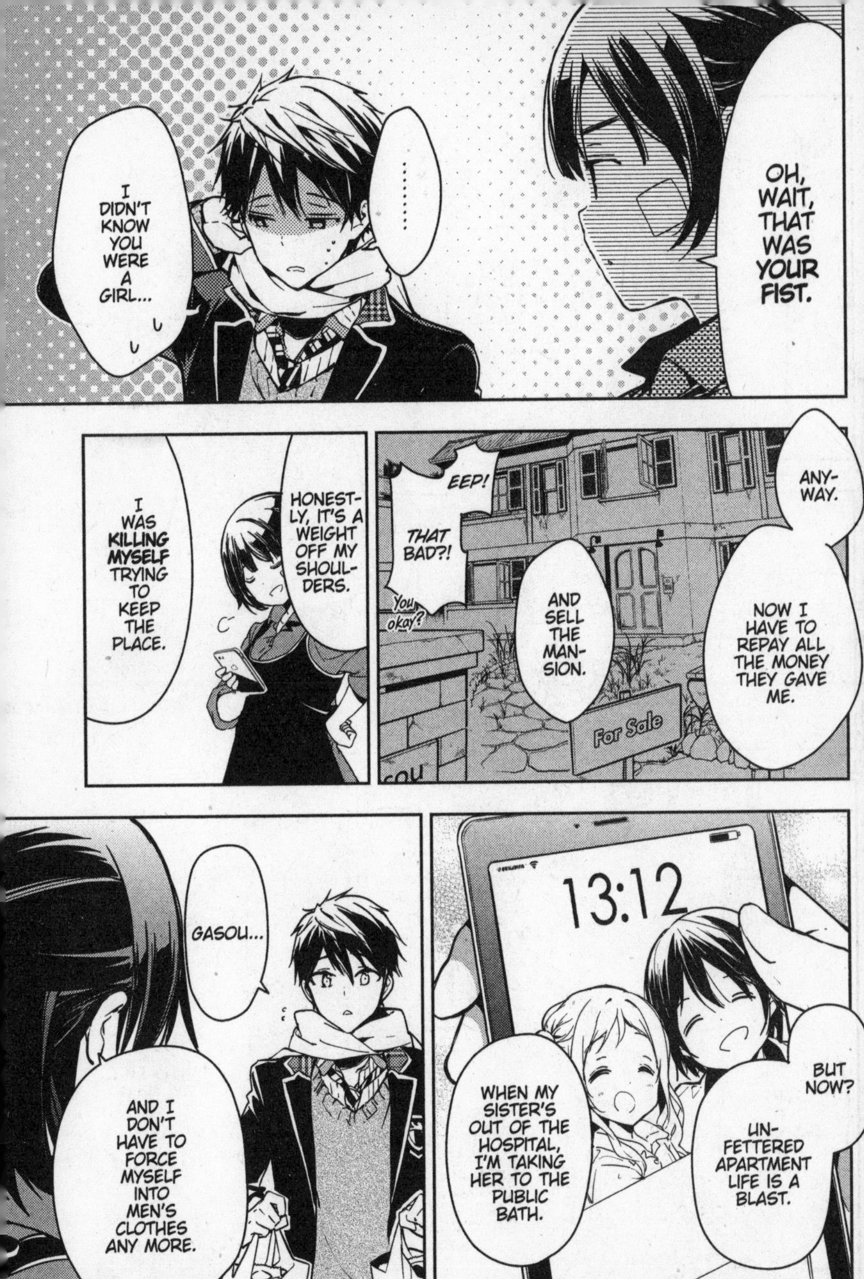
OH, WAIT, THAT WAS YOUR FIST.
......
I DIDN'T KNOW YOU WERE A GIRL...
ANYWAY.
NOW I HAVE TO REPAY ALL THE MONEY THEY GAVE ME.
AND SELL THE MANSION.
EEP!
THAT BAD?!
You okay?
For Sale
HONESTLY, IT'S A WEIGHT OFF MY SHOULDERS.
I WAS KILLING MYSELF TRYING TO KEEP THE PLACE.
13:12
BUT NOW?
UNFETTERED APARTMENT LIFE IS A BLAST.
WHEN MY SISTER'S OUT OF THE HOSPITAL, I'M TAKING HER TO THE PUBLIC BATH.
GASOU...
AND I DON'T HAVE TO FORCE MYSELF INTO MEN'S CLOTHES ANY MORE.

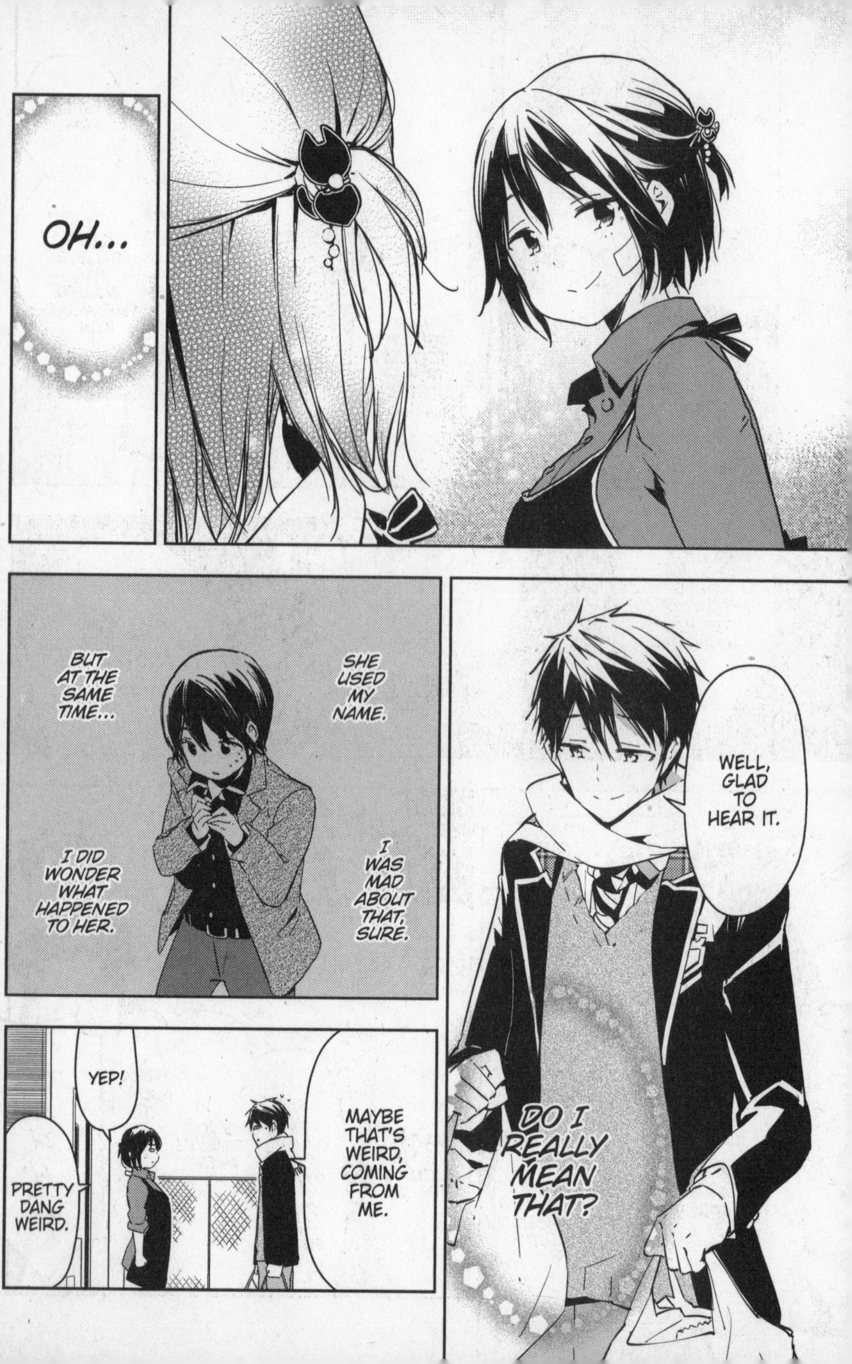
OH...
WELL, GLAD TO HEAR IT.
DO I REALLY MEAN THAT?
SHE USED MY NAME.
I WAS MAD ABOUT THAT, SURE.
BUT AT THE SAME TIME...
I DID WONDER WHAT HAPPENED TO HER.
MAYBE THAT'S WEIRD, COMING FROM ME.
YEP!
PRETTY DANG WEIRD.

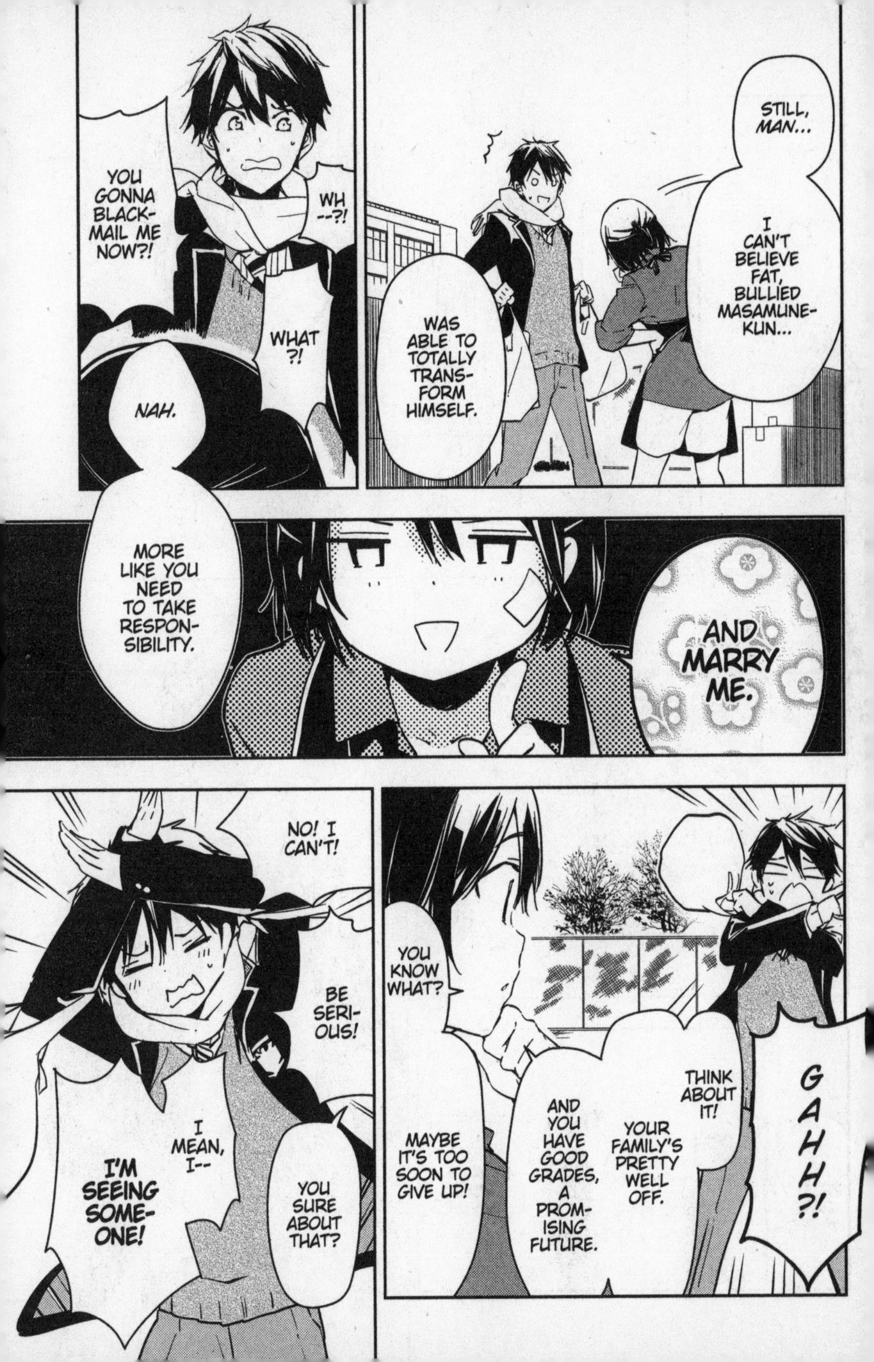
STILL, MAN...
I CAN'T BELIEVE FAT, BULLIED MASAMUNE-KUN...
WAS ABLE TO TOTALLY TRANSFORM HIMSELF.
WH--?!
YOU GONNA BLACKMAIL ME NOW?!
WHAT?!
NAH.
MORE LIKE YOU NEED TO TAKE RESPONSIBILITY.
AND MARRY ME.
GAHH?!
THINK ABOUT IT!
YOU KNOW WHAT?
YOUR FAMILY'S PRETTY WELL OFF.
AND YOU HAVE GOOD GRADES, A PROMISING FUTURE.
MAYBE IT'S TOO SOON TO GIVE UP!
NO! I CAN'T!
BE SERIOUS!
I MEAN, I--
YOU SURE ABOUT THAT?
I'M SEEING SOMEONE!

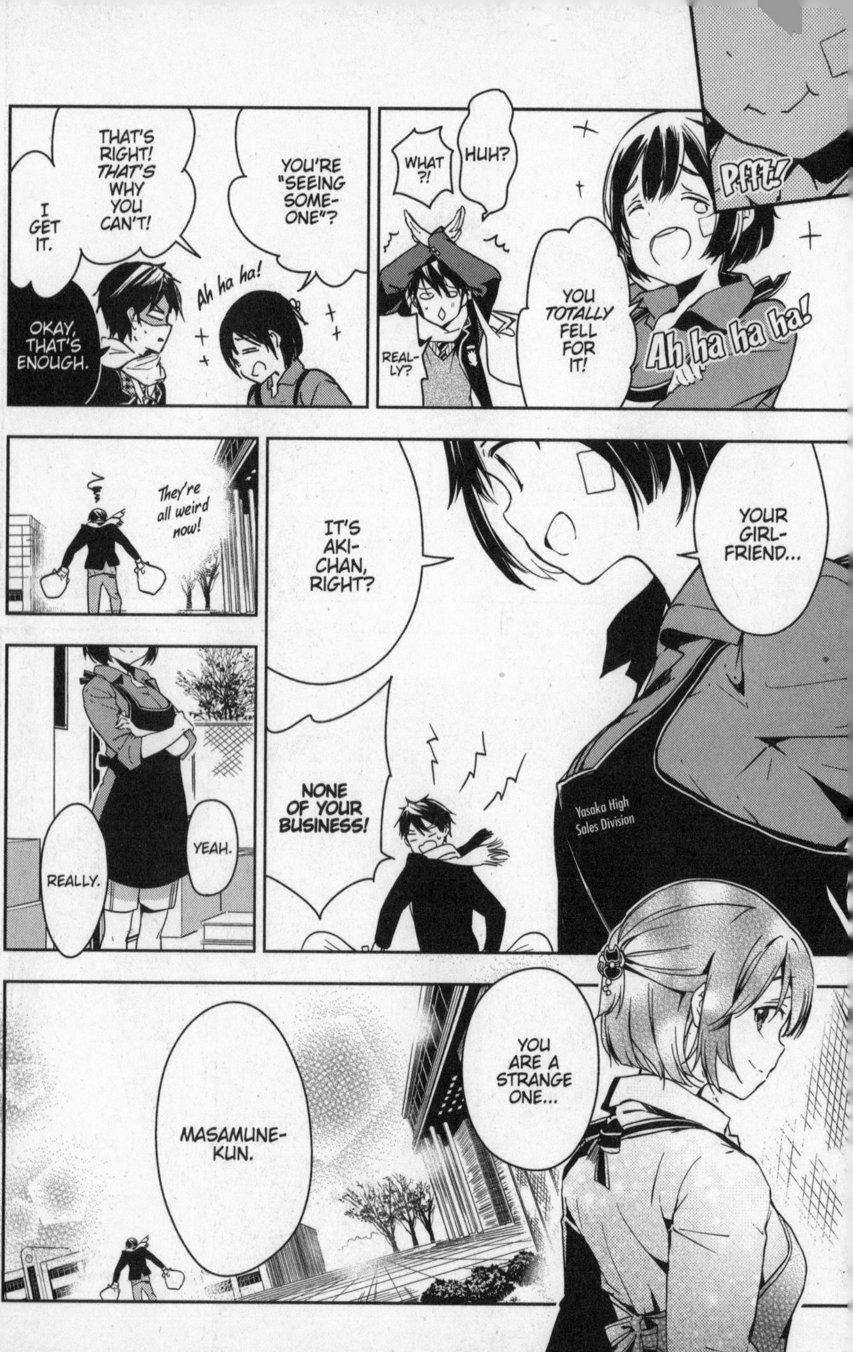
Pfft!
Ah ha ha ha!
YOU TOTALLY FELL FOR IT!
HUH?
WHAT ?!
REALLY?
YOU'RE "SEEING SOMEONE"?
Ah ha ha!
THAT'S RIGHT! THAT'S WHY YOU CAN'T!
I GET IT.
OKAY, THAT'S ENOUGH.
YOUR GIRLFRIEND...
IT'S AKI-CHAN, RIGHT?
Yasaka High Sales Division
NONE OF YOUR BUSINESS!
They're all weird now!
YEAH.
REALLY.
YOU ARE A STRANGE ONE...
MASAMUNE-KUN.

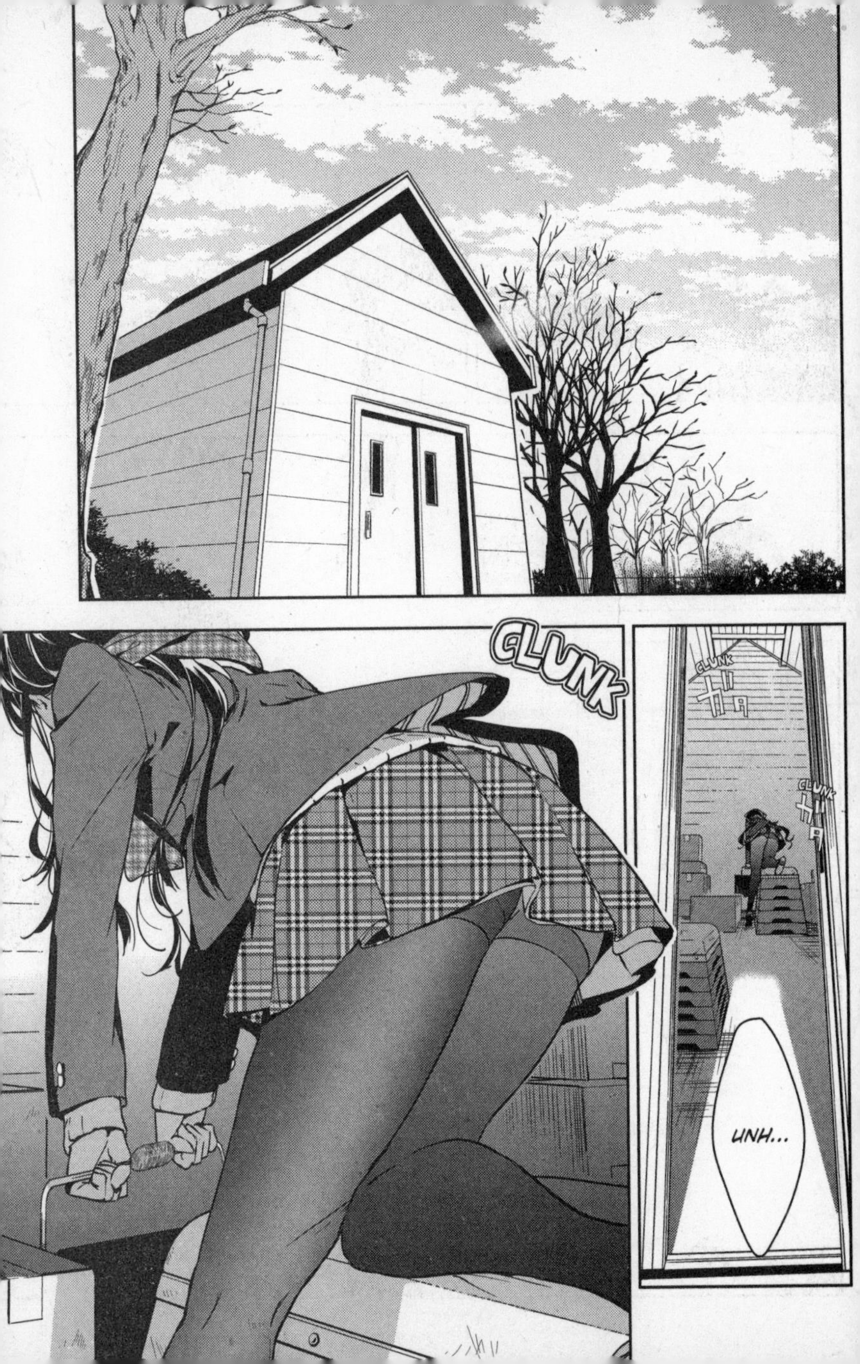
CLUNK
CLUNK
UNH...
CLUNK

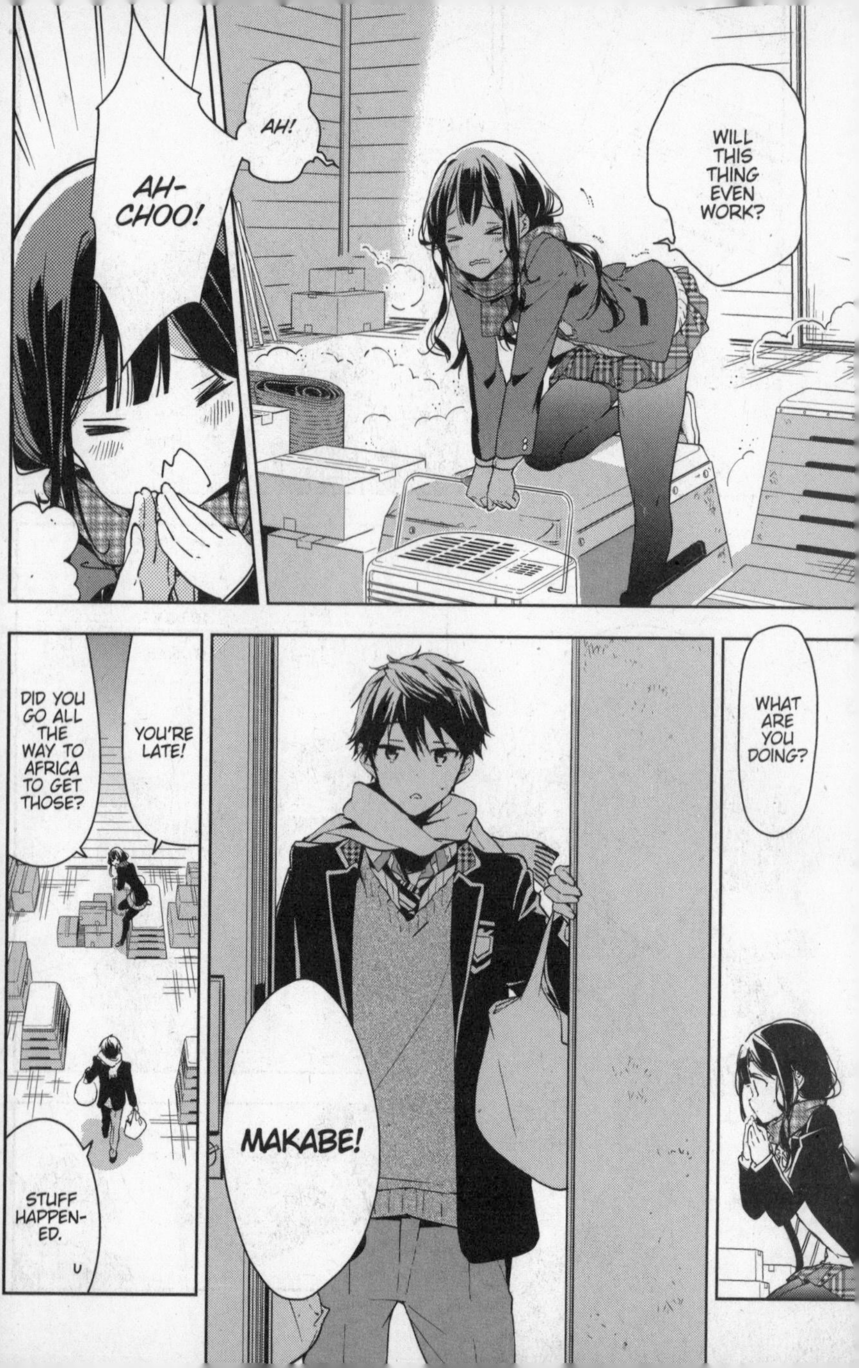
WILL THIS THING EVEN WORK?
AH!
AH-CHOO!
WHAT ARE YOU DOING?
MAKABE!
YOU'RE LATE!
DID YOU GO ALL THE WAY TO AFRICA TO GET THOSE?
STUFF HAPPEN-ED.

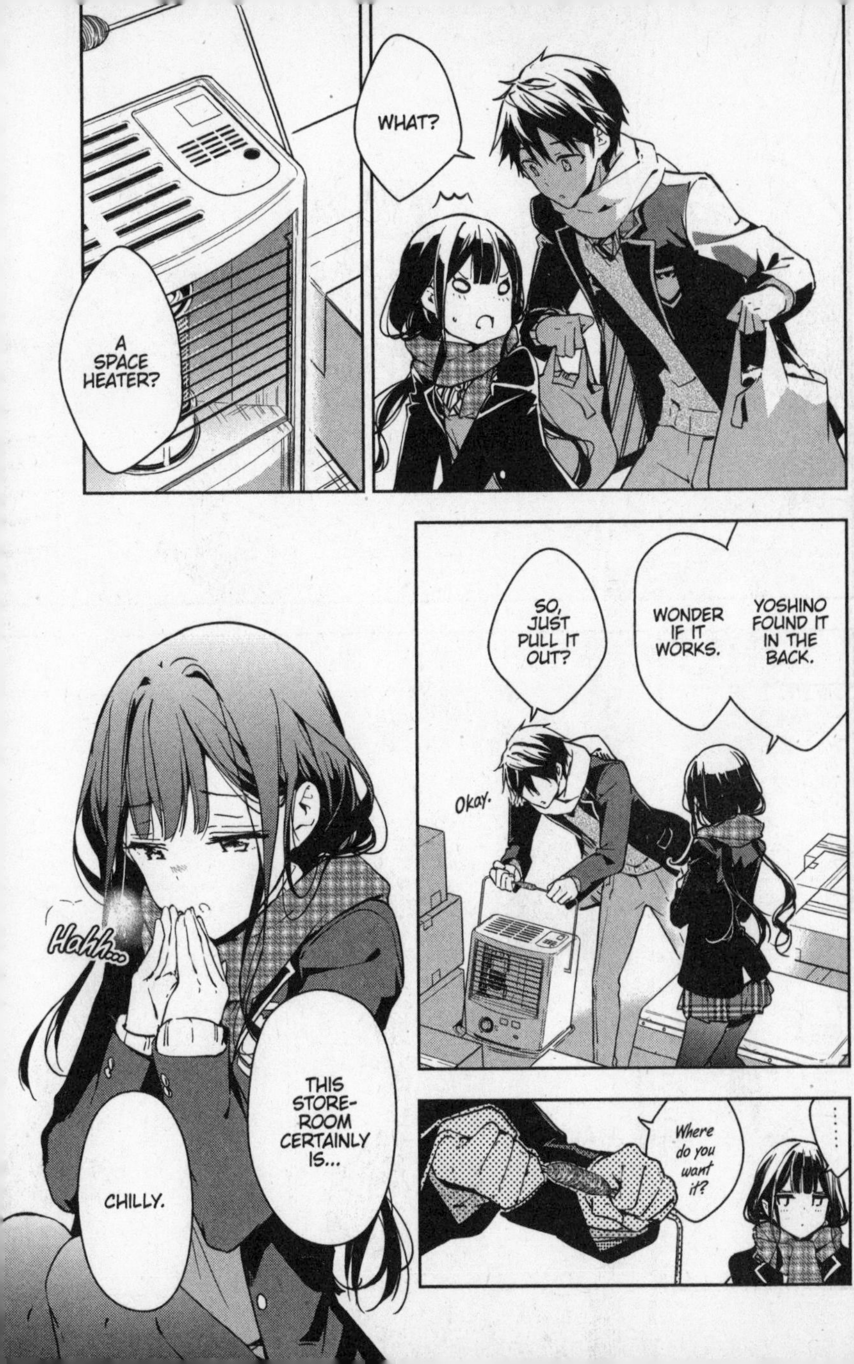
WHAT?
A SPACE HEATER?
YOSHINO FOUND IT IN THE BACK.
WONDER IF IT WORKS.
SO, JUST PULL IT OUT?
Okay.
......
Where do you want it?
Hahh...
THIS STOREROOM CERTAINLY IS...
CHILLY.

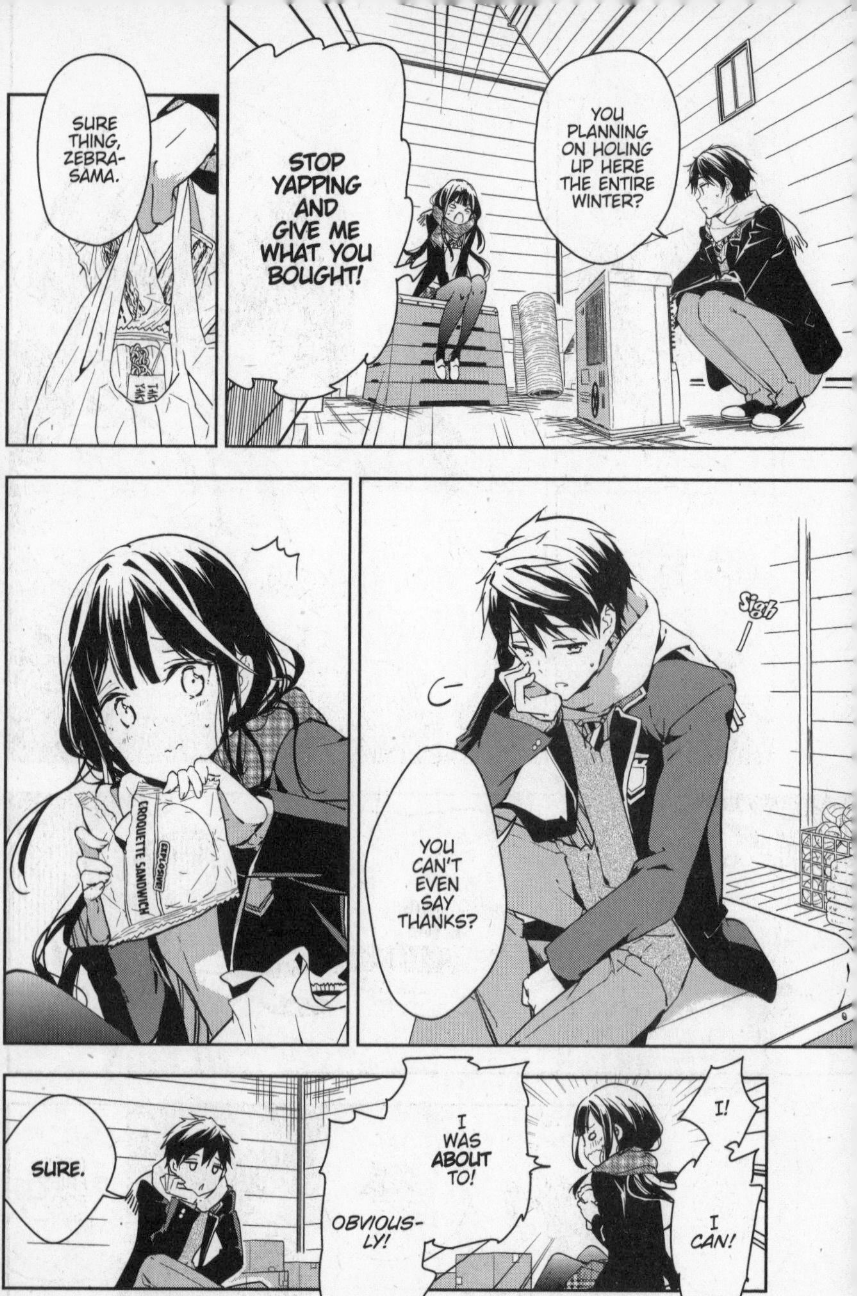
YOU PLANNING ON HOLING UP HERE THE ENTIRE WINTER?
STOP YAPPING AND GIVE ME WHAT YOU BOUGHT!
SURE THING, ZEBRA-SAMA.
Sigh
YOU CAN'T EVEN SAY THANKS?
EXPLOSIVE
CROQUETTE SANDWICH
I!
I CAN!
I WAS ABOUT TO!
OBVIOUS-LY!
SURE.

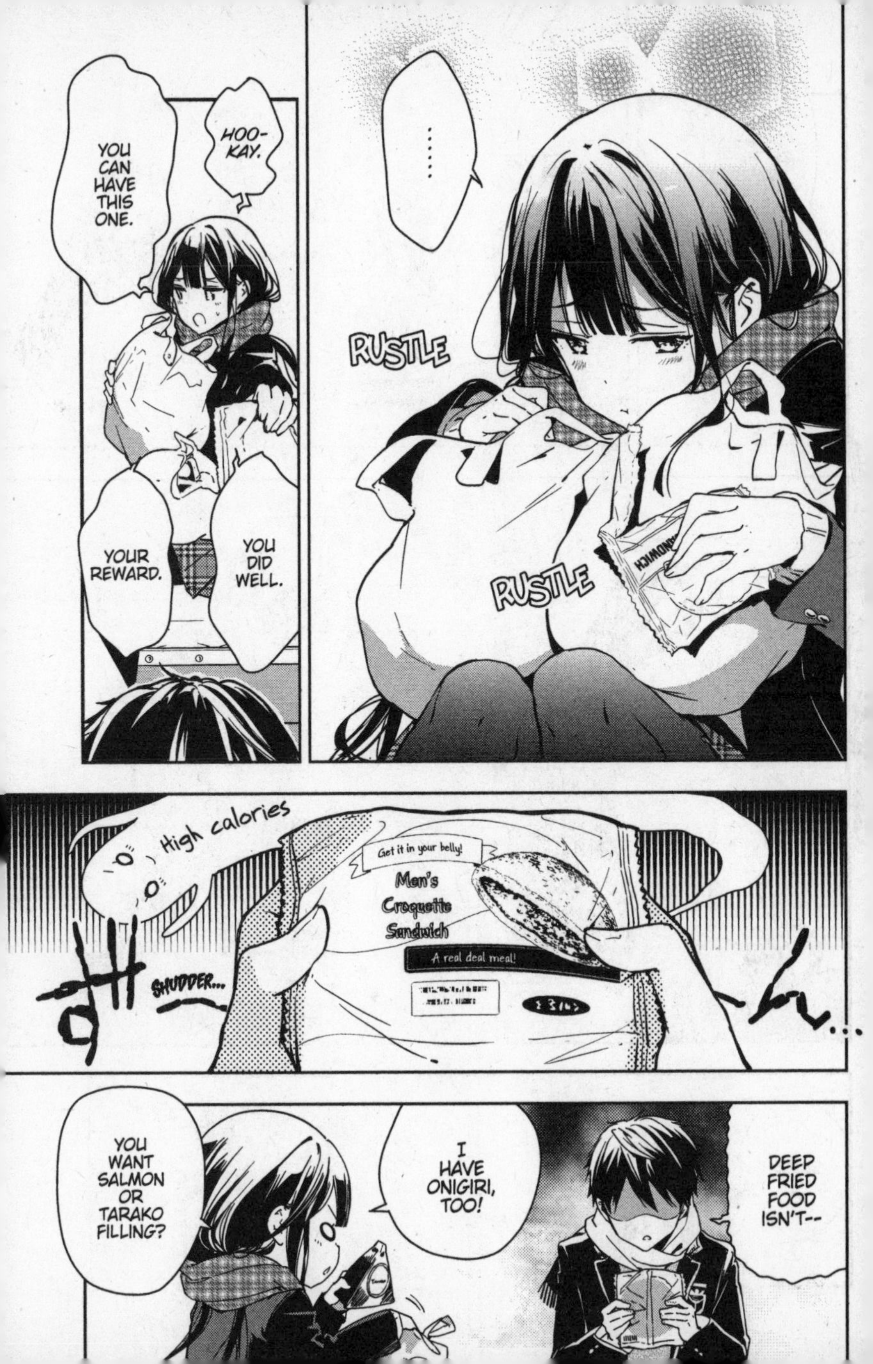
......
RUSTLE
RUSTLE
HOO-KAY.
YOU CAN HAVE THIS ONE.
YOU DID WELL.
YOUR REWARD.
High calories
Get it in your belly!
Men's Croquette Sandwich
A real deal meal!
SHUDDER...
DEEP FRIED FOOD ISN'T--
I HAVE ONIGIRI, TOO!
YOU WANT SALMON OR TARAKO FILLING?

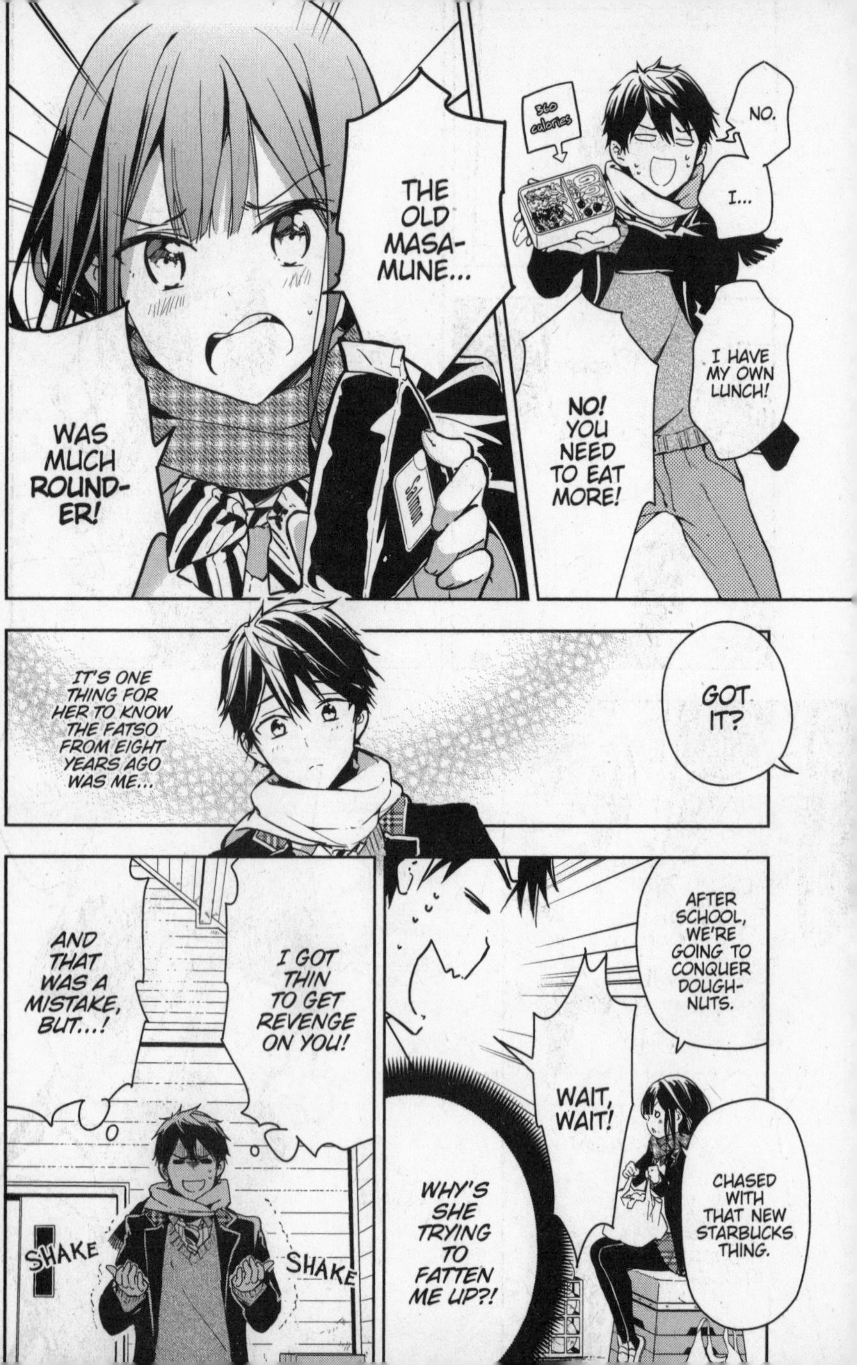
360 calories
NO.
I...
I HAVE MY OWN LUNCH!
NO! YOU NEED TO EAT MORE!
THE OLD MASAMUNE...
WAS MUCH ROUNDER!
GOT IT?
IT'S ONE THING FOR HER TO KNOW THE FATSO FROM EIGHT YEARS AGO WAS ME...
AFTER SCHOOL, WE'RE GOING TO CONQUER DOUGHNUTS.
CHASED WITH THAT NEW STARBUCKS THING.
WAIT, WAIT!
WHY'S SHE TRYING TO FATTEN ME UP?!
I GOT THIN TO GET REVENGE ON YOU!
AND THAT WAS A MISTAKE, BUT...!
SHAKE
SHAKE

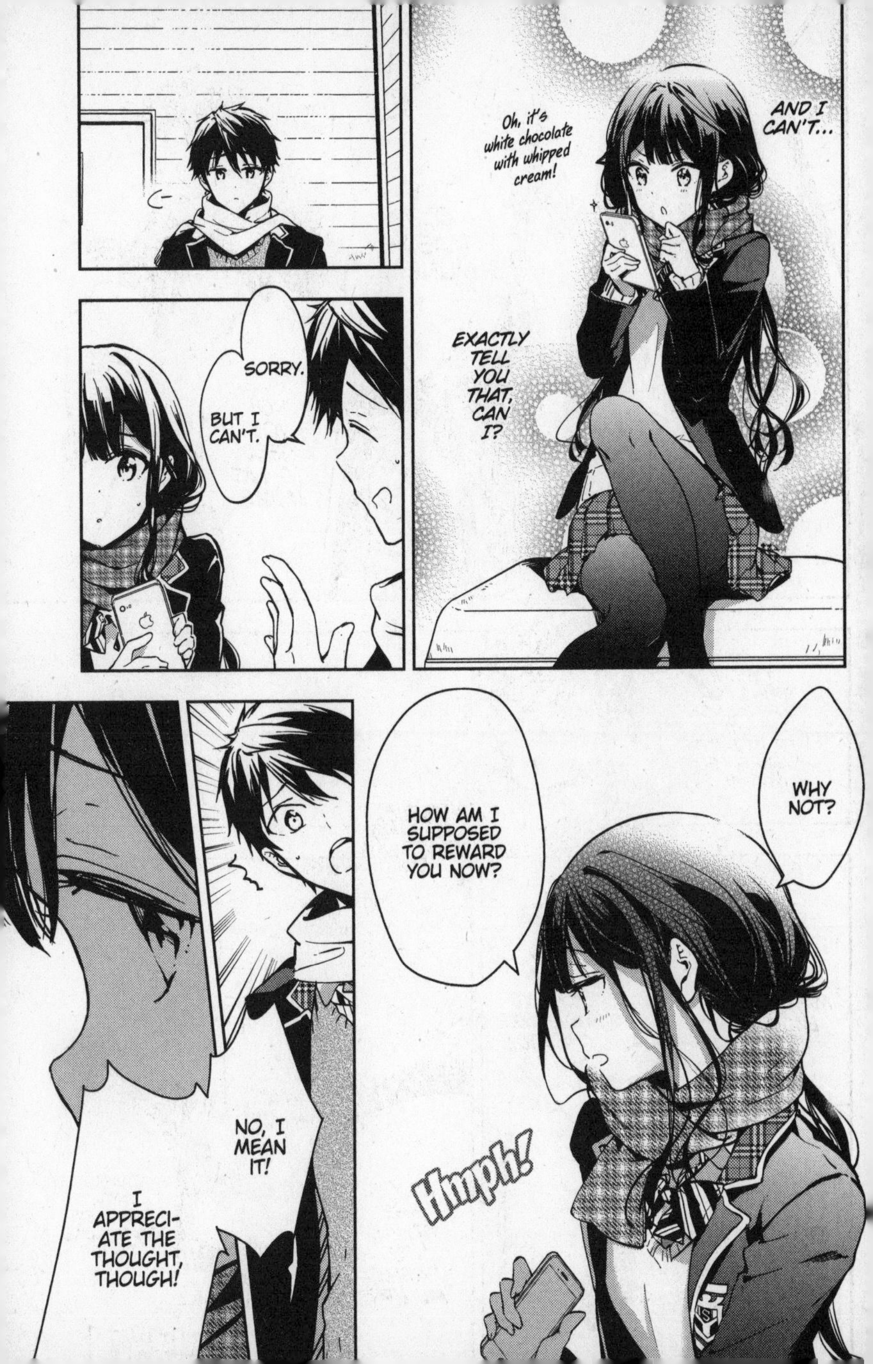
Oh, it's white chocolate with whipped cream!
AND I CAN'T...
EXACTLY TELL YOU THAT, CAN I?
SORRY.
BUT I CAN'T.
WHY NOT?
HOW AM I SUPPOSED TO REWARD YOU NOW?
Hmph!
NO, I MEAN IT!
I APPRECIATE THE THOUGHT, THOUGH!

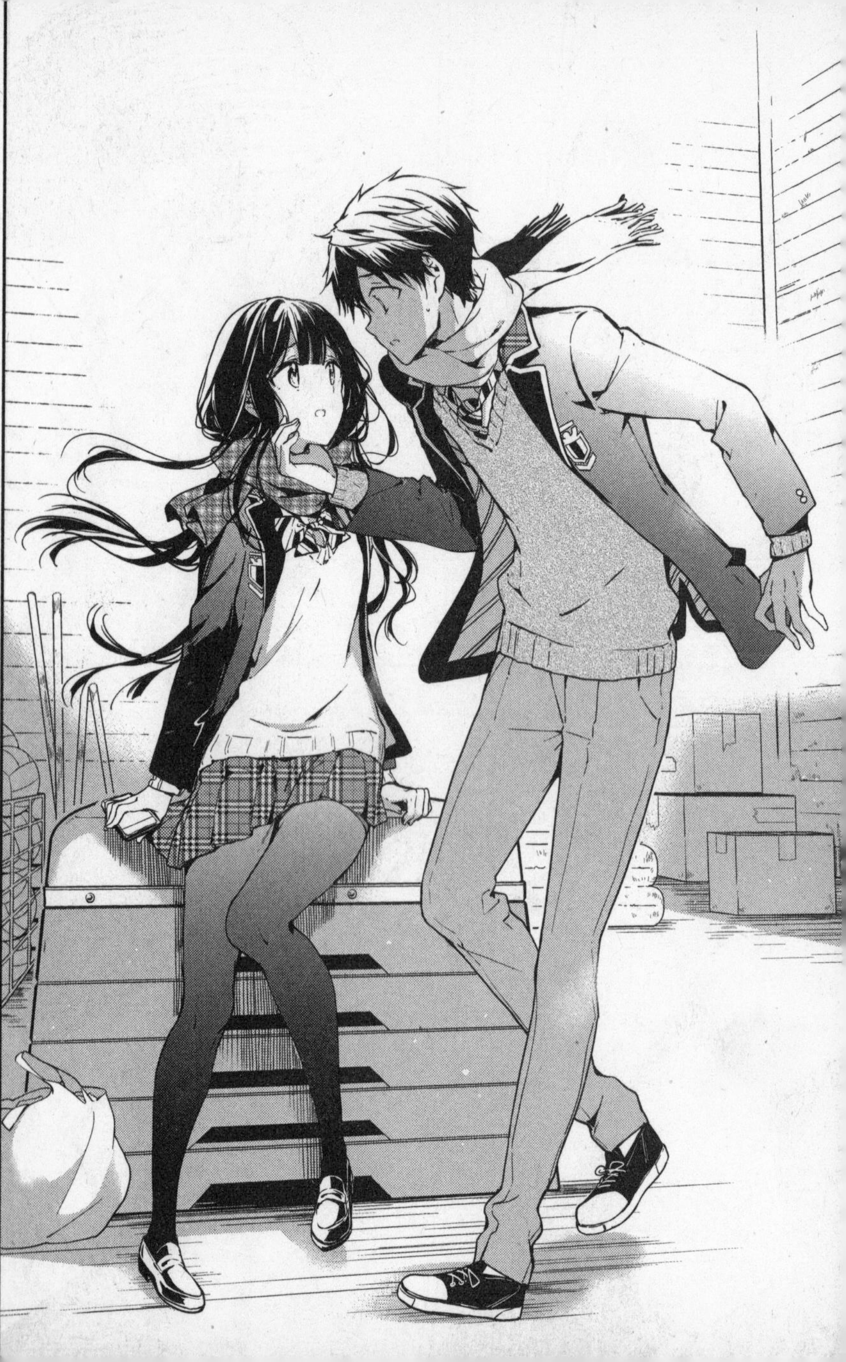

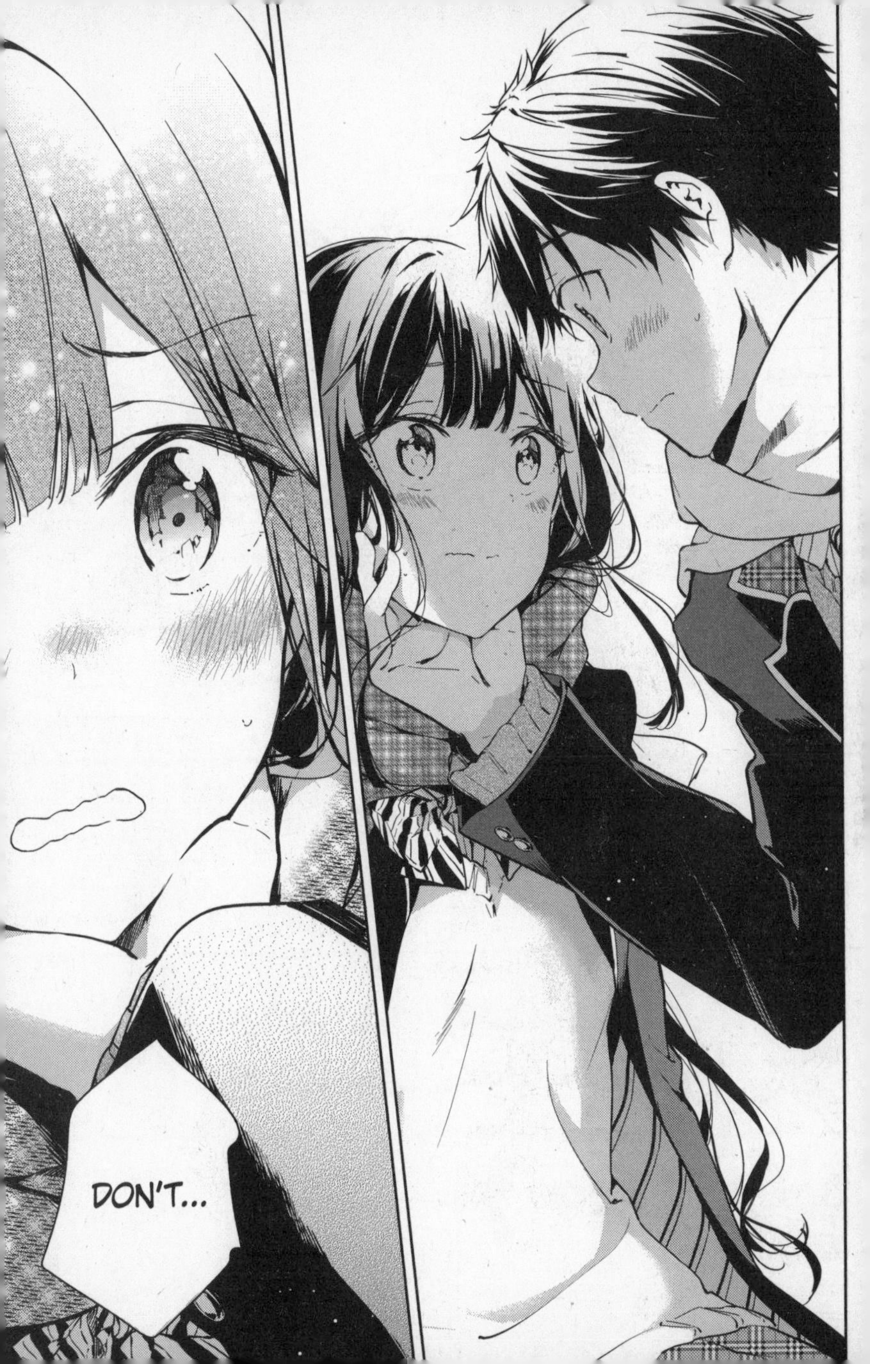
DON'T...

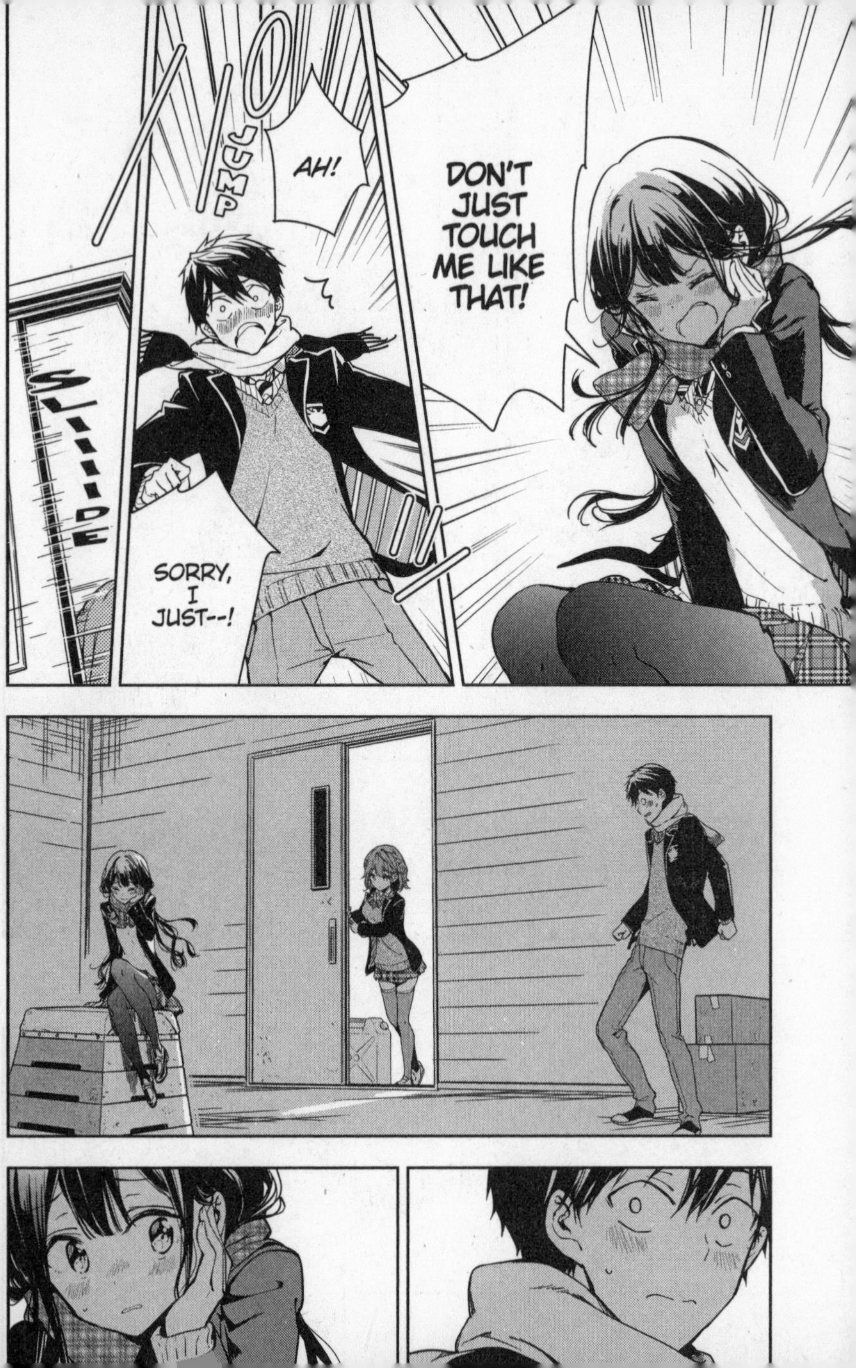
DON'T JUST TOUCH ME LIKE THAT!
AH!
JUMP
SLIIIIDE
SORRY, I JUST--!

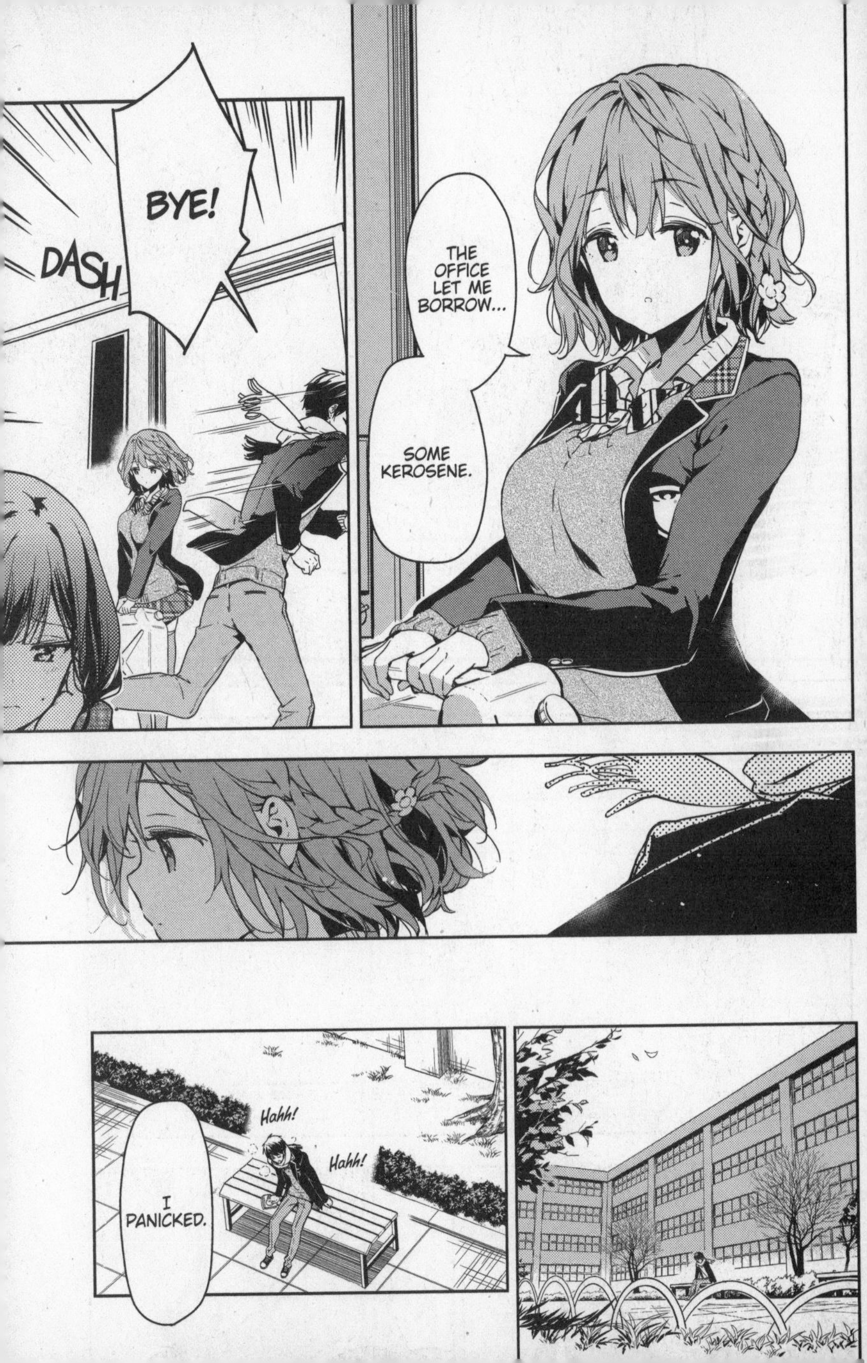
THE OFFICE LET ME BORROW...
SOME KEROSENE.
BYE!
DASH
Hahh!
Hahh!
I PANICKED.

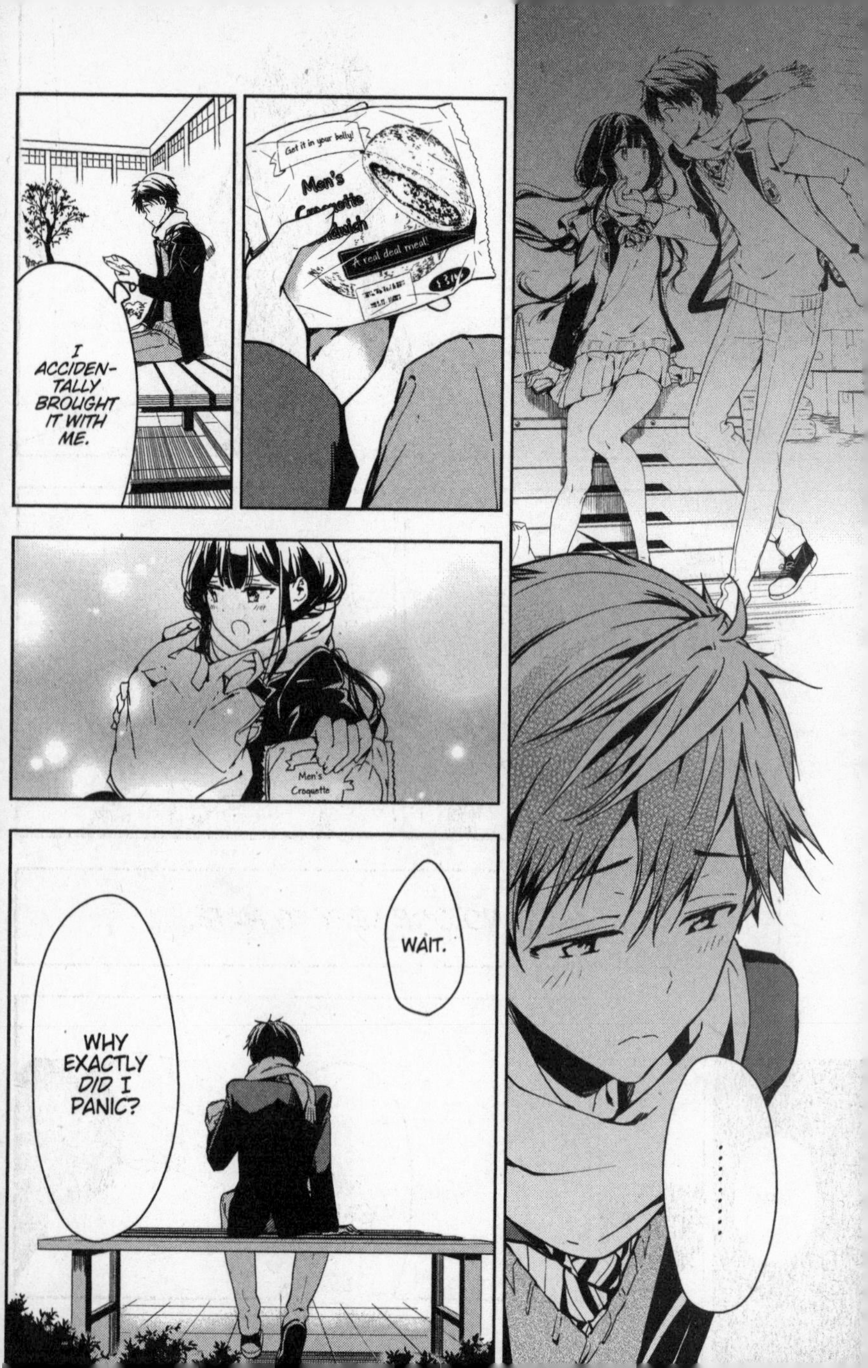
......
Get it in your belly!
Men's
A real deal meal!
I ACCIDENTALLY BROUGHT IT WITH ME.
Men's Croquette
WAIT.
WHY EXACTLY DID I PANIC?

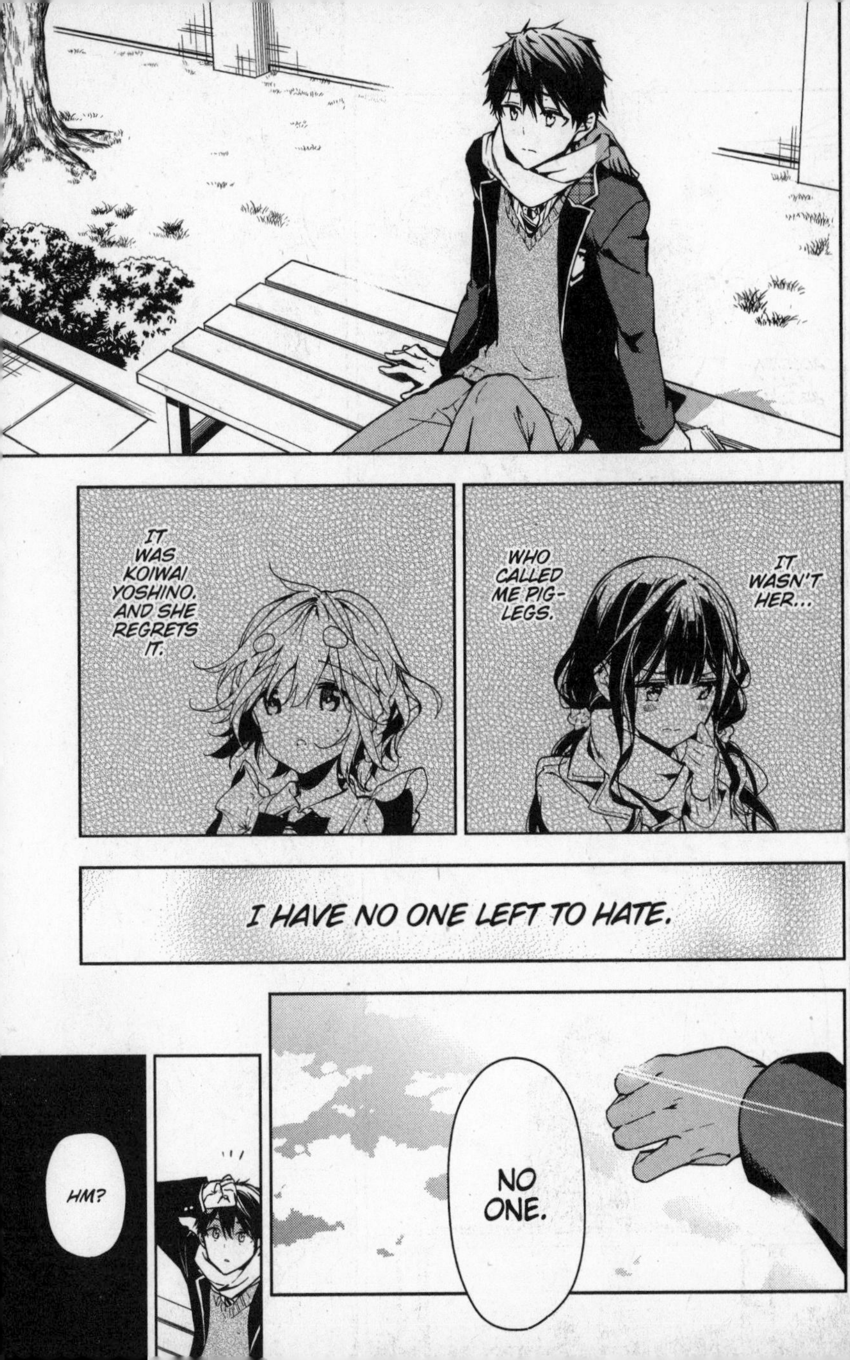
IT WASN'T HER...
WHO CALLED ME PIG-LEGS.
IT WAS KOIWAI YOSHINO. AND SHE REGRETS IT.
I HAVE NO ONE LEFT TO HATE.
NO ONE.
HM?

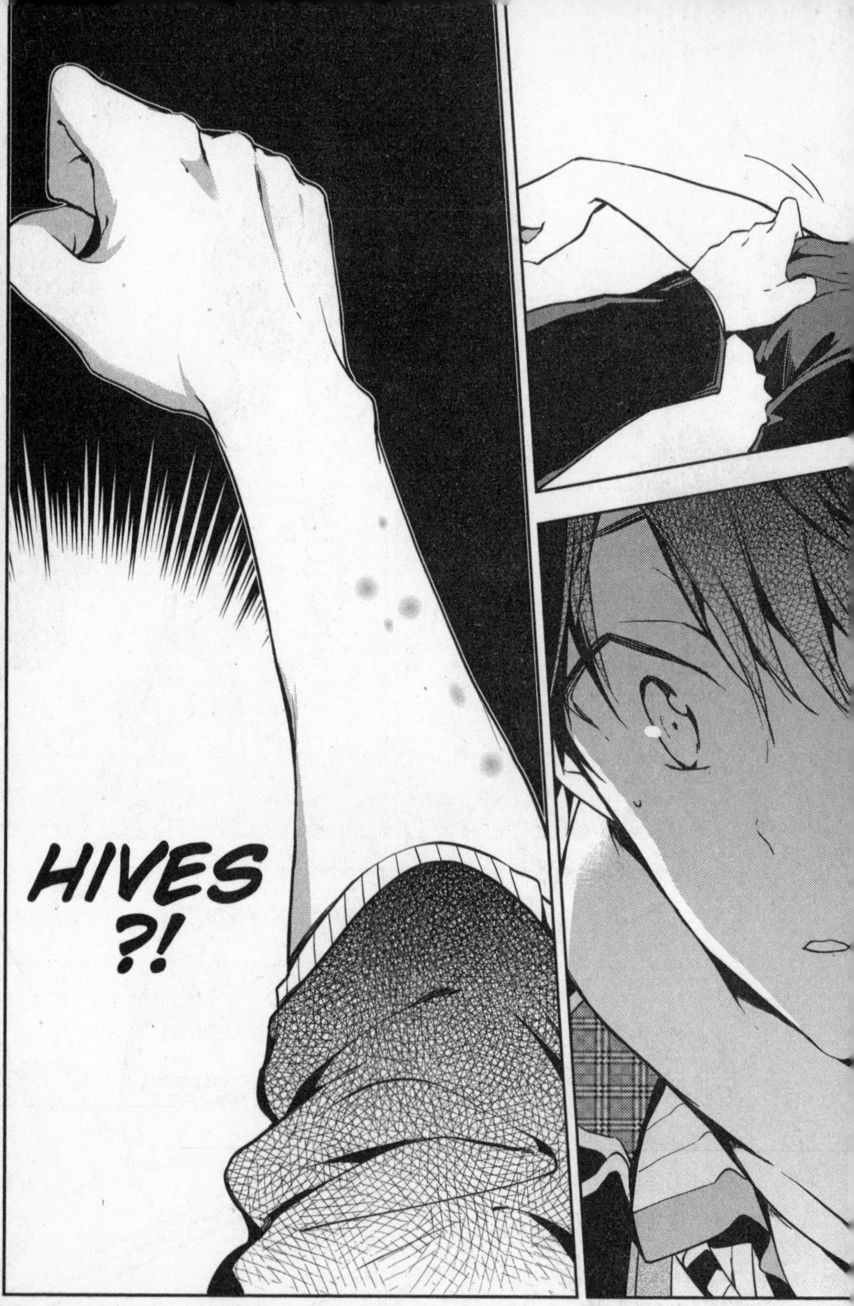
HIVES ?!

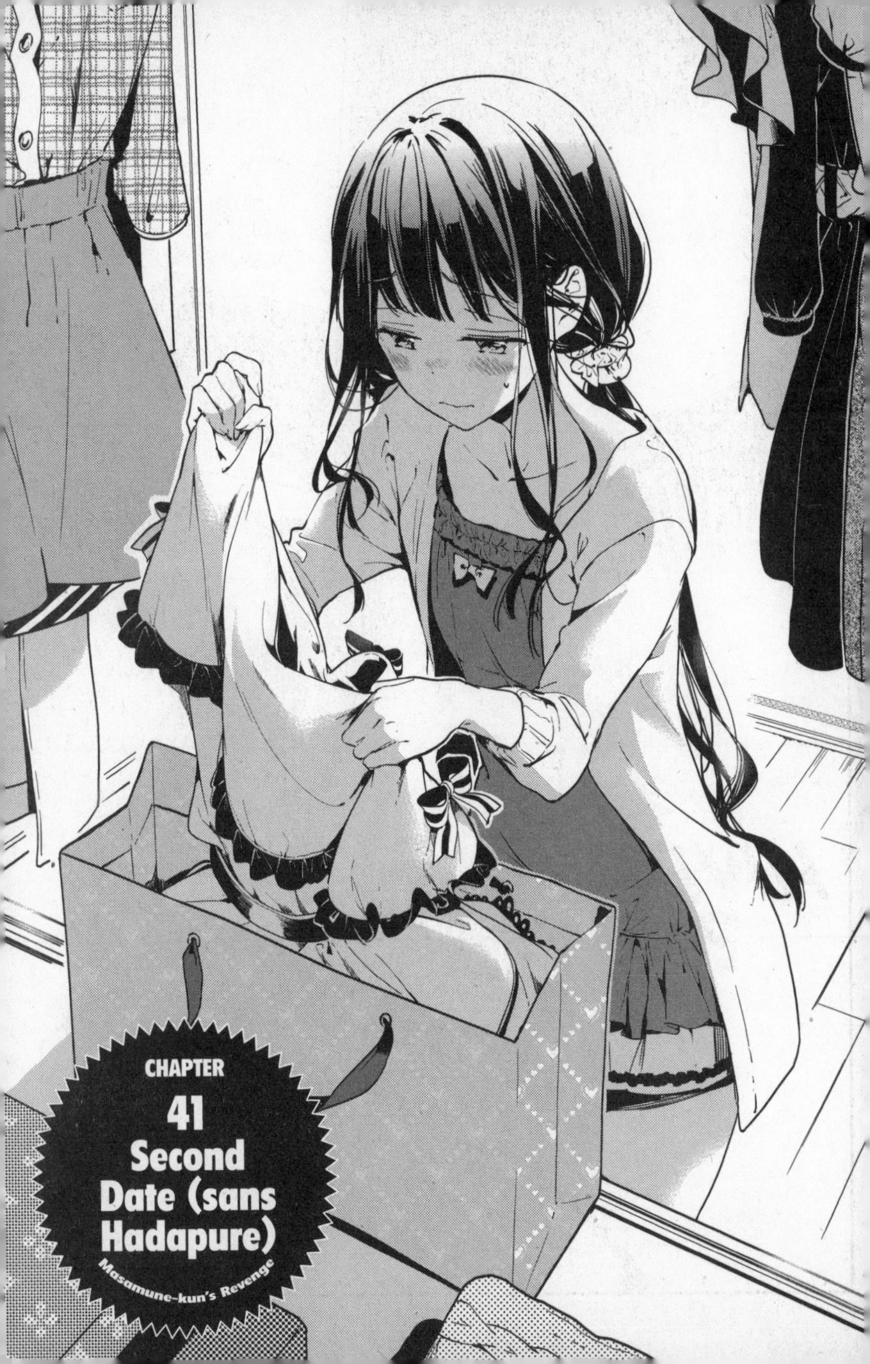
CHAPTER
41
Second Date (sans Hadapure)
Masamune-kun's Revenge

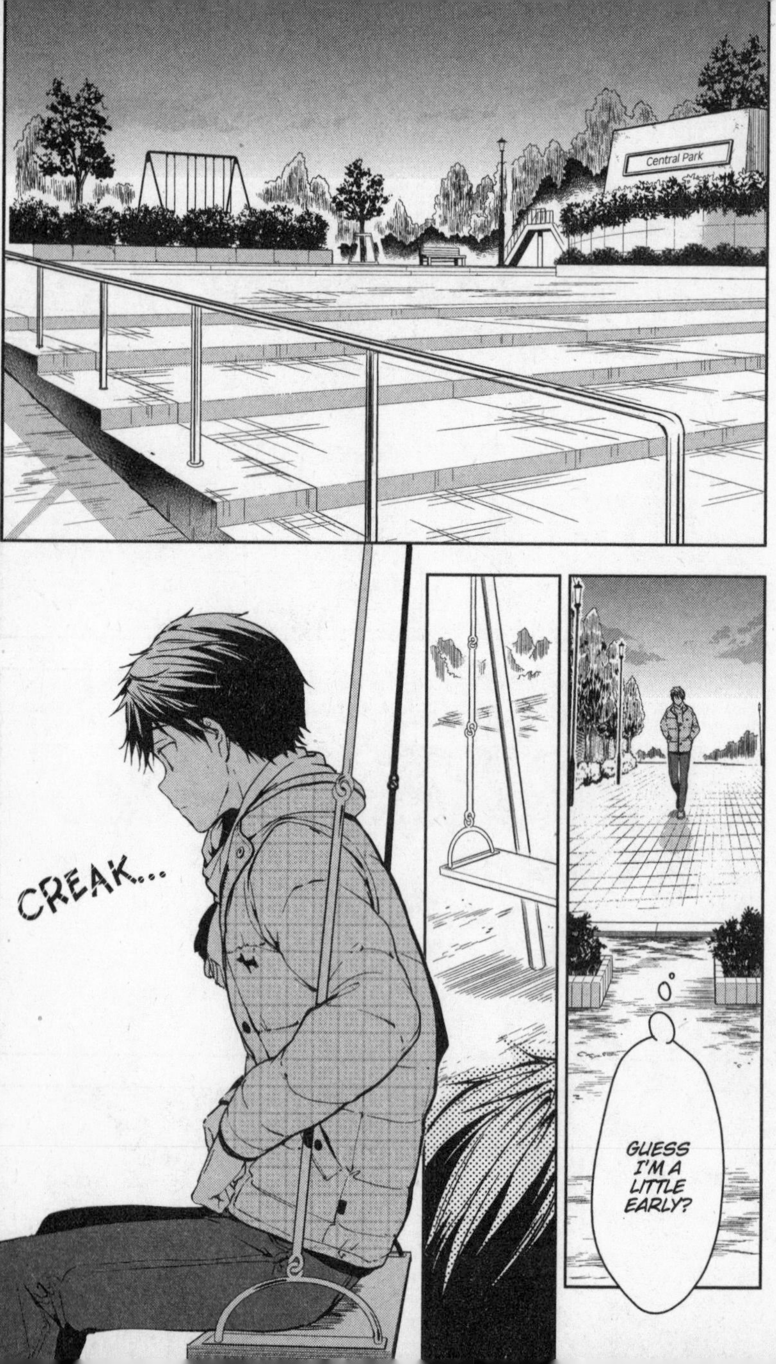
Central Park
GUESS I'M A LITTLE EARLY?
CREAK...

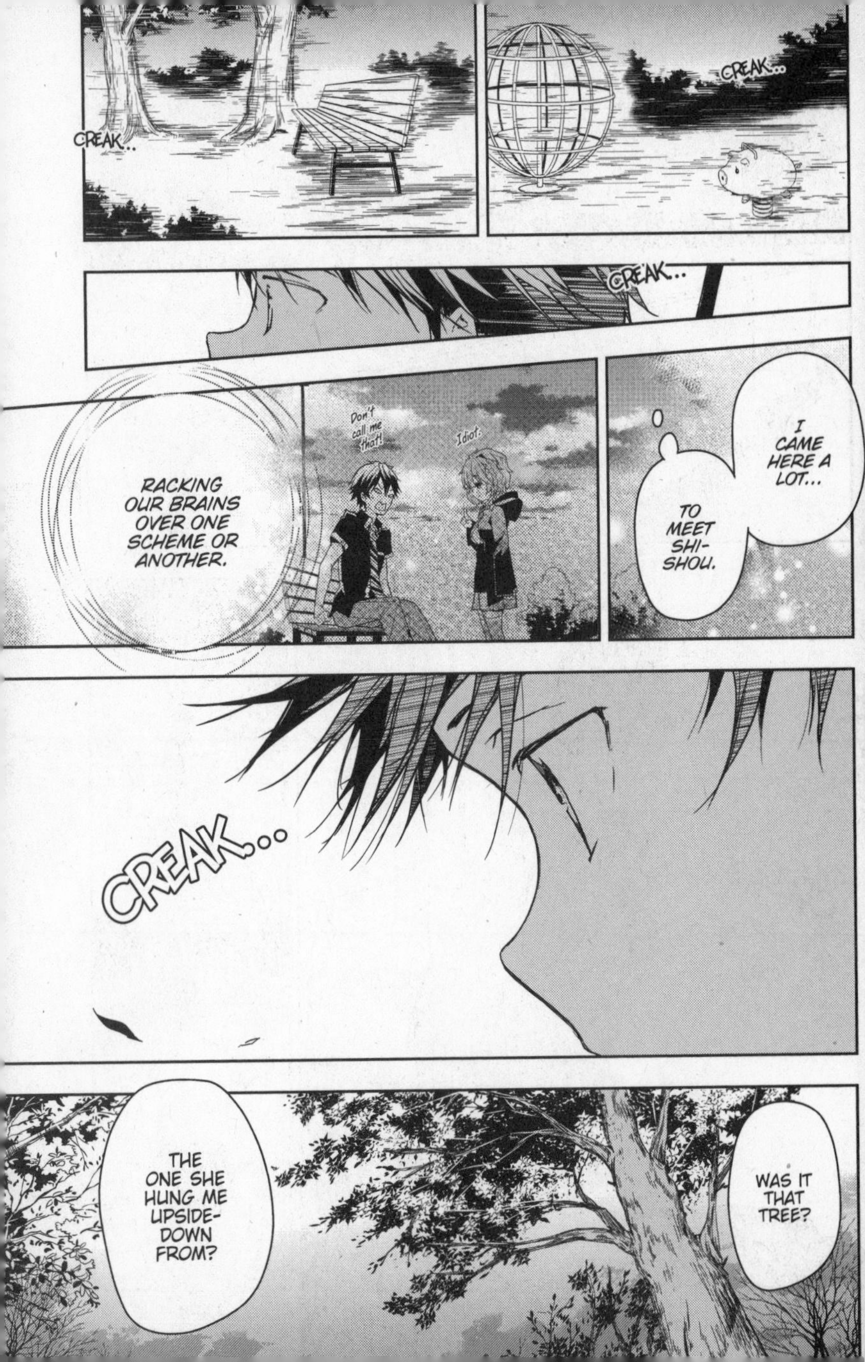
CREAK...
CREAK..
CREAK...
I CAME HERE A LOT...
TO MEET SHI-SHOU.
Idiot.
Don't call me that!
RACKING OUR BRAINS OVER ONE SCHEME OR ANOTHER.
CREAK...
WAS IT THAT TREE?
THE ONE SHE HUNG ME UPSIDE-DOWN FROM?

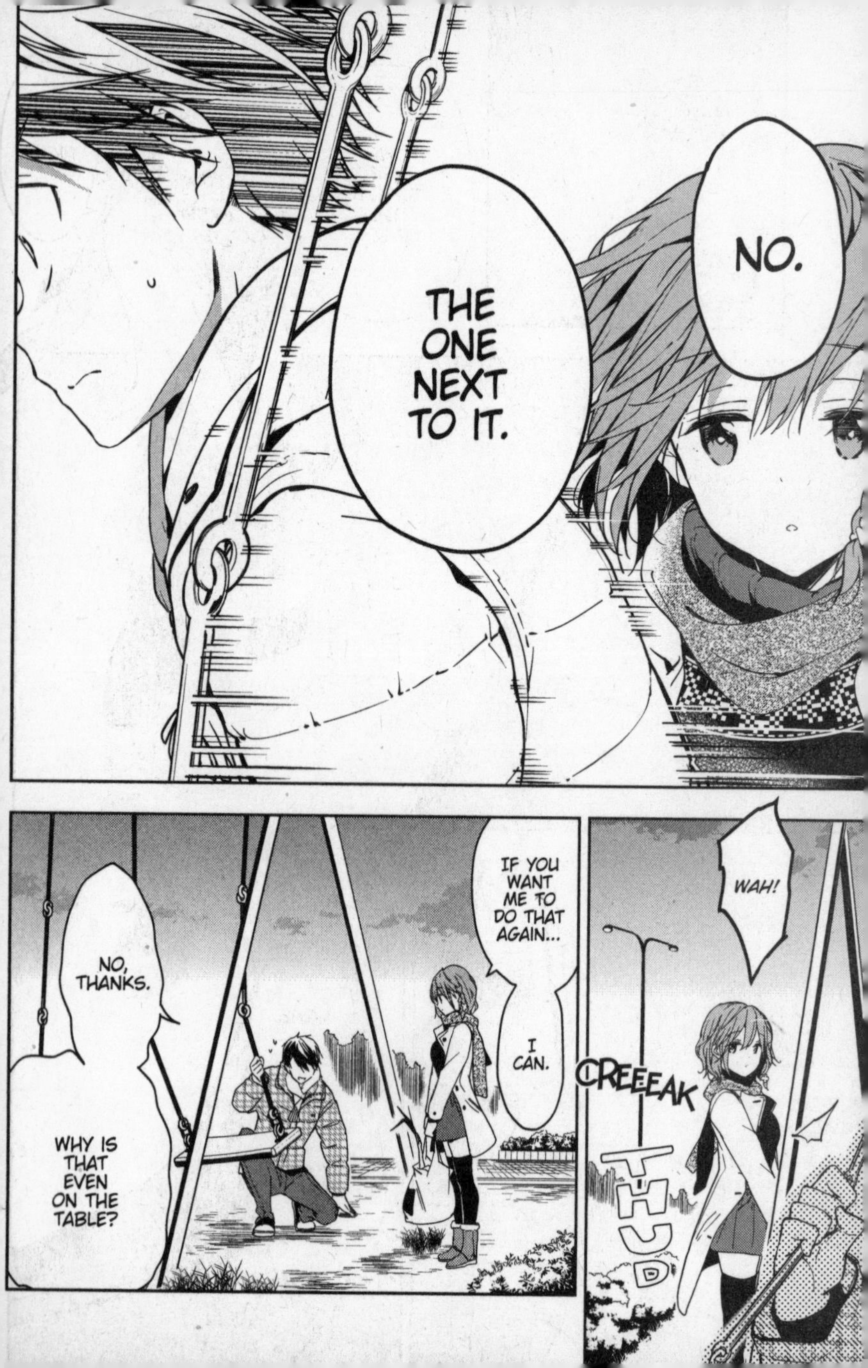
NO.
THE ONE NEXT TO IT.
WAH!
CREEEAK
THUD
IF YOU WANT ME TO DO THAT AGAIN...
I CAN.
NO, THANKS.
WHY IS THAT EVEN ON THE TABLE?

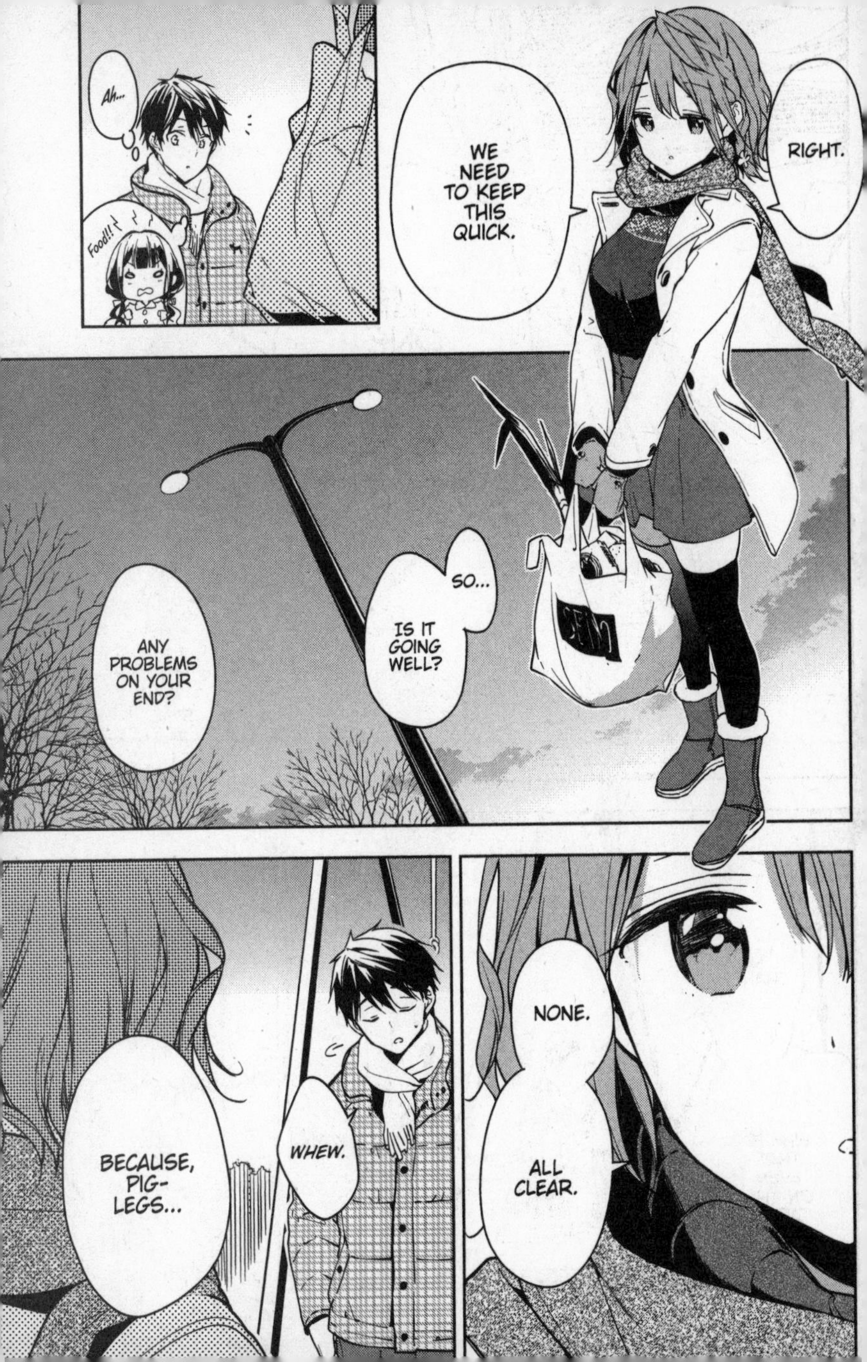
RIGHT.
WE NEED TO KEEP THIS QUICK.
Ah...
Food!!
SO...
IS IT GOING WELL?
ANY PROBLEMS ON YOUR END?
NONE.
ALL CLEAR.
WHEW.
BECAUSE, PIG-LEGS...

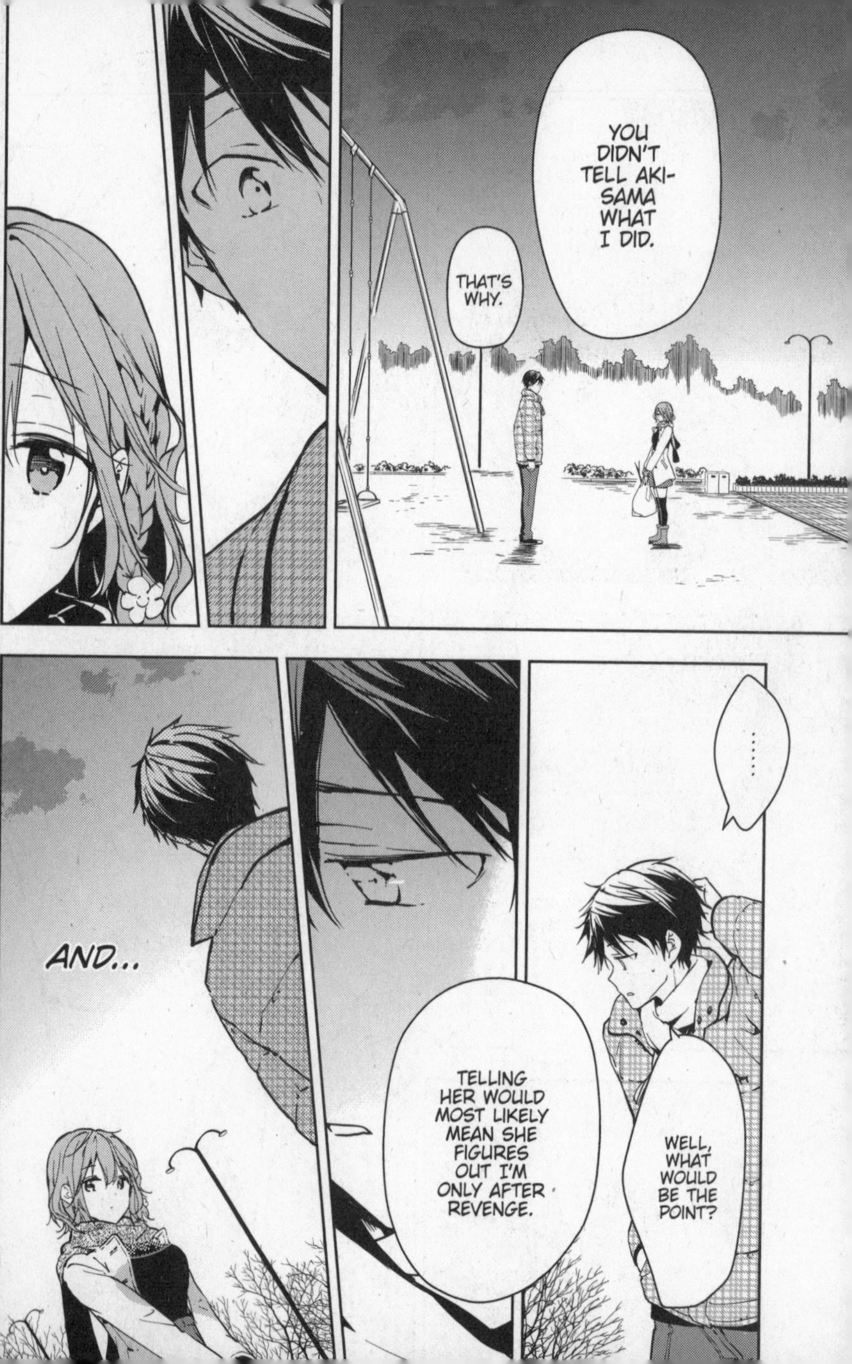
YOU DIDN'T TELL AKI-SAMA WHAT I DID.
THAT'S WHY.
......
WELL, WHAT WOULD BE THE POINT?
TELLING HER WOULD MOST LIKELY MEAN SHE FIGURES OUT I'M ONLY AFTER REVENGE.
AND...

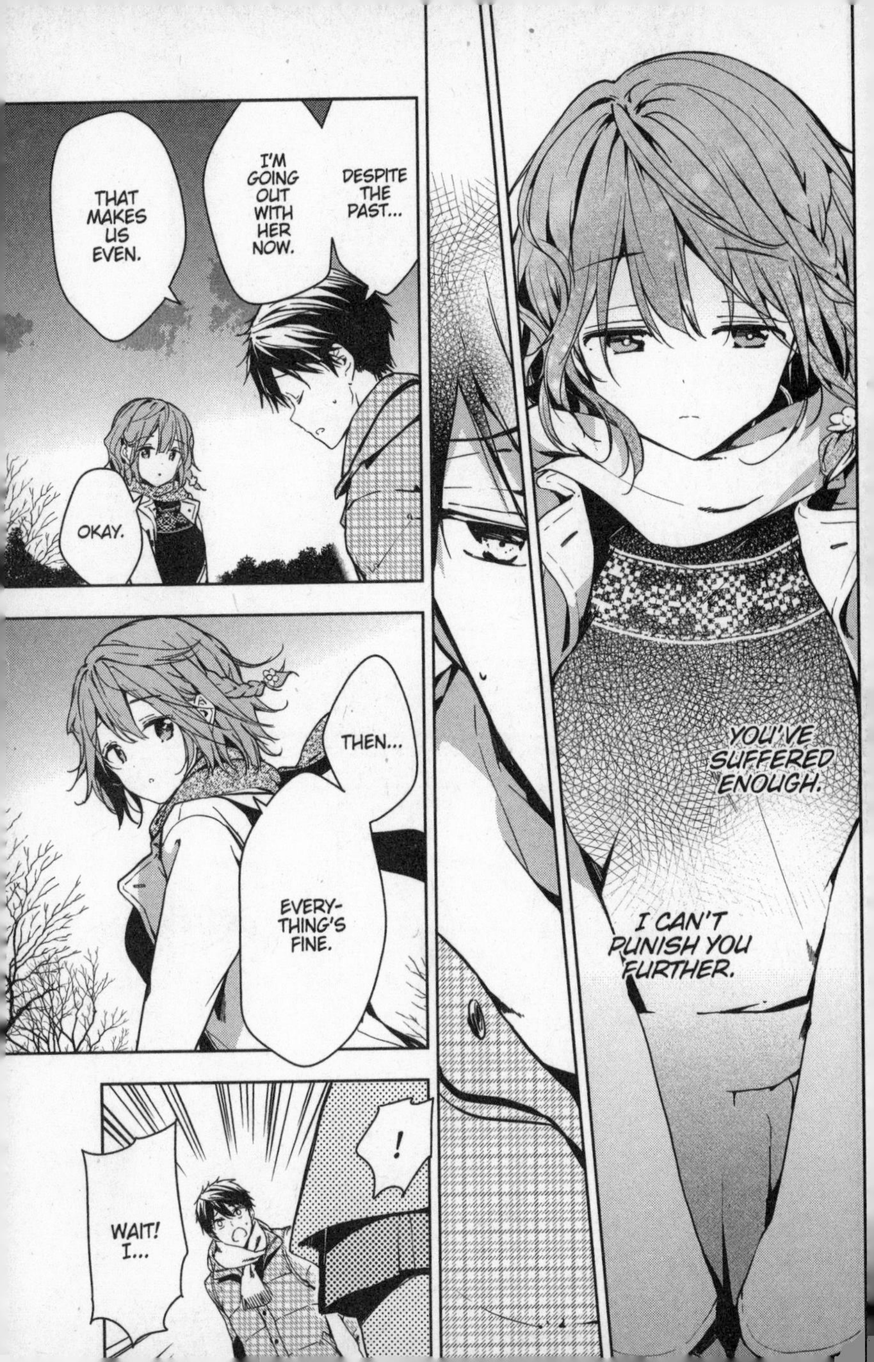
YOU'VE SUFFERED ENOUGH.
I CAN'T PUNISH YOU FURTHER.
DESPITE THE PAST...
I'M GOING OUT WITH HER NOW.
THAT MAKES US EVEN.
OKAY.
THEN...
EVERYTHING'S FINE.
!
WAIT! I...

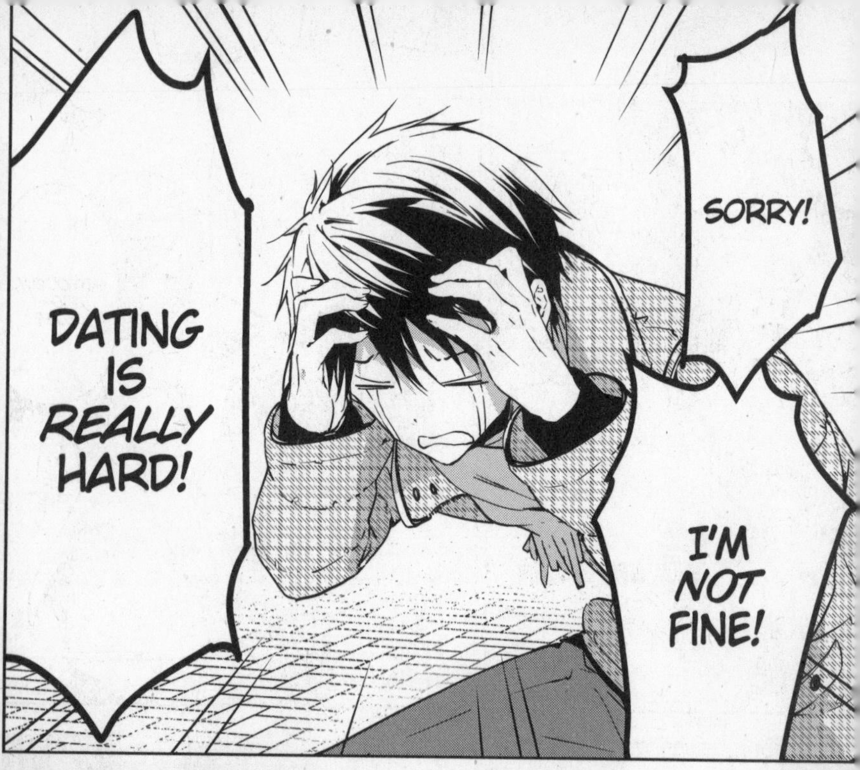
SORRY!
I'M *NOT* FINE!
DATING IS *REALLY* HARD!
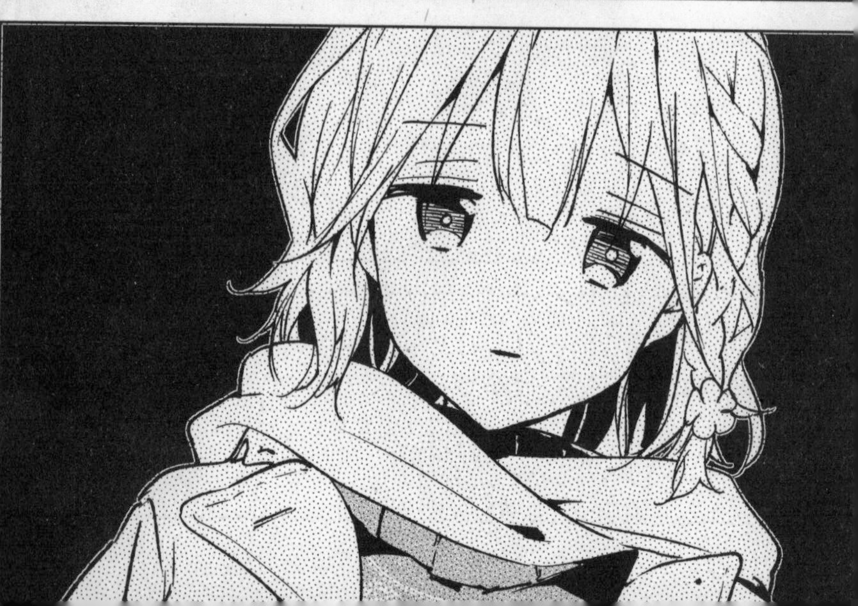

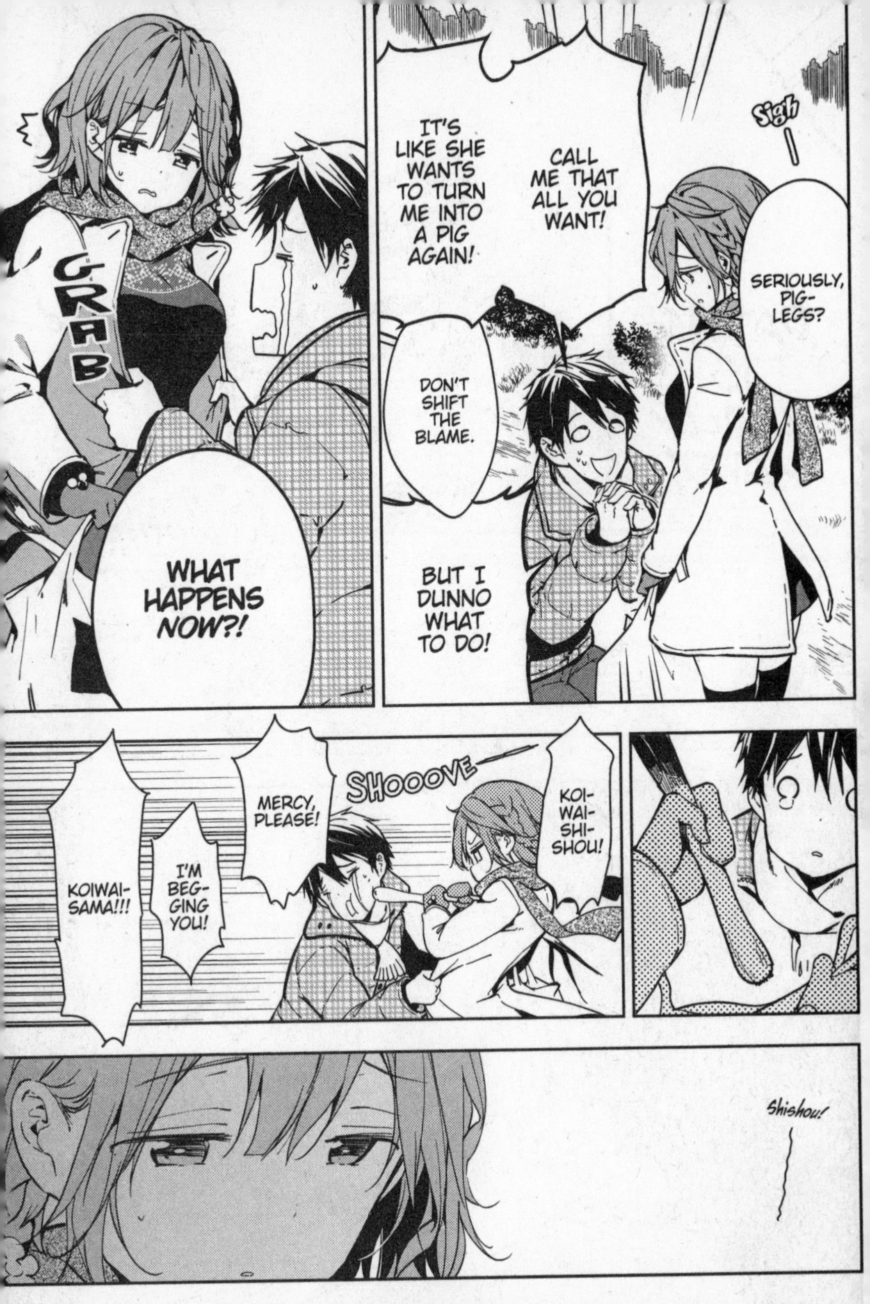
Sigh
SERIOUSLY, PIG-LEGS?
CALL ME THAT ALL YOU WANT!
IT'S LIKE SHE WANTS TO TURN ME INTO A PIG AGAIN!
DON'T SHIFT THE BLAME.
BUT I DUNNO WHAT TO DO!
GRAB
WHAT HAPPENS NOW?!
KOI-WAI-SHI-SHOU!
SHOOOVE
MERCY, PLEASE!
I'M BEG-GING YOU!
KOIWAI-SAMA!!!
Shishou!

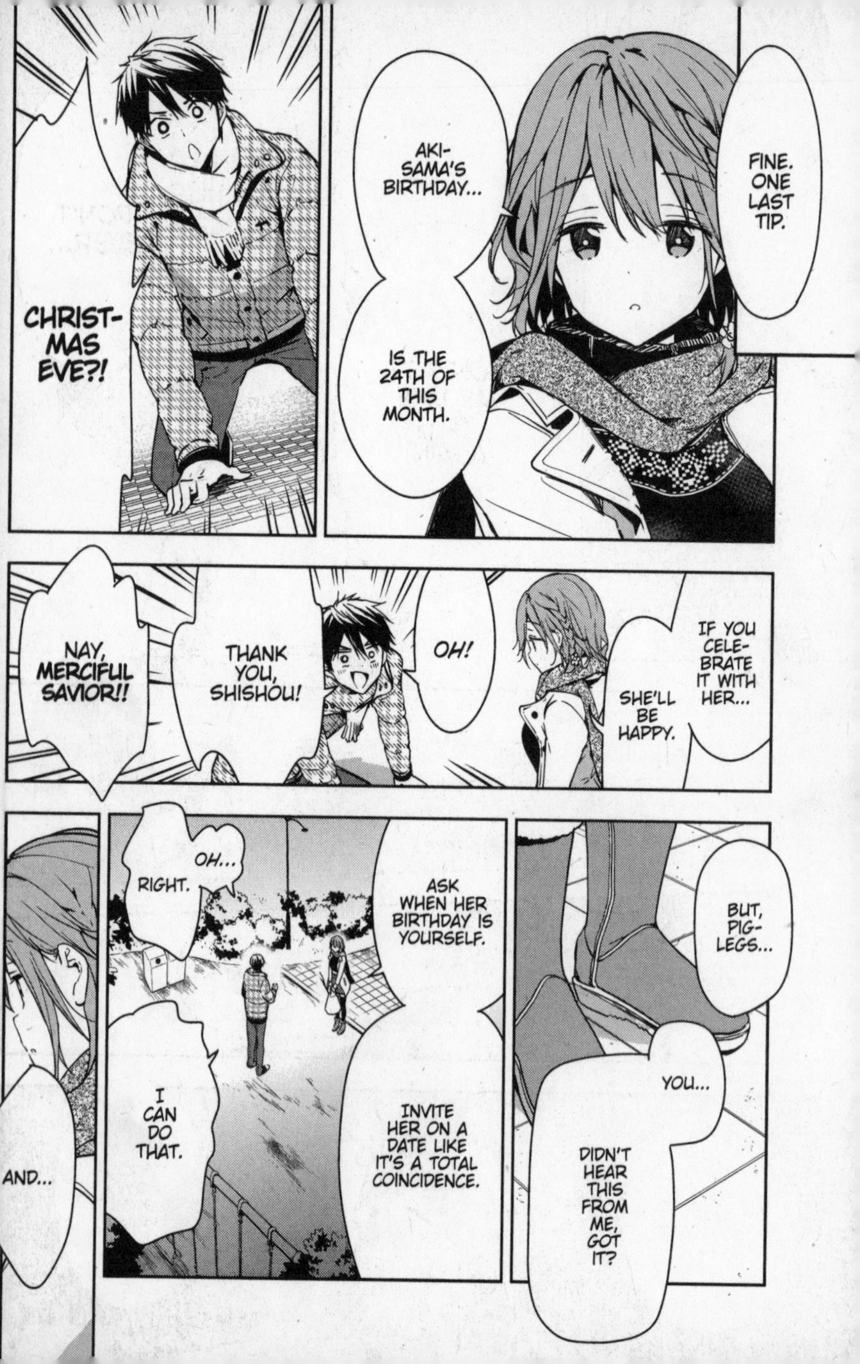

FINE. ONE LAST TIP.
AKI-SAMA'S BIRTHDAY...
IS THE 24TH OF THIS MONTH.
CHRISTMAS EVE?!
IF YOU CELEBRATE IT WITH HER...
SHE'LL BE HAPPY.
OH!
THANK YOU, SHISHOU!
NAY, MERCIFUL SAVIOR!!
BUT, PIG-LEGS...
YOU...
DIDN'T HEAR THIS FROM ME, GOT IT?
ASK WHEN HER BIRTHDAY IS YOURSELF.
INVITE HER ON A DATE LIKE IT'S A TOTAL COINCIDENCE.
OH... RIGHT.
I CAN DO THAT.
AND...

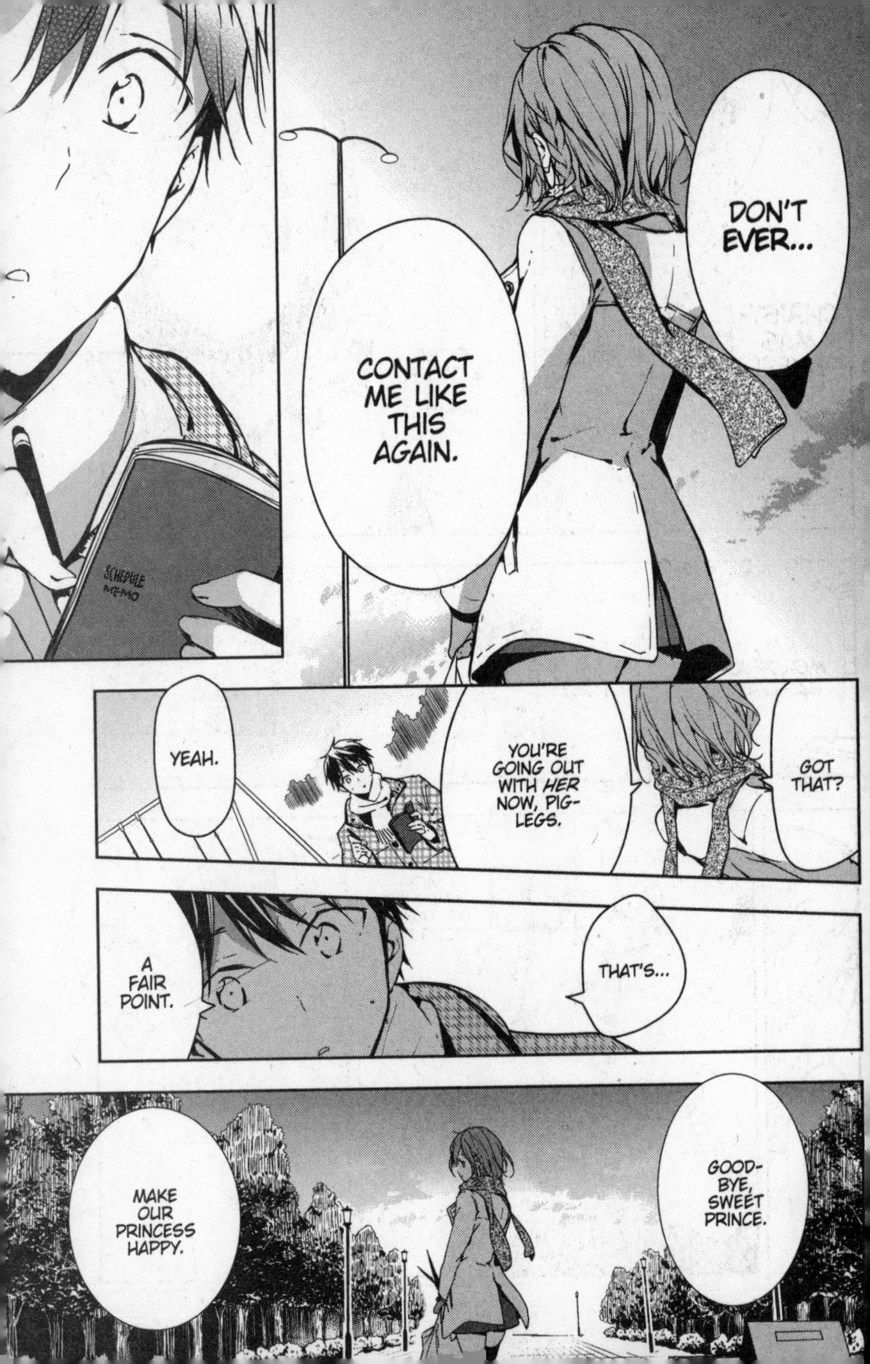
DON'T EVER...
CONTACT ME LIKE THIS AGAIN.
SCHEDULE MEMO
GOT THAT?
YOU'RE GOING OUT WITH *HER* NOW, PIG-LEGS.
YEAH.
THAT'S...
A FAIR POINT.
GOOD-BYE, SWEET PRINCE.
MAKE OUR PRINCESS HAPPY.

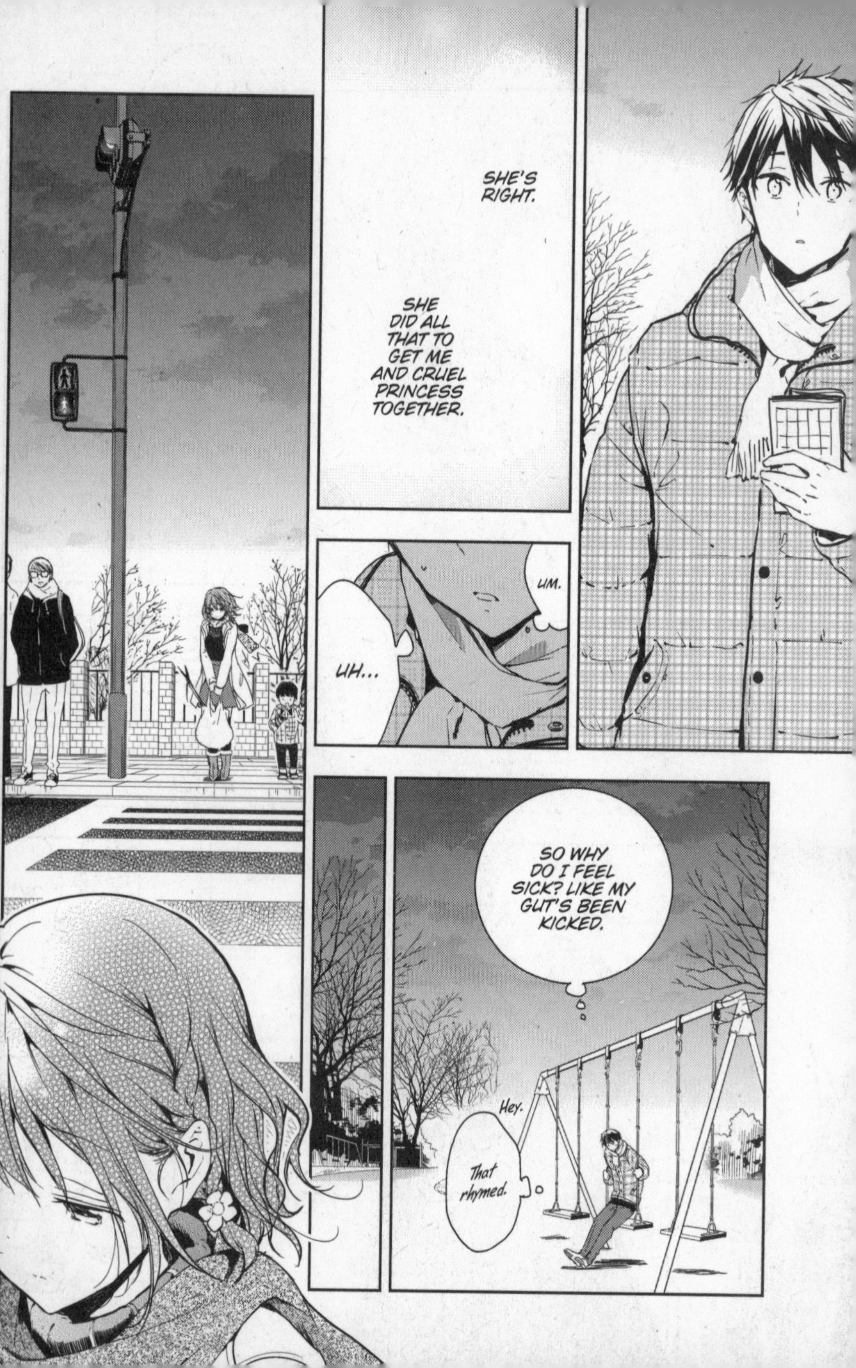
SHE'S RIGHT.
SHE DID ALL THAT TO GET ME AND CRUEL PRINCESS TOGETHER.
UM.
UH...
SO WHY DO I FEEL SICK? LIKE MY GUT'S BEEN KICKED.
Hey.
That rhymed.

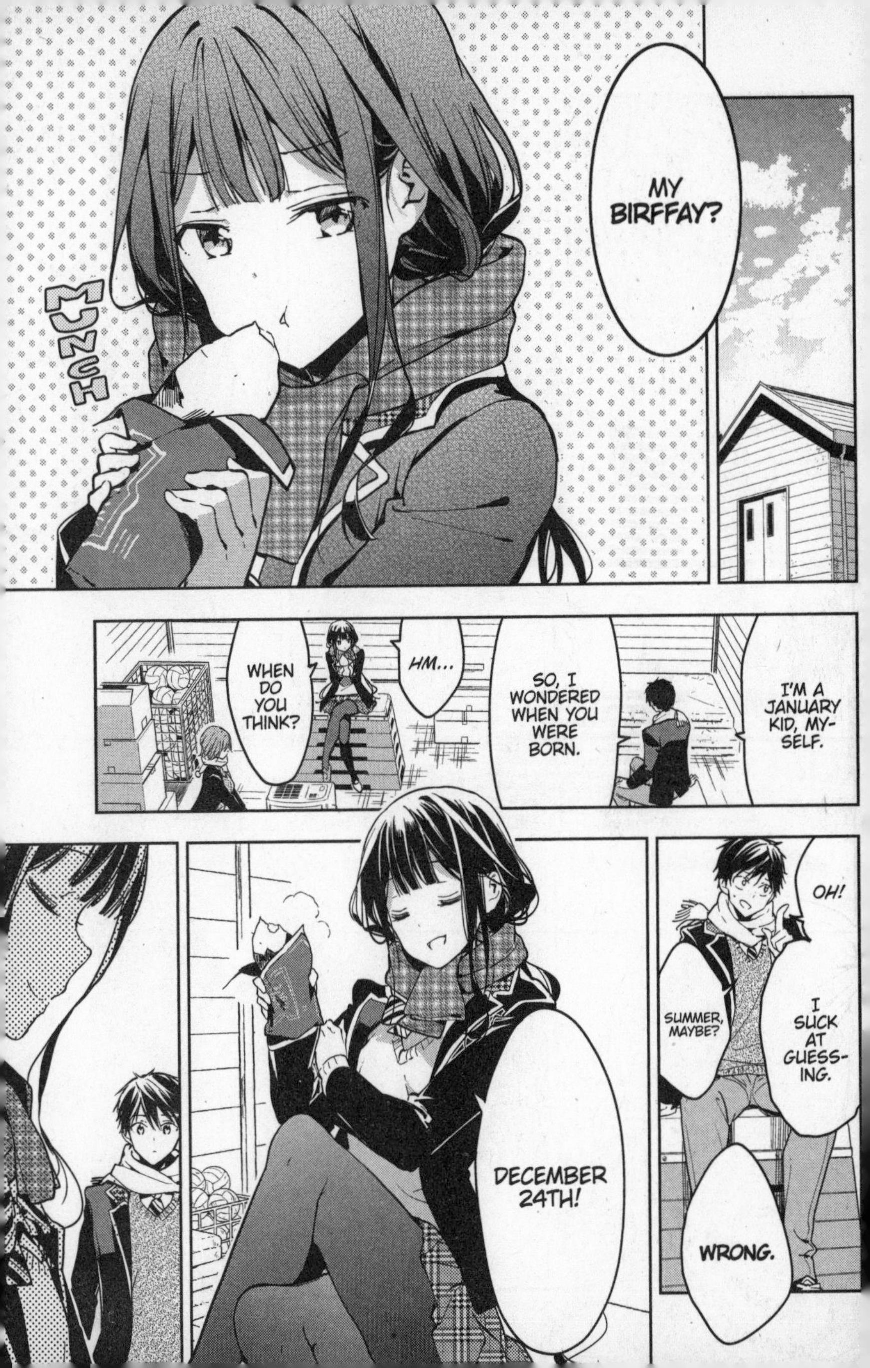
MY BIRFFAY?
MUNCH
I'M A JANUARY KID, MY-SELF.
SO, I WONDERED WHEN YOU WERE BORN.
HM...
WHEN DO YOU THINK?
OH!
I SUCK AT GUESS-ING.
SUMMER, MAYBE?
WRONG.
DECEMBER 24TH!

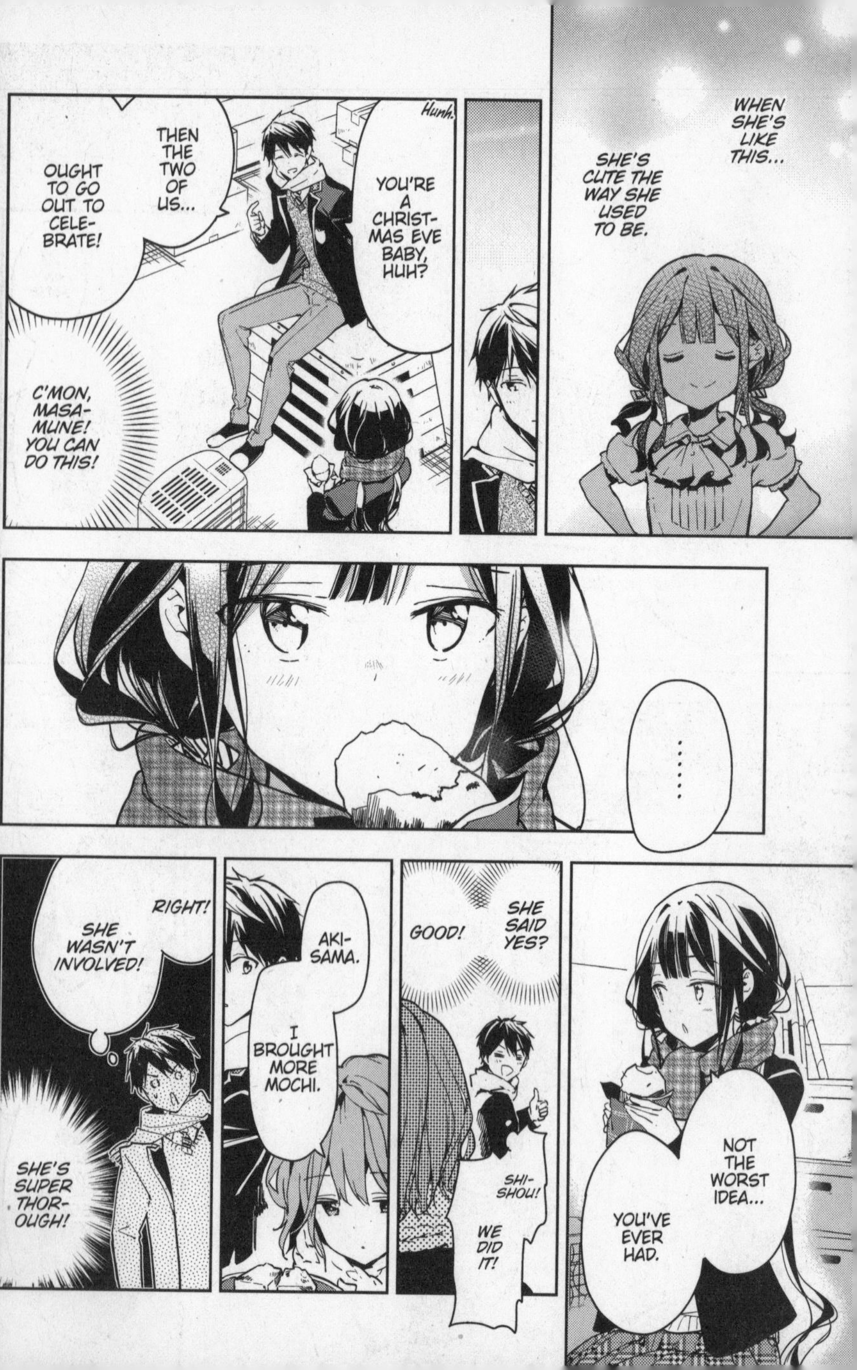
WHEN SHE'S LIKE THIS...
SHE'S CUTE THE WAY SHE USED TO BE.
Hunh.
YOU'RE A CHRIST-MAS EVE BABY, HUH?
THEN THE TWO OF US...
OUGHT TO GO OUT TO CELE-BRATE!
C'MON, MASA-MUNE! YOU CAN DO THIS!
......
NOT THE WORST IDEA...
YOU'VE EVER HAD.
SHE SAID YES?
GOOD!
SHI-SHOU!
WE DID IT!
AKI-SAMA.
I BROUGHT MORE MOCHI.
RIGHT!
SHE WASN'T INVOLVED!
SHE'S SUPER THOR-OUGH!

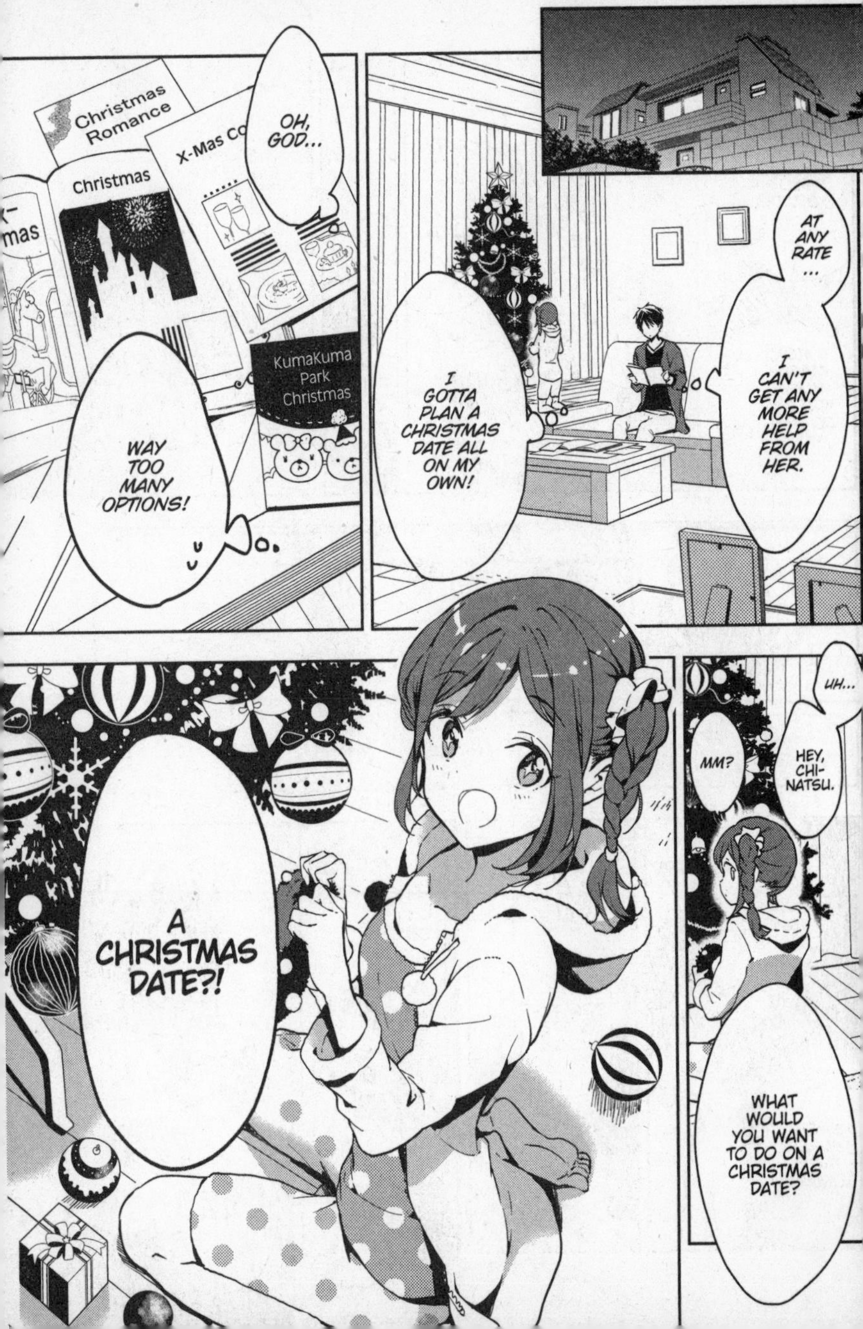
AT ANY RATE...
I CAN'T GET ANY MORE HELP FROM HER.
I GOTTA PLAN A CHRISTMAS DATE ALL ON MY OWN!
OH, GOD...
Christmas Romance
X-Mas Co
Christmas
X-mas
KumaKuma Park Christmas
WAY TOO MANY OPTIONS!
UH...
HEY, CHI-NATSU.
MM?
WHAT WOULD YOU WANT TO DO ON A CHRISTMAS DATE?
A CHRISTMAS DATE?!

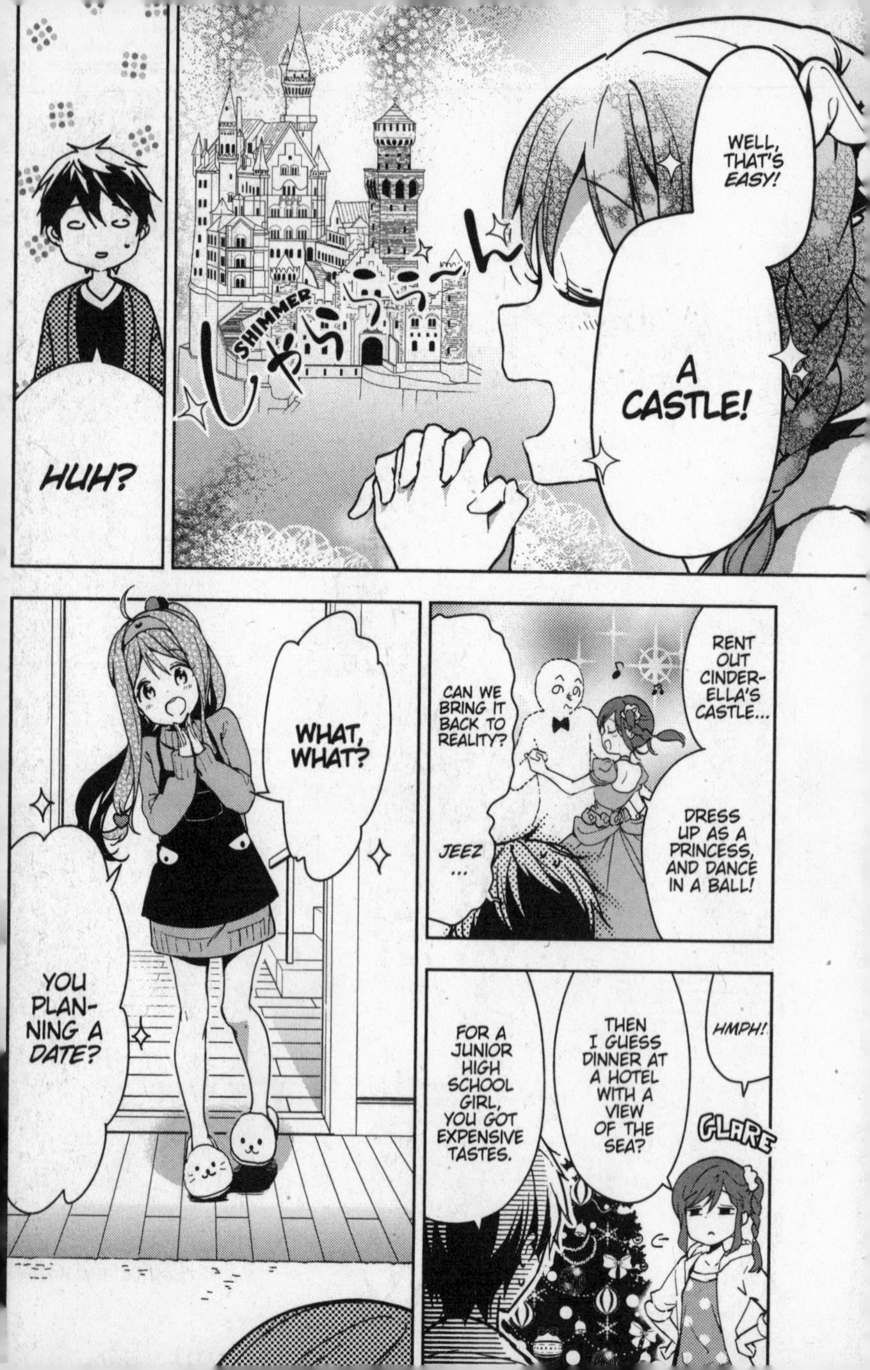
WELL, THAT'S *EASY!*
A CASTLE!
SHIMMER
HUH?
RENT OUT CINDERELLA'S CASTLE...
DRESS UP AS A PRINCESS, AND DANCE IN A BALL!
CAN WE BRING IT BACK TO REALITY?
JEEZ...
HMPH!
THEN I GUESS DINNER AT A HOTEL WITH A VIEW OF THE SEA?
GLARE
FOR A JUNIOR HIGH SCHOOL GIRL, YOU GOT EXPENSIVE TASTES.
WHAT, WHAT?
YOU PLAN-NING A *DATE?*

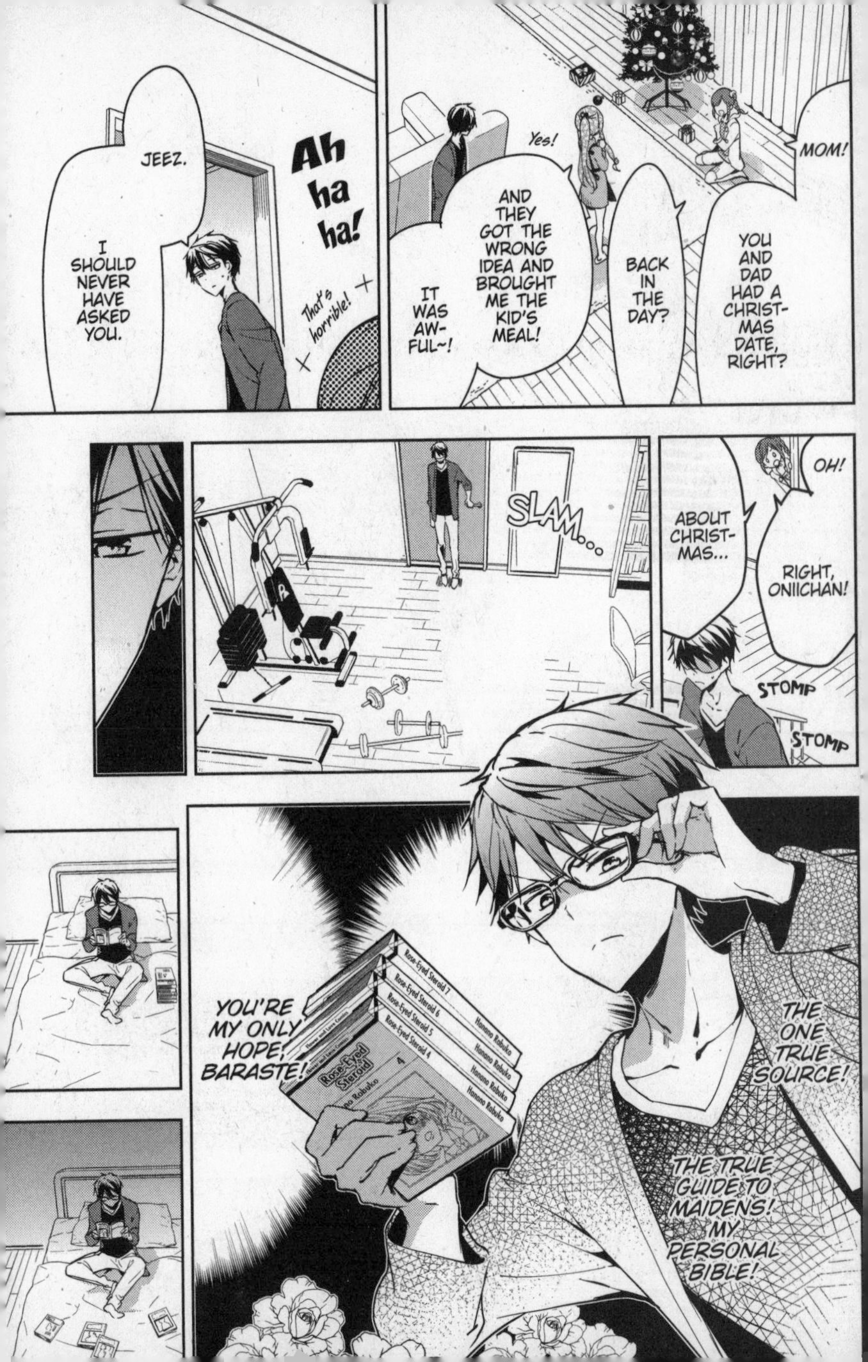
MOM!
YOU AND DAD HAD A CHRIST-MAS DATE, RIGHT?
BACK IN THE DAY?
Yes!
AND THEY GOT THE WRONG IDEA AND BROUGHT ME THE KID'S MEAL!
IT WAS AW-FUL~!
Ah ha ha!
That's horrible!
JEEZ.
I SHOULD NEVER HAVE ASKED YOU.
OH!
RIGHT, ONIICHAN!
ABOUT CHRIST-MAS...
STOMP
STOMP
SLAM...
THE ONE TRUE SOURCE!
YOU'RE MY ONLY HOPE, BARASTE!
Rose-Eyed Steroid 7
Rose-Eyed Steroid 6
Rose-Eyed Steroid 5
Rose-Eyed Steroid 4
Hanano Rabuko
Hanano Rabuko
Hanano Rabuko
Hanano Rabuko
Rose-Eyed Steroid
THE TRUE GUIDE TO MAIDENS! MY PERSONAL BIBLE!

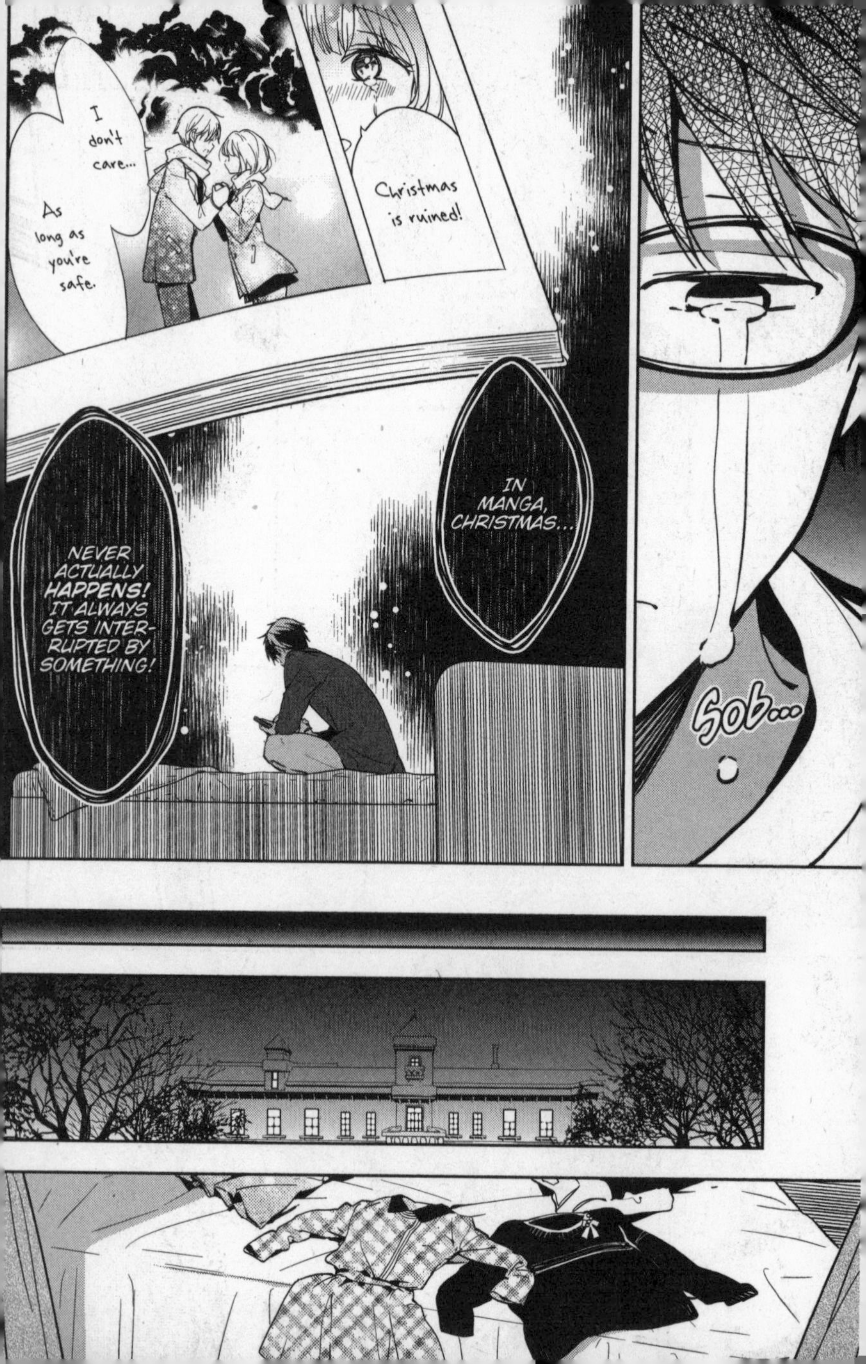
Sob...
Christmas is ruined!
I don't care... As long as you're safe.
IN MANGA, CHRISTMAS...
NEVER ACTUALLY HAPPENS! IT ALWAYS GETS INTER-RUPTED BY SOMETHING!

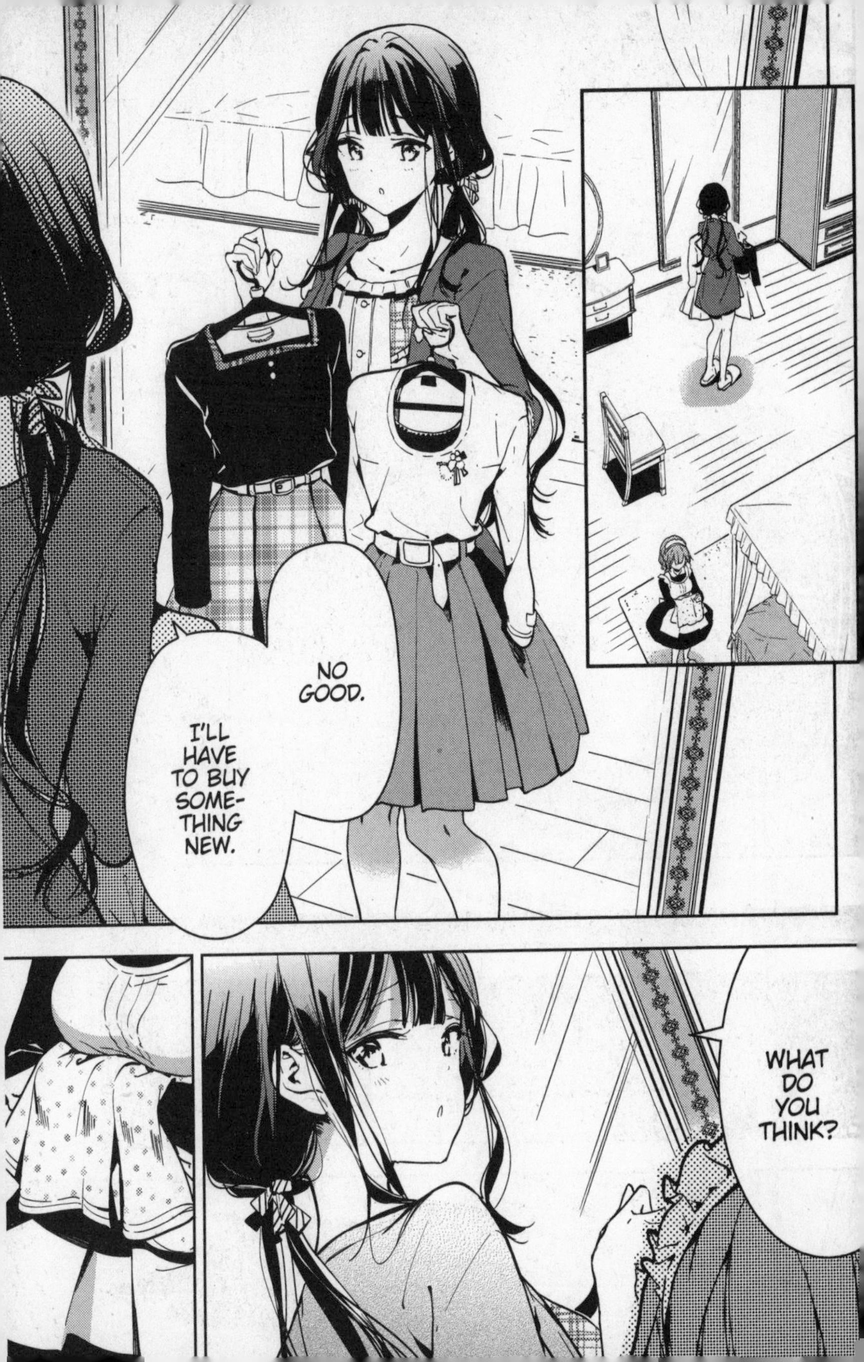
NO GOOD.
I'LL HAVE TO BUY SOME-THING NEW.
WHAT DO YOU THINK?

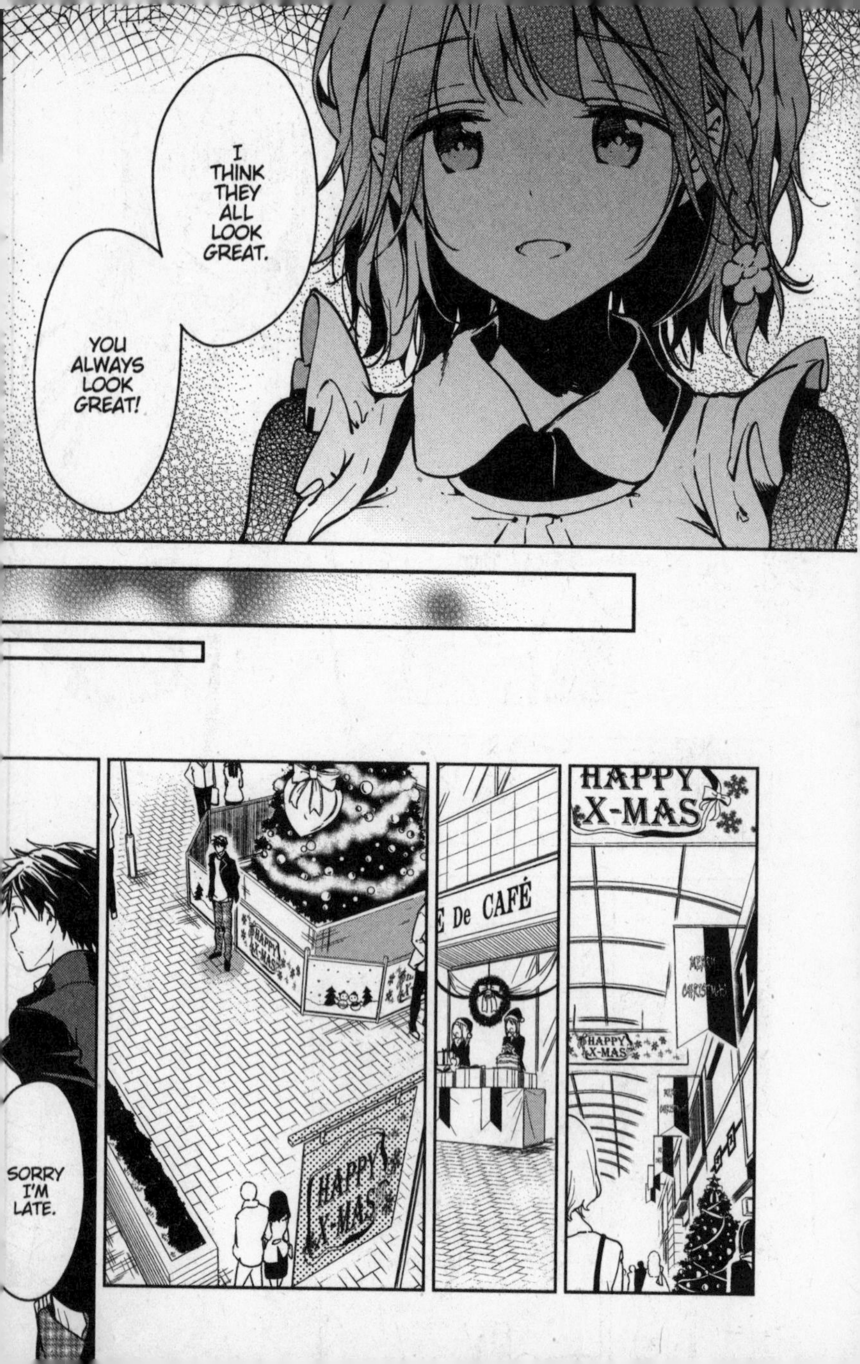
I THINK THEY ALL LOOK GREAT.
YOU ALWAYS LOOK GREAT!
HAPPY X-MAS
HAPPY X-MAS
E De CAFÉ
HAPPY X-MAS
HAPPY X-MAS
SORRY I'M LATE.

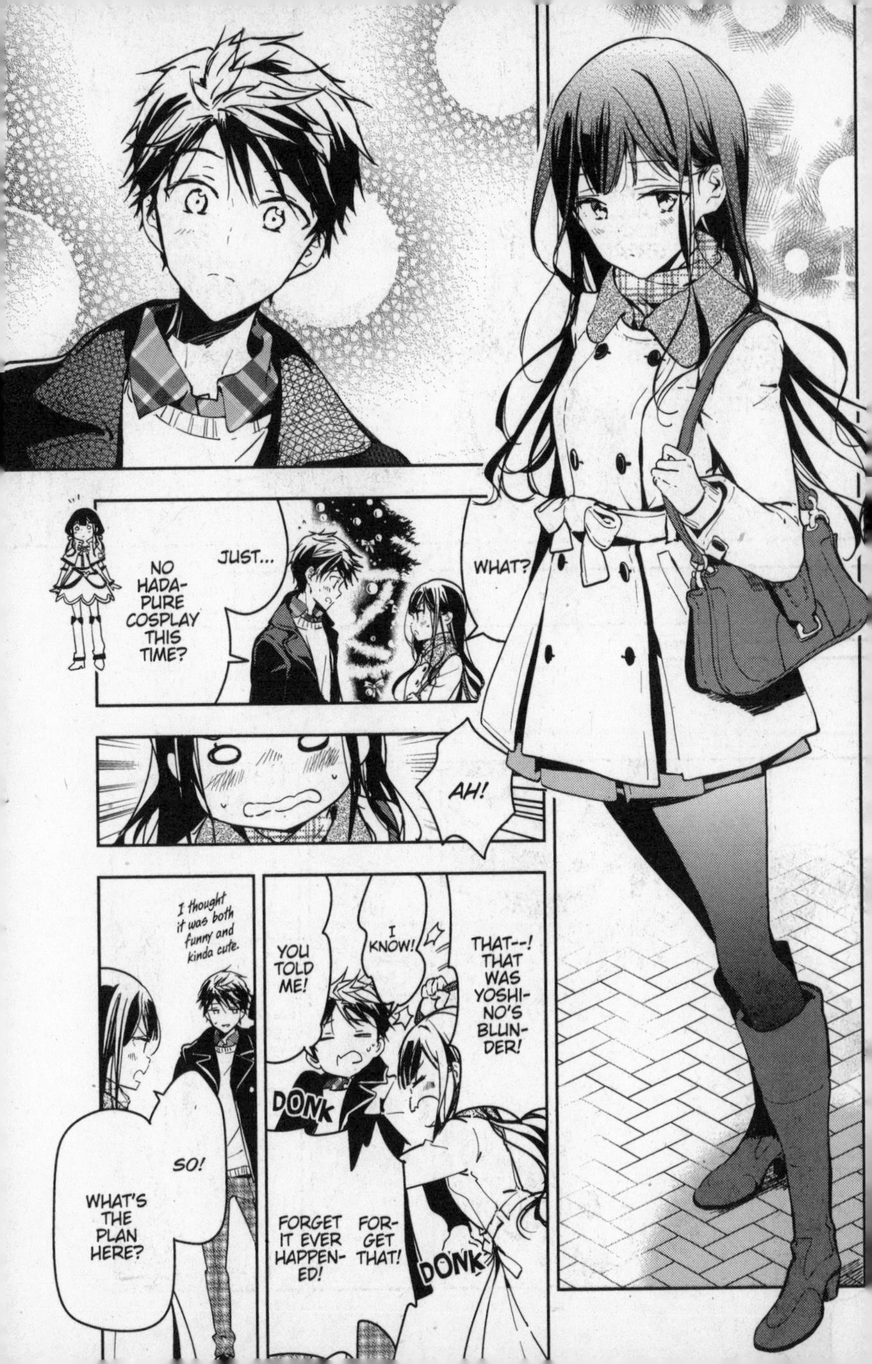
WHAT?
JUST...
NO HADA-PURE COSPLAY THIS TIME?
AH!
THAT--! THAT WAS YOSHINO'S BLUNDER!
I KNOW!
YOU TOLD ME!
DONK
FORGET THAT!
FORGET IT EVER HAPPENED!
DONK
I thought it was both funny and kinda cute.
SO!
WHAT'S THE PLAN HERE?

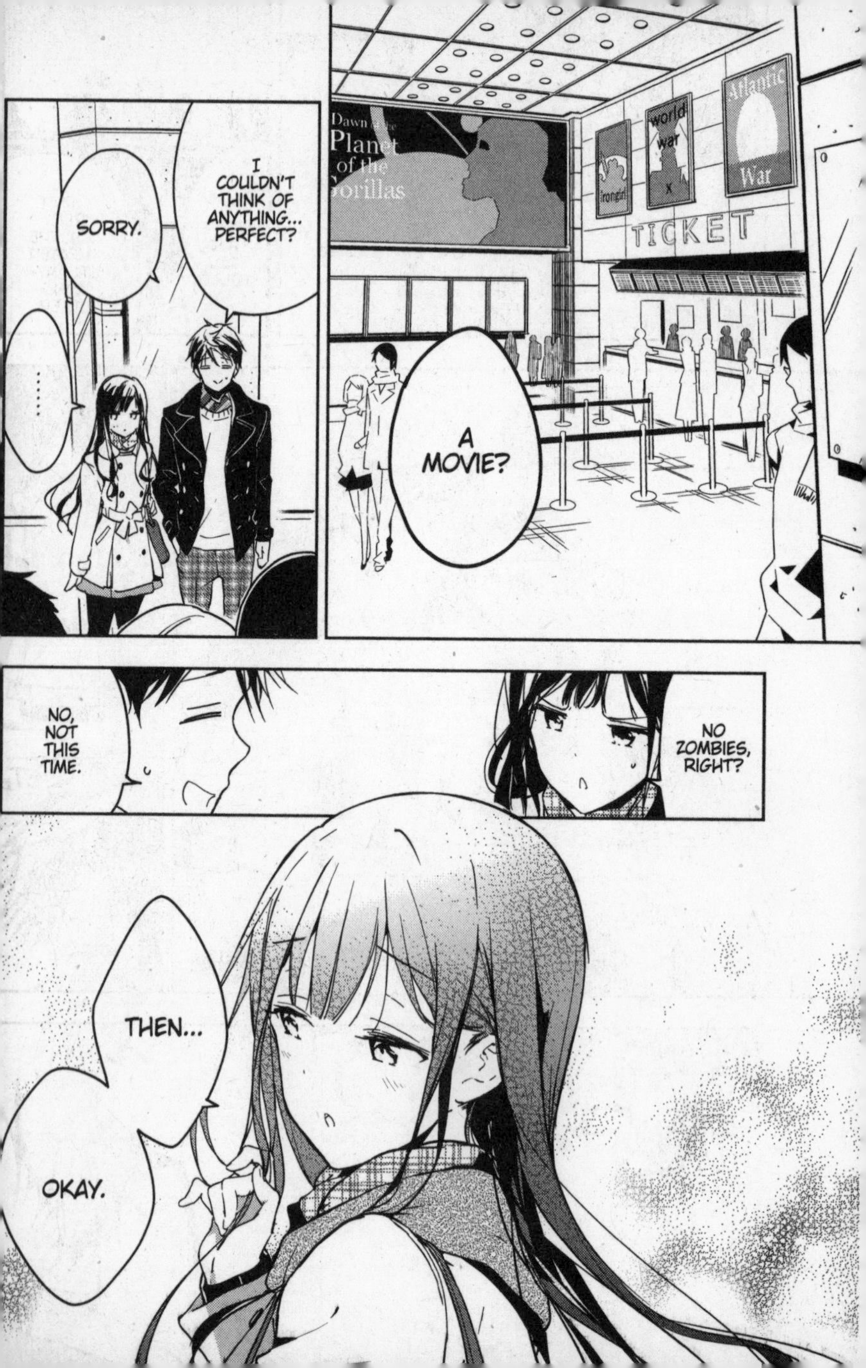
Planet
of the
world war
x
Atlantic
War
TICKET
A MOVIE?
I COULDN'T THINK OF ANYTHING... PERFECT?
SORRY.
......
NO ZOMBIES, RIGHT?
NO, NOT THIS TIME.
THEN...
OKAY.

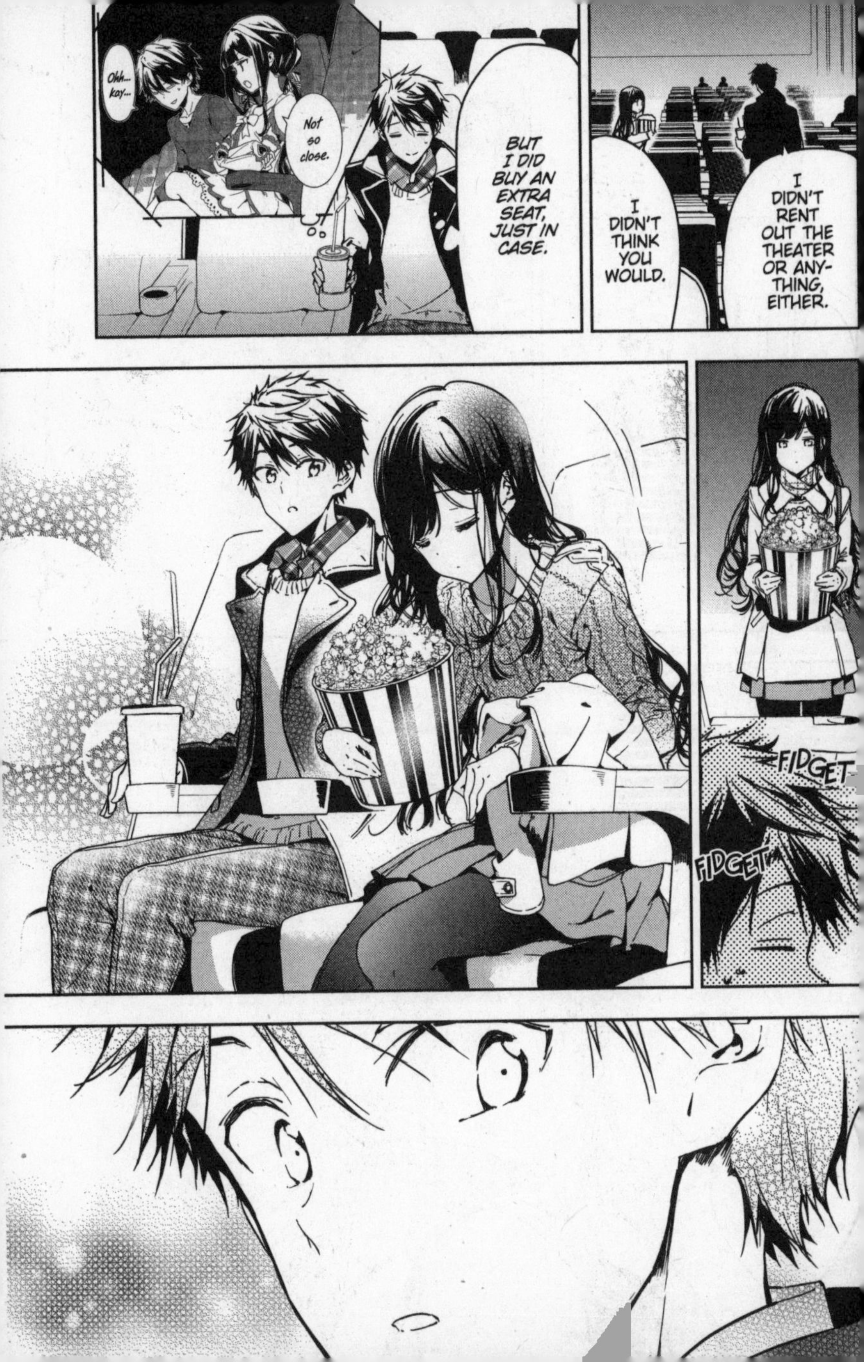
I DIDN'T RENT OUT THE THEATER OR ANYTHING, EITHER.
I DIDN'T THINK YOU WOULD.
BUT I DID BUY AN EXTRA SEAT, JUST IN CASE.
Not so close.
Ohh... kay...
FIDGET
FIDGET

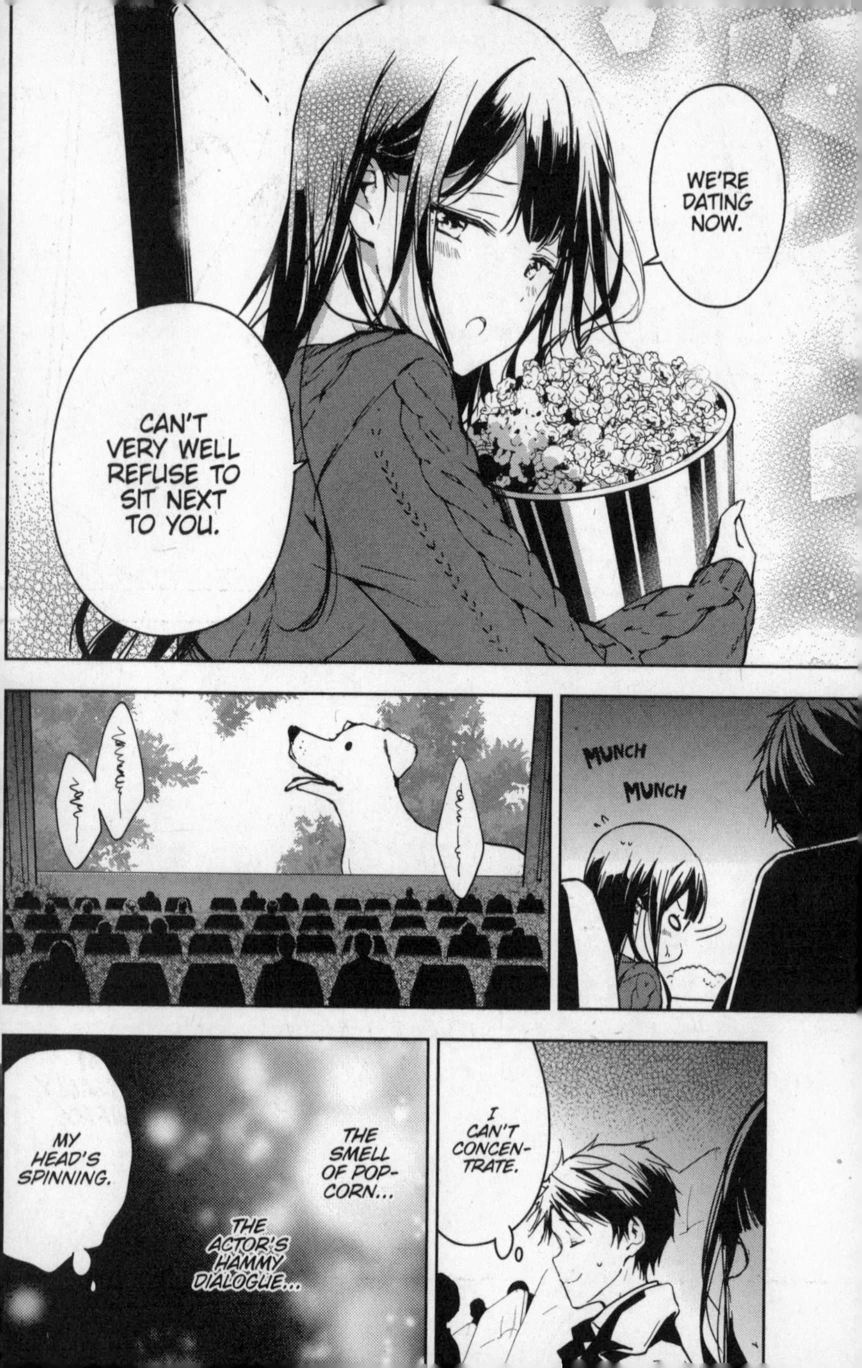
WE'RE DATING NOW.
CAN'T VERY WELL REFUSE TO SIT NEXT TO YOU.
MUNCH
MUNCH
I CAN'T CONCEN-TRATE.
THE SMELL OF POP-CORN...
THE ACTOR'S HAMMY DIALOGUE...
MY HEAD'S SPINNING.

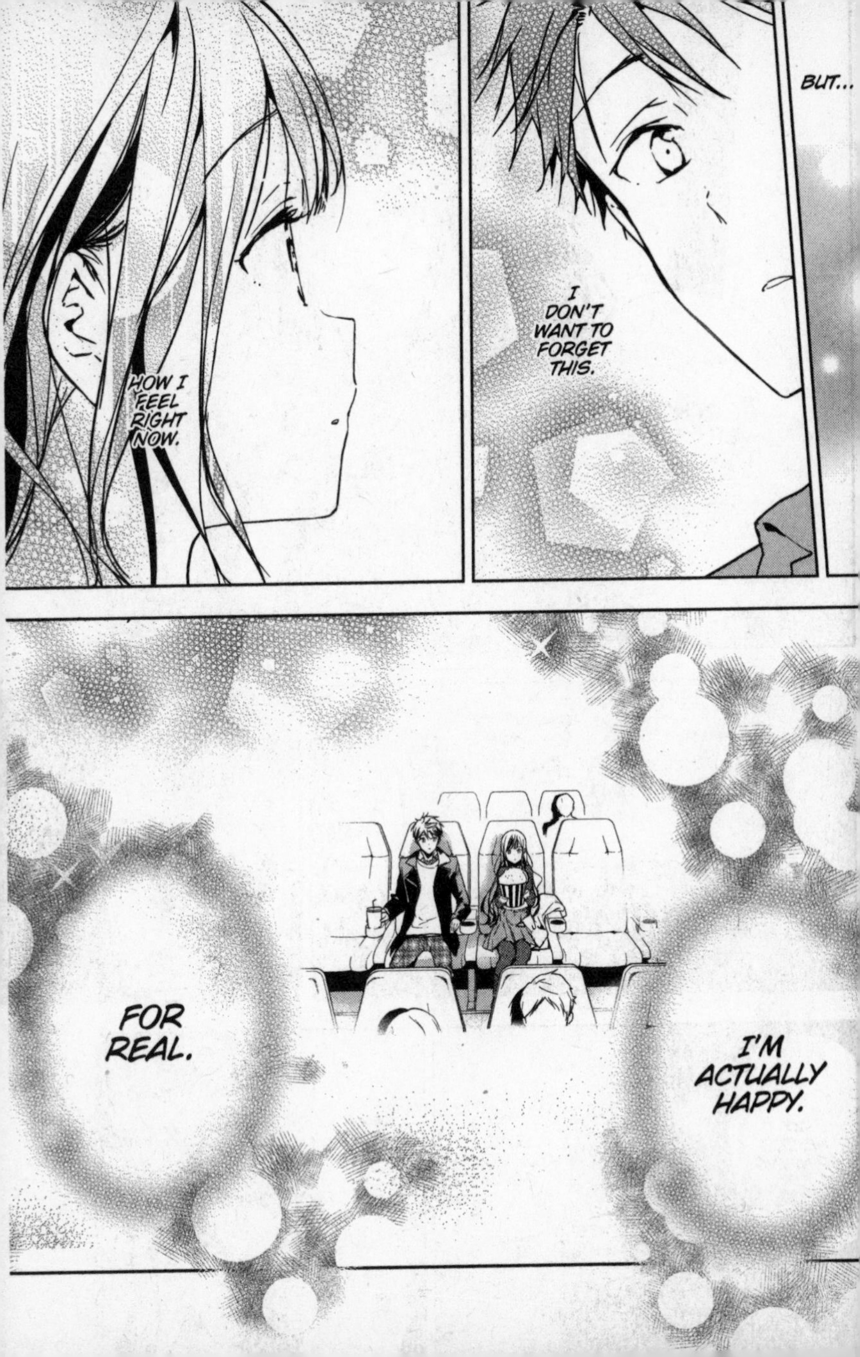
BUT...
I DON'T WANT TO FORGET THIS.
HOW I FEEL RIGHT NOW.
I'M ACTUALLY HAPPY.
FOR REAL.

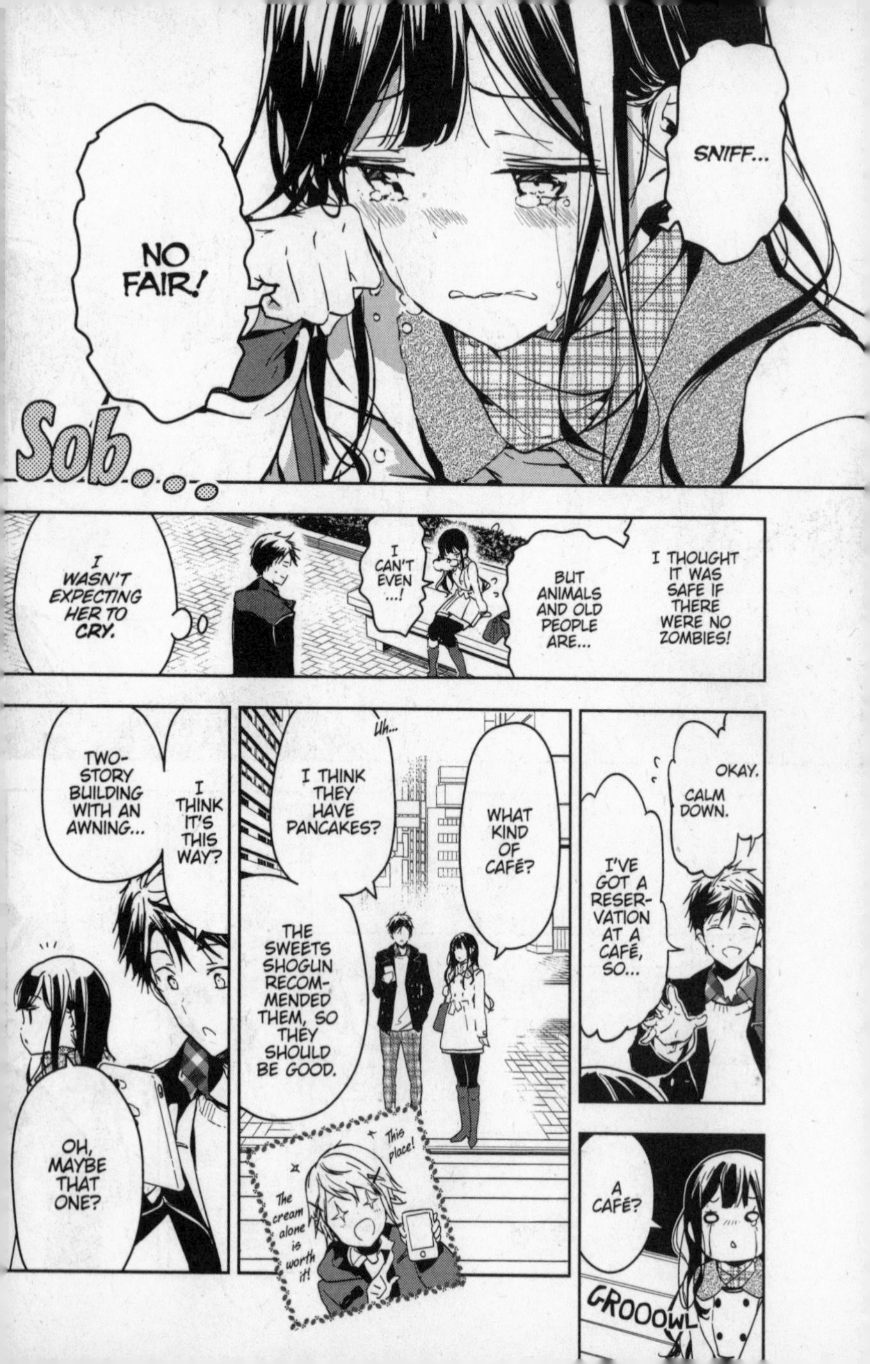
SNIFF...
NO FAIR!
Sob....
I THOUGHT IT WAS SAFE IF THERE WERE NO ZOMBIES!
BUT ANIMALS AND OLD PEOPLE ARE...
I CAN'T EVEN ...!
I WASN'T EXPECTING HER TO CRY.
OKAY. CALM DOWN.
I'VE GOT A RESERVATION AT A CAFÉ, SO...
A CAFÉ?
GROOOWL
WHAT KIND OF CAFÉ?
Uh...
I THINK THEY HAVE PANCAKES?
THE SWEETS SHOGUN RECOMMENDED THEM, SO THEY SHOULD BE GOOD.
This place!
The cream alone is worth it!
I THINK IT'S THIS WAY?
TWO-STORY BUILDING WITH AN AWNING...
OH, MAYBE THAT ONE?

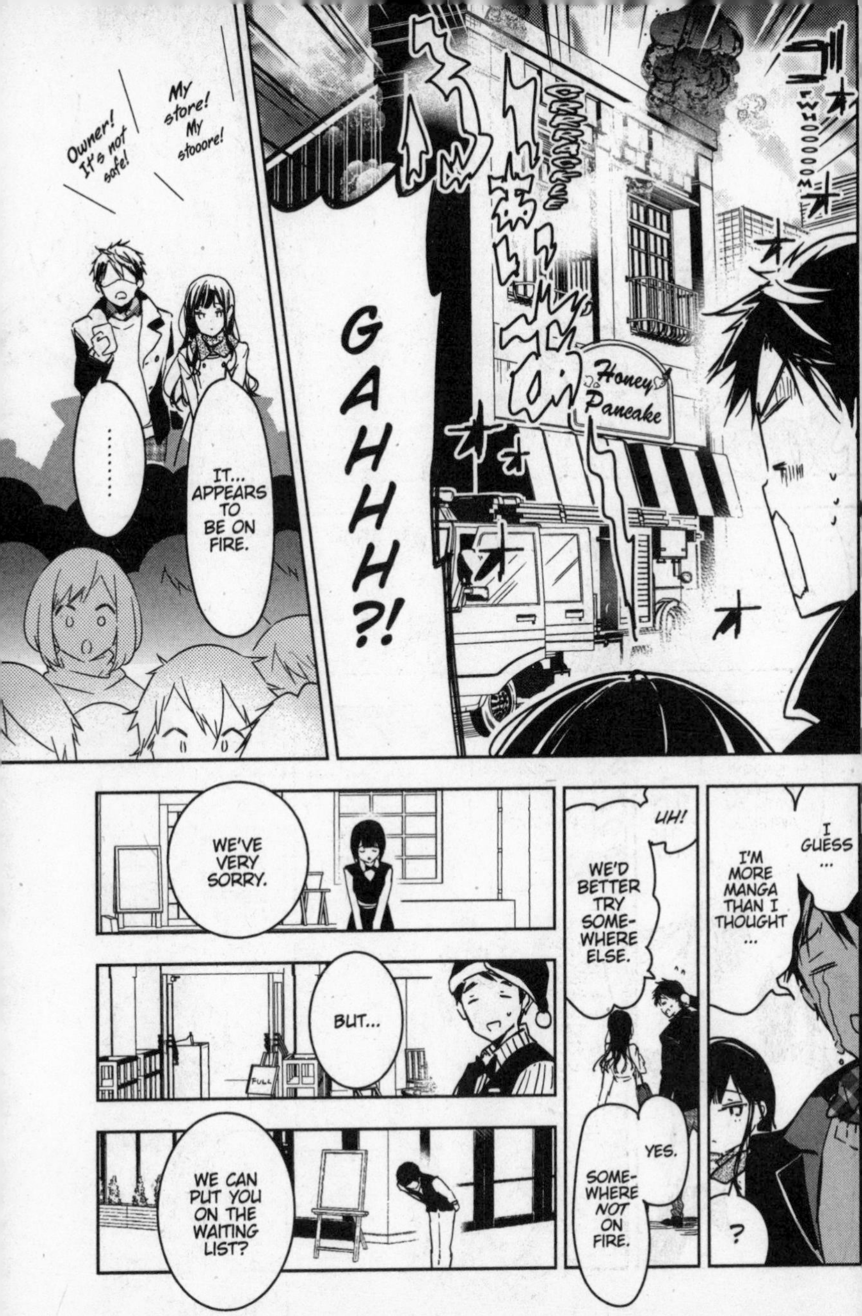
WHOOOOOOM
GAHHH?!
Honey Pancake
My store! My stooore!
Owner! It's not safe!
IT... APPEARS TO BE ON FIRE.
......
I GUESS ...
I'M MORE MANGA THAN I THOUGHT ...
?
UH!
WE'D BETTER TRY SOME-WHERE ELSE.
YES.
SOME-WHERE NOT ON FIRE.
WE'VE VERY SORRY.
BUT...
FULL
WE CAN PUT YOU ON THE WAITING LIST?

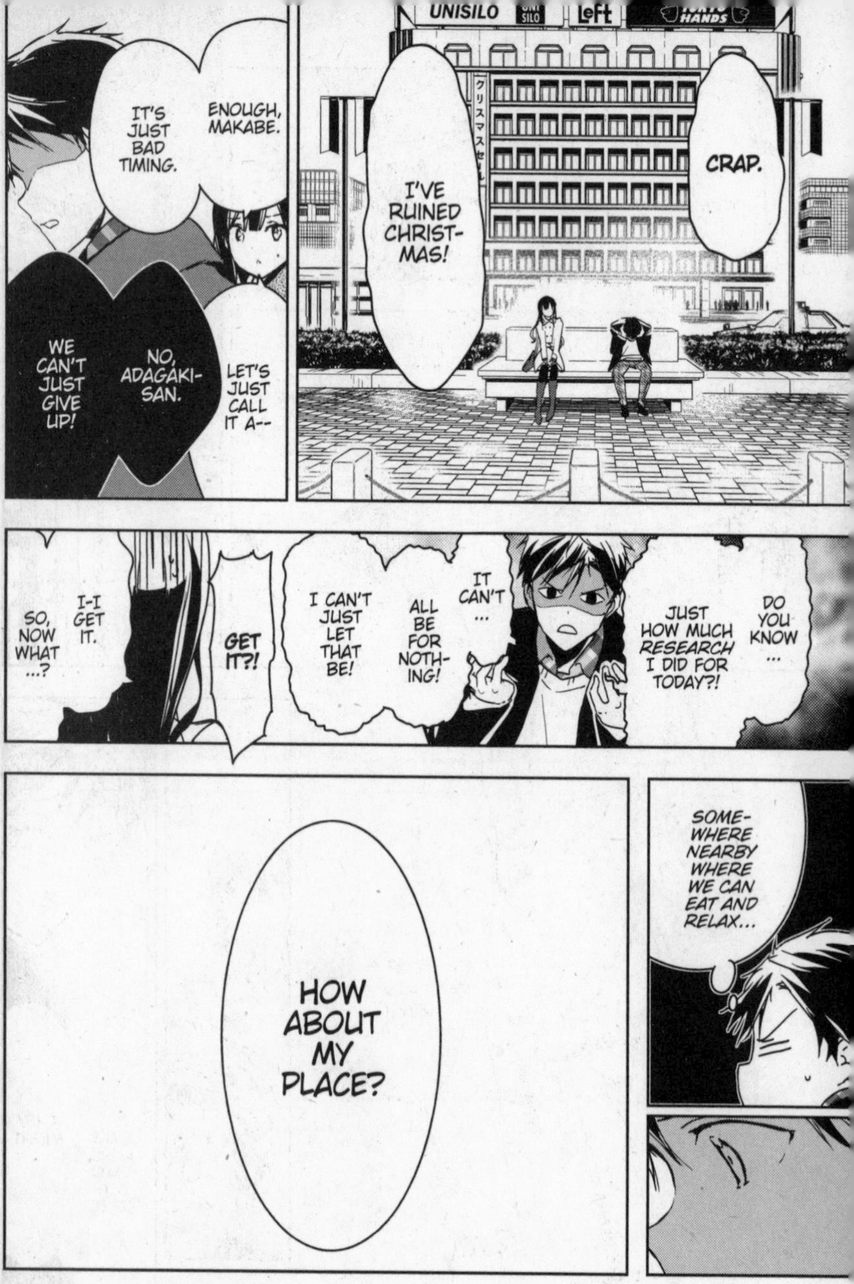
UNISILO
CRAP.
I'VE RUINED CHRISTMAS!
ENOUGH, MAKABE.
IT'S JUST BAD TIMING.
LET'S JUST CALL IT A--
NO, ADAGAKI-SAN.
WE CAN'T JUST GIVE UP!
DO YOU KNOW ...
JUST HOW MUCH RESEARCH I DID FOR TODAY?!
IT CAN'T ...
ALL BE FOR NOTHING!
I CAN'T JUST LET THAT BE!
GET IT?!
I-I GET IT.
SO, NOW WHAT ...?
SOMEWHERE NEARBY WHERE WE CAN EAT AND RELAX...
HOW ABOUT MY PLACE?

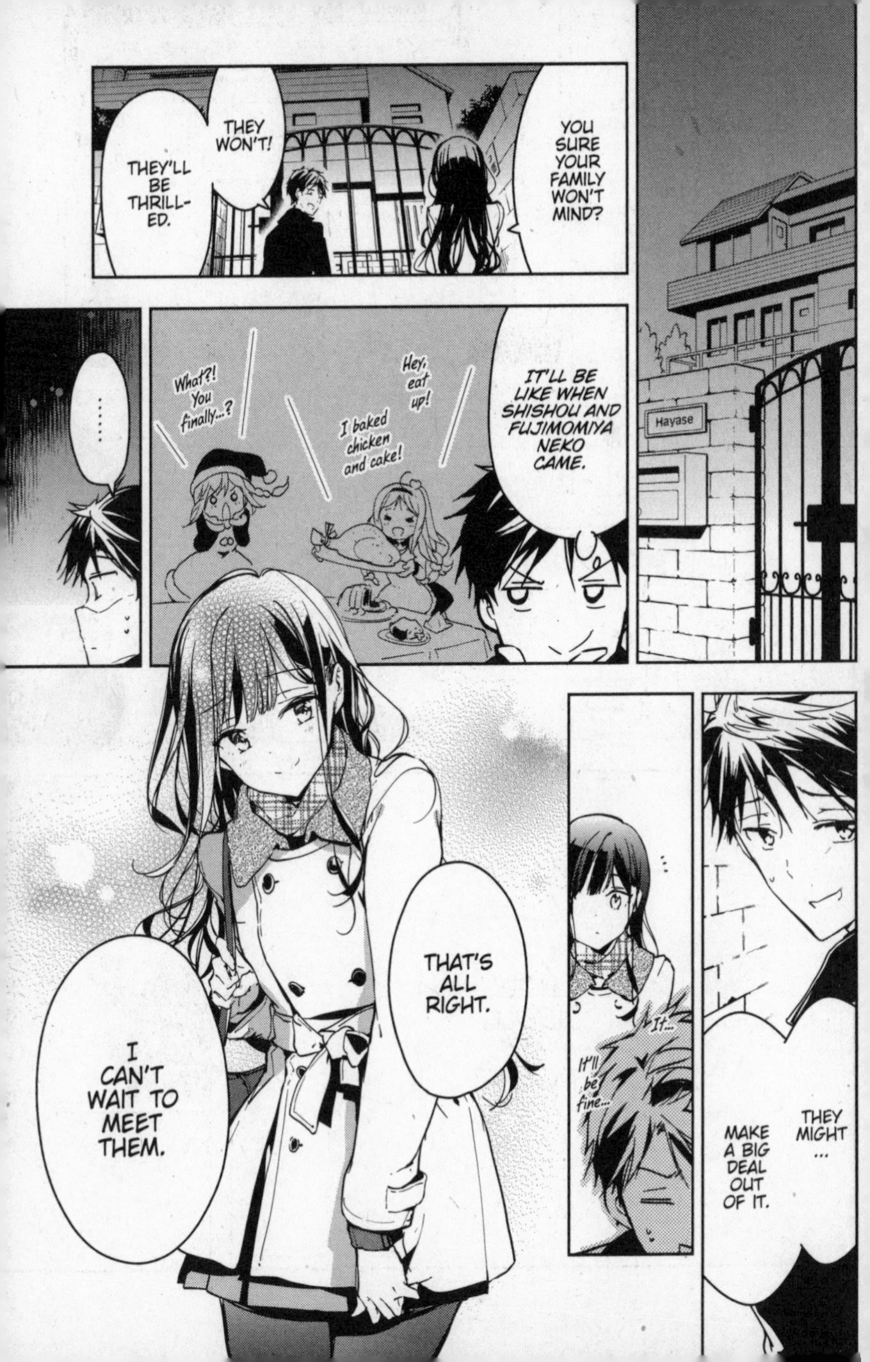
Hayase
YOU SURE YOUR FAMILY WON'T MIND?
THEY WON'T!
THEY'LL BE THRILL-ED.
IT'LL BE LIKE WHEN SHISHOU AND FUJIMOMIYA NEKO CAME.
Hey, eat up!
I baked chicken and cake!
What?! You finally...?
......
THEY MIGHT...
MAKE A BIG DEAL OUT OF IT.
It...
It'll be fine...
THAT'S ALL RIGHT.
I CAN'T WAIT TO MEET THEM.

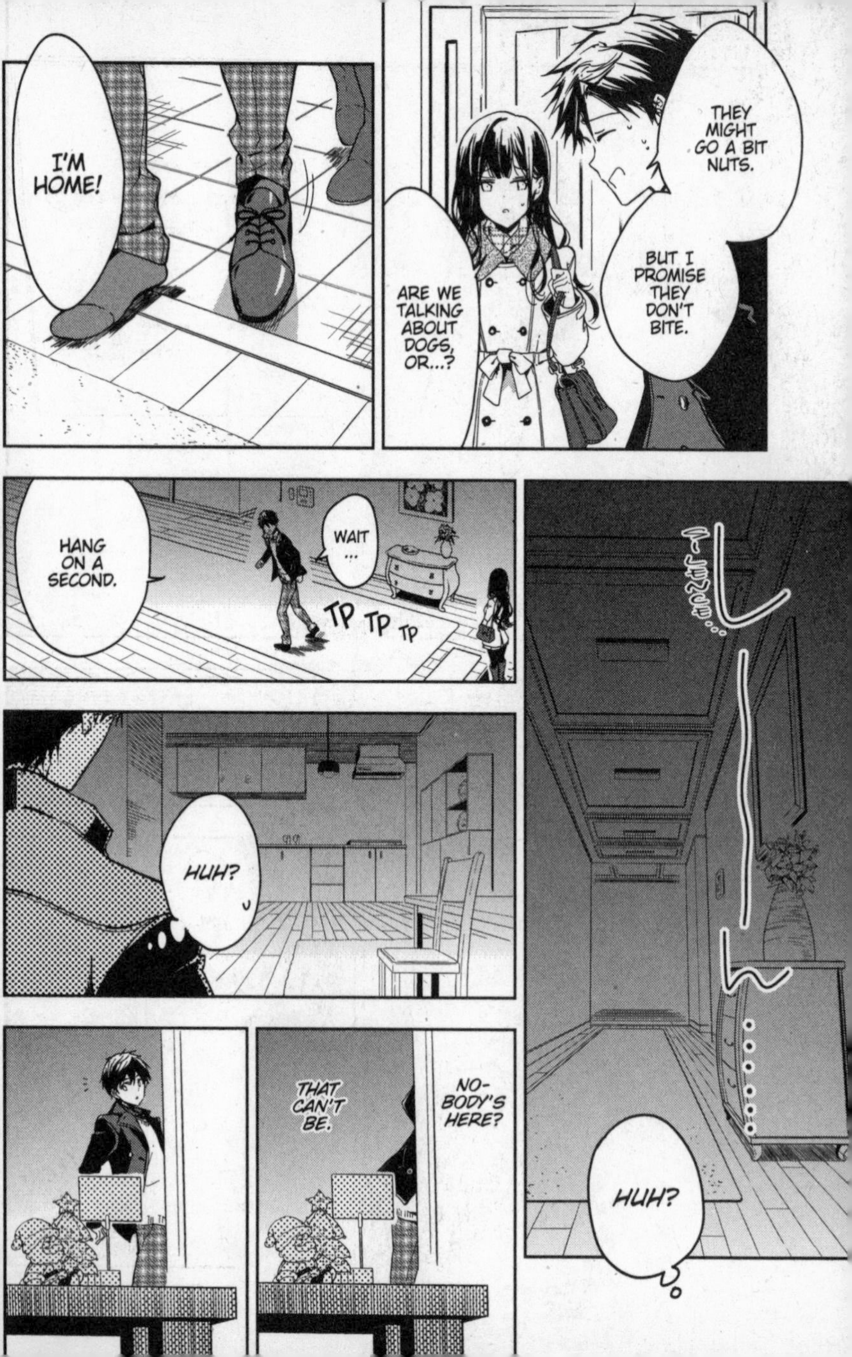
THEY MIGHT GO A BIT NUTS.
BUT I PROMISE THEY DON'T BITE.
ARE WE TALKING ABOUT DOGS, OR...?
I'M HOME!
HANG ON A SECOND.
WAIT ...
TP TP TP
HUH?
しーーん……
HUH?
NO-BODY'S HERE?
THAT CAN'T BE.

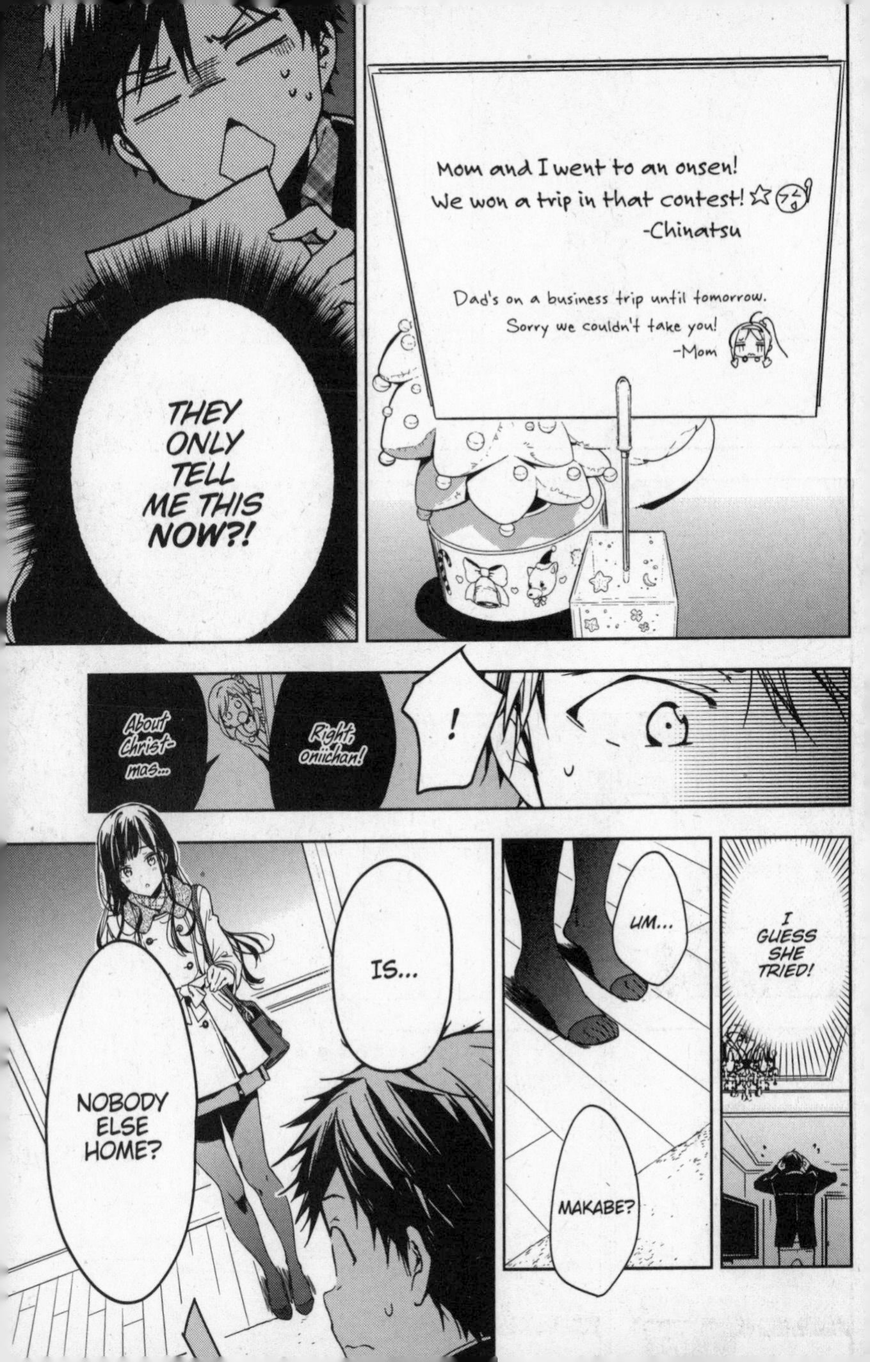

Mom and I went to an onsen! We won a trip in that contest! ☆
-Chinatsu
Dad's on a business trip until tomorrow. Sorry we couldn't take you!
-Mom
THEY ONLY TELL ME THIS NOW?!
!
Right, oniichan!
About Christmas...
I GUESS SHE TRIED!
UM...
MAKABE?
IS...
NOBODY ELSE HOME?

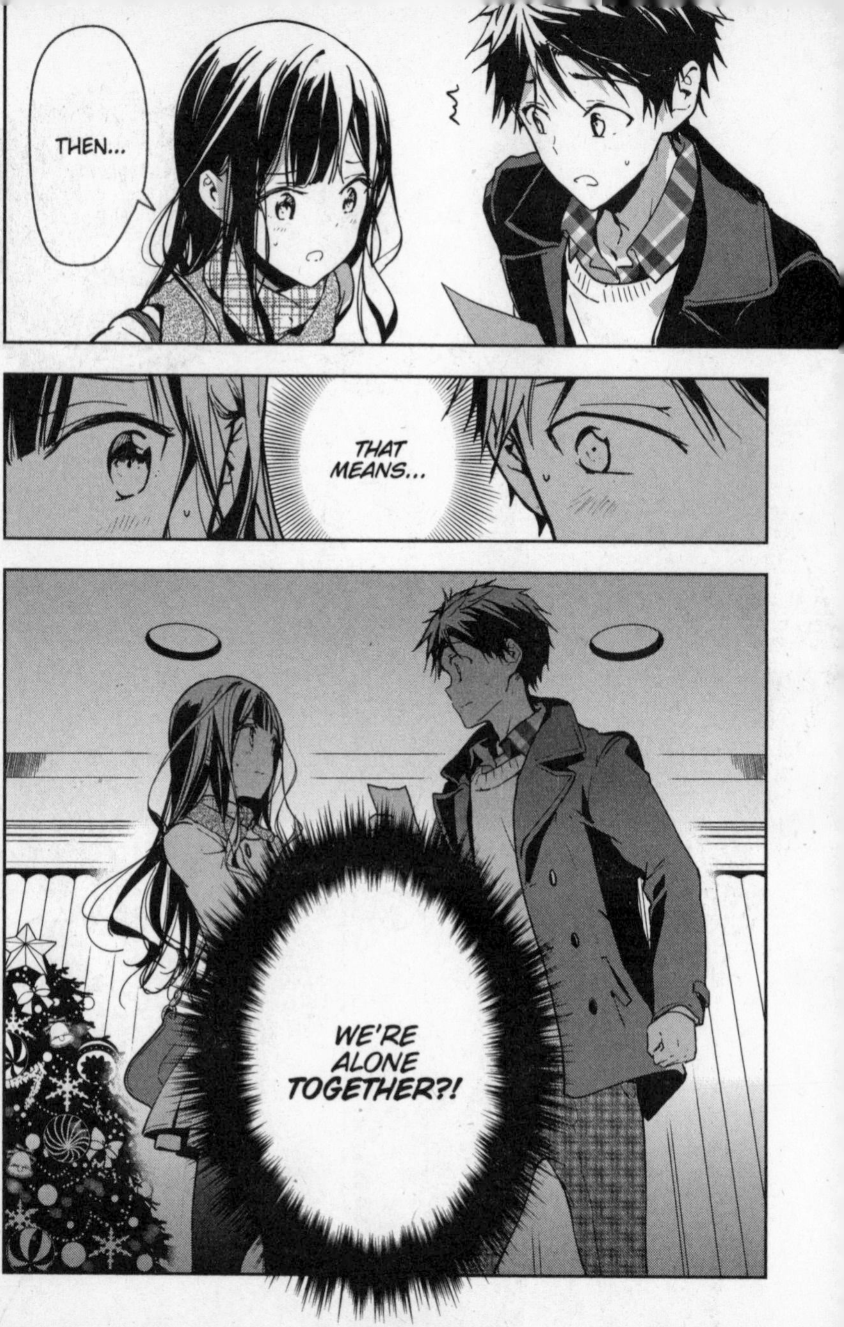
THEN...
THAT MEANS...
WE'RE ALONE TOGETHER?!

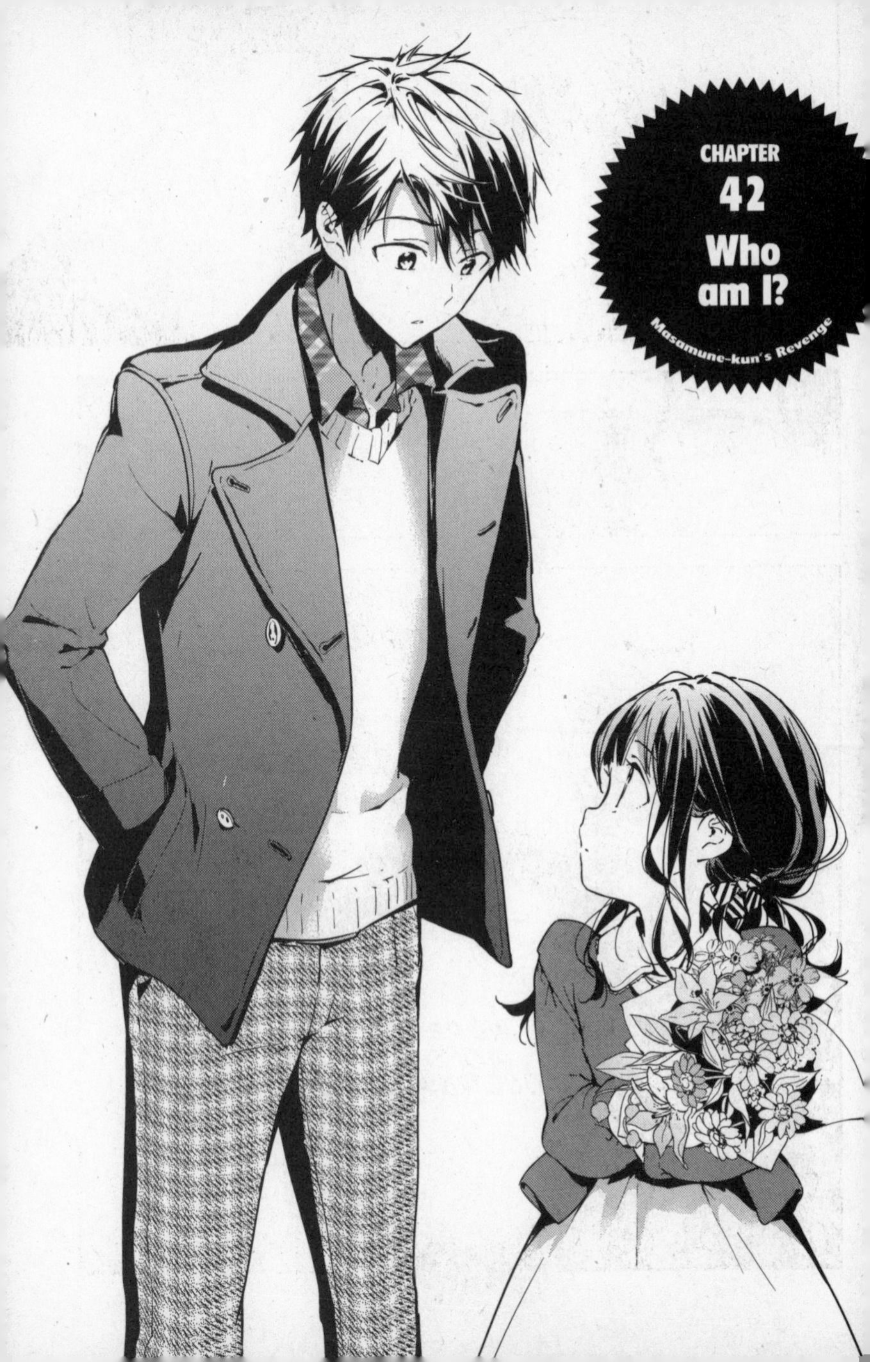
CHAPTER
42
Who am I?
Masamune-kun's Revenge

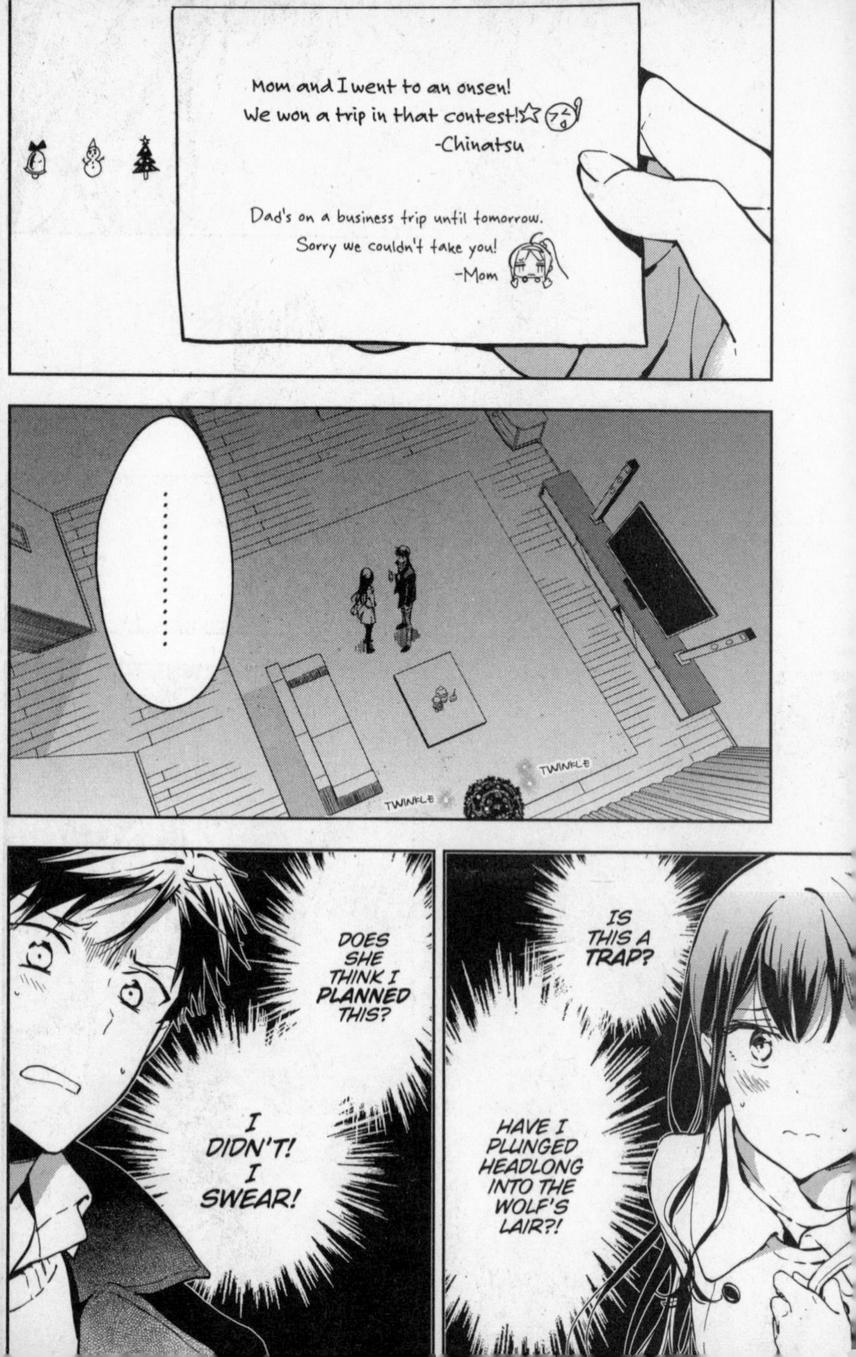
Mom and I went to an onsen! We won a trip in that contest!☆
-Chinatsu
Dad's on a business trip until tomorrow. Sorry we couldn't take you!
-Mom
......
TWINKLE
TWINKLE
IS THIS A TRAP?
HAVE I PLUNGED HEADLONG INTO THE WOLF'S LAIR?!
DOES SHE THINK I PLANNED THIS?
I DIDN'T! I SWEAR!

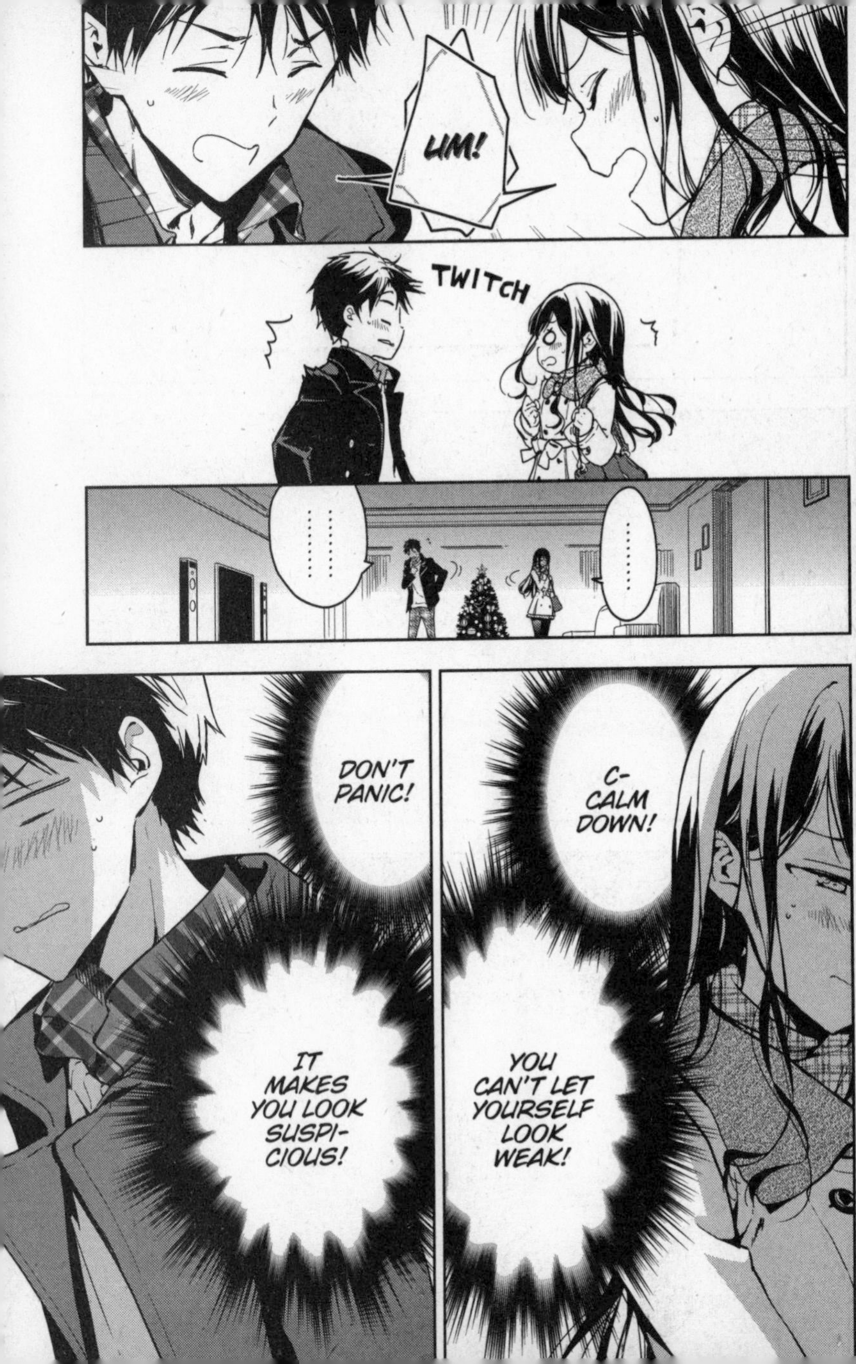
UM!
TWITCH
......
......
C- CALM DOWN!
YOU CAN'T LET YOURSELF LOOK WEAK!
DON'T PANIC!
IT MAKES YOU LOOK SUSPI- CIOUS!

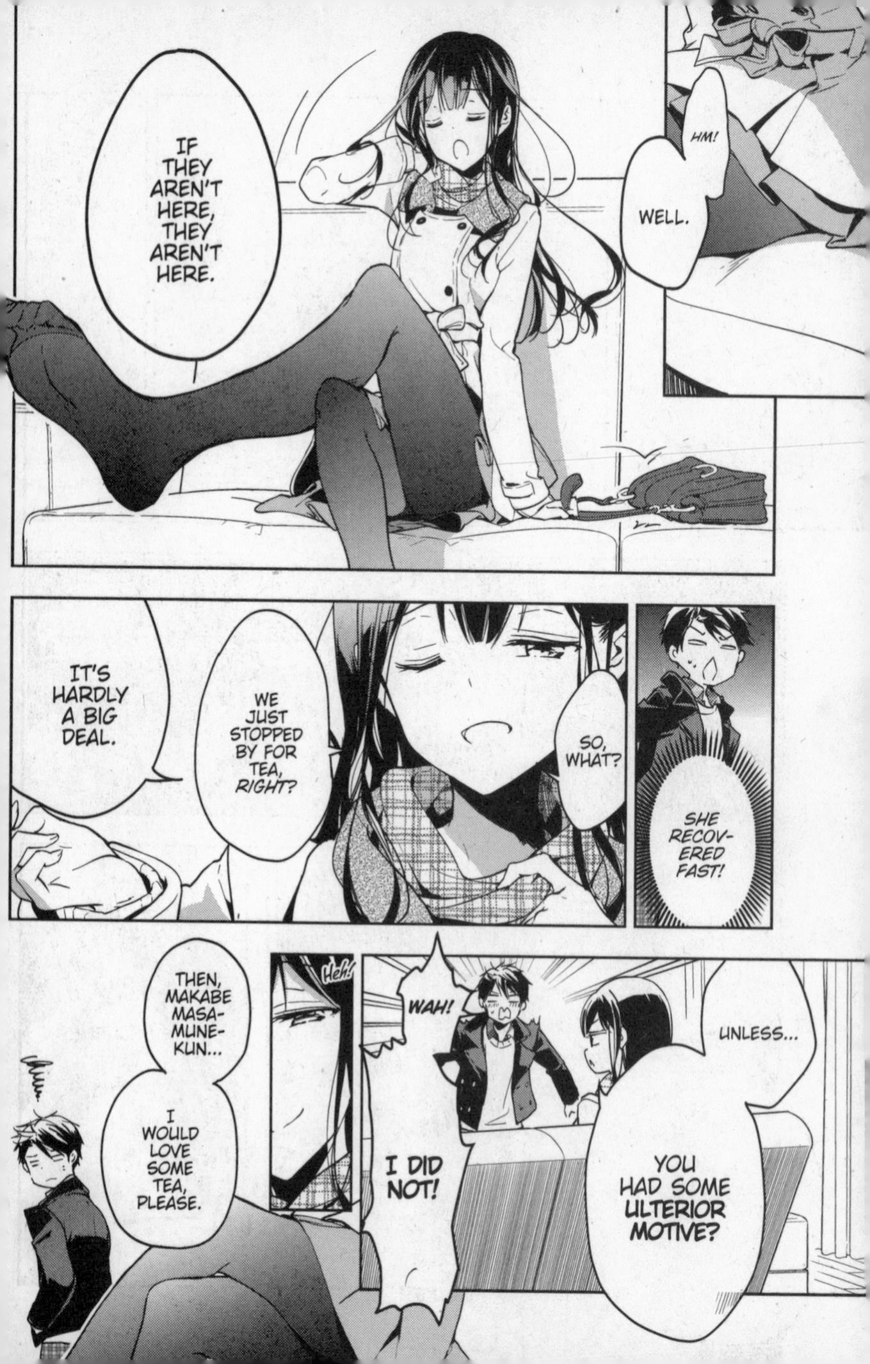
HM!
WELL.
IF THEY AREN'T HERE, THEY AREN'T HERE.
SHE RECOVERED FAST!
SO, WHAT?
WE JUST STOPPED BY FOR TEA, *RIGHT?*
IT'S HARDLY A BIG DEAL.
UNLESS...
YOU HAD SOME ULTERIOR MOTIVE?
WAH!
I DID NOT!
Heh!
THEN, MAKABE MASAMUNE-KUN...
I WOULD LOVE SOME TEA, PLEASE.

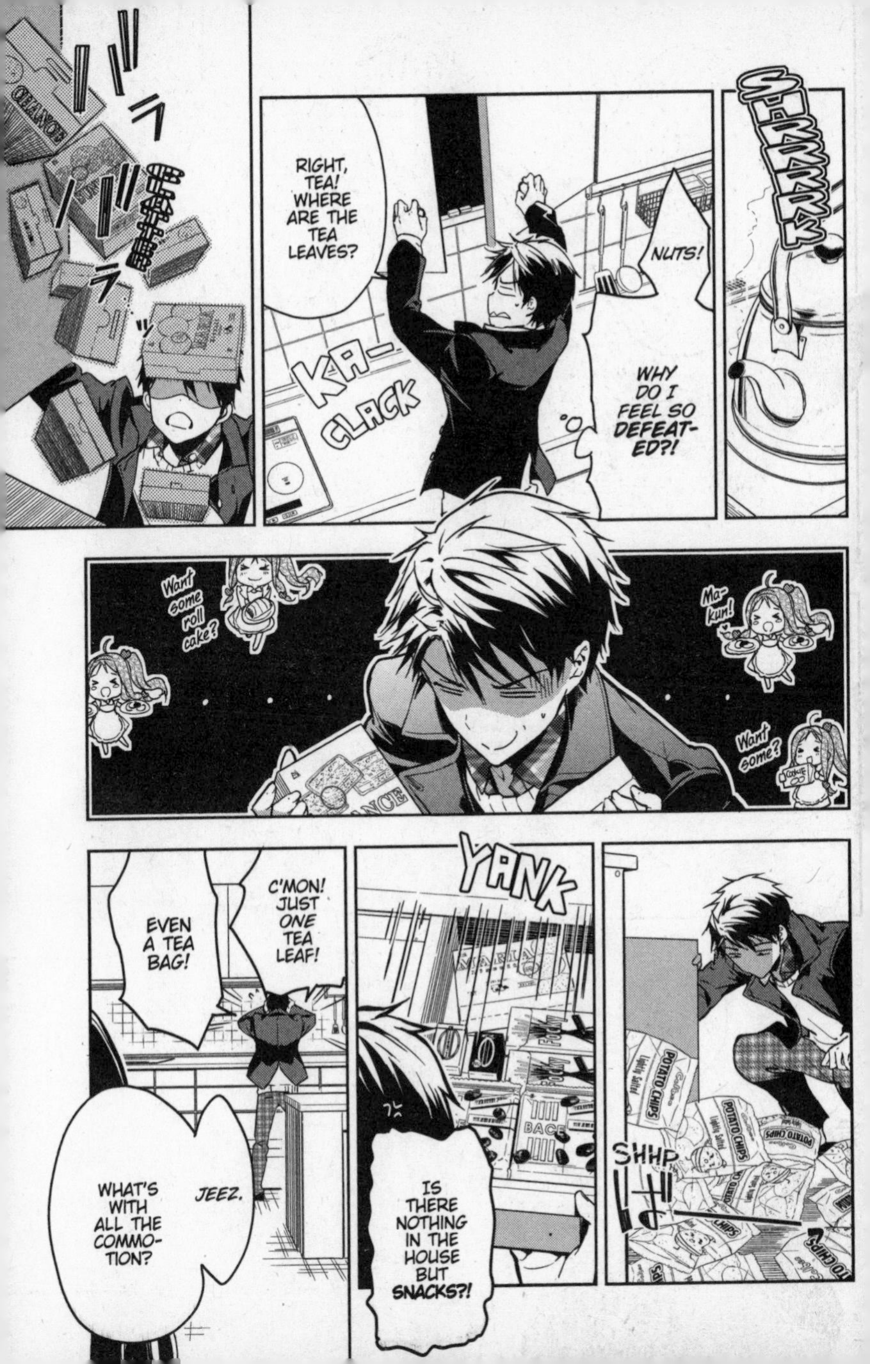
SPRAAAAY
RIGHT, TEA! WHERE ARE THE TEA LEAVES?
NUTS!
WHY DO I FEEL SO DEFEATED?!
KA-CLACK
Ma-kun!
Want some?
Want some roll cake?
YANK
IS THERE NOTHING IN THE HOUSE BUT SNACKS?!
C'MON! JUST ONE TEA LEAF!
EVEN A TEA BAG!
JEEZ.
WHAT'S WITH ALL THE COMMOTION?

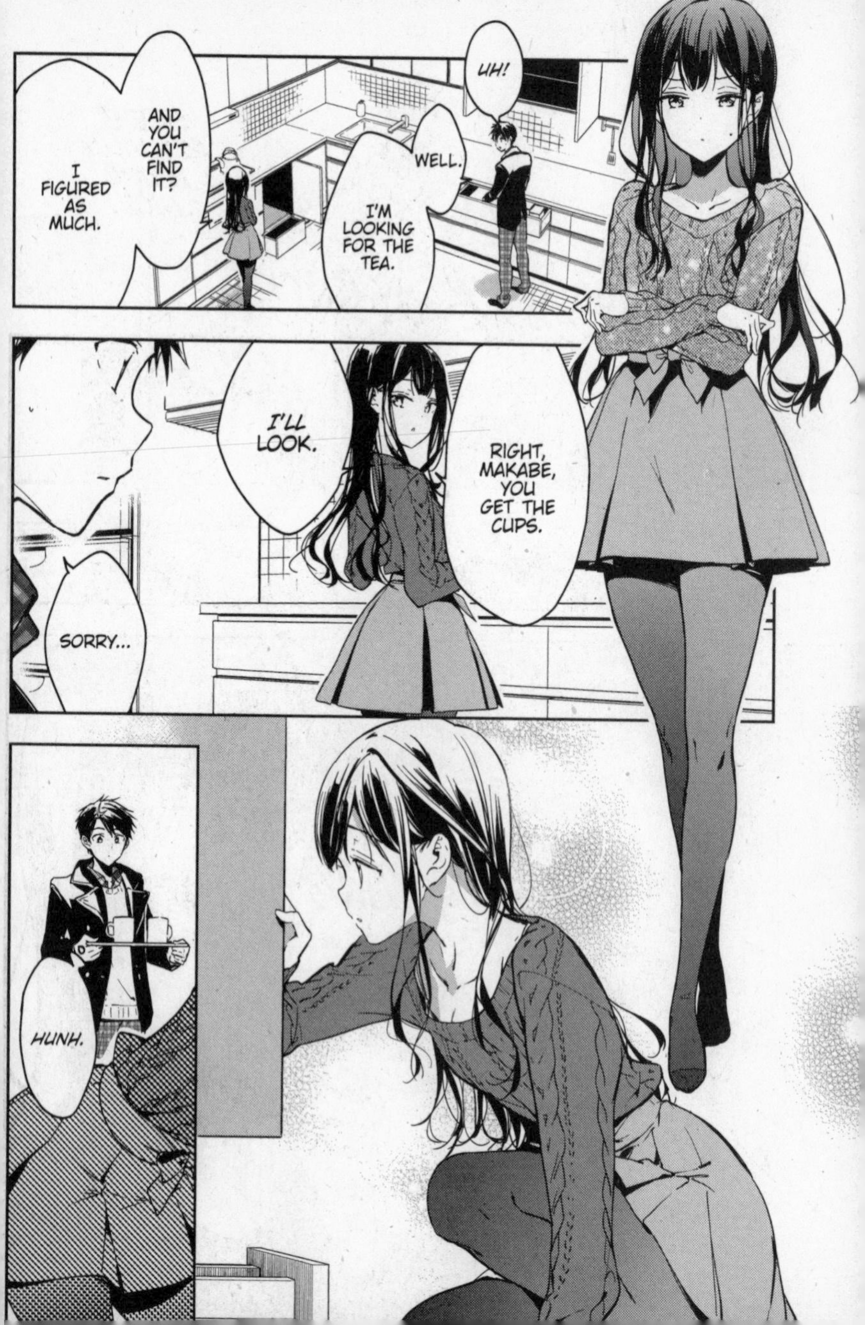
UH!
WELL.
I'M LOOKING FOR THE TEA.
AND YOU CAN'T FIND IT?
I FIGURED AS MUCH.
RIGHT, MAKABE, YOU GET THE CUPS.
I'LL LOOK.
SORRY...
HUNH.

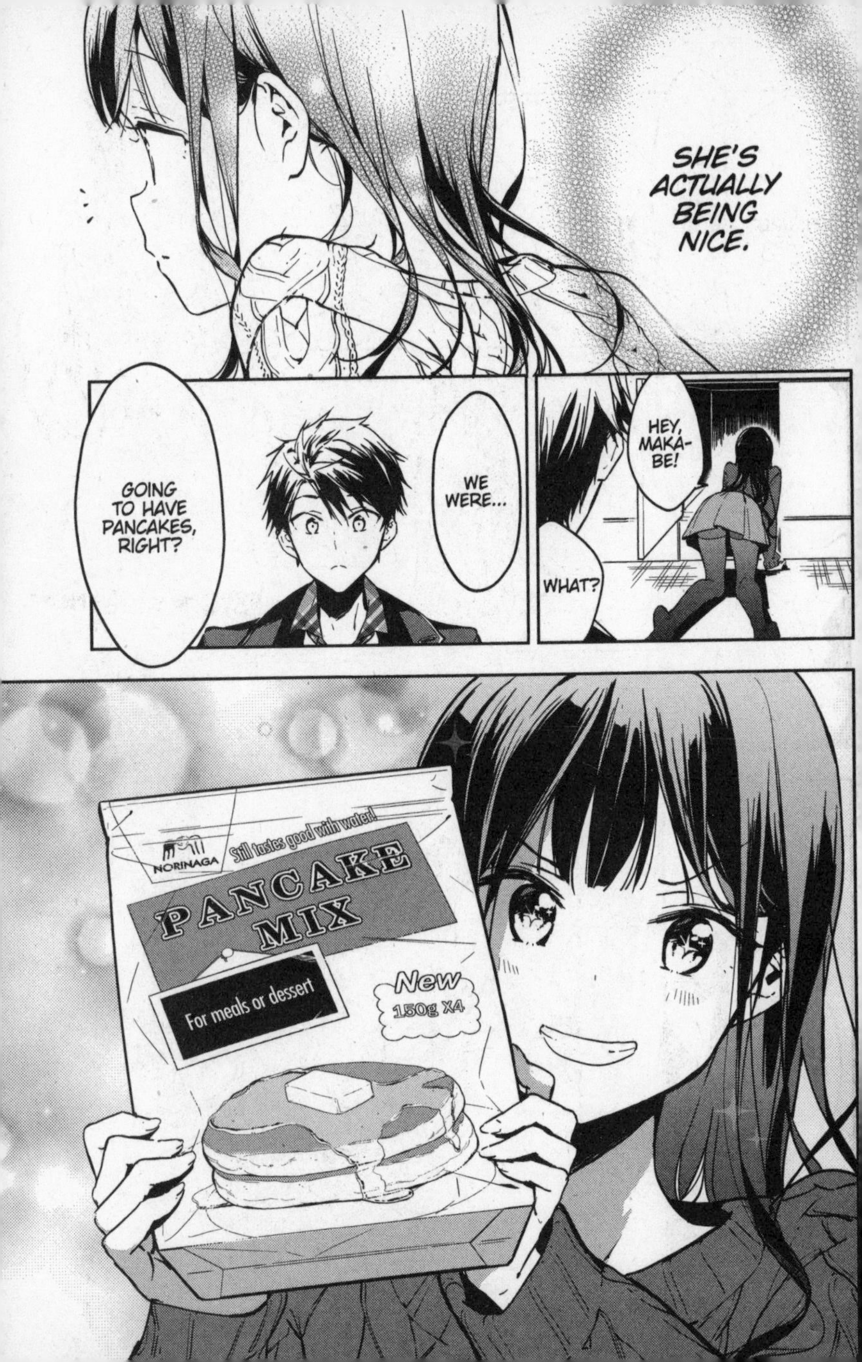
SHE'S ACTUALLY BEING NICE.
HEY, MAKA-BE!
WHAT?
WE WERE...
GOING TO HAVE PANCAKES, RIGHT?
NORINAGA
Still tastes good with water!
PANCAKE MIX
For meals or dessert
New
150g X4

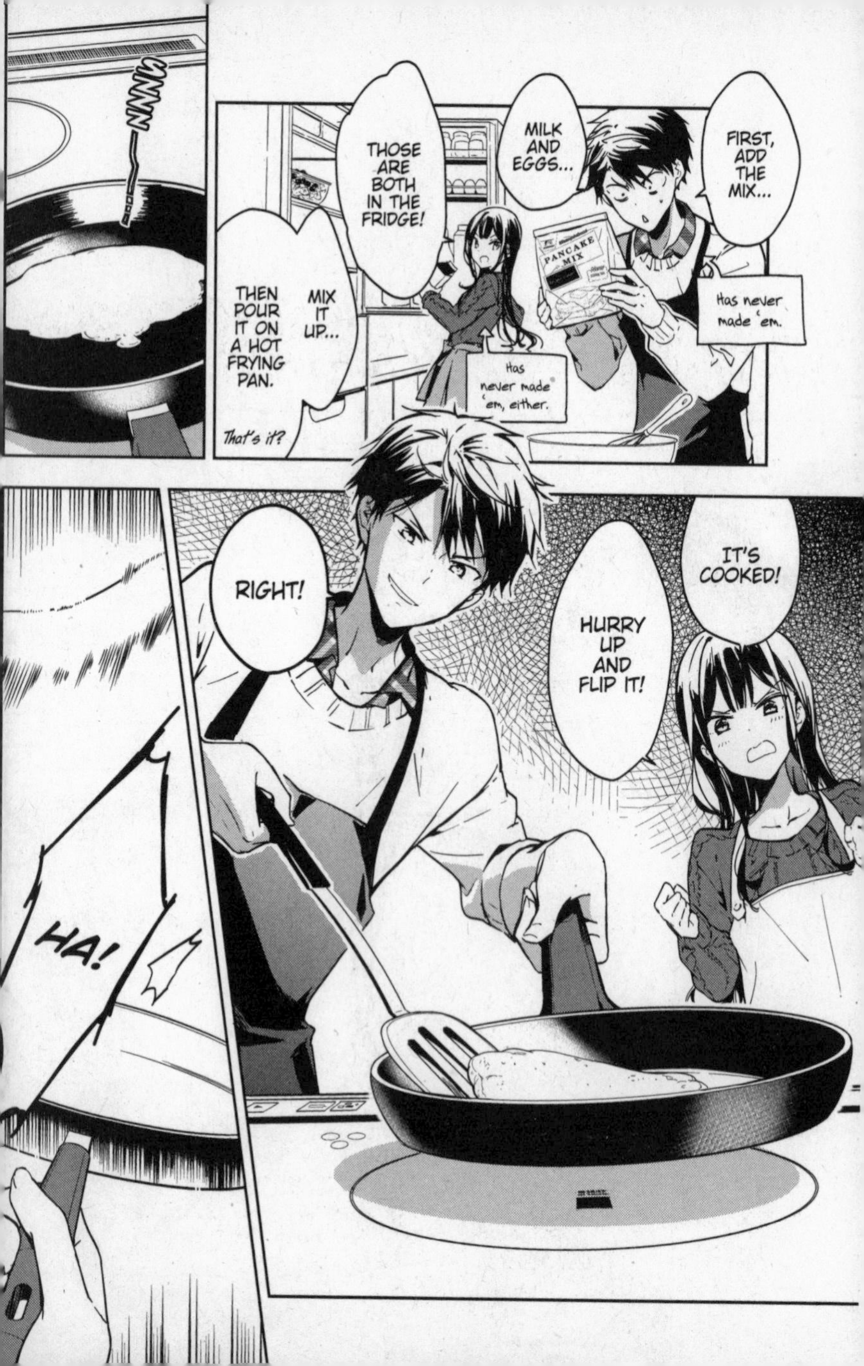
FIRST, ADD THE MIX...
MILK AND EGGS...
Has never made 'em.
THOSE ARE BOTH IN THE FRIDGE!
Has never made 'em, either.
MIX IT UP...
THEN POUR IT ON A HOT FRYING PAN.
That's it?
SNNNN
IT'S COOKED!
HURRY UP AND FLIP IT!
RIGHT!
HA!

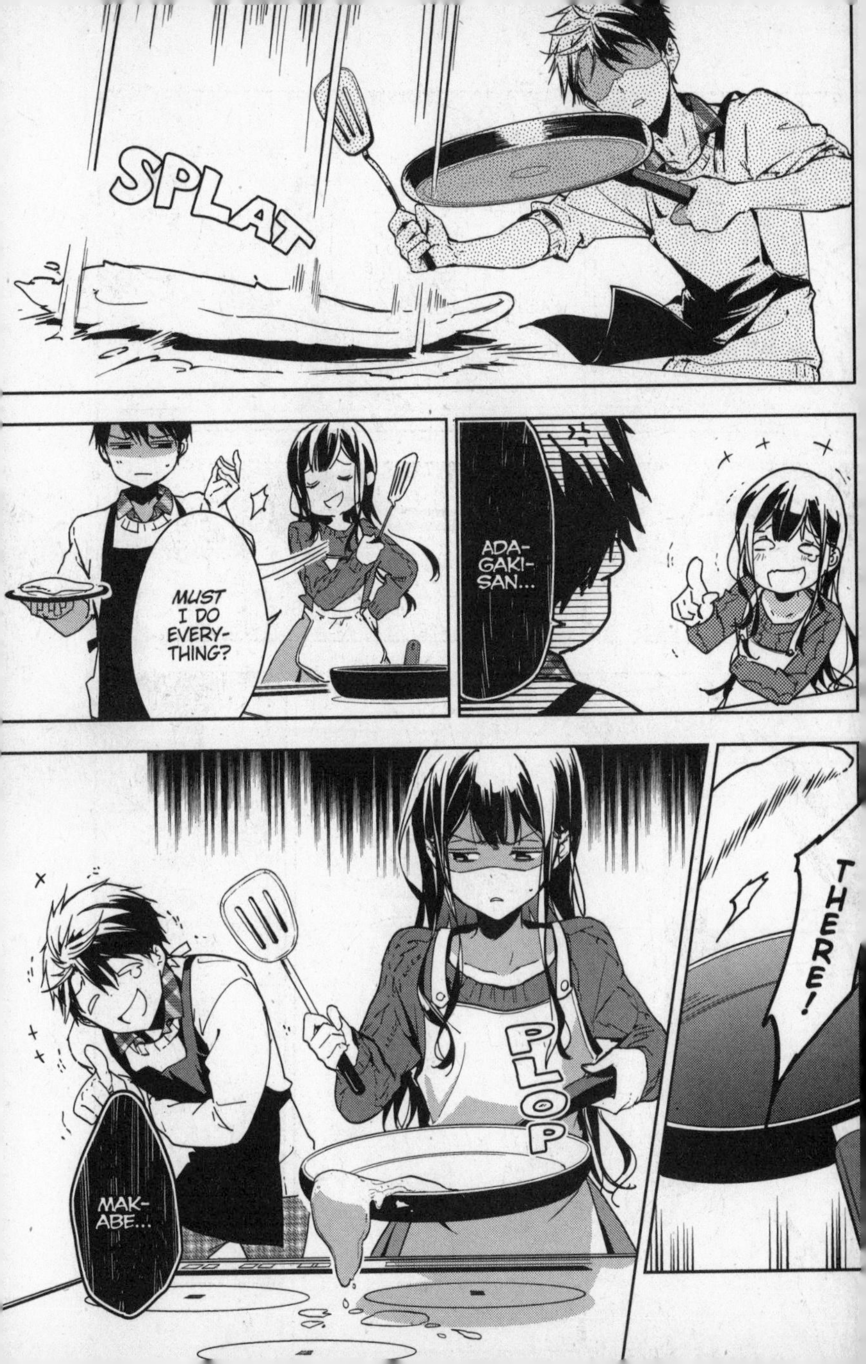
SPLAT
ADA-GAKI-SAN...
MUST I DO EVERY-THING?
THERE!
PLOP
MAK-ABE...

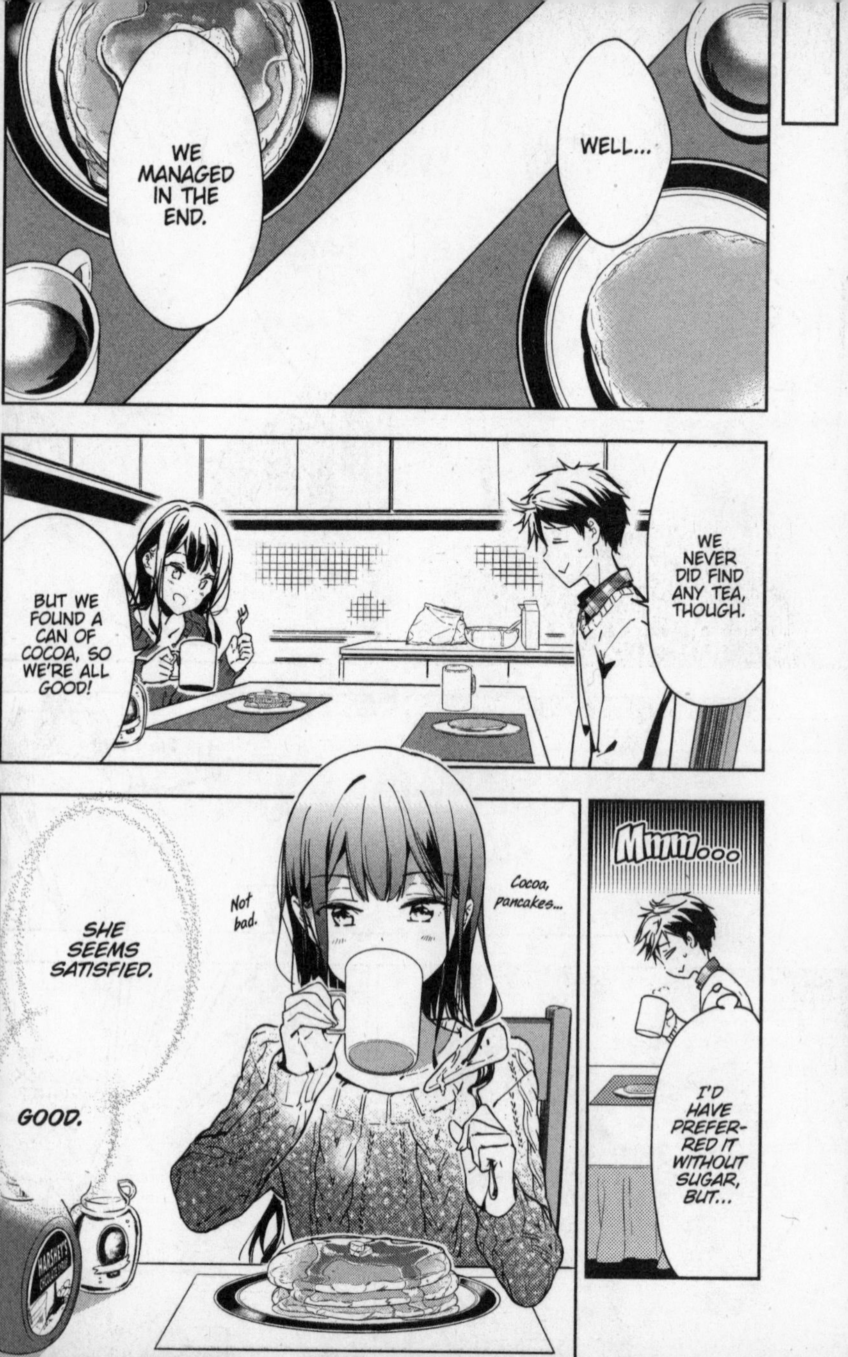
WELL...
WE MANAGED IN THE END.
WE NEVER DID FIND ANY TEA, THOUGH.
BUT WE FOUND A CAN OF COCOA, SO WE'RE ALL GOOD!
Mmm...
I'D HAVE PREFER-RED IT WITHOUT SUGAR, BUT...
Cocoa, pancakes...
Not bad.
SHE SEEMS SATISFIED.
GOOD.

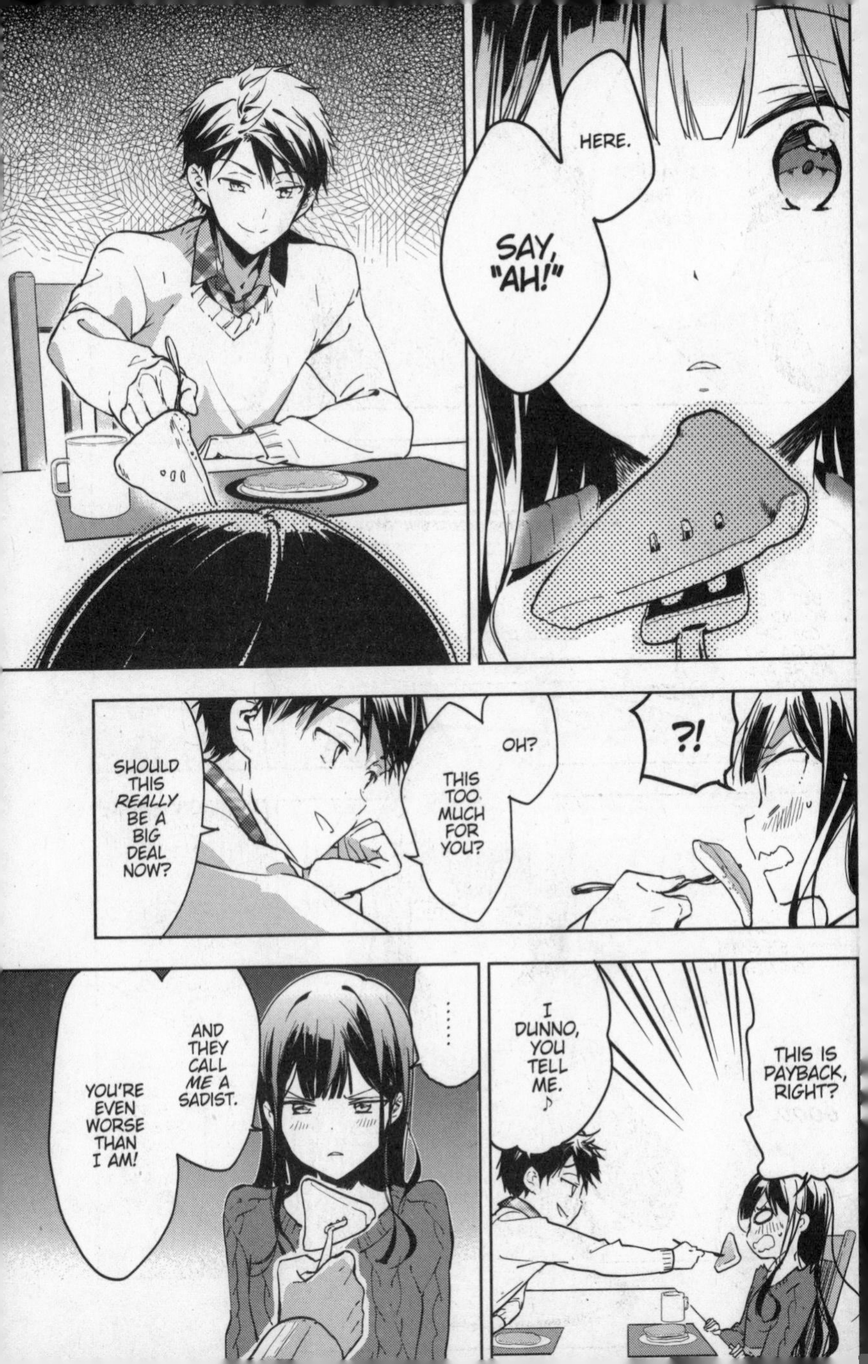
HERE.
SAY, "AH!"
?!
OH?
THIS TOO MUCH FOR YOU?
SHOULD THIS *REALLY* BE A BIG DEAL NOW?
THIS IS PAYBACK, RIGHT?
I DUNNO, YOU TELL ME. ♪
......
AND THEY CALL *ME* A SADIST.
YOU'RE EVEN WORSE THAN I AM!

GRAB

CHOMP

ZING

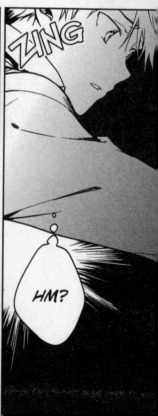

HM?

WHAT WAS THAT?

THAT FELT... WRONG.

IT'S A LITTLE BLAND.

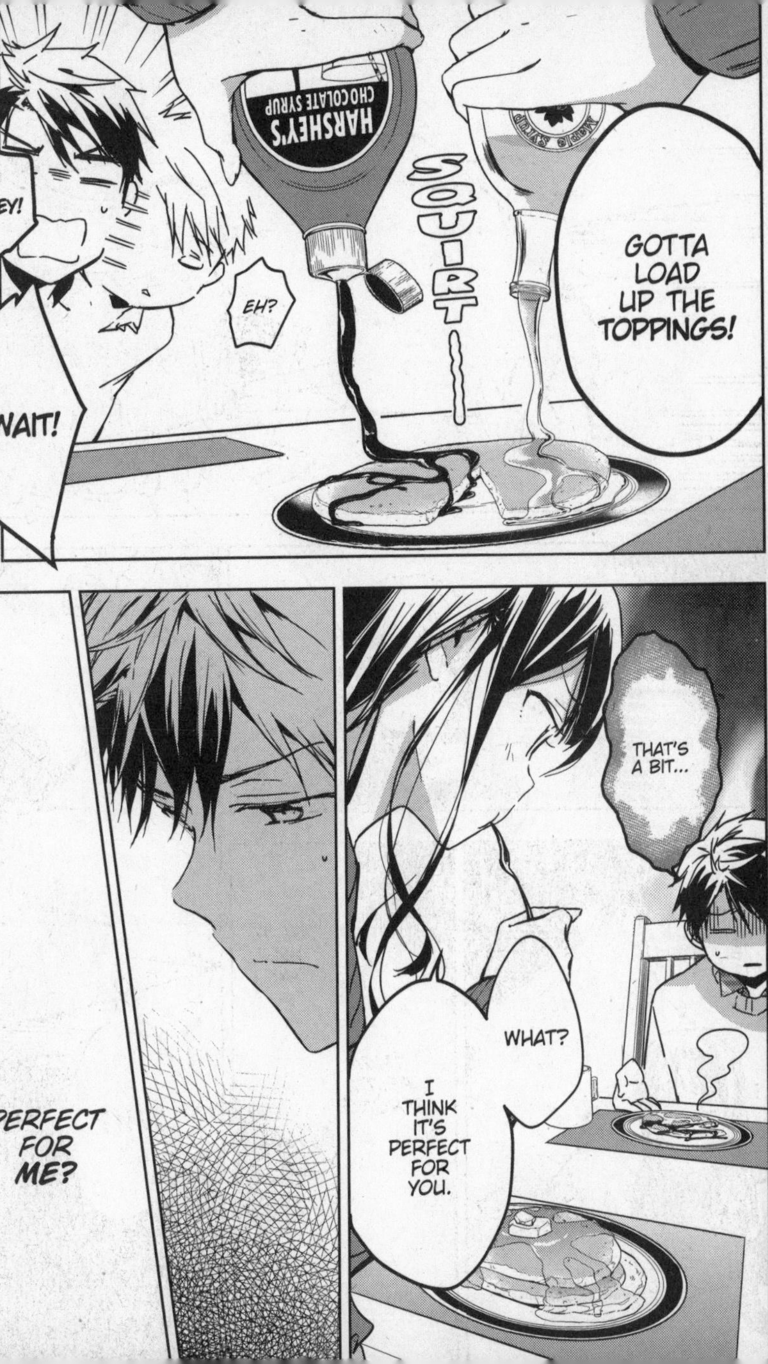
HARSHEY'S CHOCOLATE SYRUP
GOTTA LOAD UP THE TOPPINGS!
SQUIRT
EH?
HEY!
WAIT!
THAT'S A BIT...
WHAT?
I THINK IT'S PERFECT FOR YOU.
PERFECT FOR ME?

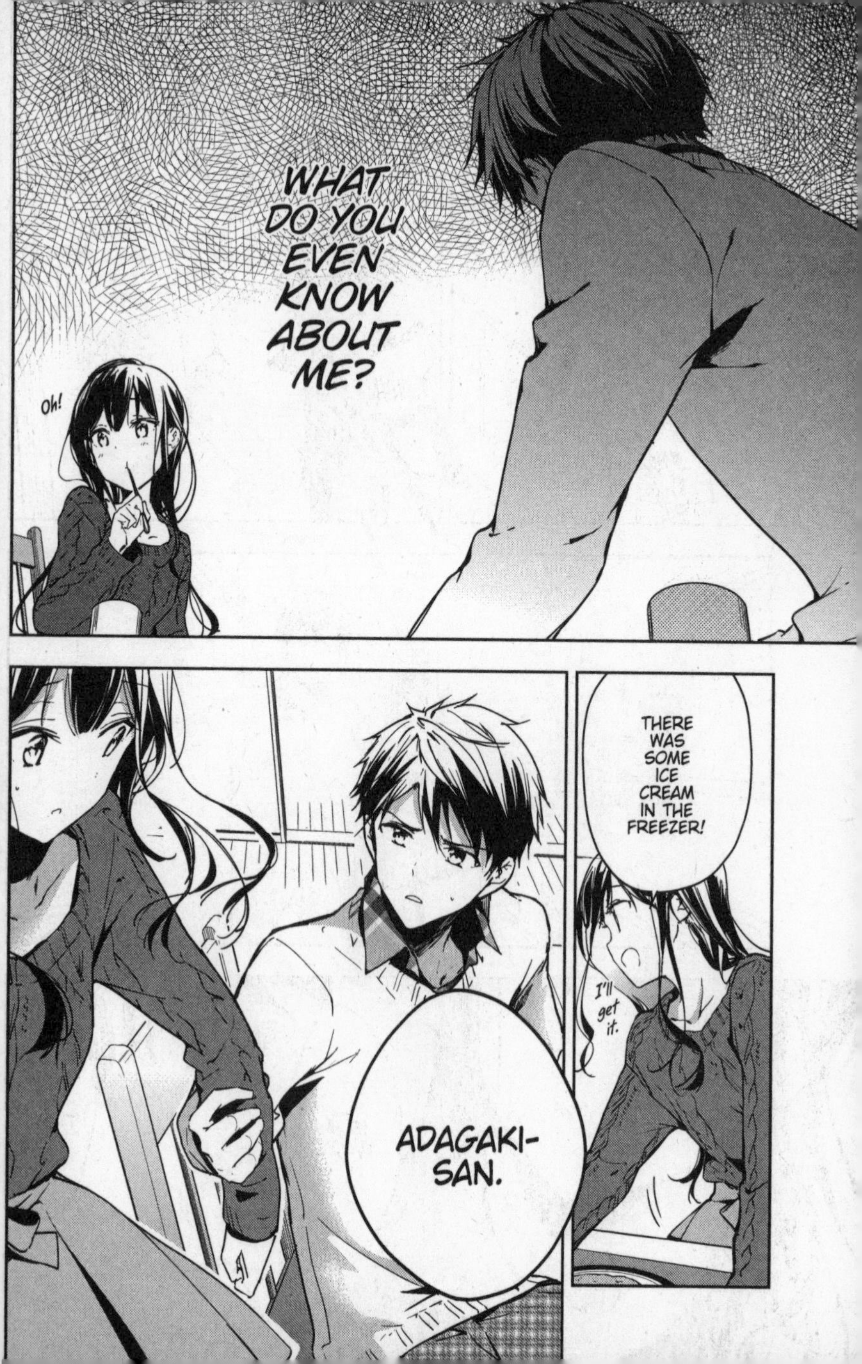
WHAT DO YOU EVEN KNOW ABOUT ME?
Oh!
THERE WAS SOME ICE CREAM IN THE FREEZER!
I'll get it.
ADAGAKI-SAN.

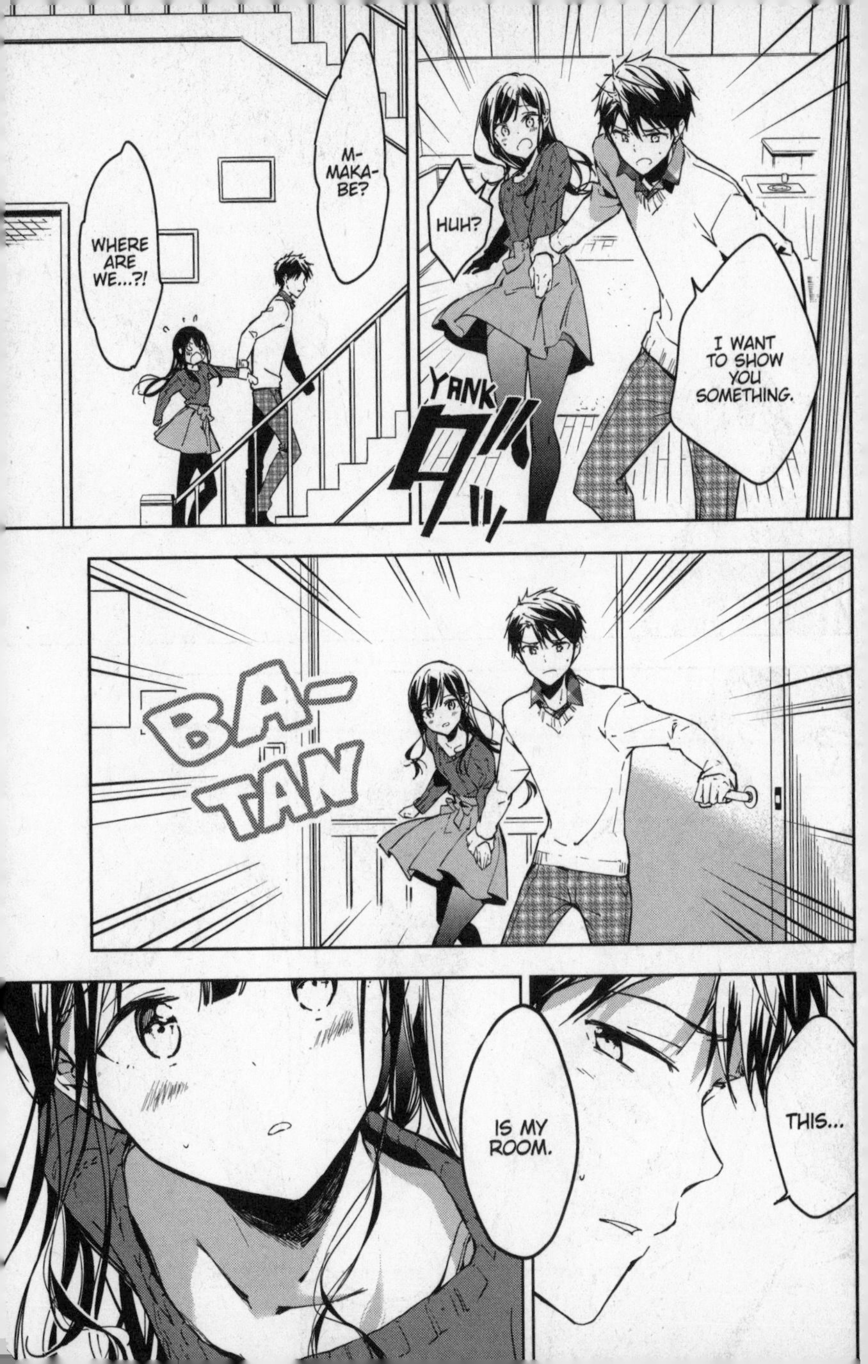
I WANT TO SHOW YOU SOMETHING.
HUH?
YANK
M-MAKABE?
WHERE ARE WE...?!
BA-TAN
THIS...
IS MY ROOM.

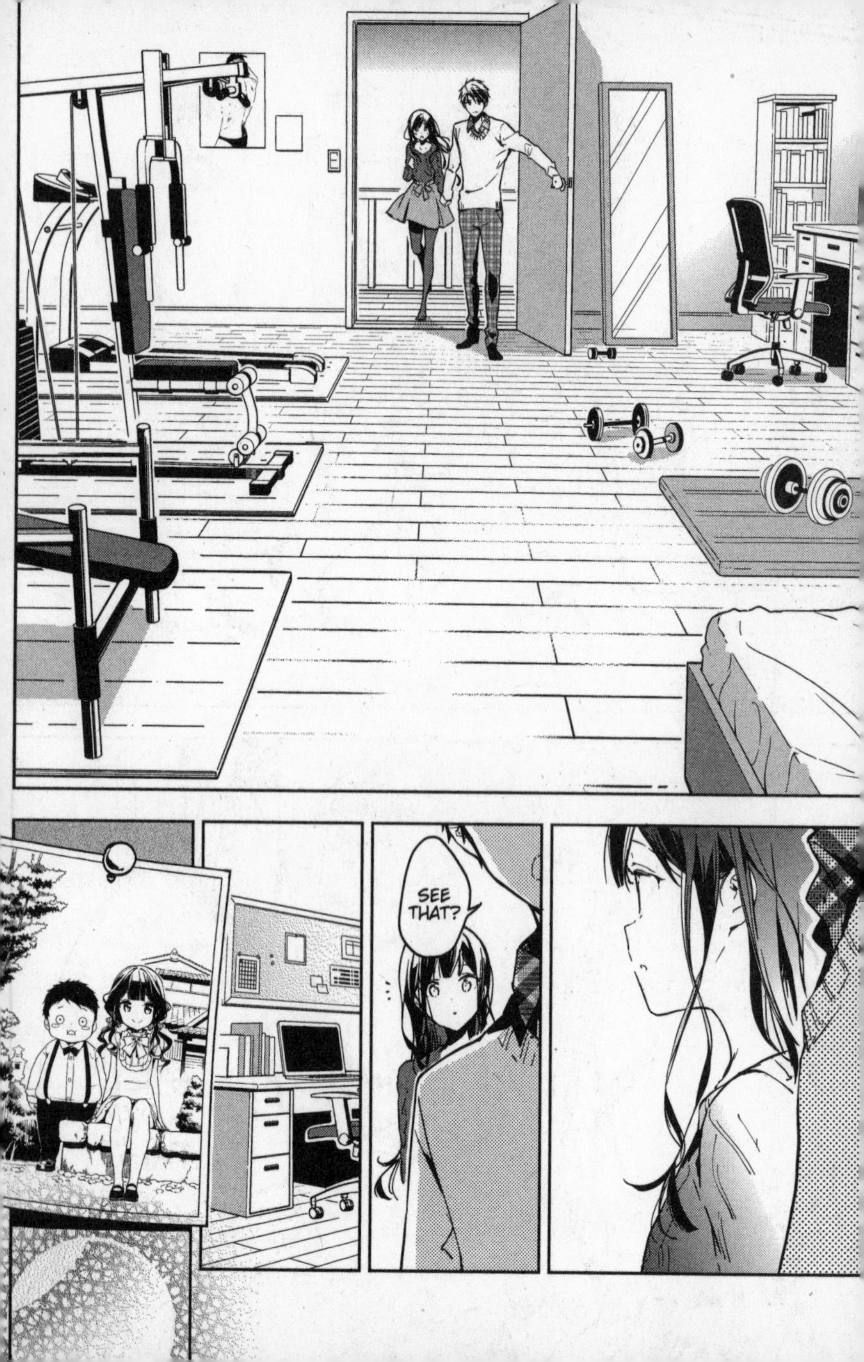
SEE THAT?

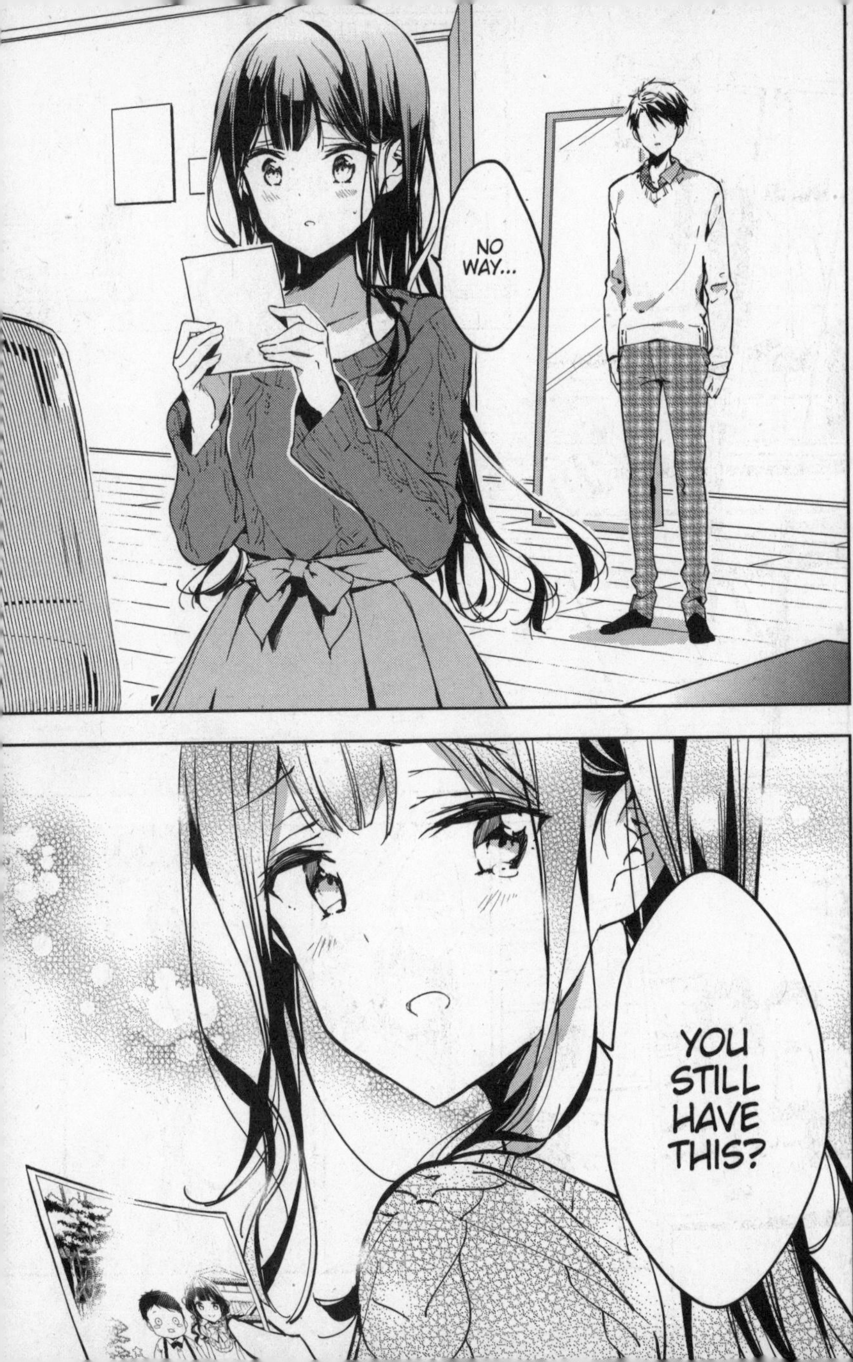
NO WAY...
YOU STILL HAVE THIS?

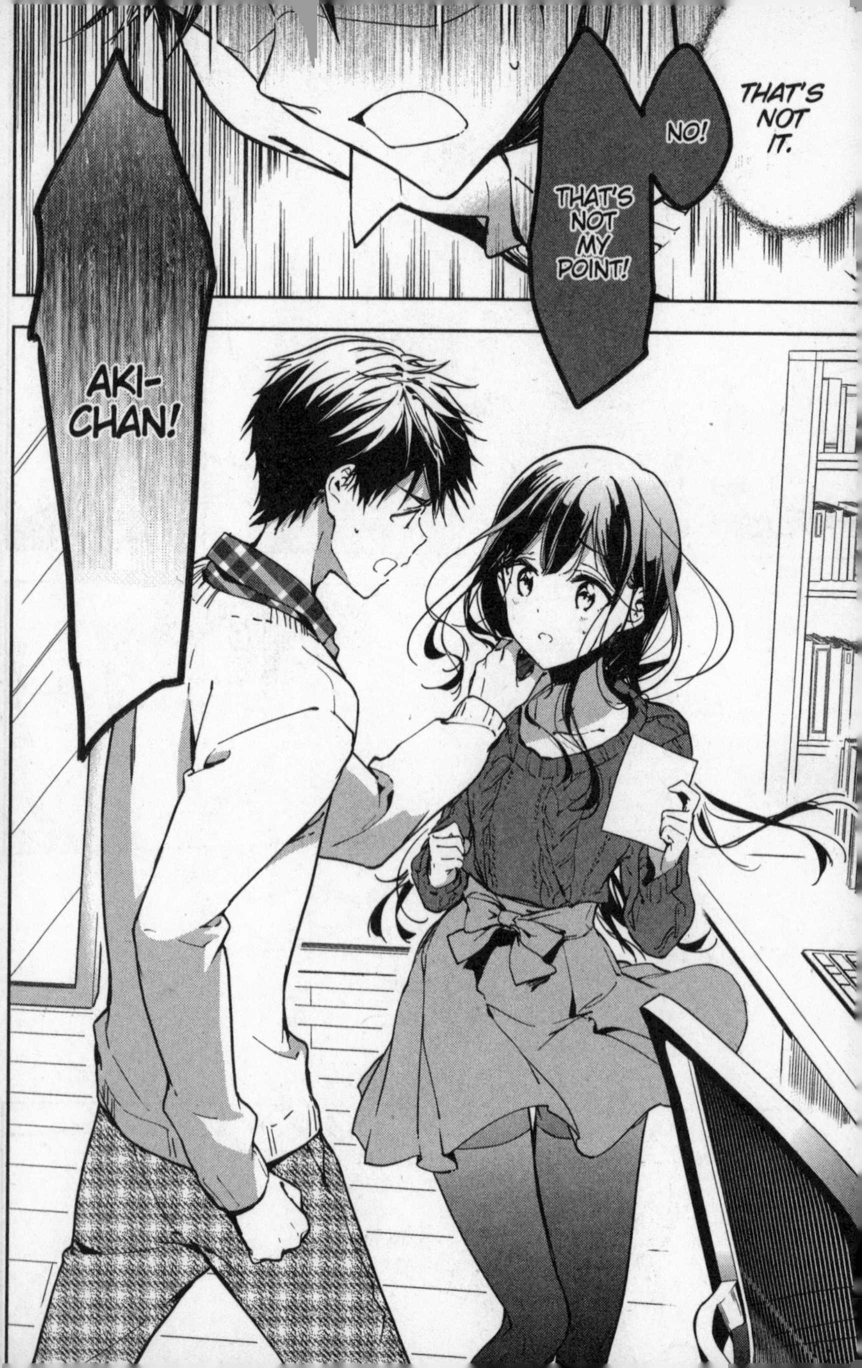
THAT'S NOT IT.
NO!
THAT'S NOT MY POINT!
AKI-CHAN!

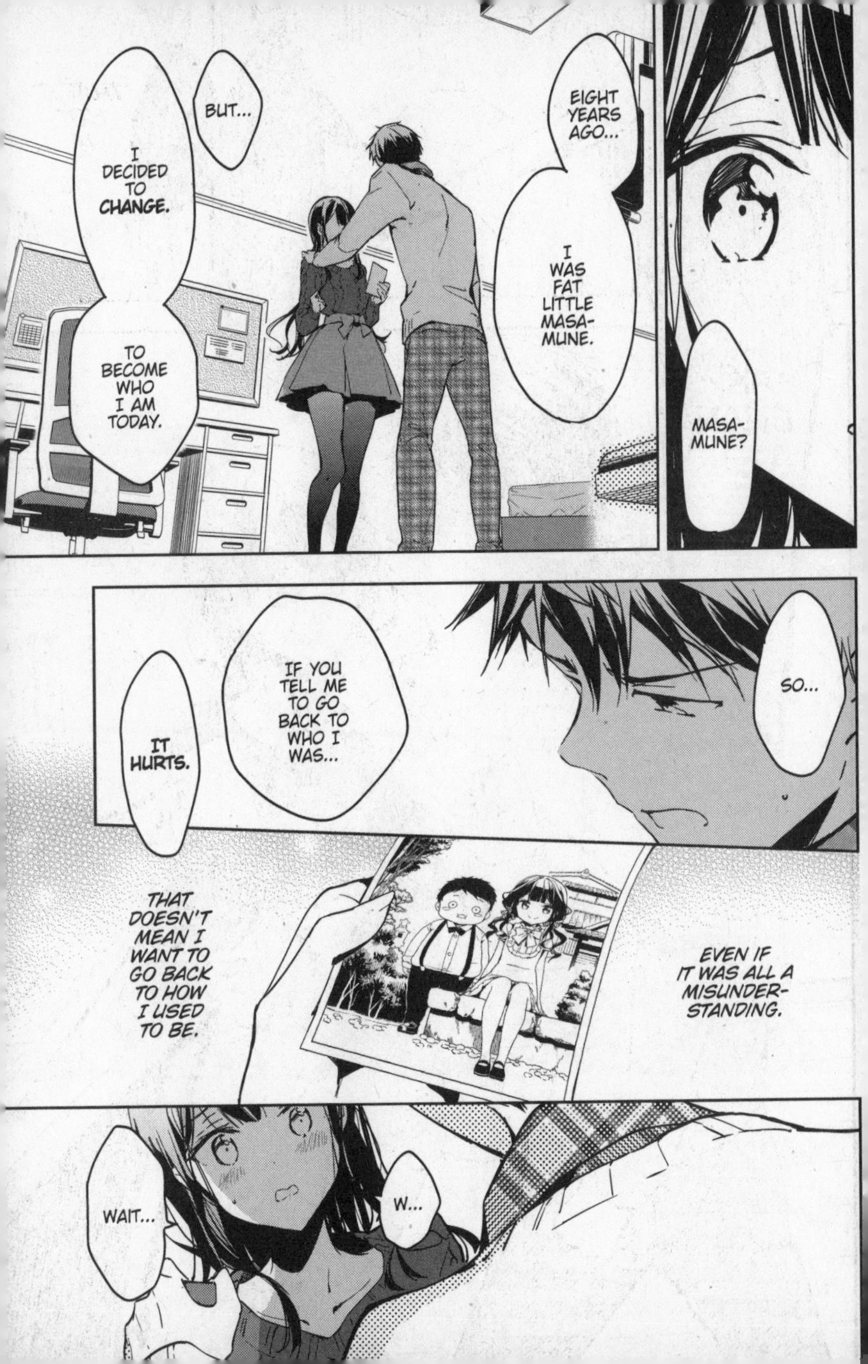
MASA-MUNE?
EIGHT YEARS AGO...
I WAS FAT LITTLE MASA-MUNE.
BUT...
I DECIDED TO **CHANGE.**
TO BECOME WHO I AM TODAY.
SO...
IF YOU TELL ME TO GO BACK TO WHO I WAS...
IT **HURTS.**
EVEN IF IT WAS ALL A MISUNDER-STANDING.
THAT DOESN'T MEAN I WANT TO GO BACK TO HOW I USED TO BE.
W...
WAIT...

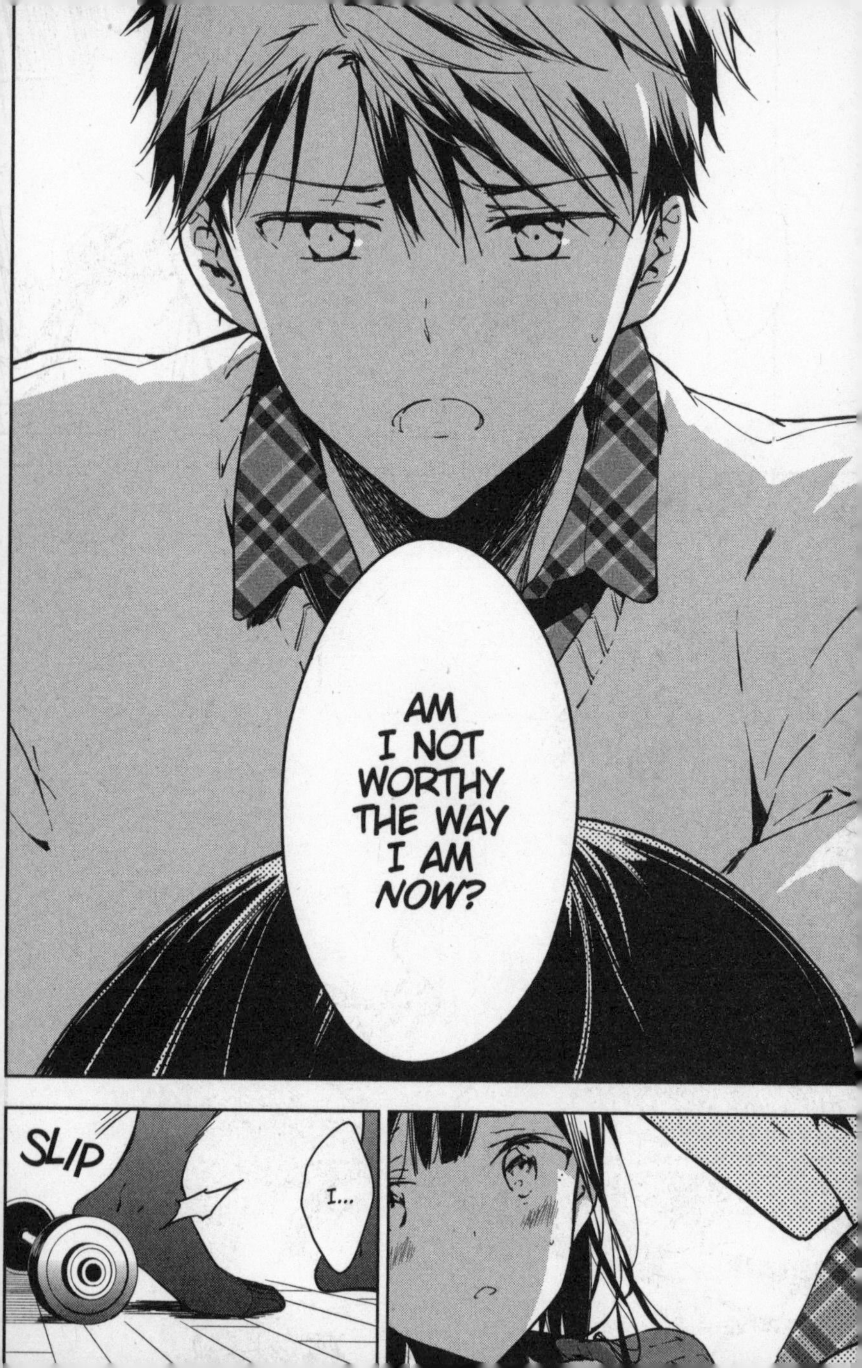
AM I NOT WORTHY THE WAY I AM NOW?
I...
SLIP

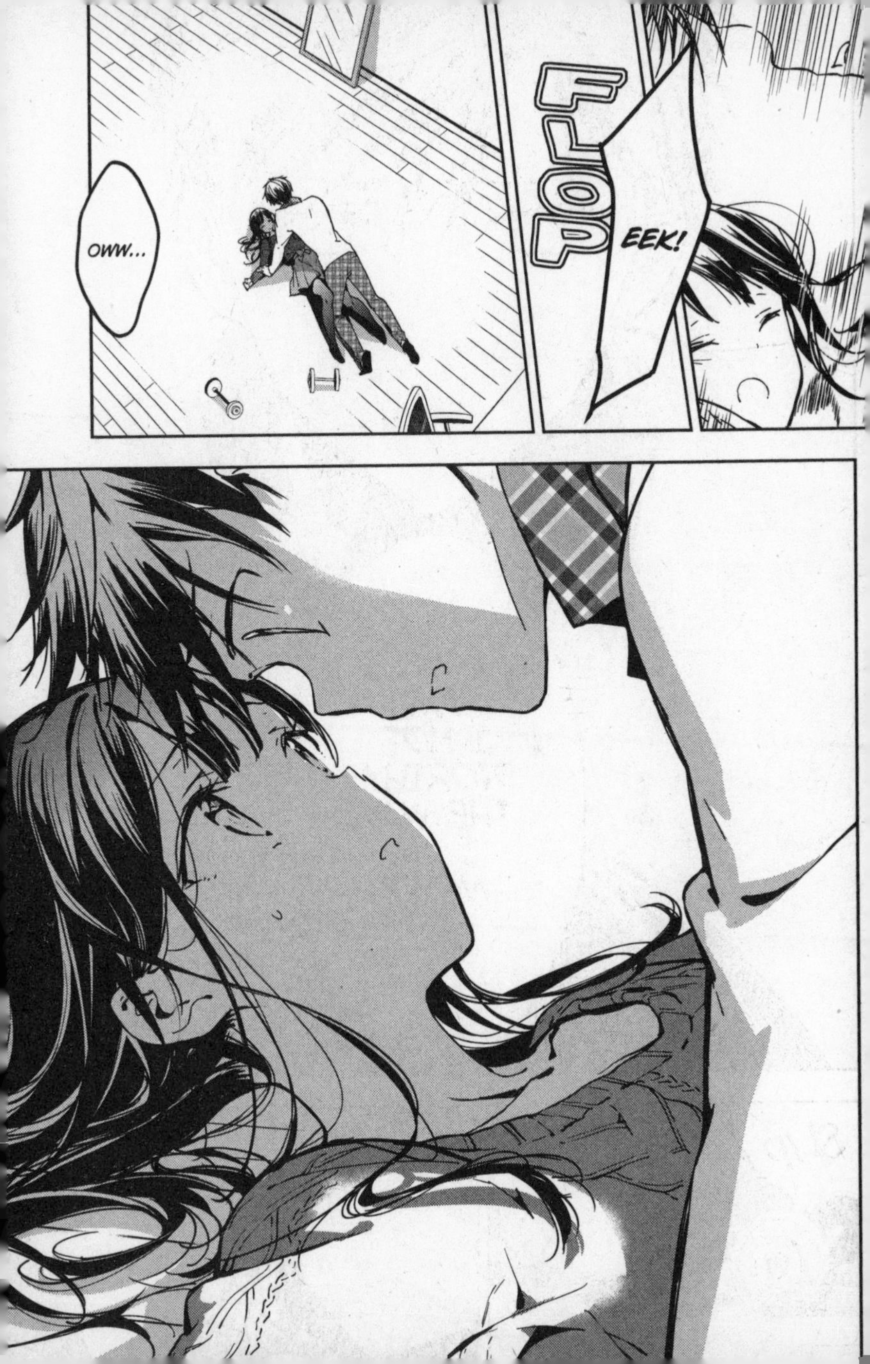
EEK!
FLOP
OWW...

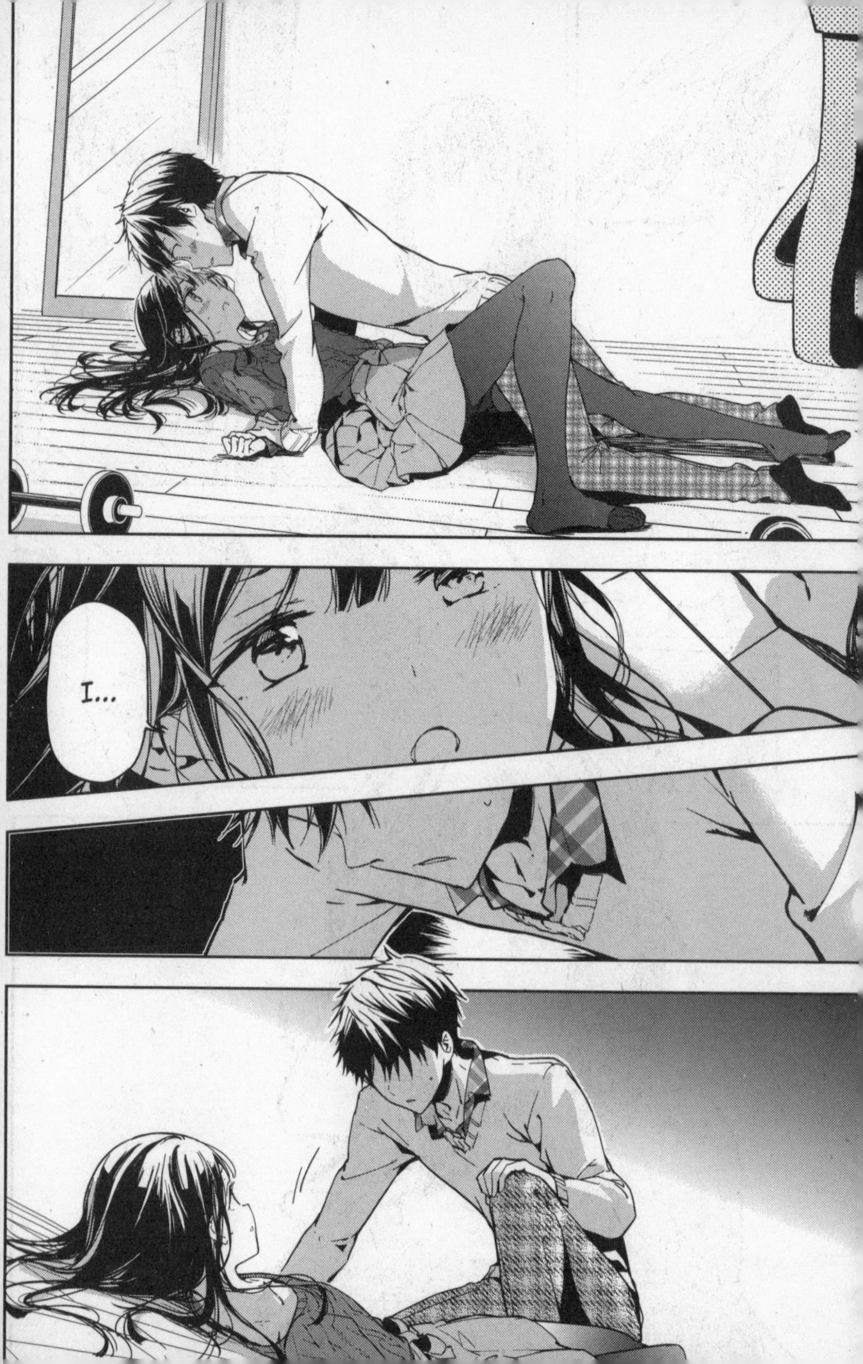
I...

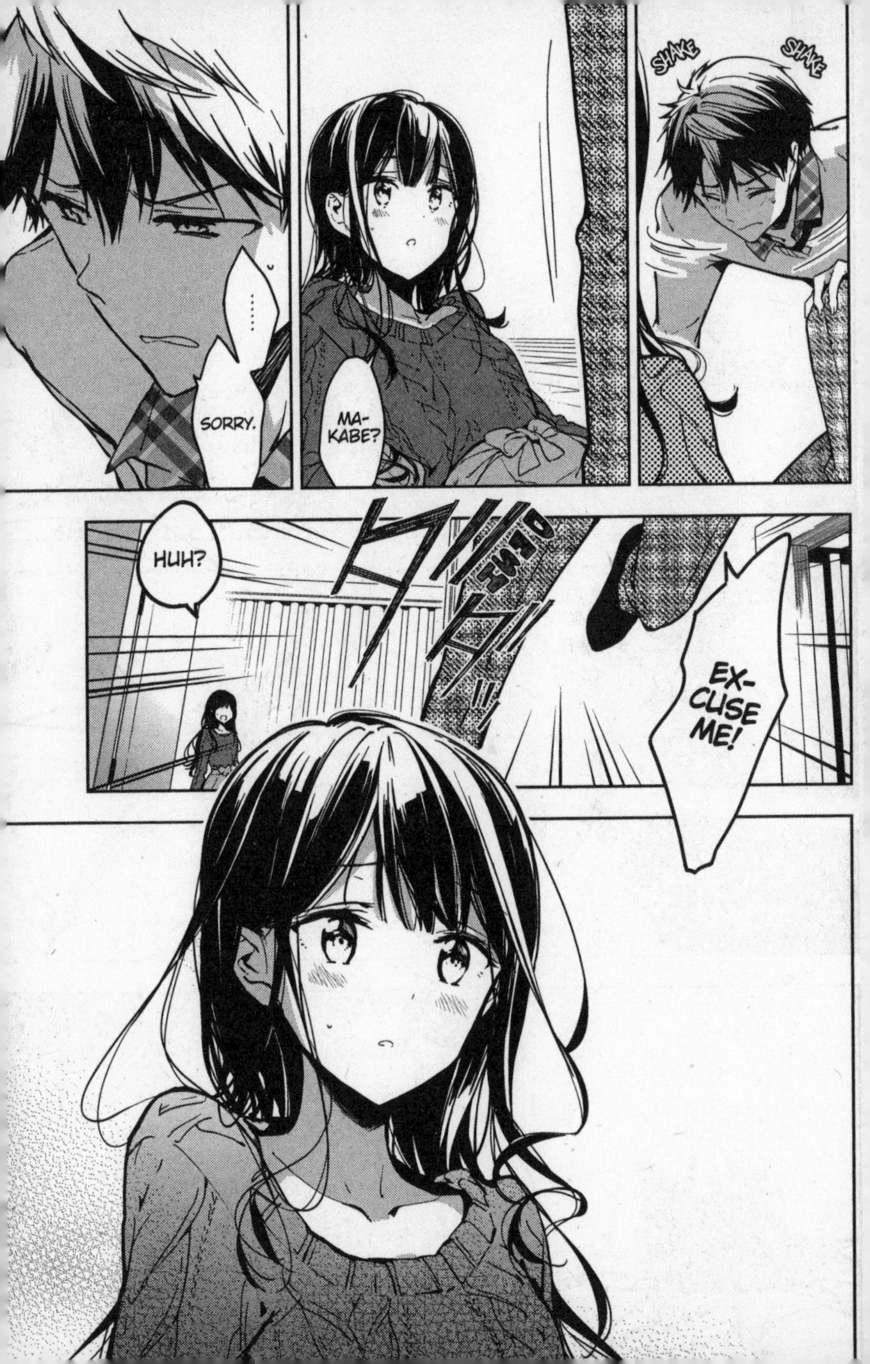
SHAKE
SHAKE
MA-KABE?
...
SORRY.
EX-CUSE ME!
DASH
HUH?

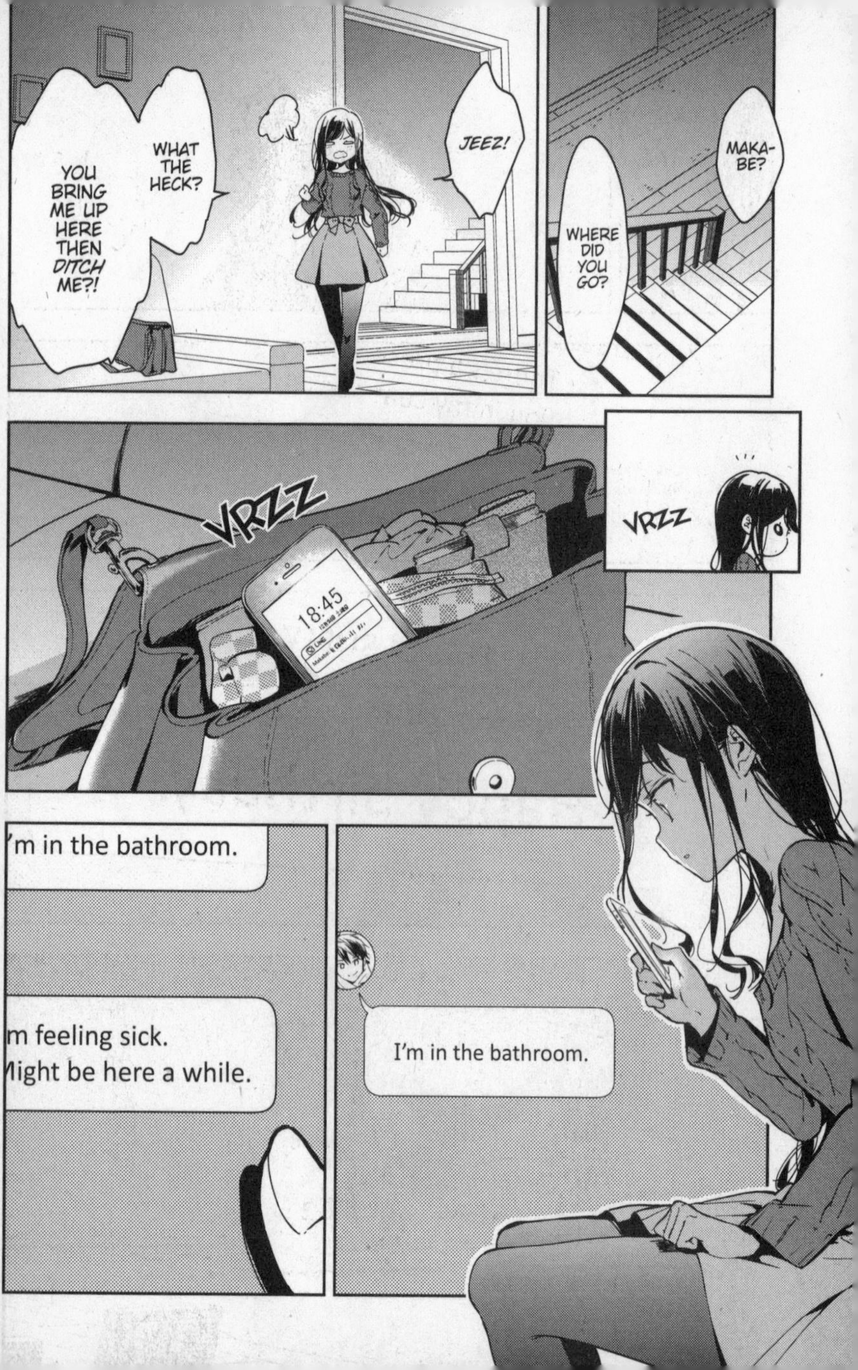
MAKA-BE?
WHERE DID YOU GO?
JEEZ!
WHAT THE HECK?
YOU BRING ME UP HERE THEN DITCH ME?!
VRZZ
VRZZ
18:45
I’m in the bathroom.
’m in the bathroom.
m feeling sick.
ight be here a while.

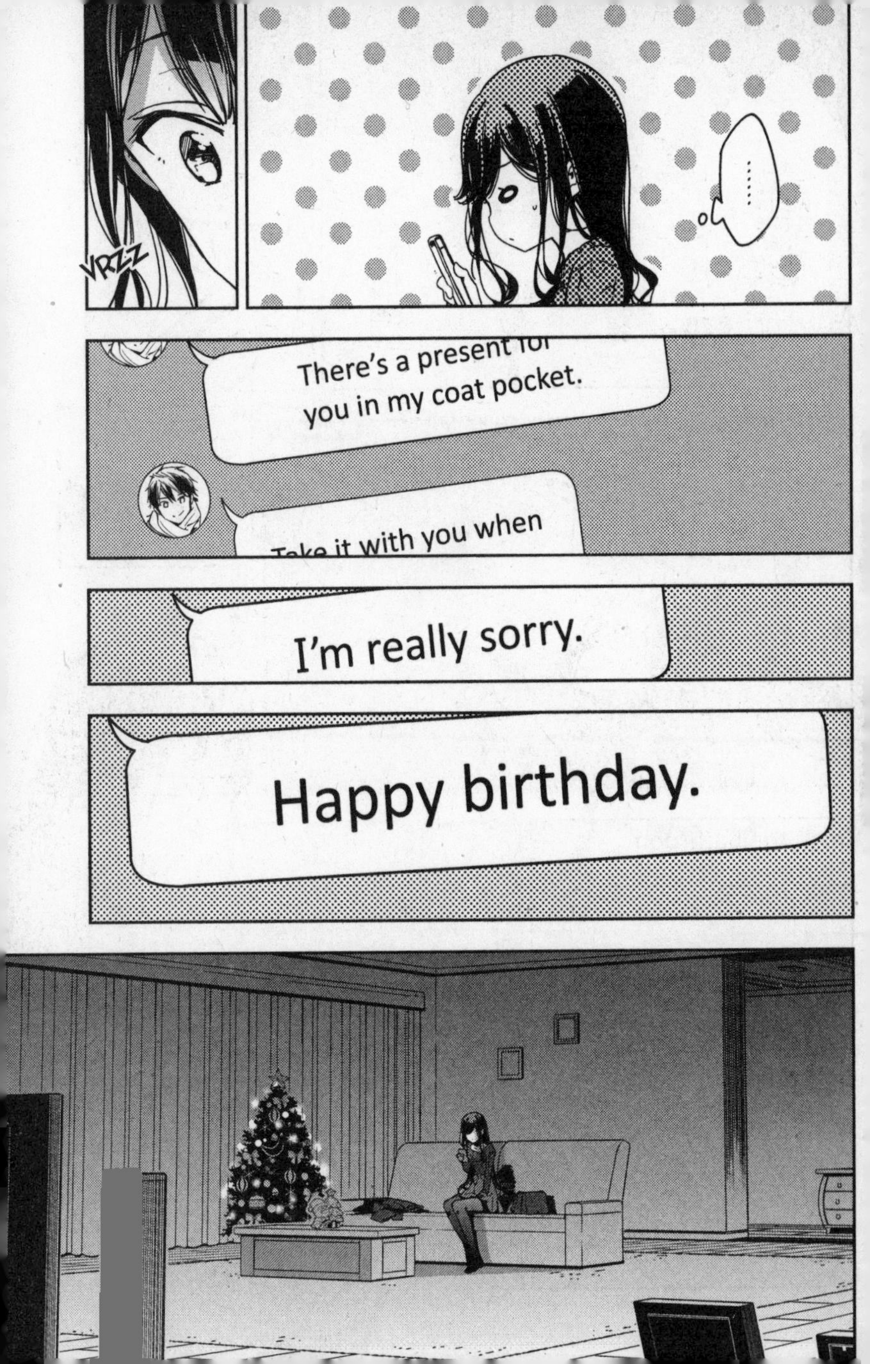
......
VRZZ
There's a present for
you in my coat pocket.
Take it with you when
I'm really sorry.
Happy birthday.

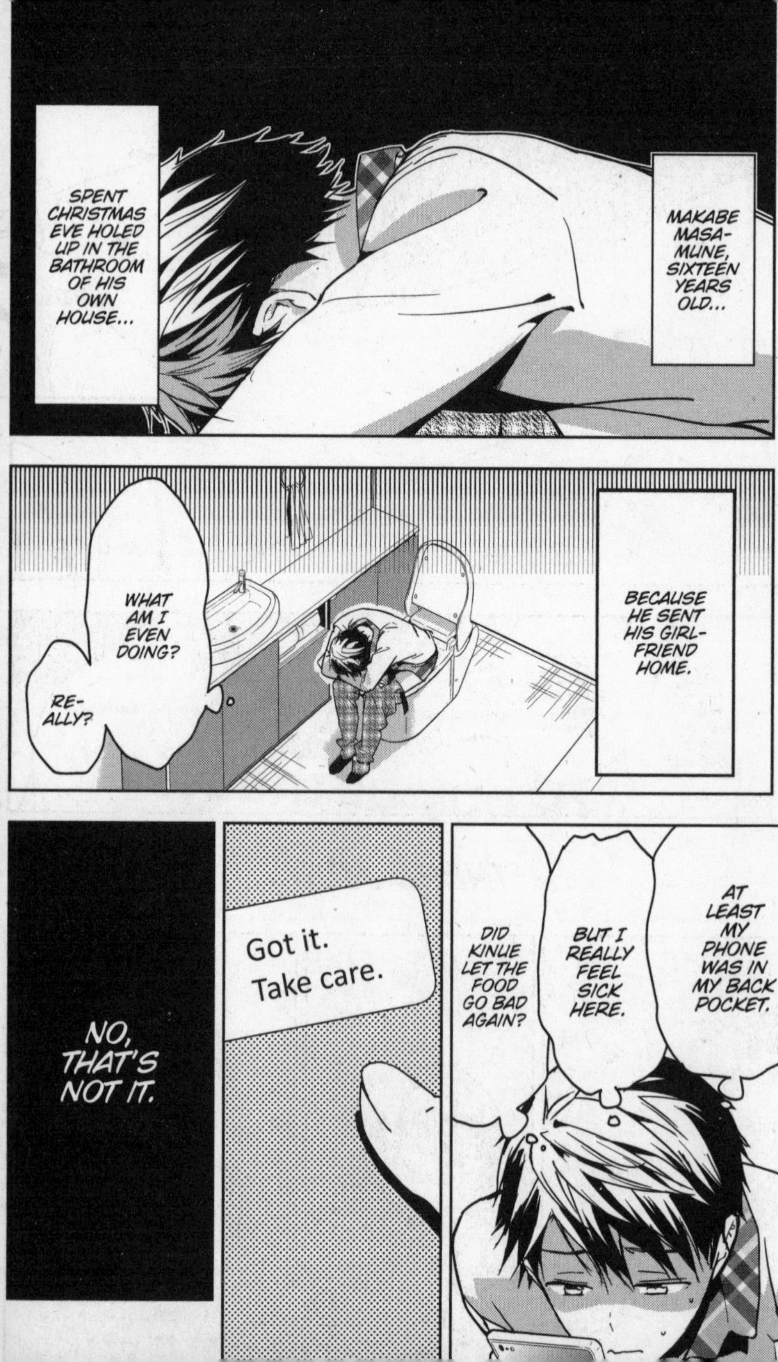
MAKABE MASA-MUNE, SIXTEEN YEARS OLD...
SPENT CHRISTMAS EVE HOLED UP IN THE BATHROOM OF HIS OWN HOUSE...
BECAUSE HE SENT HIS GIRL-FRIEND HOME.
WHAT AM I EVEN DOING? RE-ALLY?
AT LEAST MY PHONE WAS IN MY BACK POCKET.
BUT I REALLY FEEL SICK HERE.
DID KINUE LET THE FOOD GO BAD AGAIN?
Got it. Take care.
NO, THAT'S NOT IT.

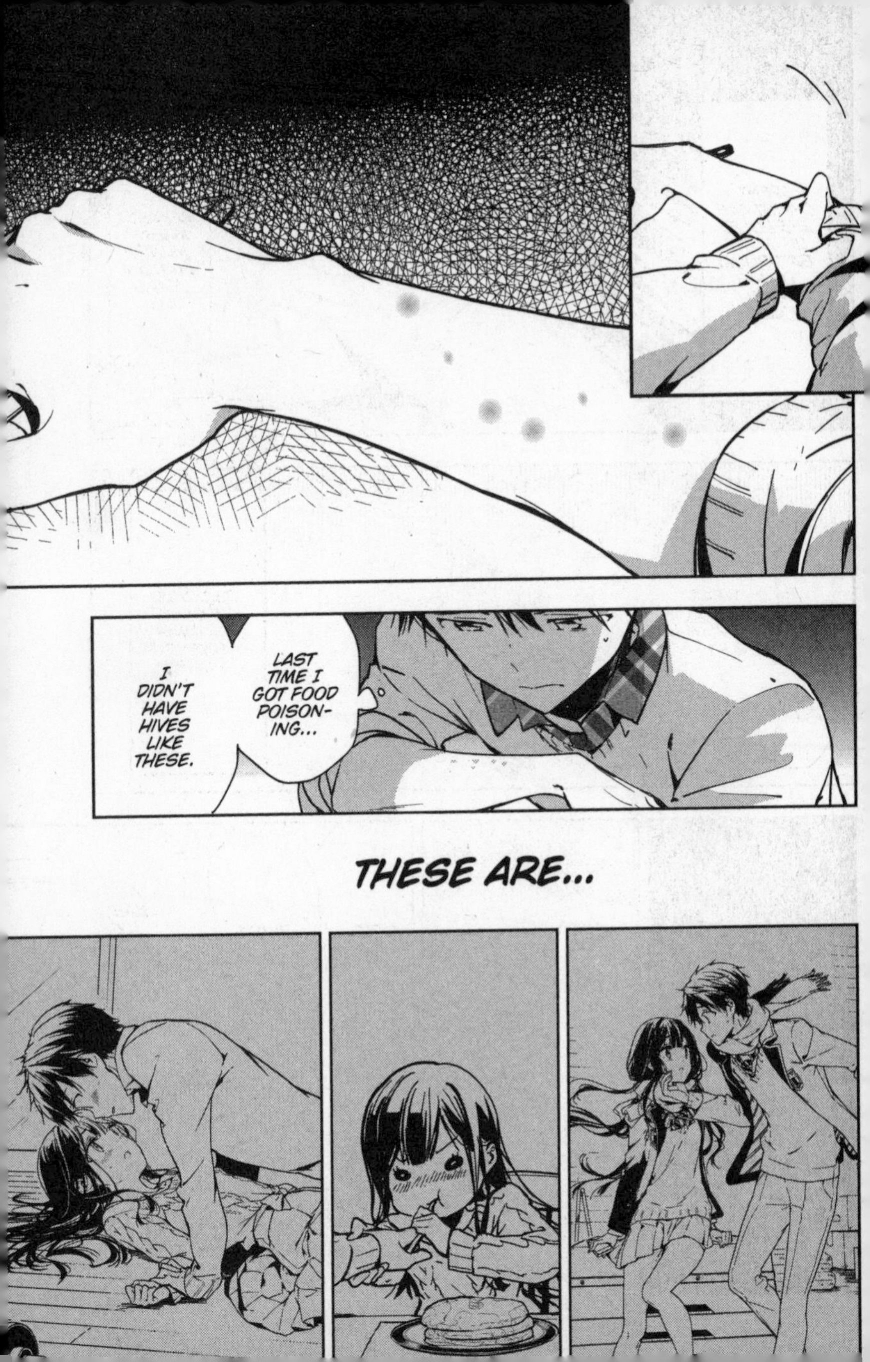

LAST TIME I GOT FOOD POISONING...
I DIDN'T HAVE HIVES LIKE THESE.
THESE ARE...

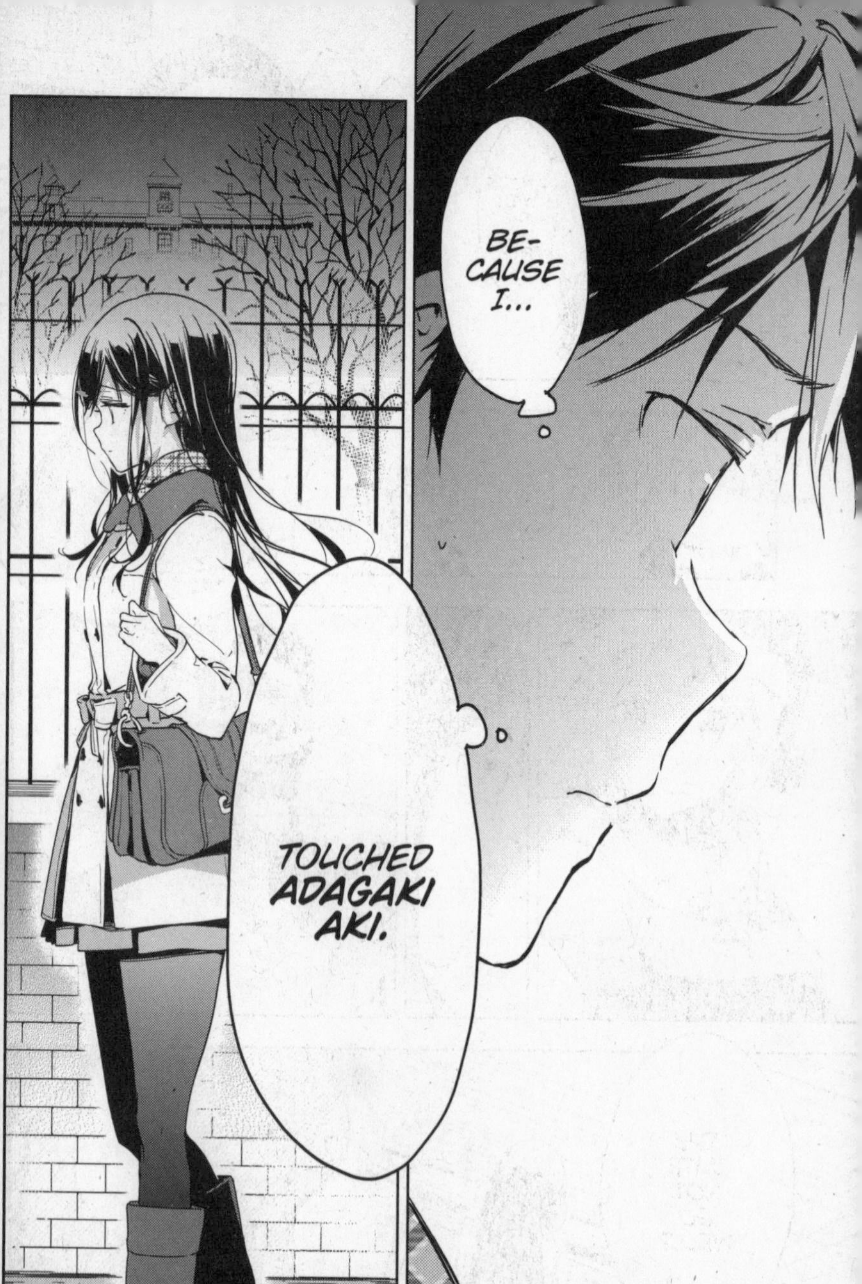
BE-CAUSE I...
TOUCHED ADAGAKI AKI.

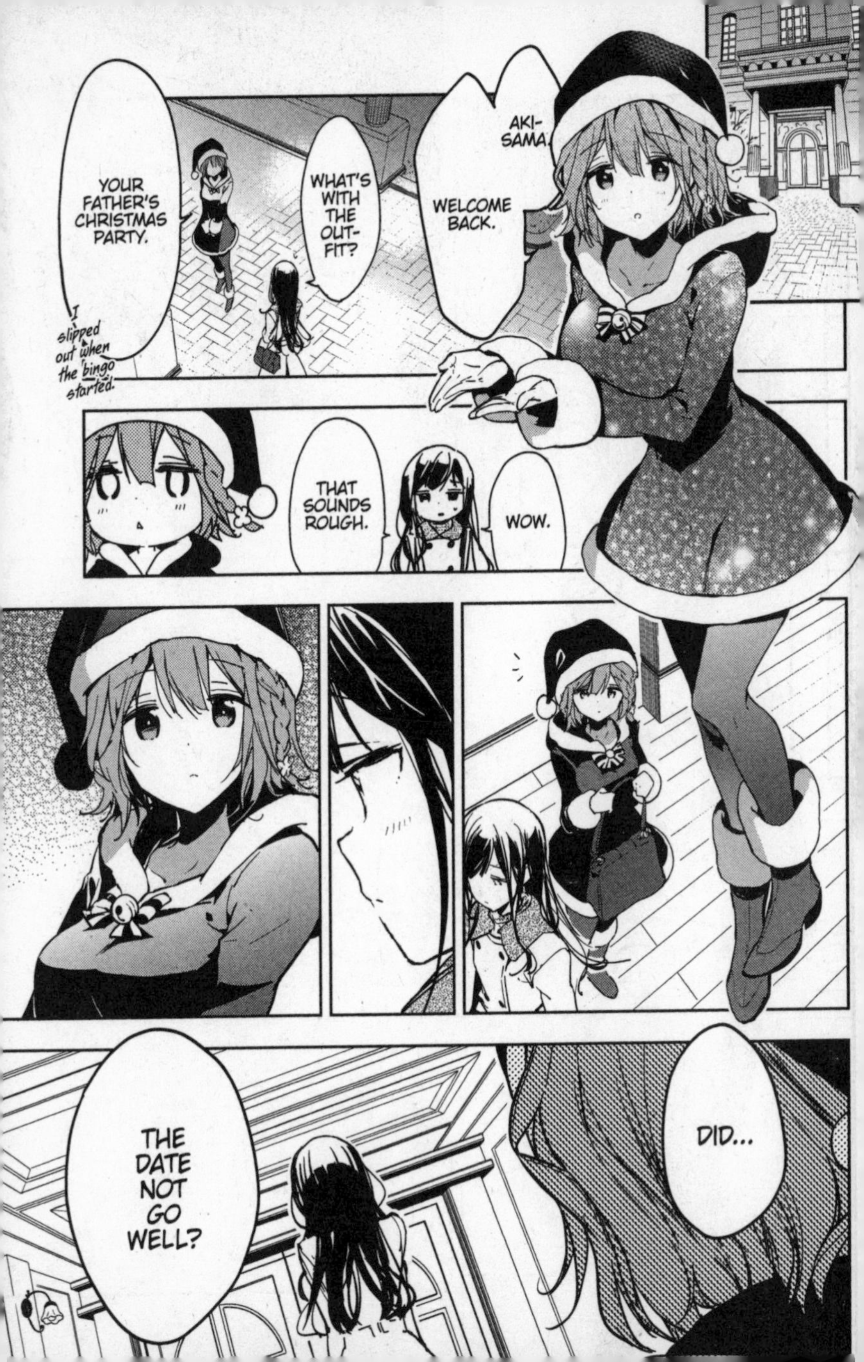
AKI-SAMA!
WELCOME BACK.
WHAT'S WITH THE OUT-FIT?
YOUR FATHER'S CHRISTMAS PARTY.
I slipped out when the bingo started.
WOW.
THAT SOUNDS ROUGH.
DID...
THE DATE NOT GO WELL?

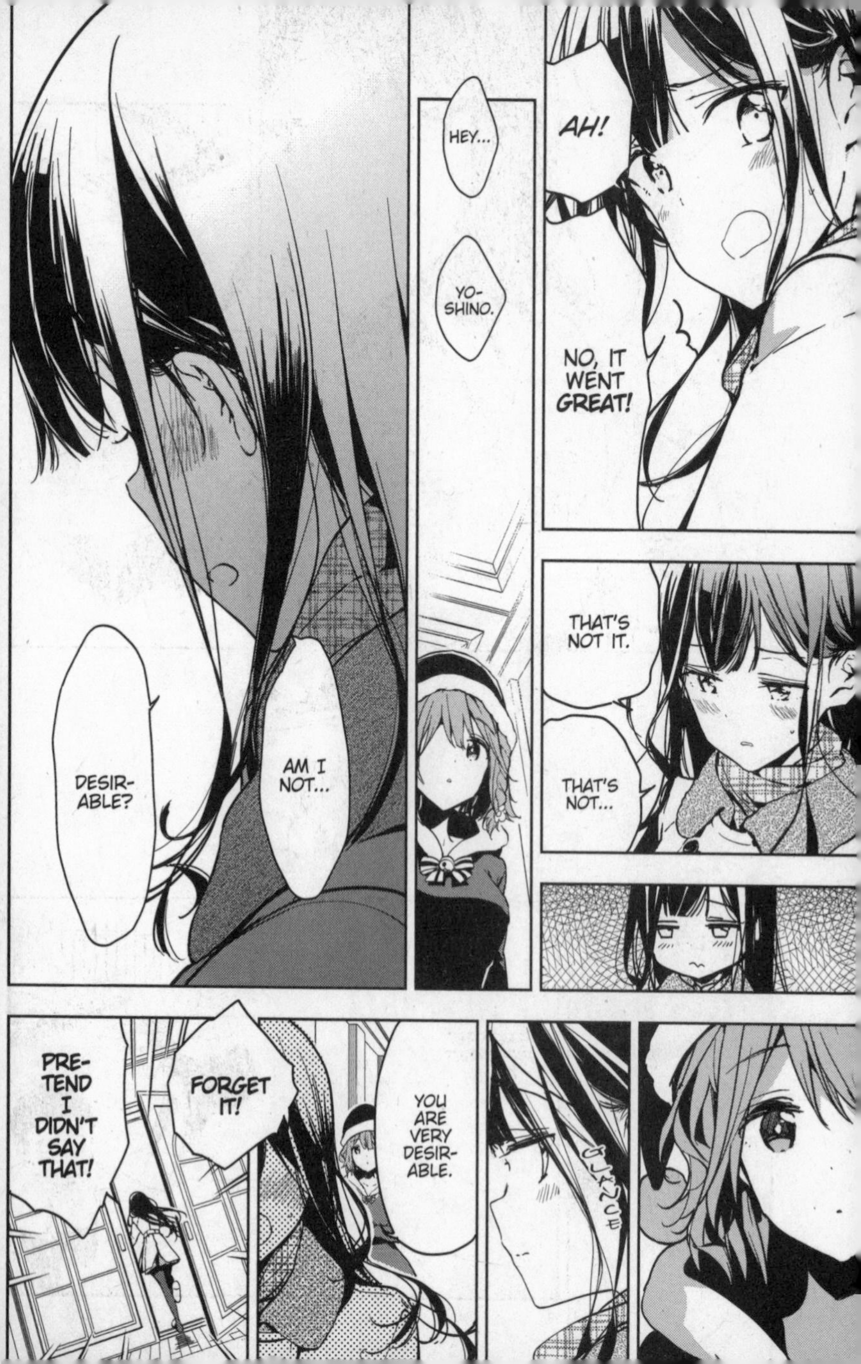
AH!
NO, IT WENT GREAT!
THAT'S NOT IT.
THAT'S NOT...
HEY...
YO-SHINO.
AM I NOT...
DESIR-ABLE?
GLANCE
YOU ARE VERY DESIR-ABLE.
FORGET IT!
PRE-TEND I DIDN'T SAY THAT!

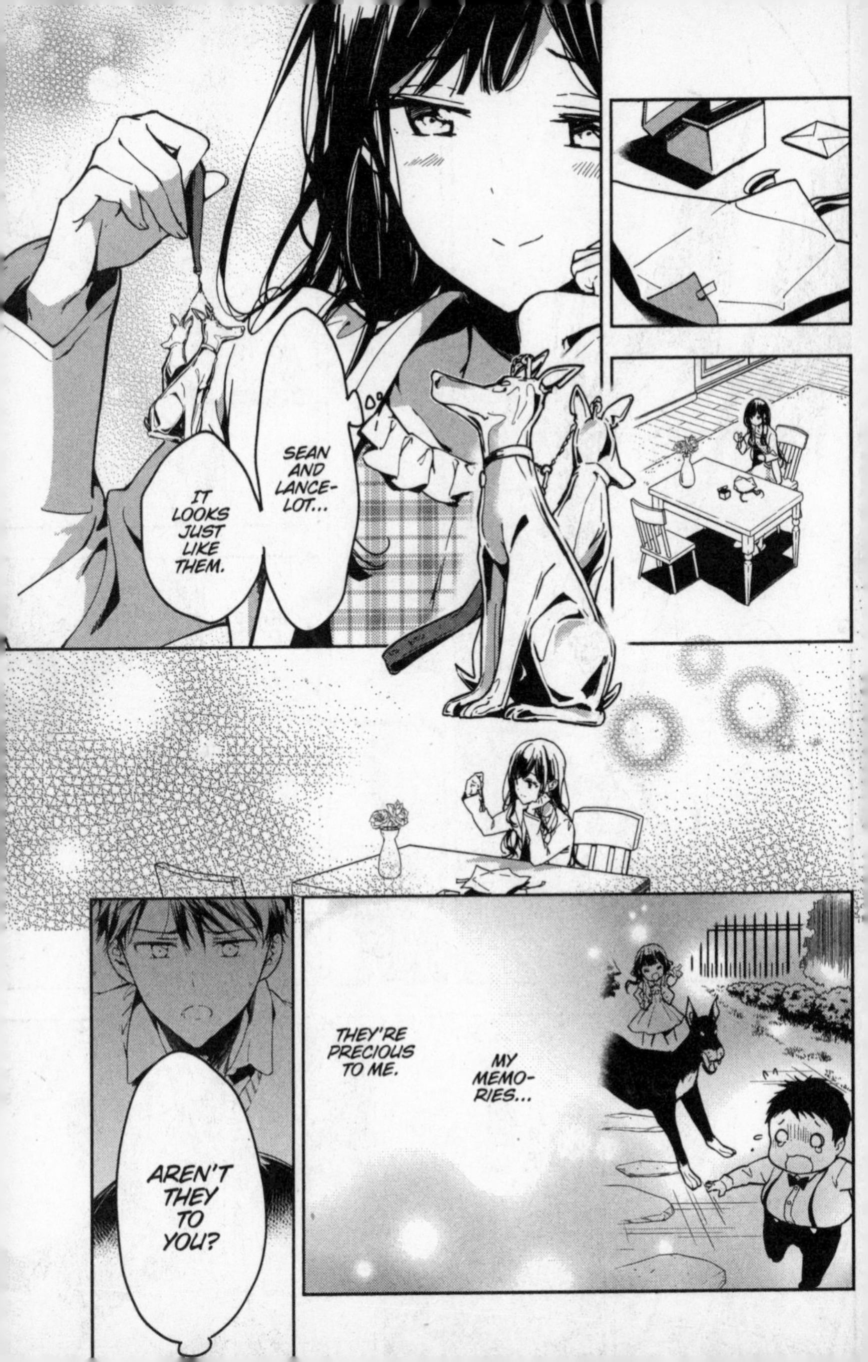
SEAN AND LANCE-LOT...
IT LOOKS JUST LIKE THEM.
MY MEMO-RIES...
THEY'RE PRECIOUS TO ME.
AREN'T THEY TO YOU?

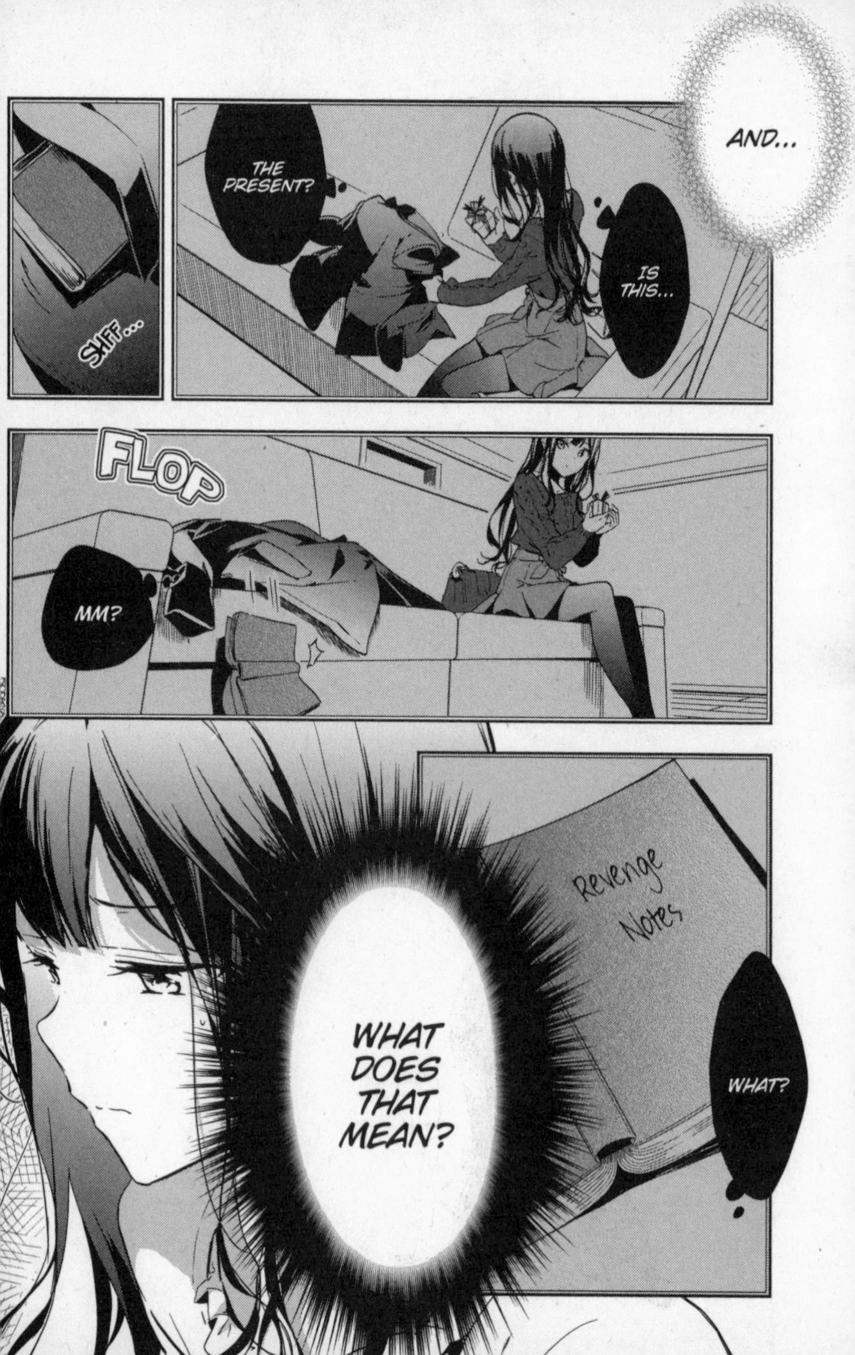
AND...
IS THIS...
THE PRESENT?
SHFF...
FLOP
MM?
WHAT?
Revenge Notes
WHAT DOES THAT MEAN?

Pancakes and cocoa...

Go well together.

9

Masamune-kun's
REVENGE

Presented by Hazuki Takeoka & TIV

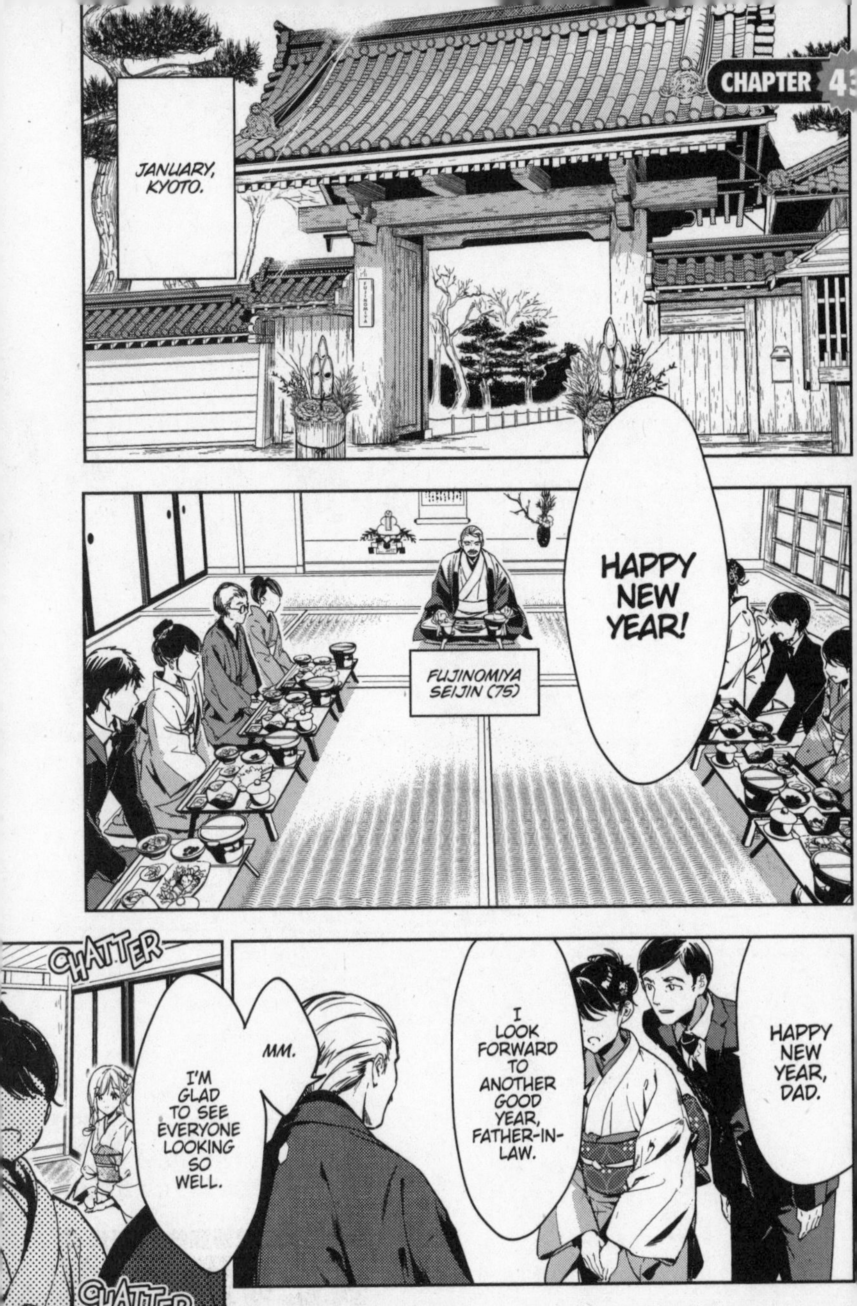
CHAPTER 43
JANUARY, KYOTO.
FUJINOMIYA
HAPPY NEW YEAR!
FUJINOMIYA SEIJIN (75)
HAPPY NEW YEAR, DAD.
I LOOK FORWARD TO ANOTHER GOOD YEAR, FATHER-IN-LAW.
MM.
I'M GLAD TO SEE EVERYONE LOOKING SO WELL.
CHATTER
CHATTER

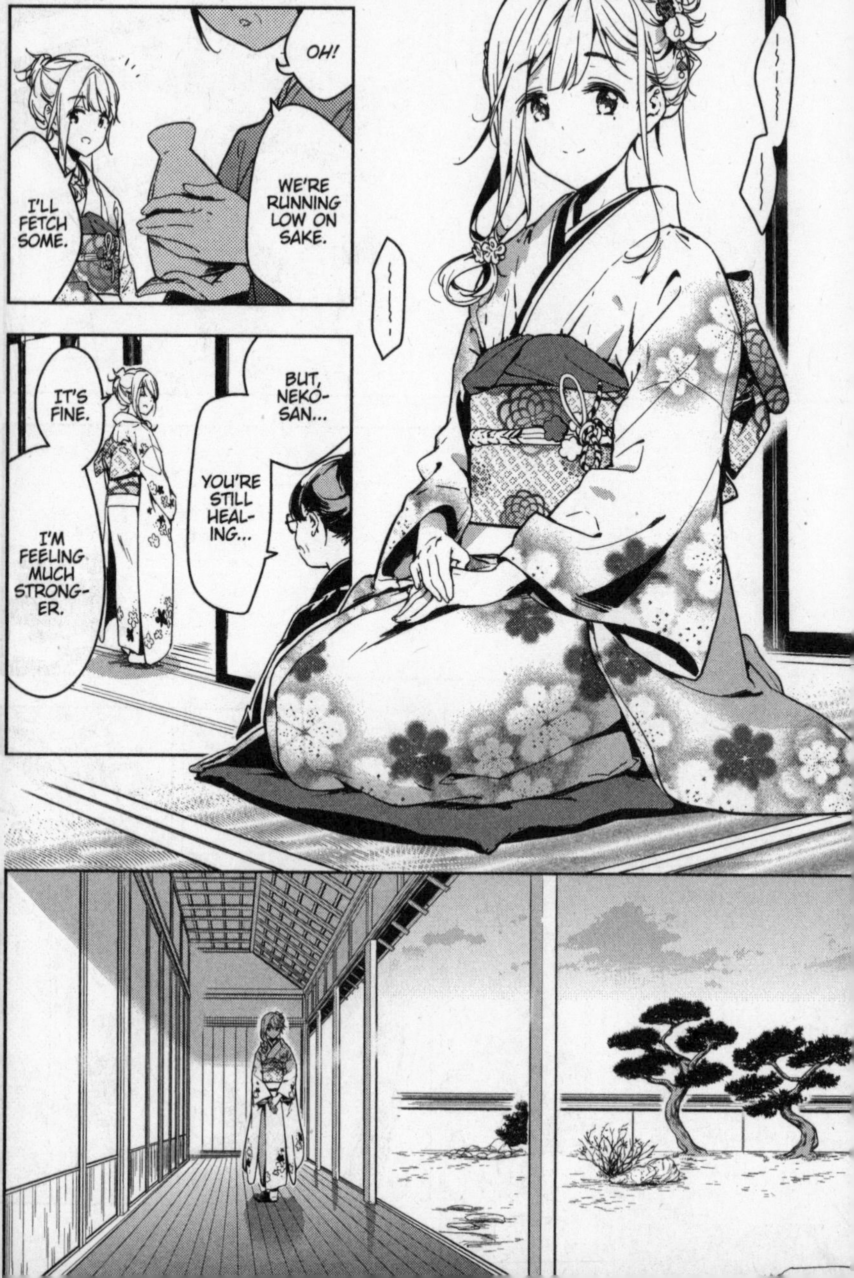

OH!
WE'RE RUNNING LOW ON SAKE.
I'LL FETCH SOME.
BUT, NEKO-SAN...
YOU'RE STILL HEAL-ING...
IT'S FINE.
I'M FEELING MUCH STRONG-ER.
...
...

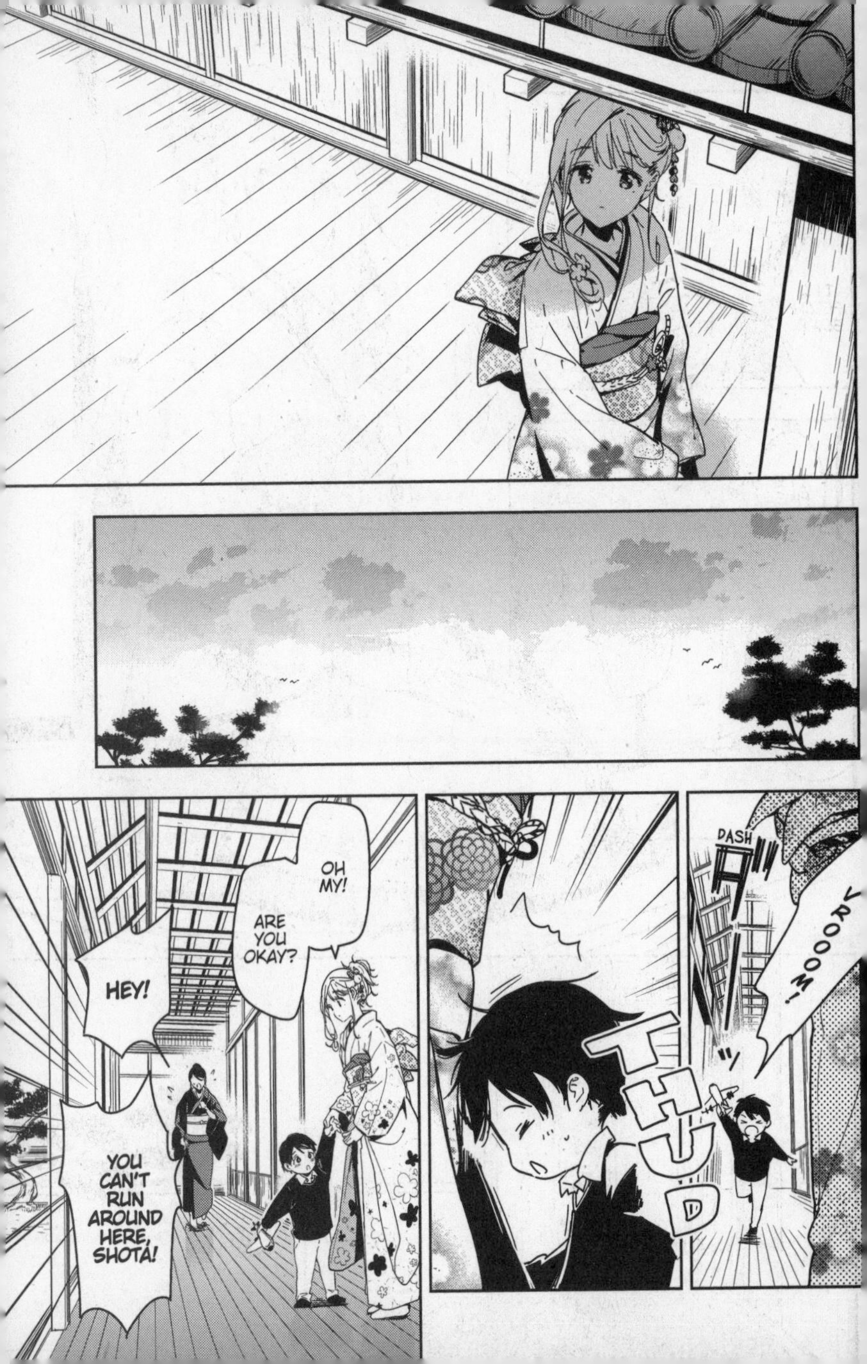
DASH
VROOOM!
THUD
OH MY!
ARE YOU OKAY?
HEY!
YOU CAN'T RUN AROUND HERE, SHOTA!

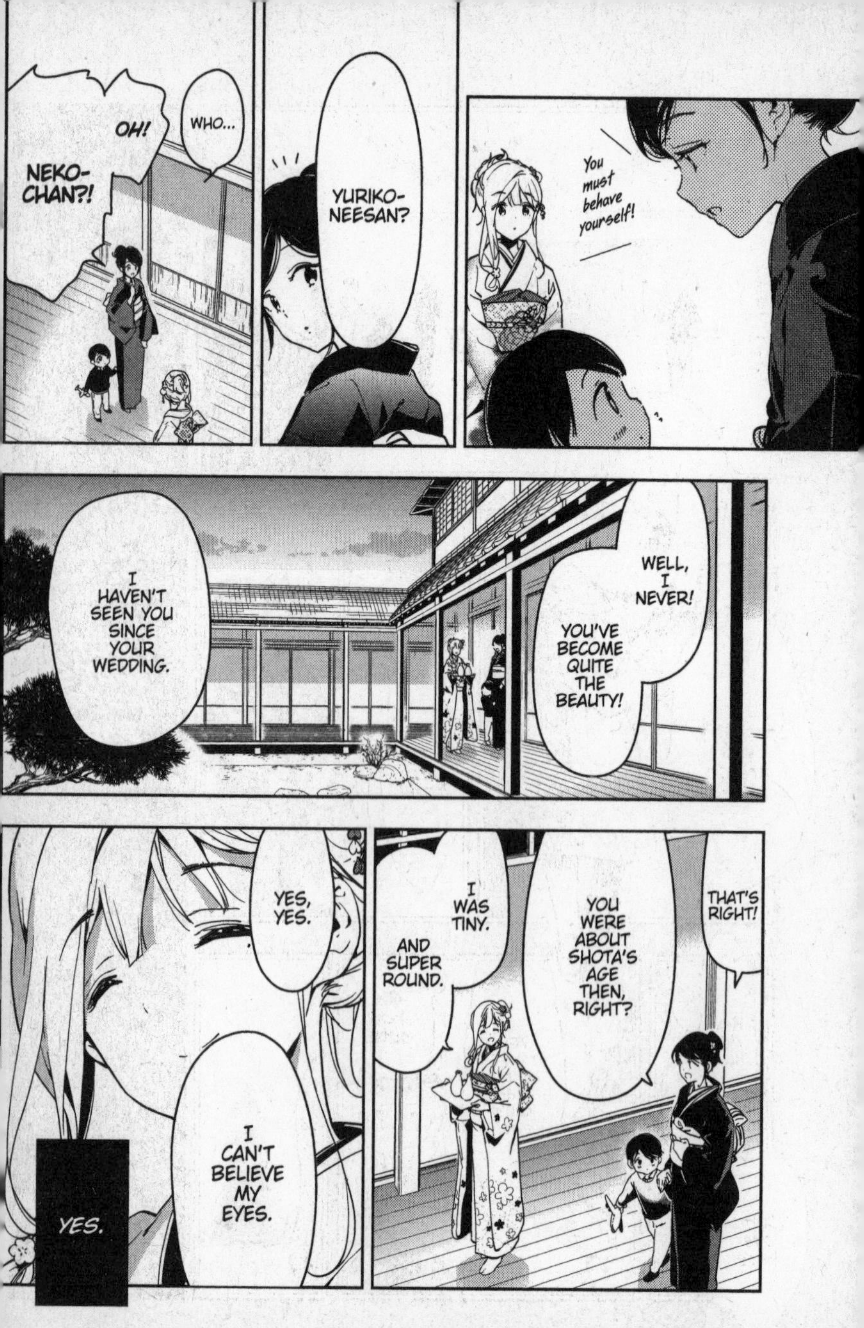
You must behave yourself!
YURIKO-NEESAN?
WHO...
OH!
NEKO-CHAN?!
WELL, I NEVER!
YOU'VE BECOME QUITE THE BEAUTY!
I HAVEN'T SEEN YOU SINCE YOUR WEDDING.
THAT'S RIGHT!
YOU WERE ABOUT SHOTA'S AGE THEN, RIGHT?
I WAS TINY.
AND SUPER ROUND.
YES, YES.
I CAN'T BELIEVE MY EYES.
YES.

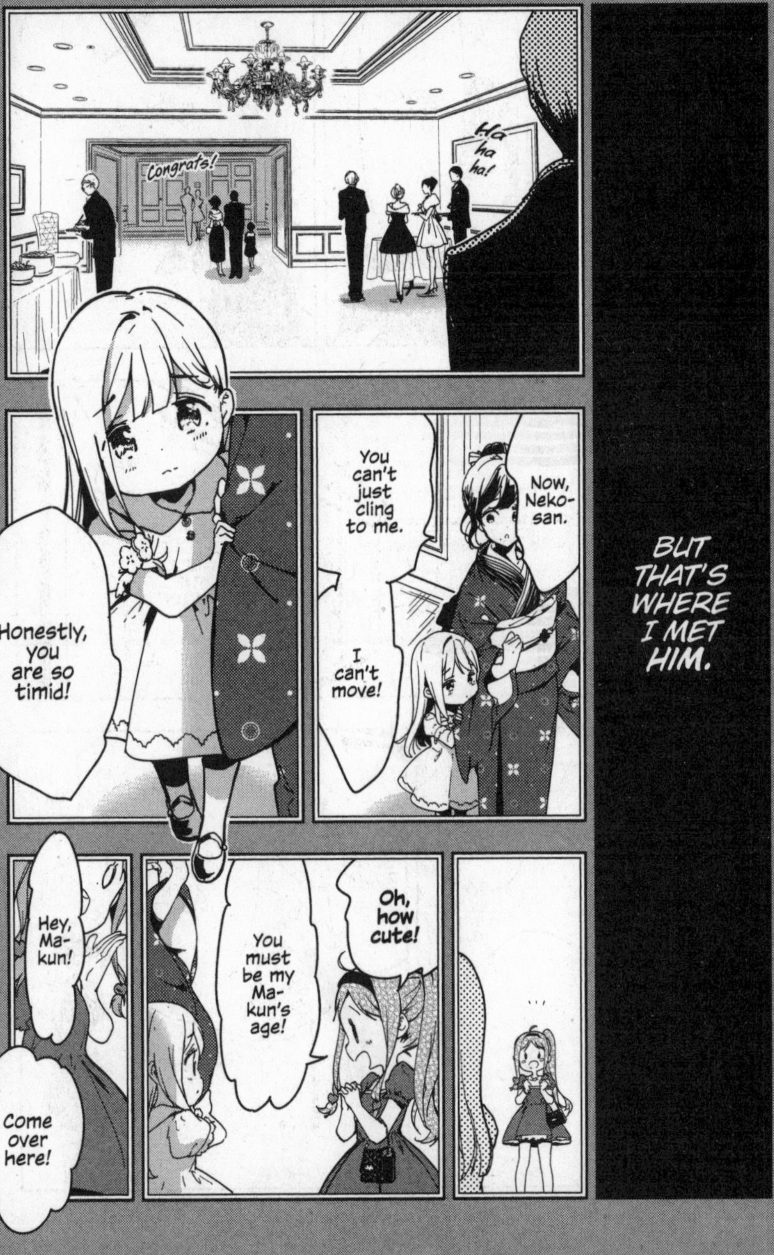
BUT THAT'S WHERE I MET HIM.
Ha ha ha!
Congrats!
Now, Neko-san.
You can't just cling to me.
I can't move!
Honestly, you are so timid!
...
Oh, how cute!
You must be my Ma-kun's age!
Hey, Ma-kun!
Come over here!

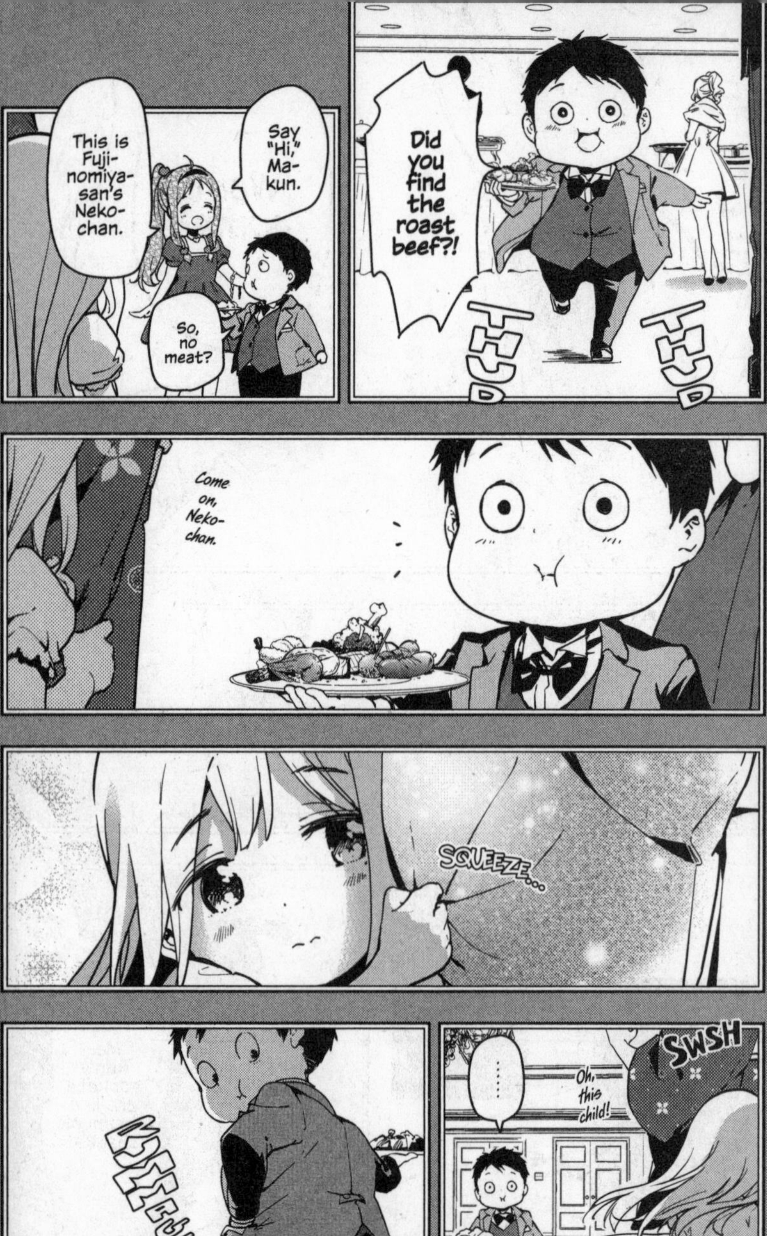
Did you find the roast beef?!
THUD
THUD
Say "Hi," Ma-kun.
This is Fuji-nomiya-san's Neko-chan.
So, no meat?
Come on, Neko-chan.
SQUEEZE...
SWSH
Oh, this child!
......

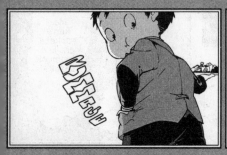

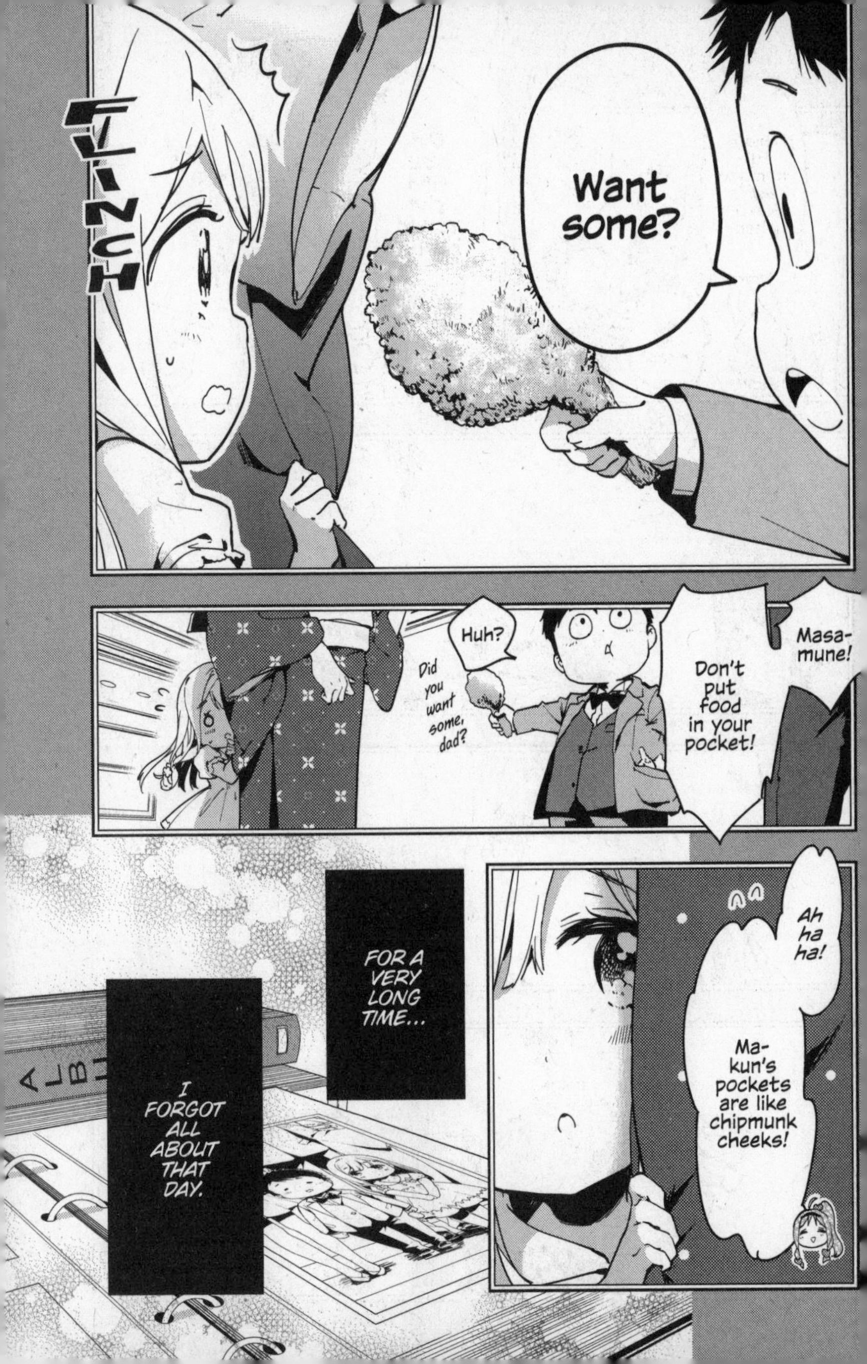
Want some?
FLINCH
Masa-mune!
Don't put food in your pocket!
Huh?
Did you want some, dad?
Ah ha ha!
Ma-kun's pockets are like chipmunk cheeks!
FOR A VERY LONG TIME...
I FORGOT ALL ABOUT THAT DAY.

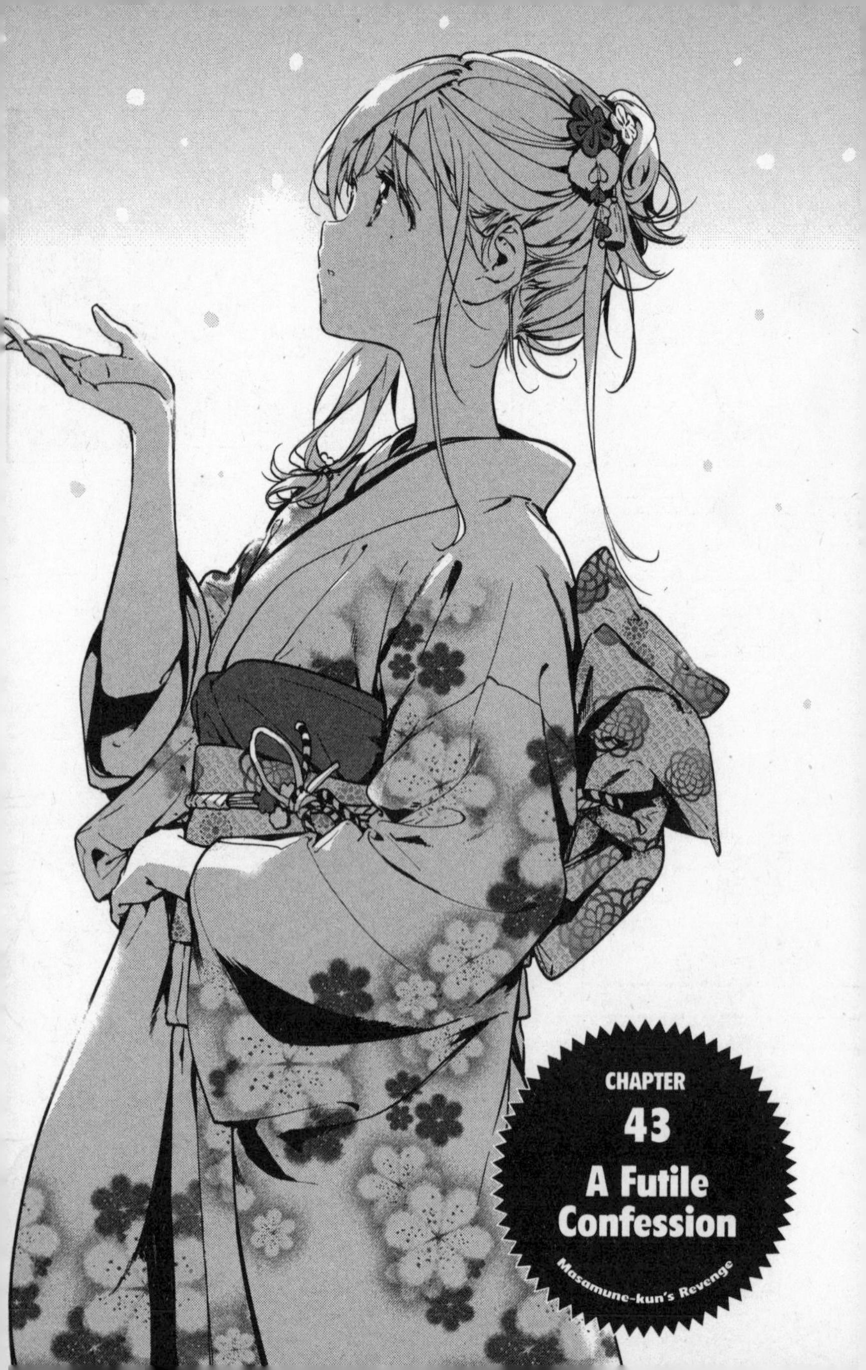
CHAPTER
43
A Futile
Confession
Masamune-kun's Revenge

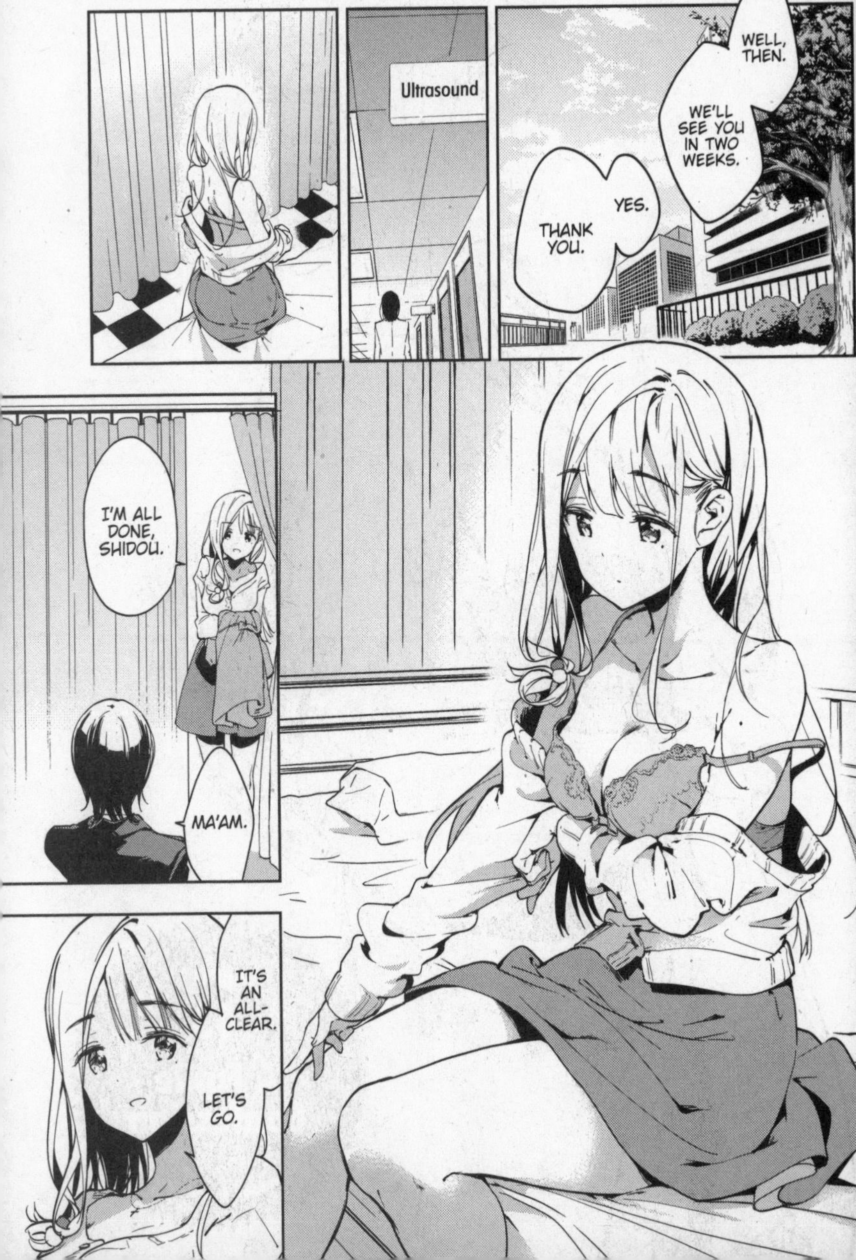
WELL, THEN.
WE'LL SEE YOU IN TWO WEEKS.
YES.
THANK YOU.
Ultrasound
I'M ALL DONE, SHIDOU.
MA'AM.
IT'S AN ALL-CLEAR.
LET'S GO.

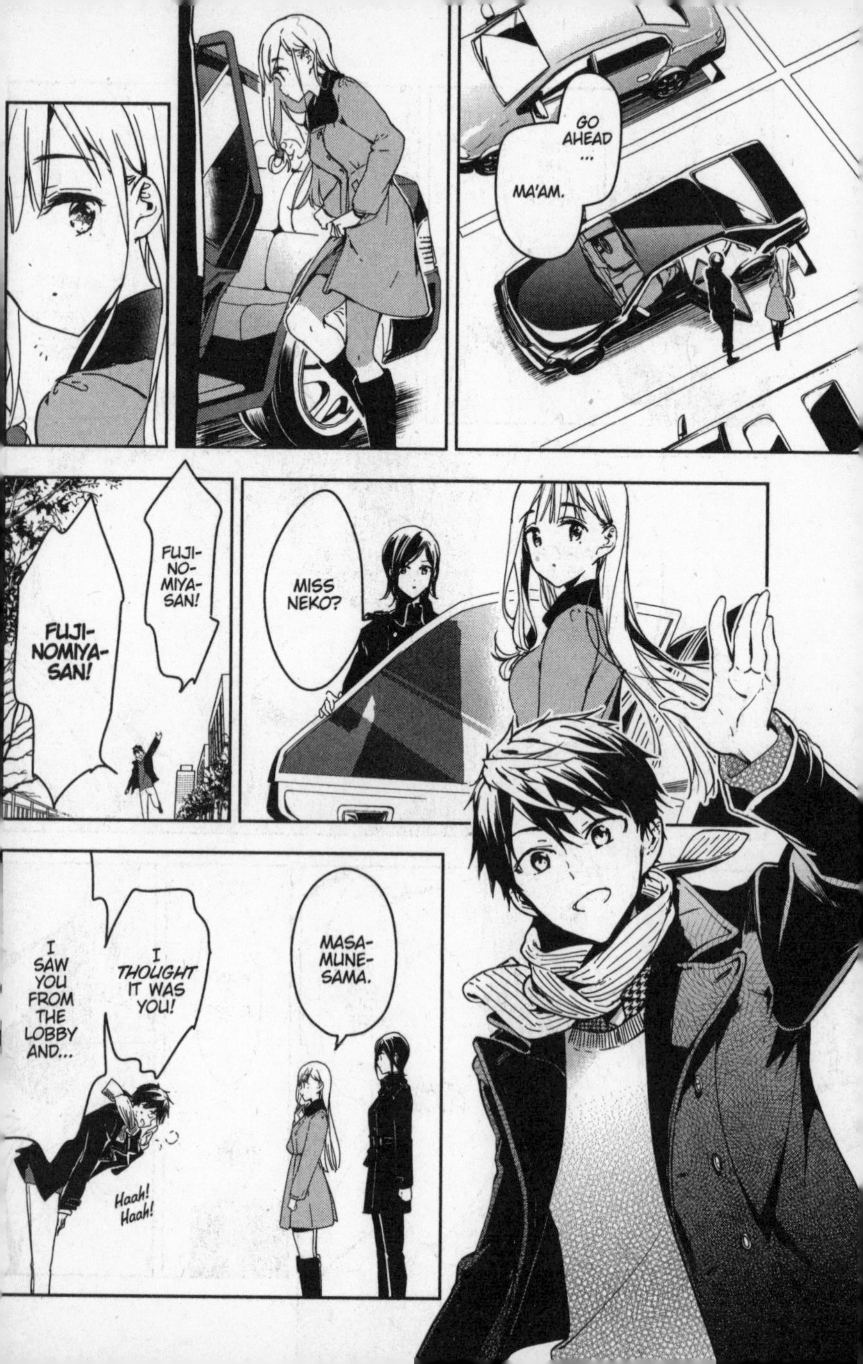
GO AHEAD... MA'AM.
MISS NEKO?
FUJI-NOMIYA-SAN!
FUJI-NOMIYA-SAN!
MASA-MUNE-SAMA.
I THOUGHT IT WAS YOU!
I SAW YOU FROM THE LOBBY AND...
Haah! Haah!

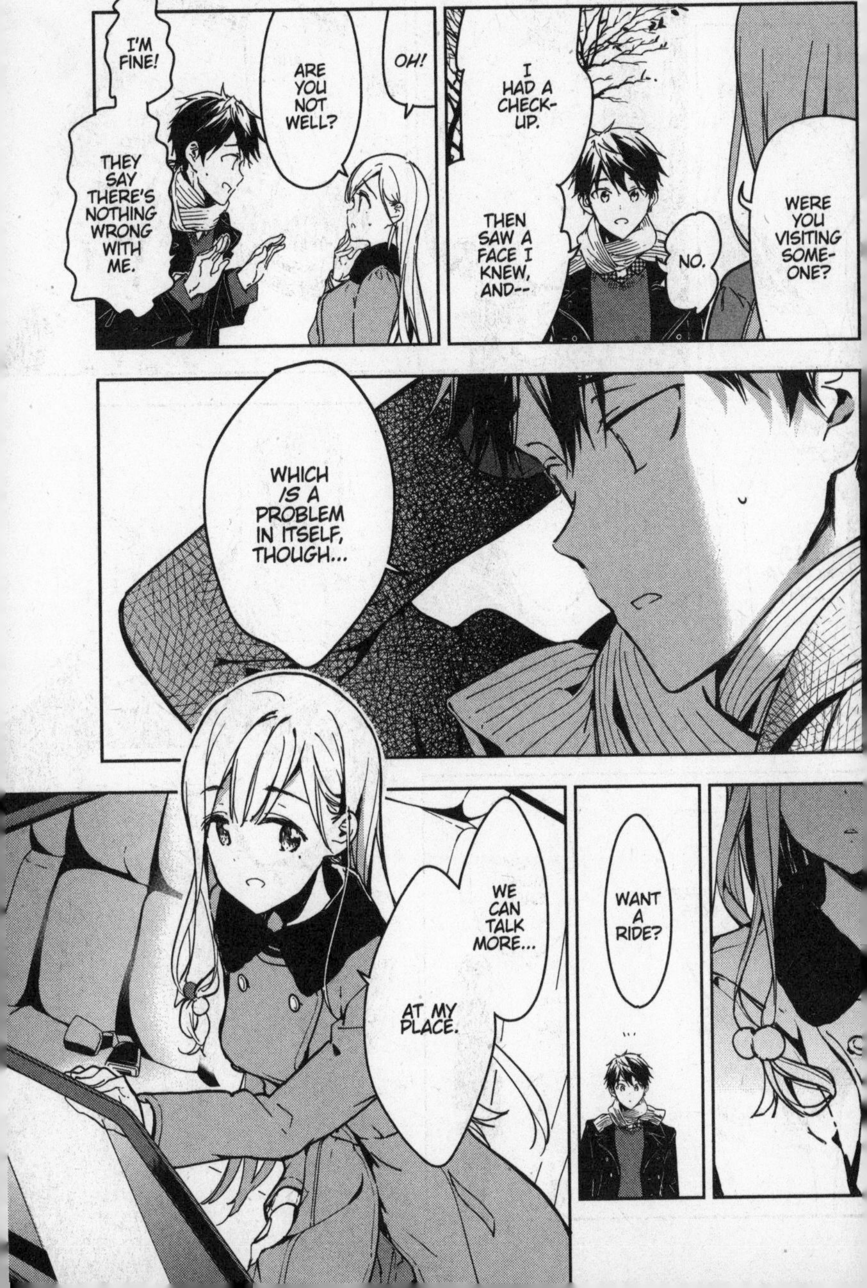
WERE YOU VISITING SOME-ONE?
NO.
I HAD A CHECK-UP.
THEN SAW A FACE I KNEW, AND--
OH!
ARE YOU NOT WELL?
I'M FINE!
THEY SAY THERE'S NOTHING WRONG WITH ME.
WHICH *IS* A PROBLEM IN ITSELF, THOUGH...
WANT A RIDE?
...
WE CAN TALK MORE...
AT MY PLACE.

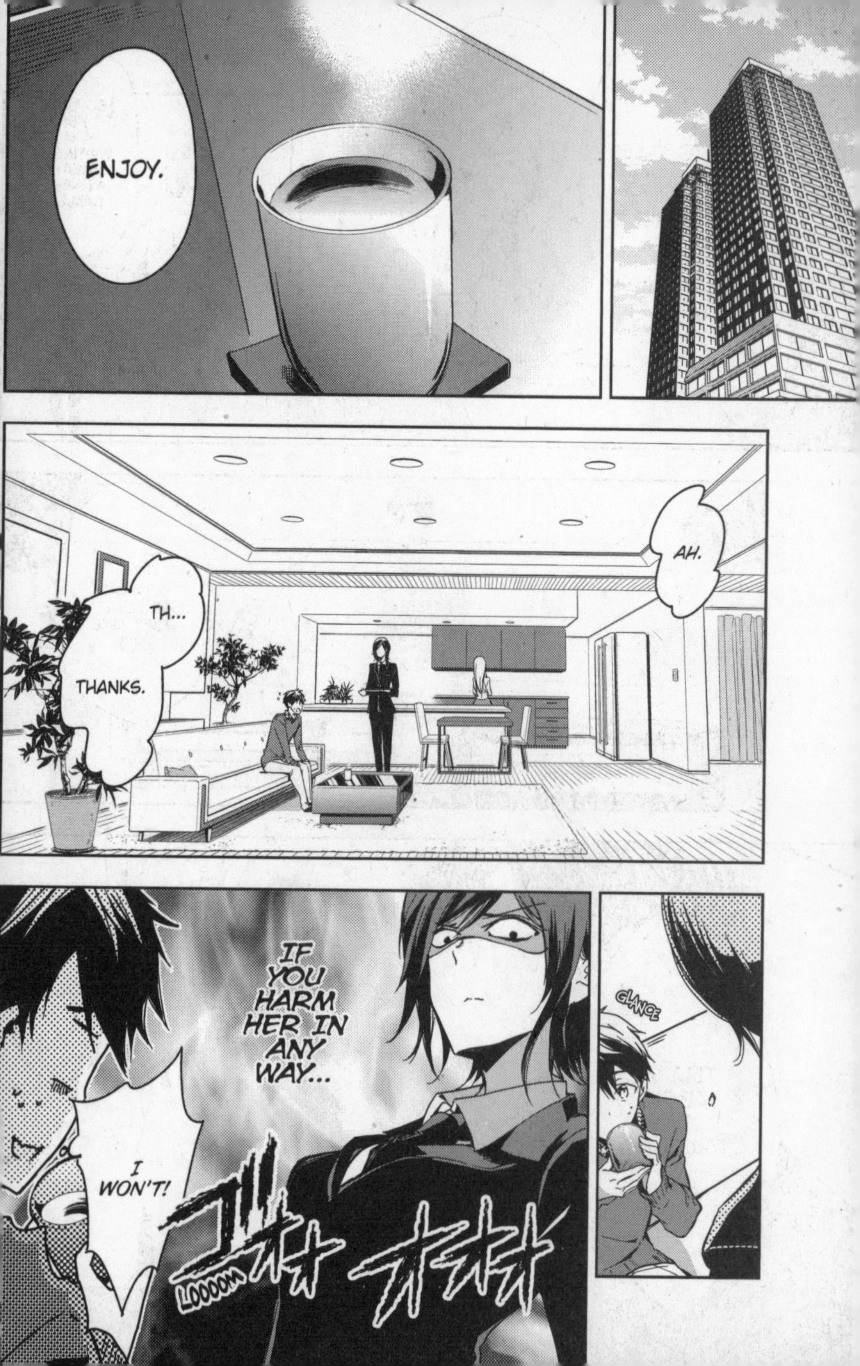
ENJOY.
AH.
TH...
THANKS.
GLANCE
IF YOU HARM HER IN ANY WAY...
I WON'T!
LOOOOM

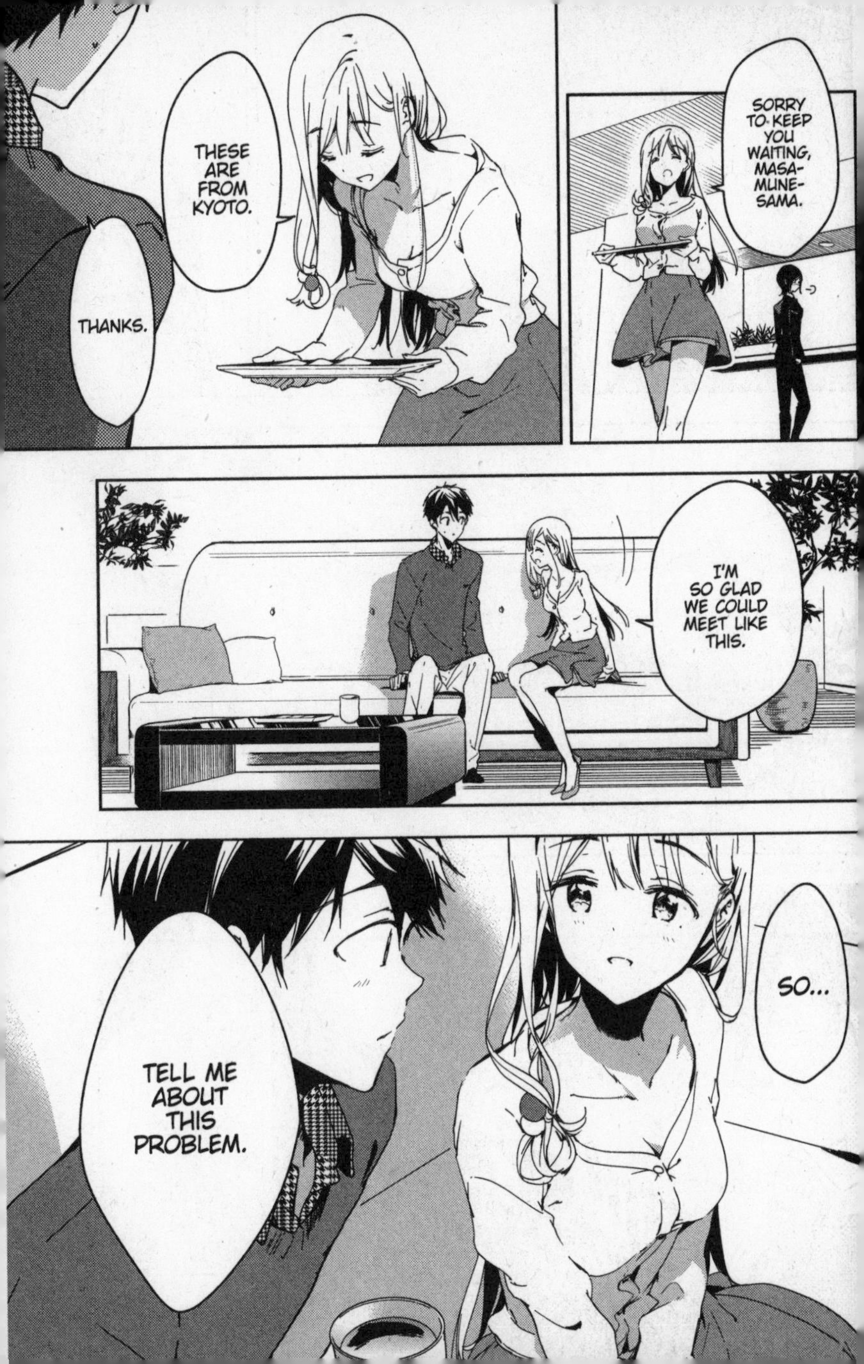
SORRY TO KEEP YOU WAITING, MASAMUNE-SAMA.
THESE ARE FROM KYOTO.
THANKS.
I'M SO GLAD WE COULD MEET LIKE THIS.
SO...
TELL ME ABOUT THIS PROBLEM.

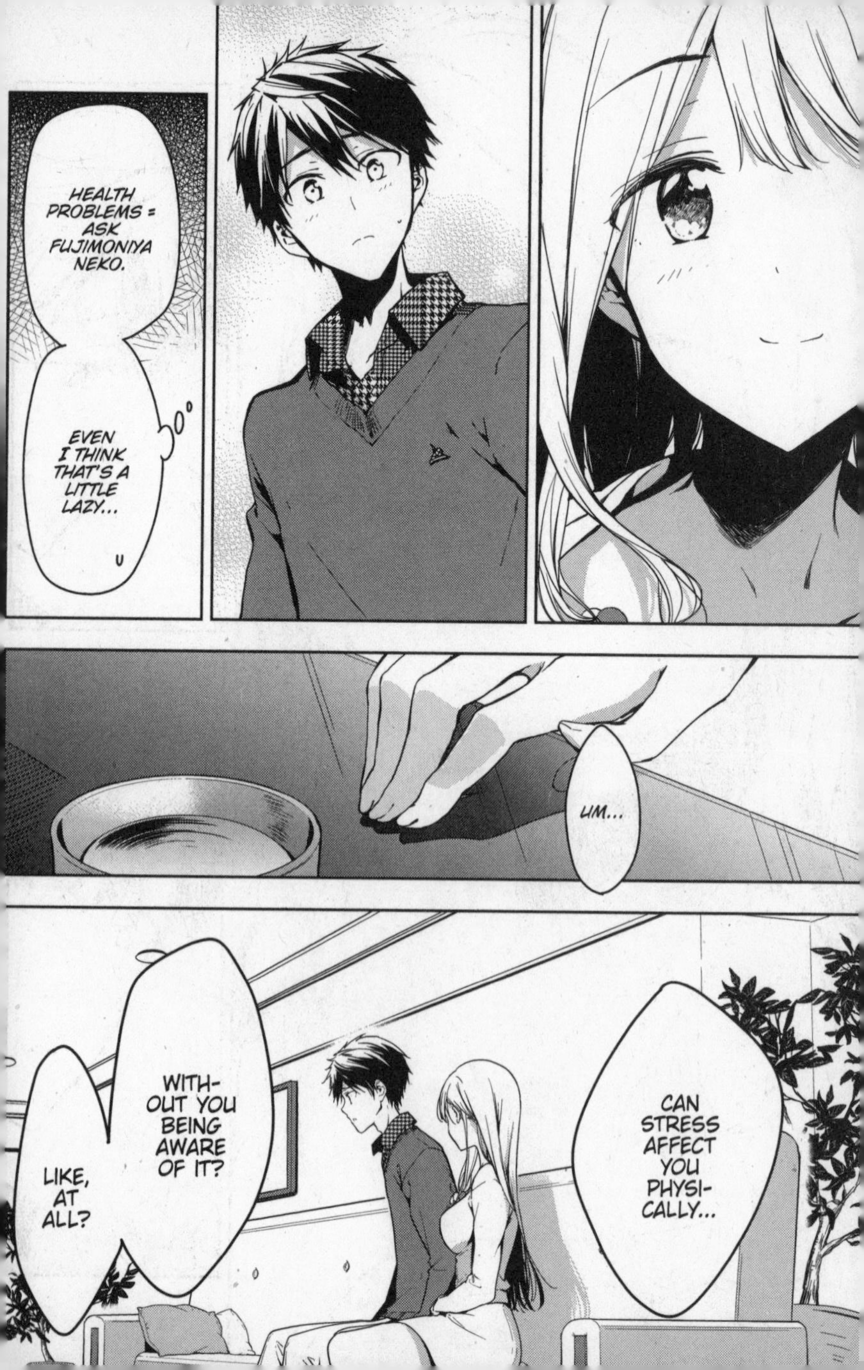
HEALTH PROBLEMS = ASK FUJIMONIYA NEKO.
EVEN I THINK THAT'S A LITTLE LAZY...
UM...
CAN STRESS AFFECT YOU PHYSICALLY...
WITHOUT YOU BEING AWARE OF IT?
LIKE, AT ALL?

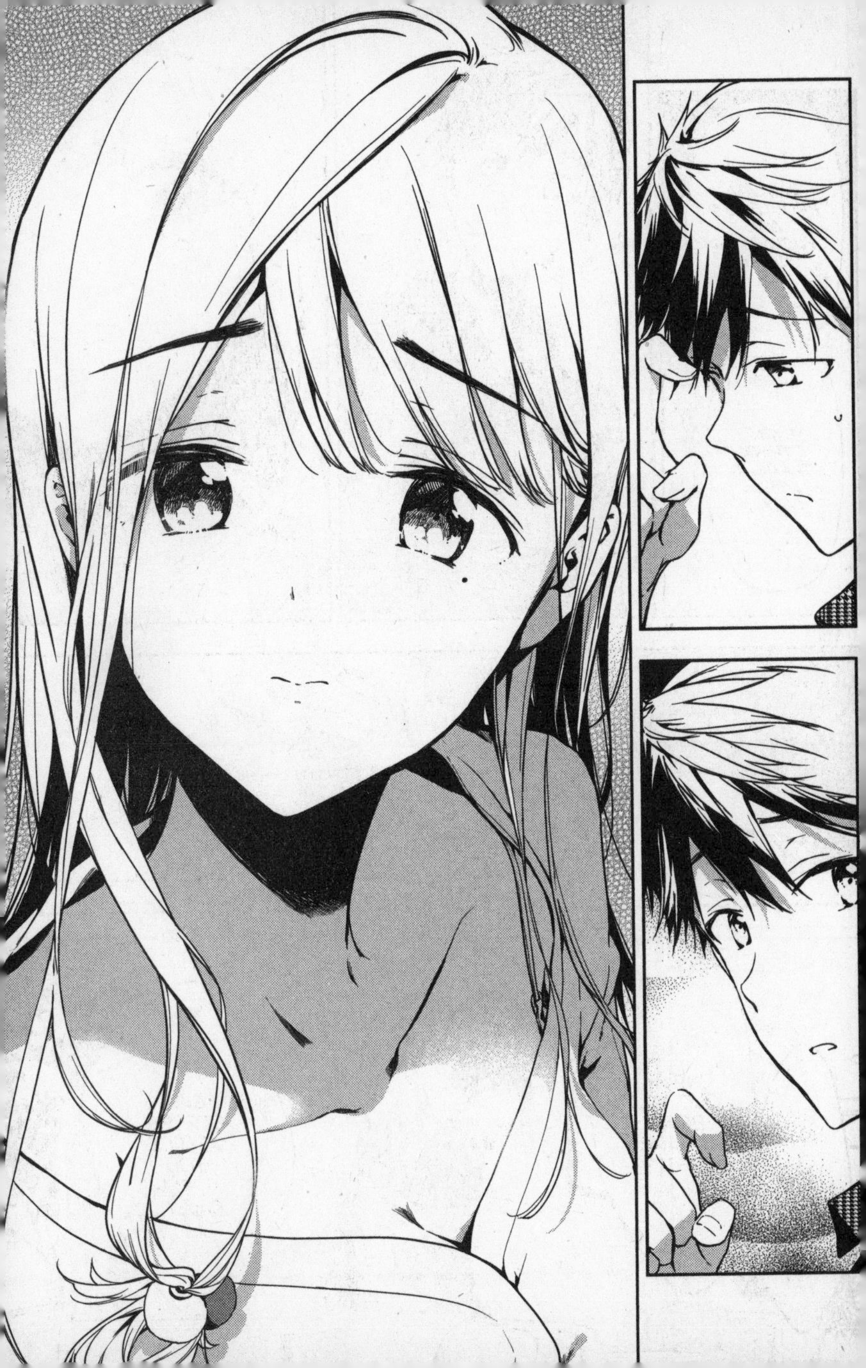

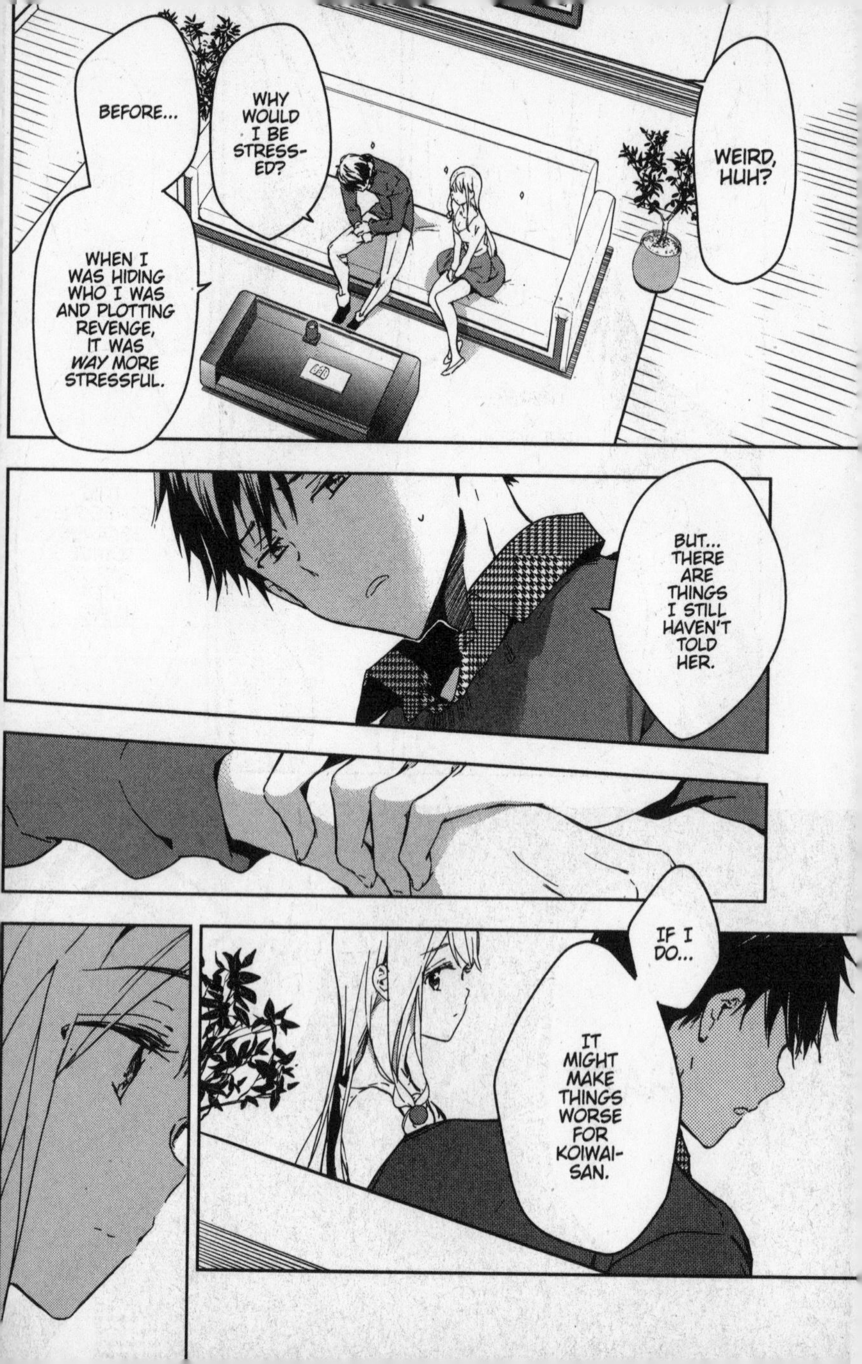
WEIRD, HUH?
WHY WOULD I BE STRESSED-ED?
BEFORE...
WHEN I WAS HIDING WHO I WAS AND PLOTTING REVENGE, IT WAS *WAY* MORE STRESSFUL.
BUT... THERE ARE THINGS I STILL HAVEN'T TOLD HER.
IF I DO...
IT MIGHT MAKE THINGS WORSE FOR KOIWAI-SAN.

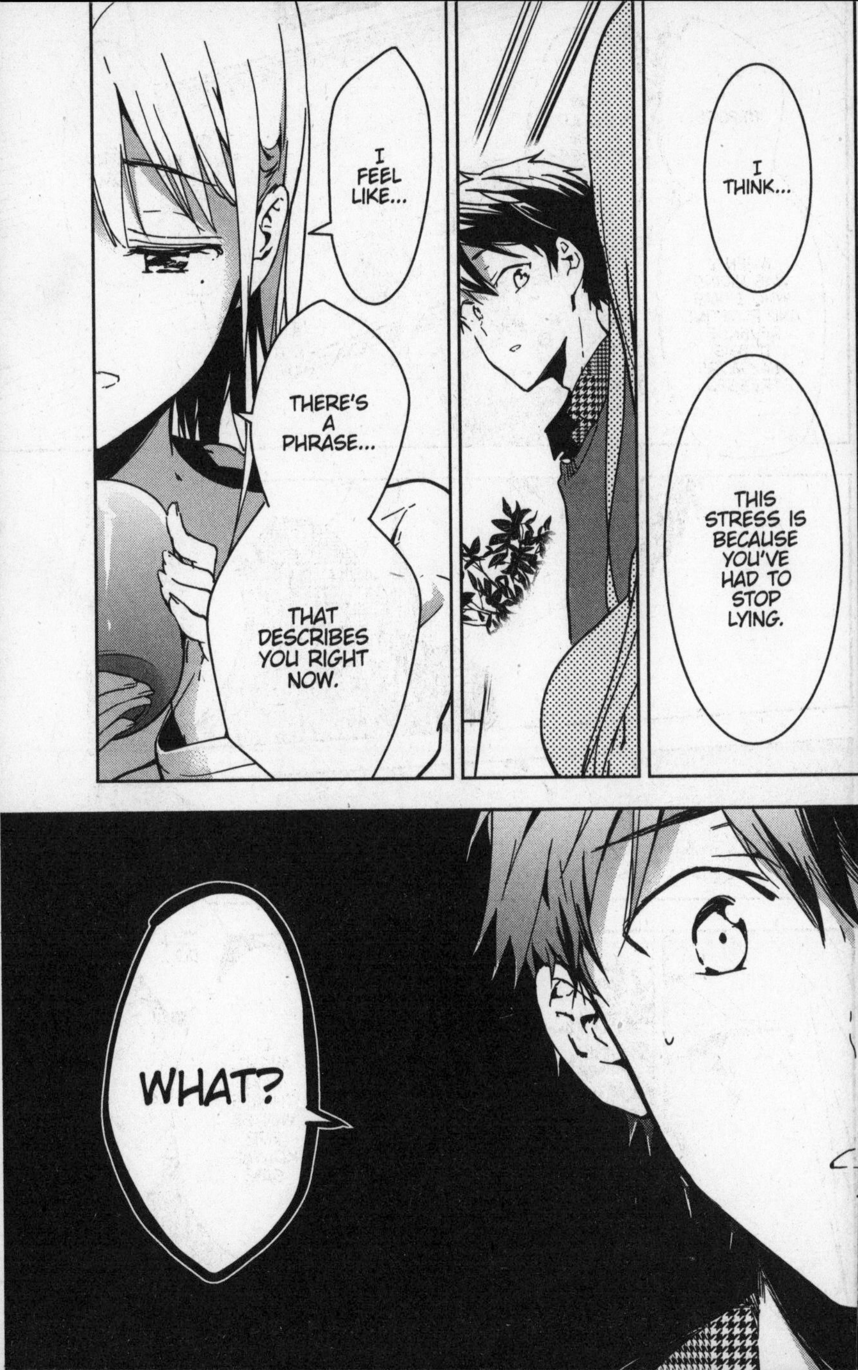
I THINK...
THIS STRESS IS BECAUSE YOU'VE HAD TO STOP LYING.
I FEEL LIKE...
THERE'S A PHRASE...
THAT DESCRIBES YOU RIGHT NOW.
WHAT?

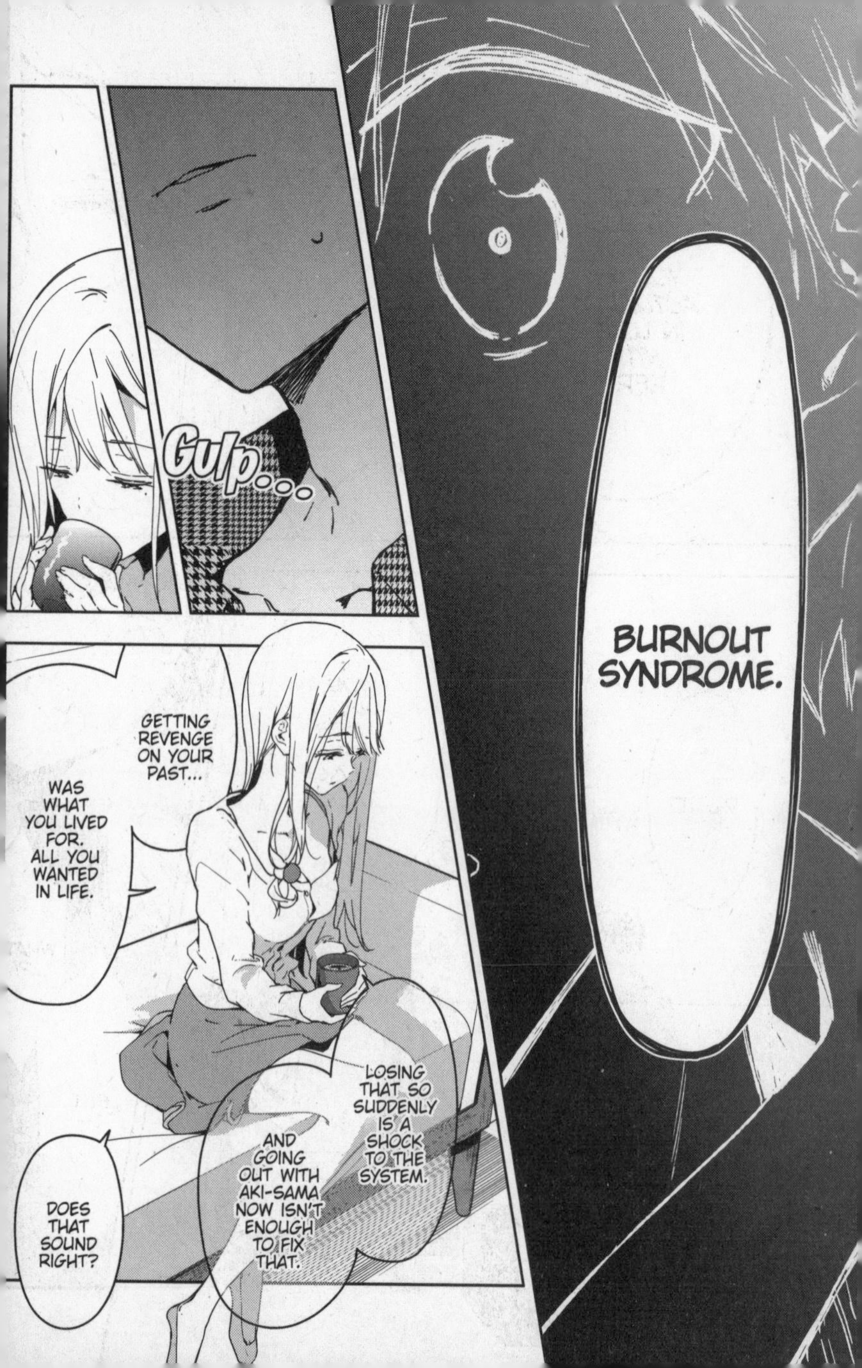
BURNOUT SYNDROME.
Gulp...
GETTING REVENGE ON YOUR PAST...
WAS WHAT YOU LIVED FOR. ALL YOU WANTED IN LIFE.
LOSING THAT SO SUDDENLY IS A SHOCK TO THE SYSTEM.
AND GOING OUT WITH AKI-SAMA NOW ISN'T ENOUGH TO FIX THAT.
DOES THAT SOUND RIGHT?

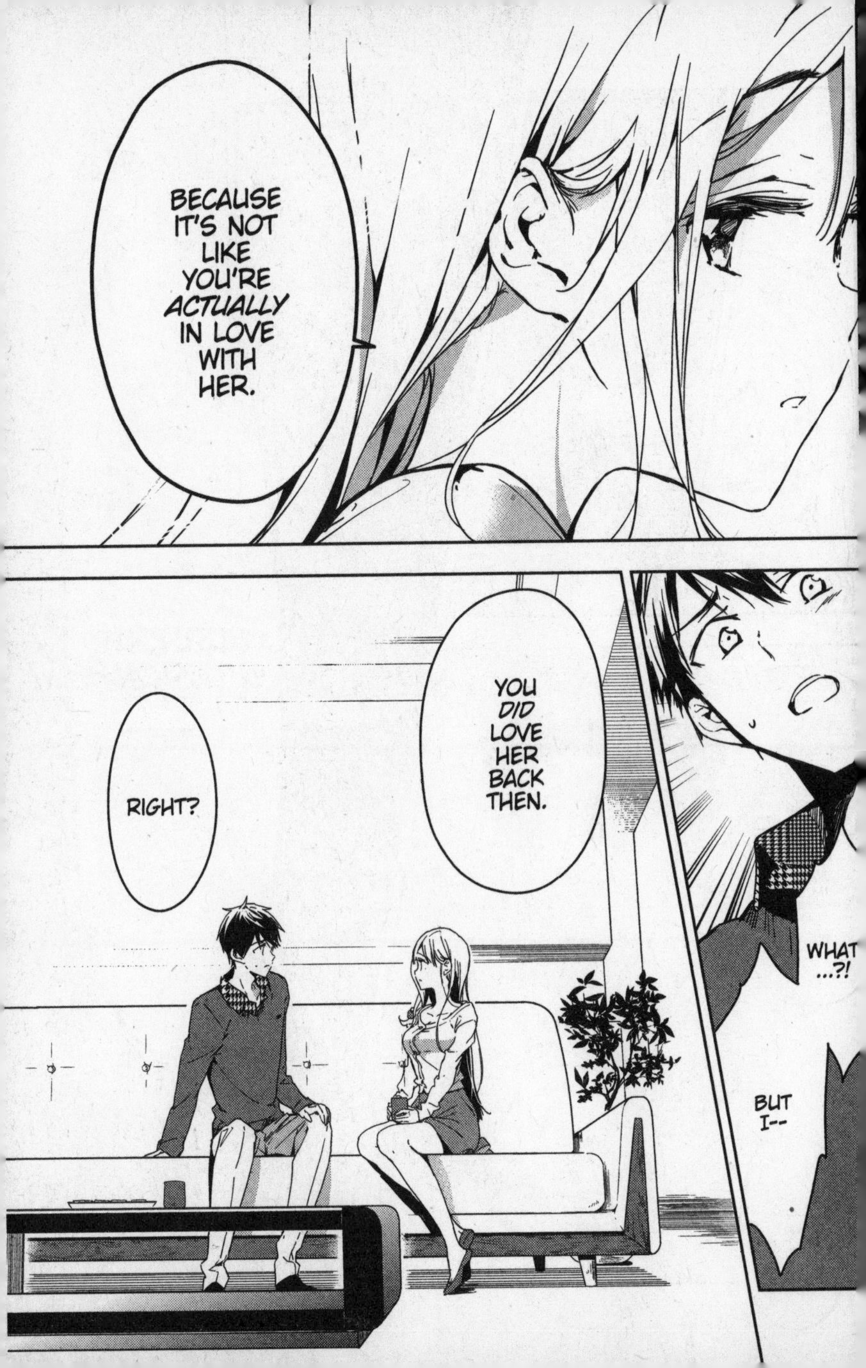
BECAUSE IT'S NOT LIKE YOU'RE *ACTUALLY* IN LOVE WITH HER.
WHAT ...?!
BUT I--
YOU *DID* LOVE HER BACK THEN.
RIGHT?

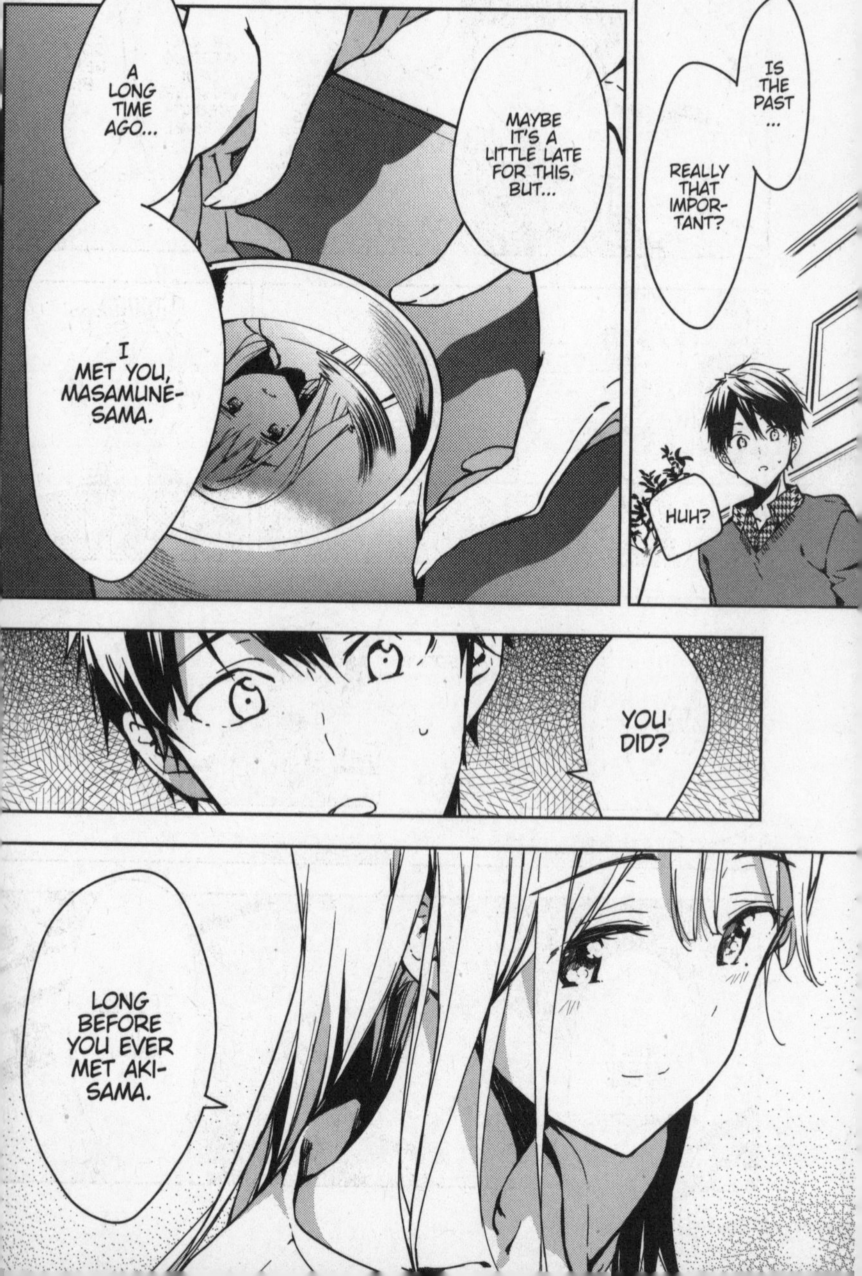
IS THE PAST... REALLY THAT IMPORTANT?
HUH?
MAYBE IT'S A LITTLE LATE FOR THIS, BUT...
A LONG TIME AGO...
I MET YOU, MASAMUNE-SAMA.
YOU DID?
LONG BEFORE YOU EVER MET AKI-SAMA.

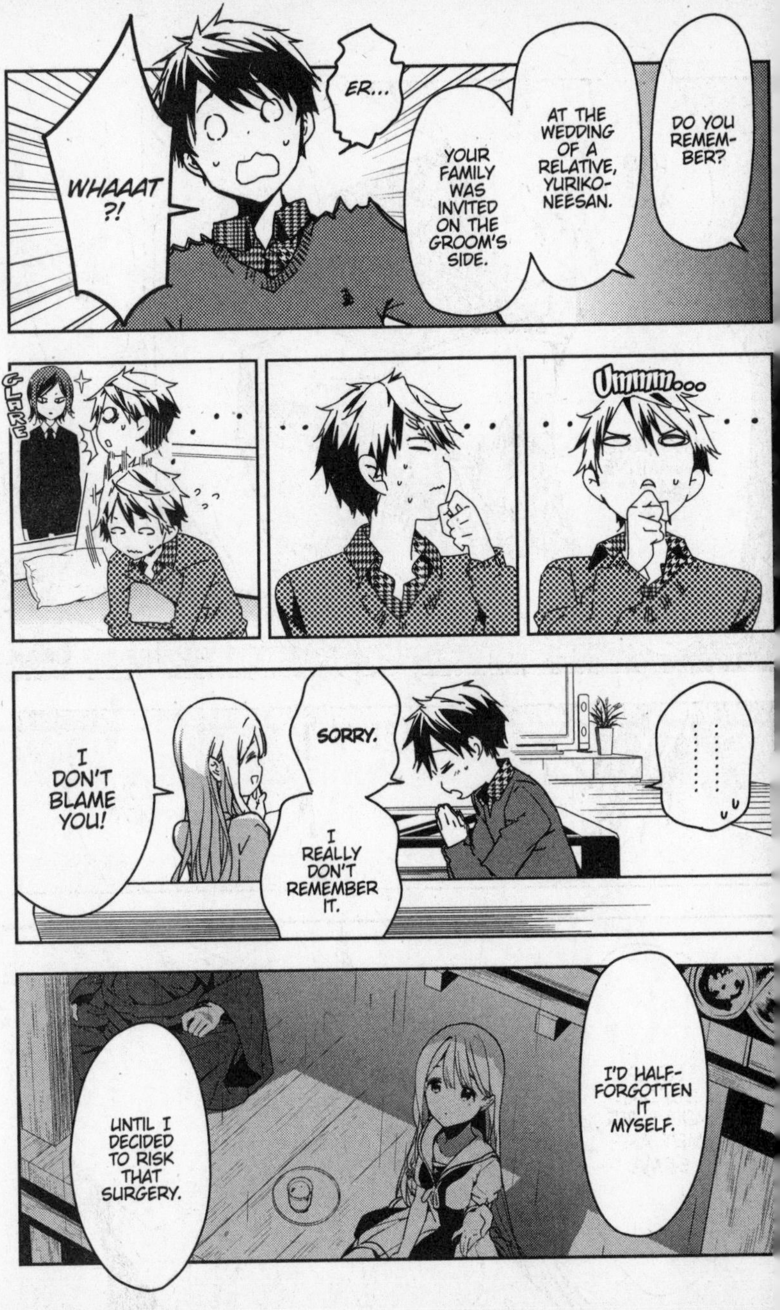

DO YOU REMEMBER?
AT THE WEDDING OF A RELATIVE, YURIKO-NEESAN.
YOUR FAMILY WAS INVITED ON THE GROOM'S SIDE.
ER...
WHAAAT?!
Ummmm...
...
...
...
GLARE
......
SORRY.
I REALLY DON'T REMEMBER IT.
I DON'T BLAME YOU!
I'D HALF-FORGOTTEN IT MYSELF.
UNTIL I DECIDED TO RISK THAT SURGERY.

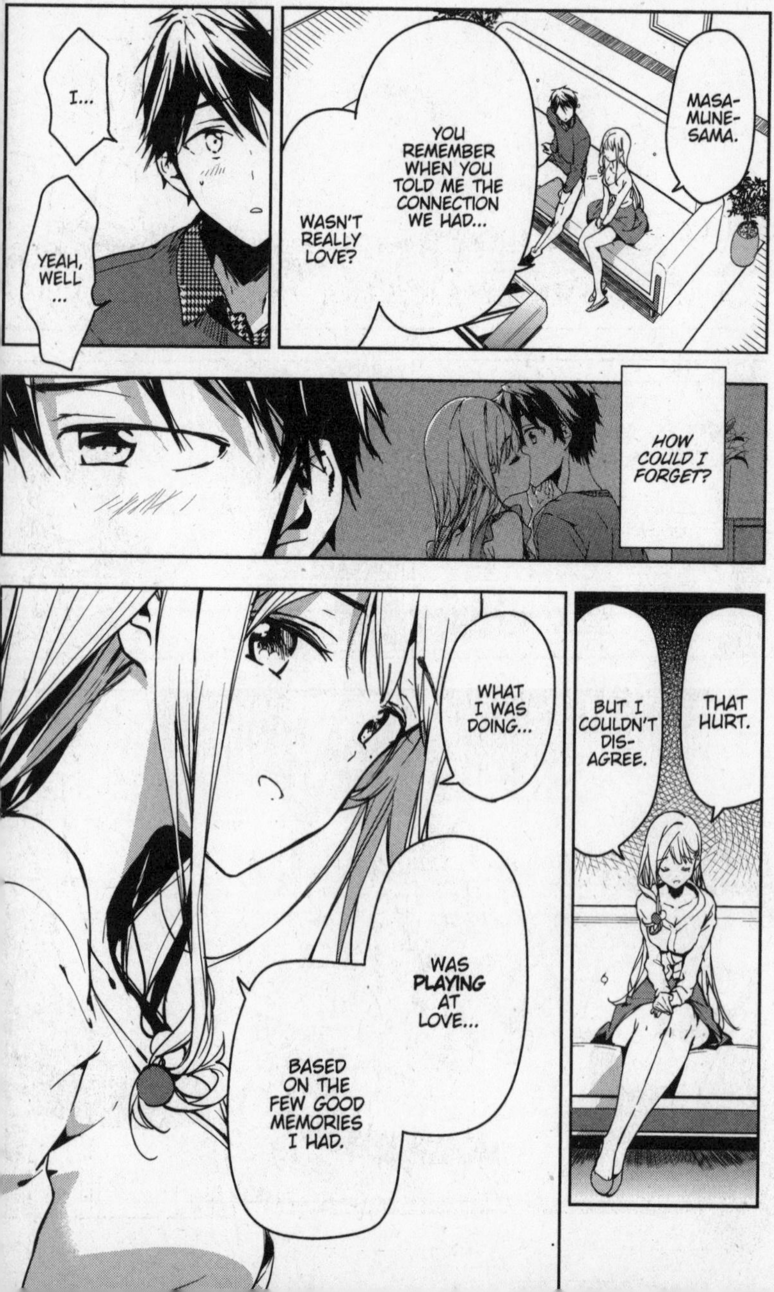
MASA-MUNE-SAMA.
YOU REMEMBER WHEN YOU TOLD ME THE CONNECTION WE HAD...
WASN'T REALLY LOVE?
I...
YEAH, WELL ...
HOW COULD I FORGET?
THAT HURT.
BUT I COULDN'T DIS-AGREE.
WHAT I WAS DOING...
WAS PLAYING AT LOVE...
BASED ON THE FEW GOOD MEMORIES I HAD.

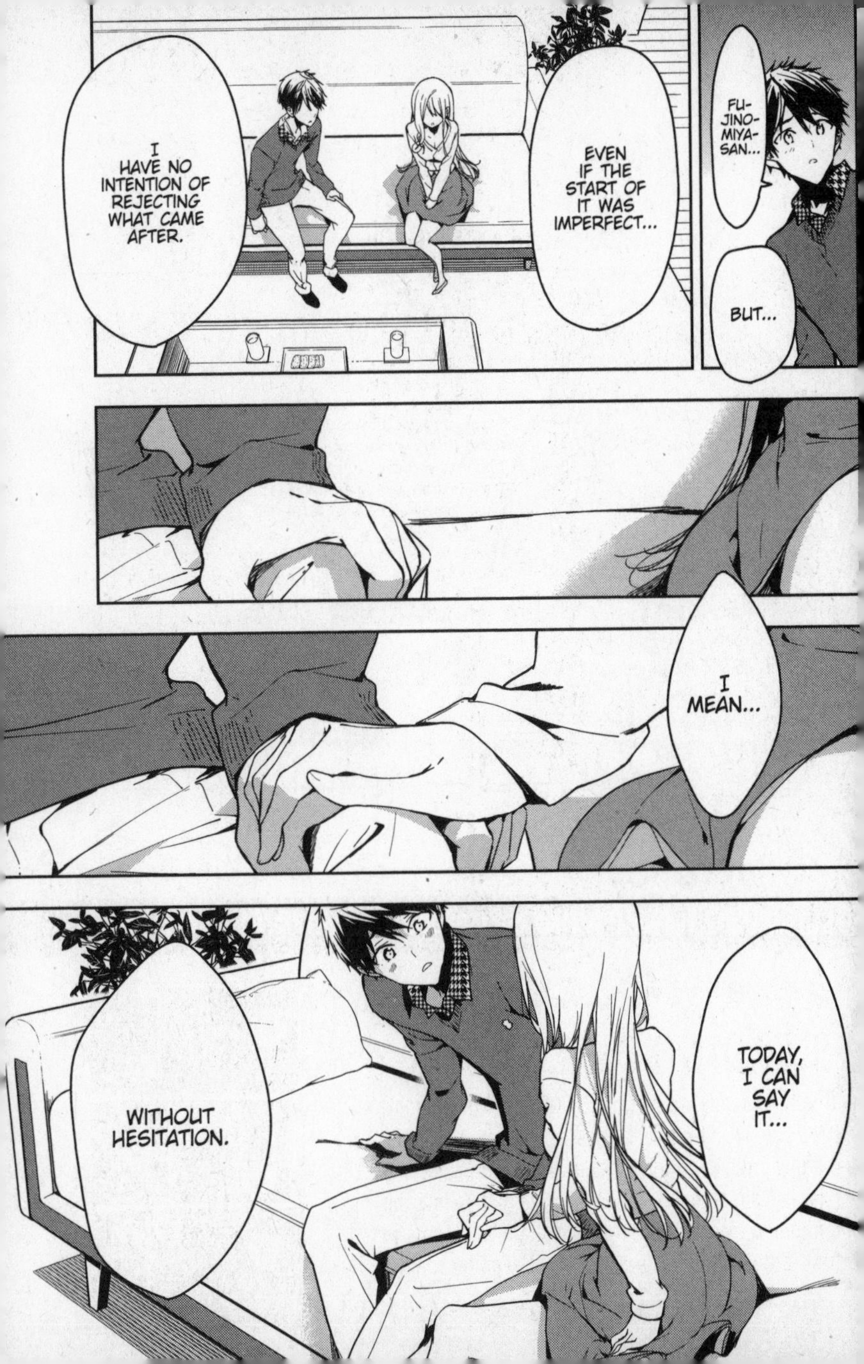
FUJINOMIYA-SAN...
BUT...
EVEN IF THE START OF IT WAS IMPERFECT...
I HAVE NO INTENTION OF REJECTING WHAT CAME AFTER.
I MEAN...
TODAY, I CAN SAY IT...
WITHOUT HESITATION.

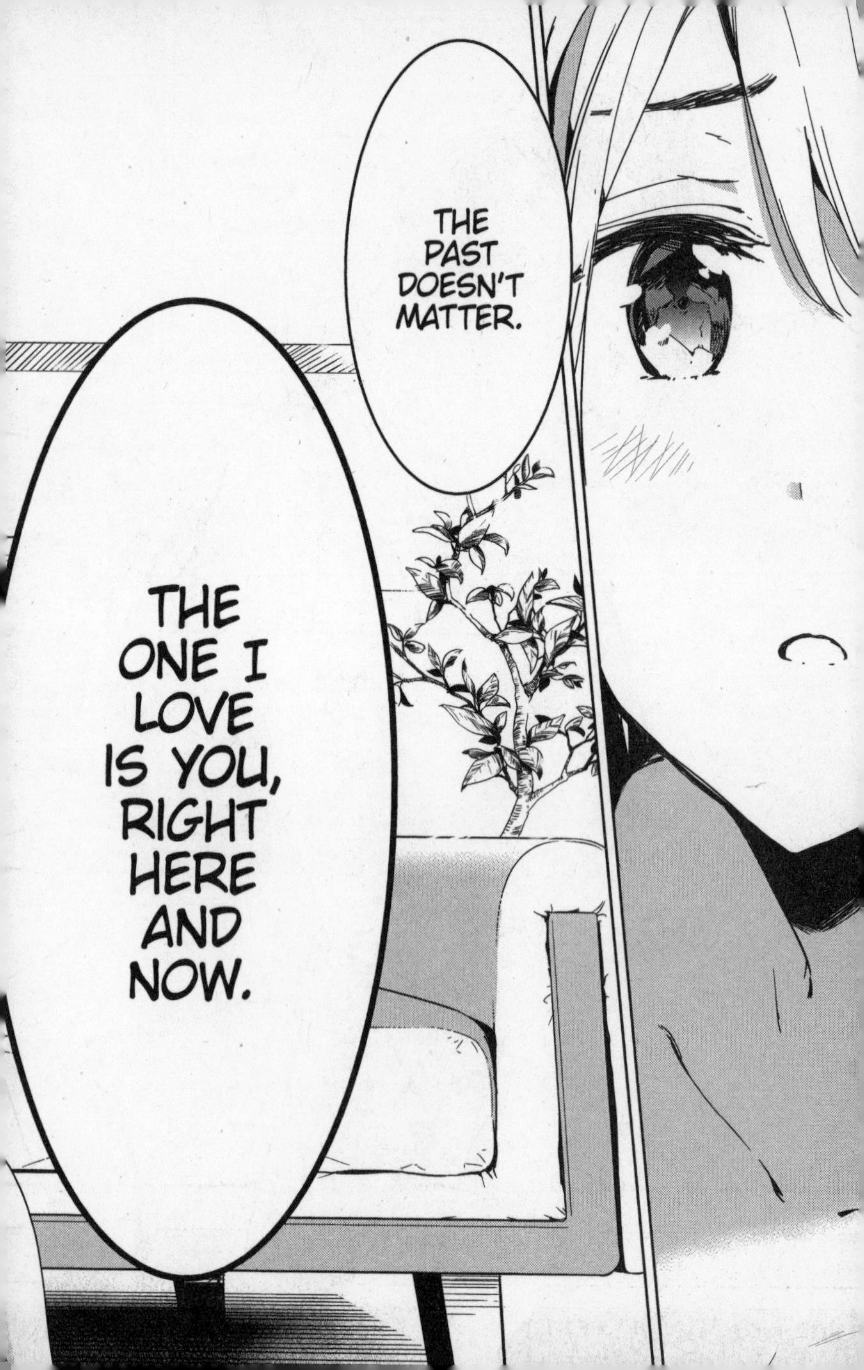
THE PAST DOESN'T MATTER.
THE ONE I LOVE IS YOU, RIGHT HERE AND NOW.

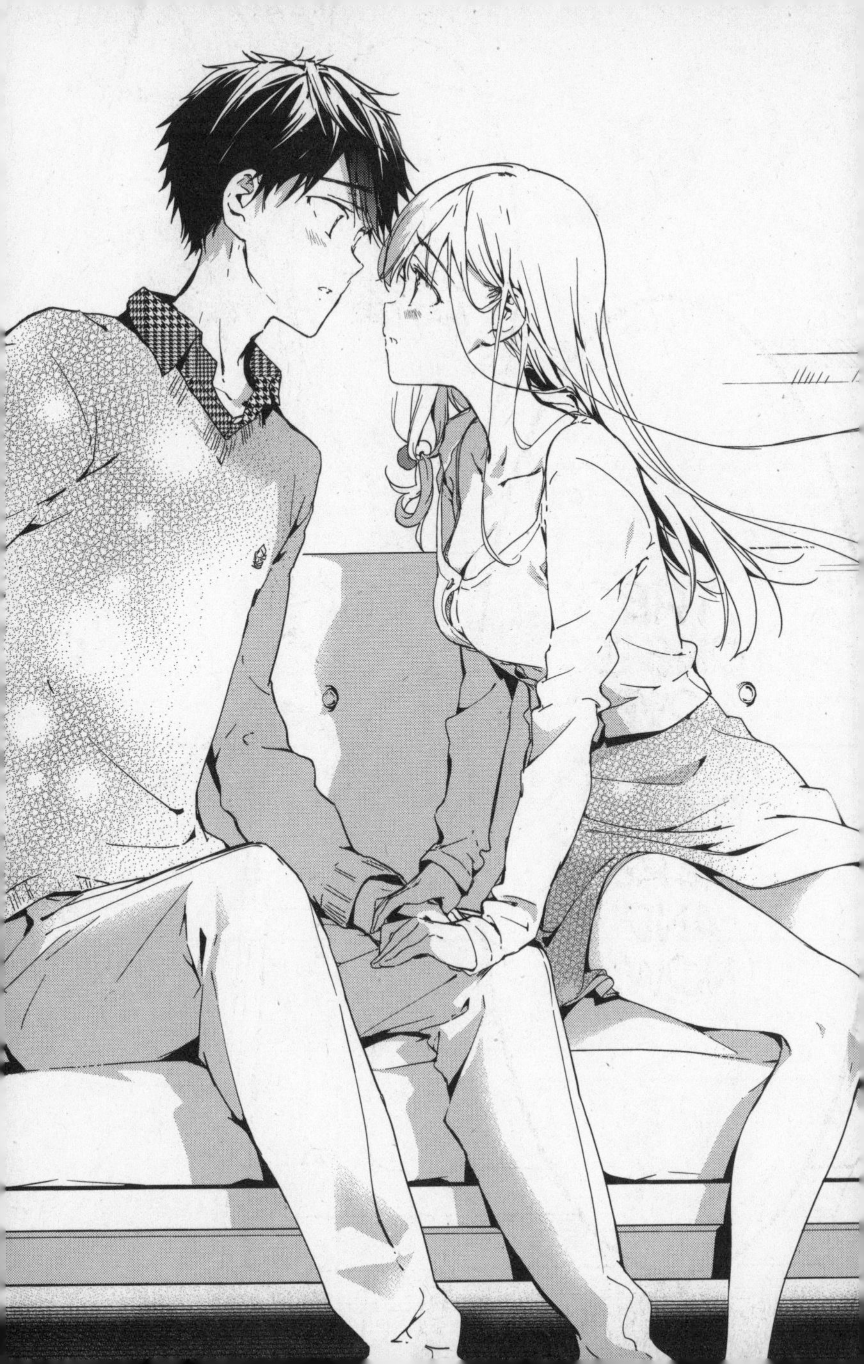

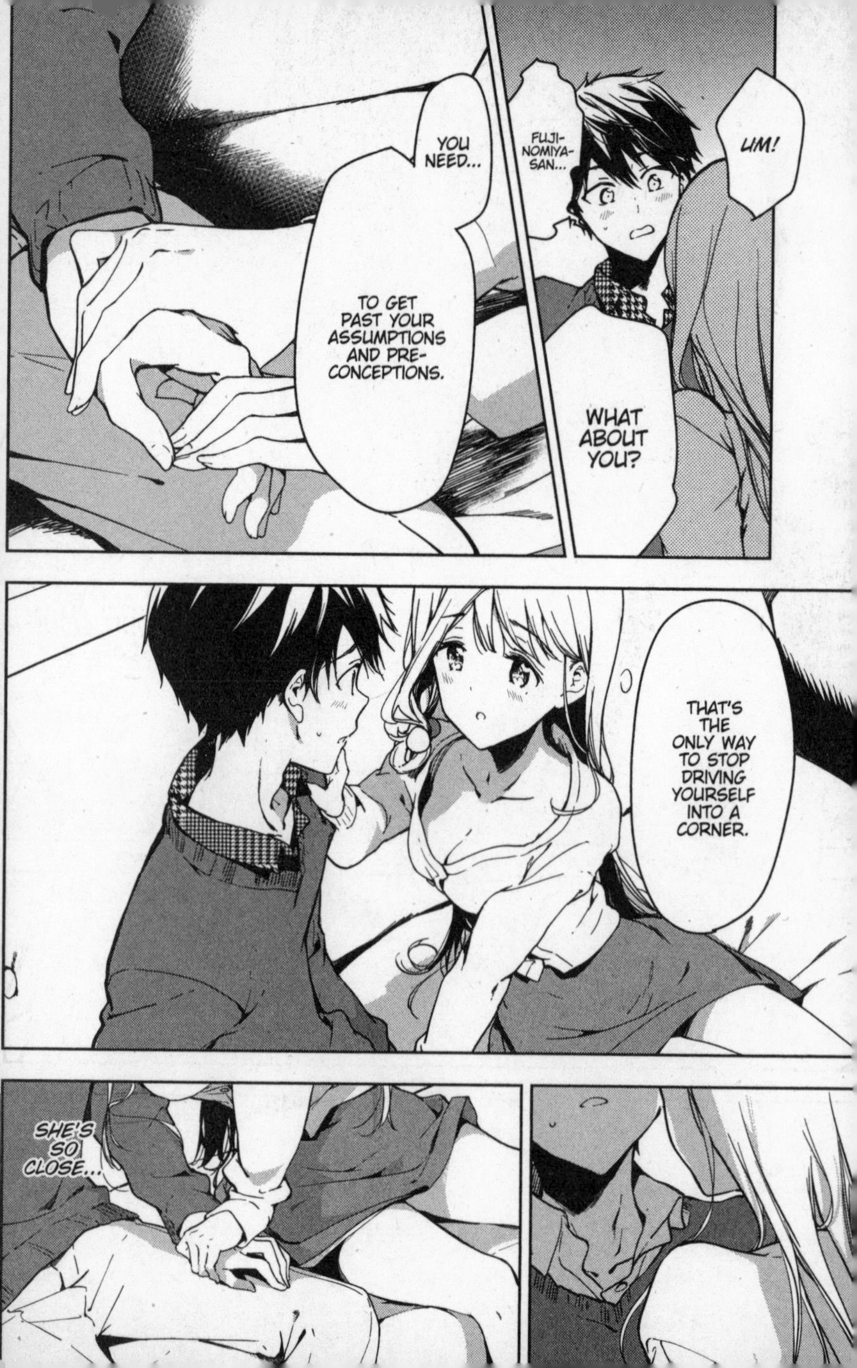
UM!
FUJI-NOMIYA-SAN...
WHAT ABOUT YOU?
YOU NEED...
TO GET PAST YOUR ASSUMPTIONS AND PRE-CONCEPTIONS.
THAT'S THE ONLY WAY TO STOP DRIVING YOURSELF INTO A CORNER.
SHE'S SO CLOSE...

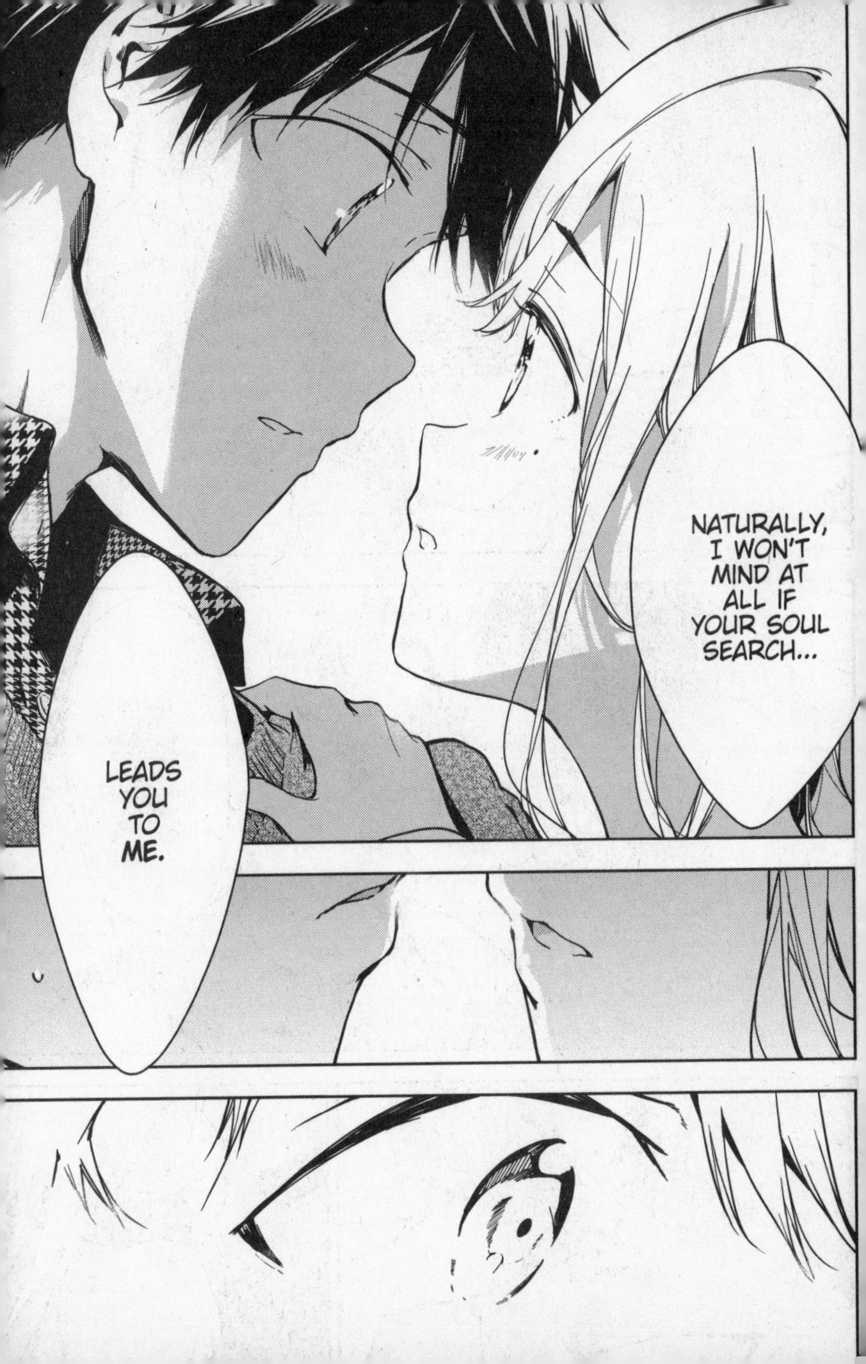
NATURALLY, I WON'T MIND AT ALL IF YOUR SOUL SEARCH...
LEADS YOU TO ME.

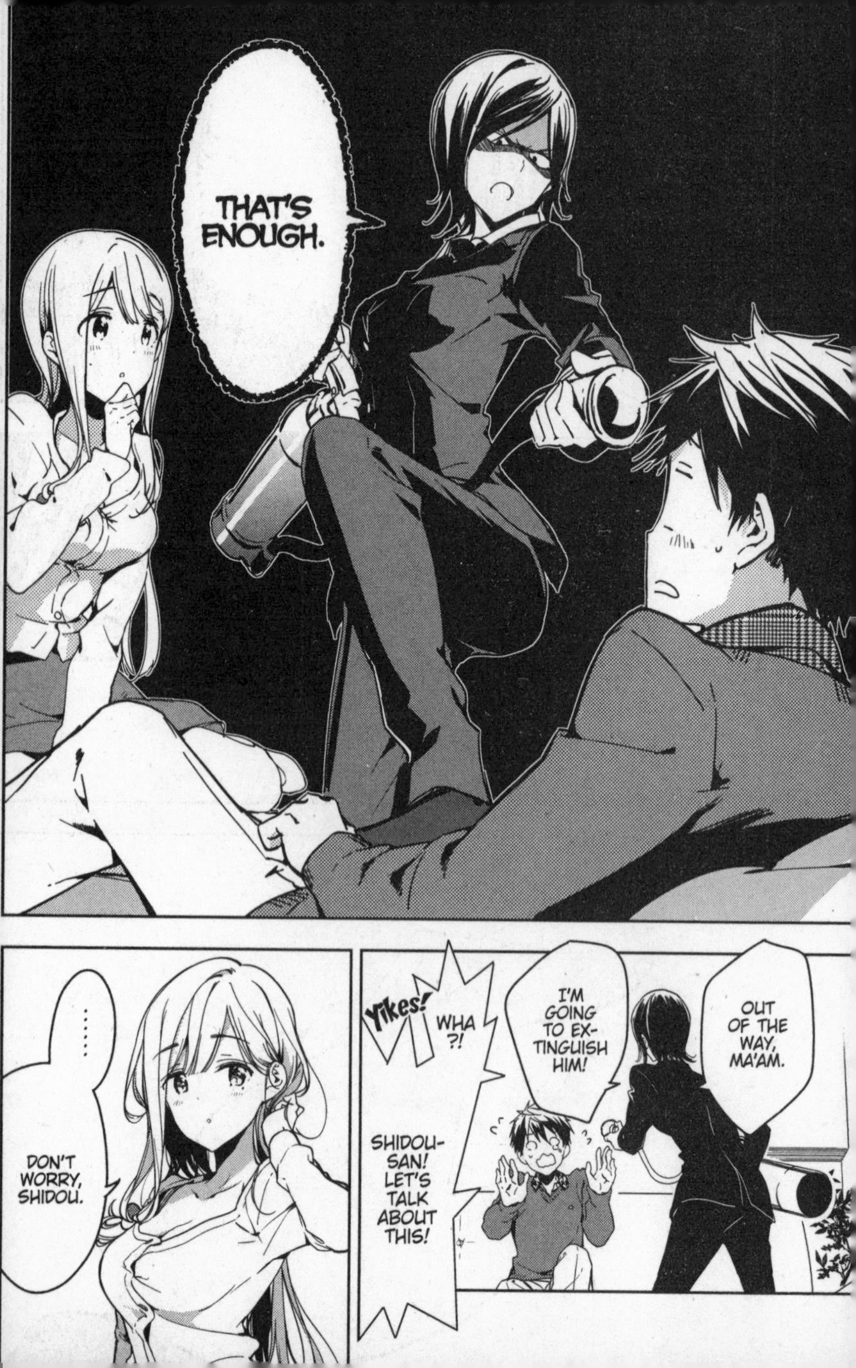
THAT'S ENOUGH.
OUT OF THE WAY, MA'AM.
I'M GOING TO EX-TINGUISH HIM!
Yikes!
WHA ?!
SHIDOU-SAN! LET'S TALK ABOUT THIS!
......
DON'T WORRY, SHIDOU.

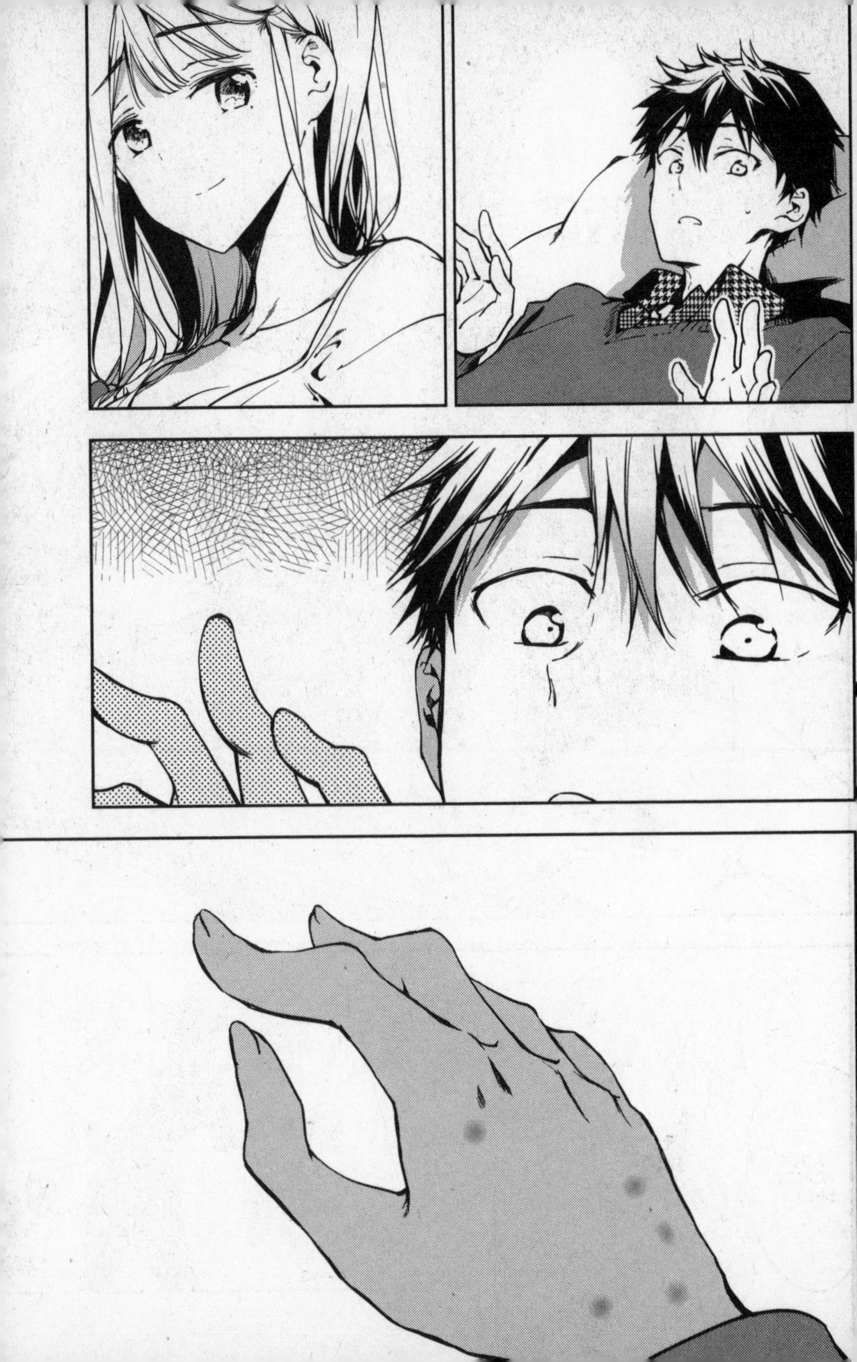

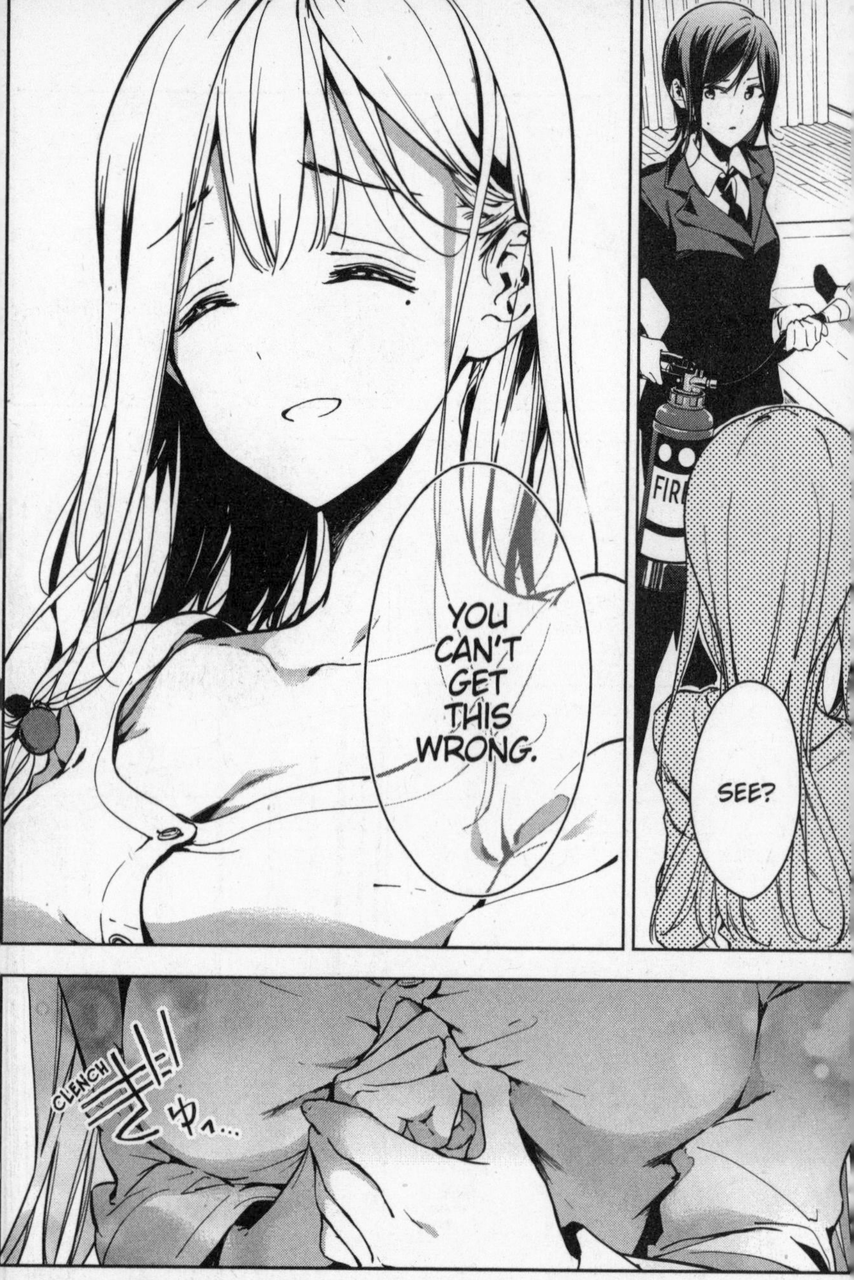
SEE?
YOU CAN'T GET THIS WRONG.
CLENCH
ぎゅ…

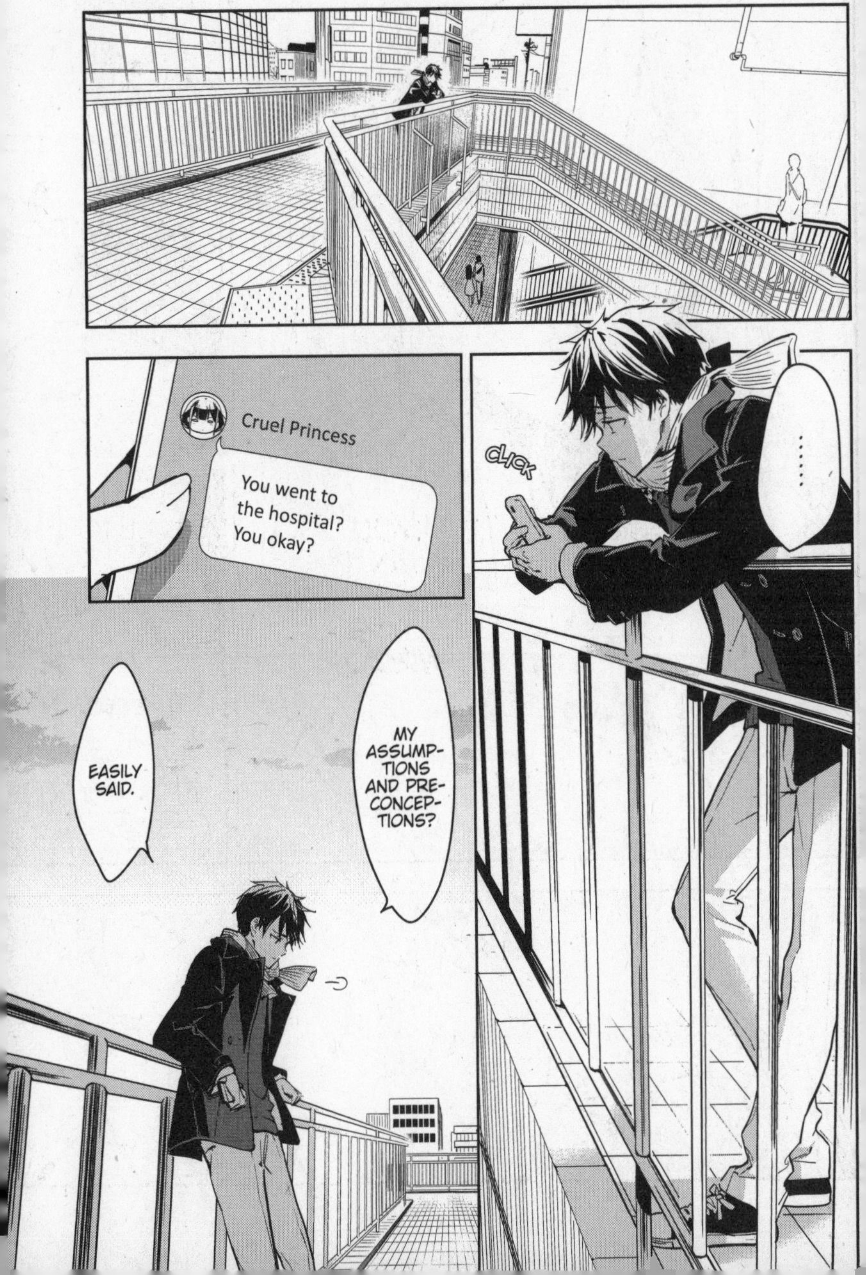
CLICK
......
Cruel Princess
You went to the hospital? You okay?
MY ASSUMPTIONS AND PRECONCEPTIONS?
EASILY SAID.

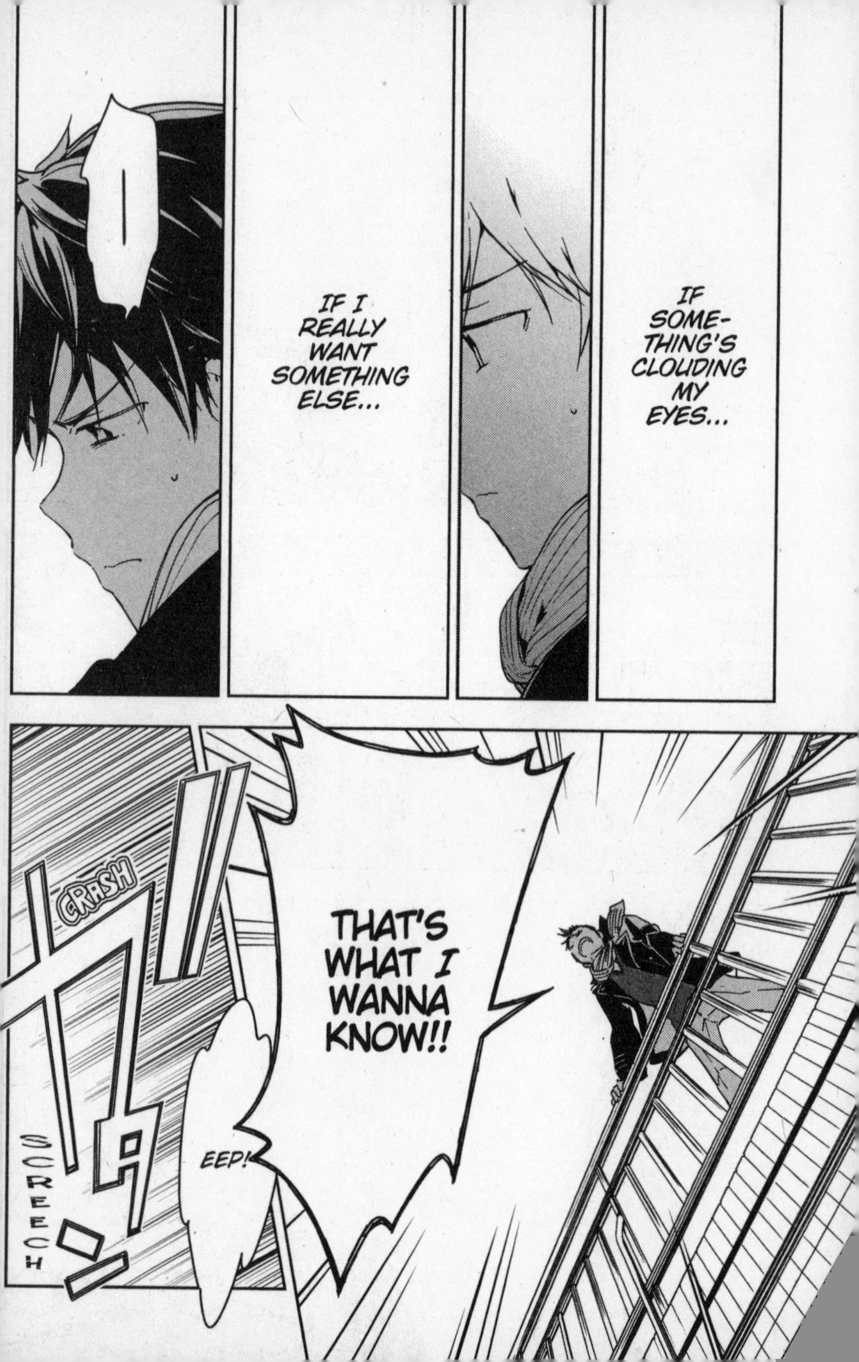
IF SOME-THING'S CLOUDING MY EYES...
IF I REALLY WANT SOMETHING ELSE...
!
THAT'S WHAT I WANNA KNOW!!
EEP!
CRASH
SCREECH

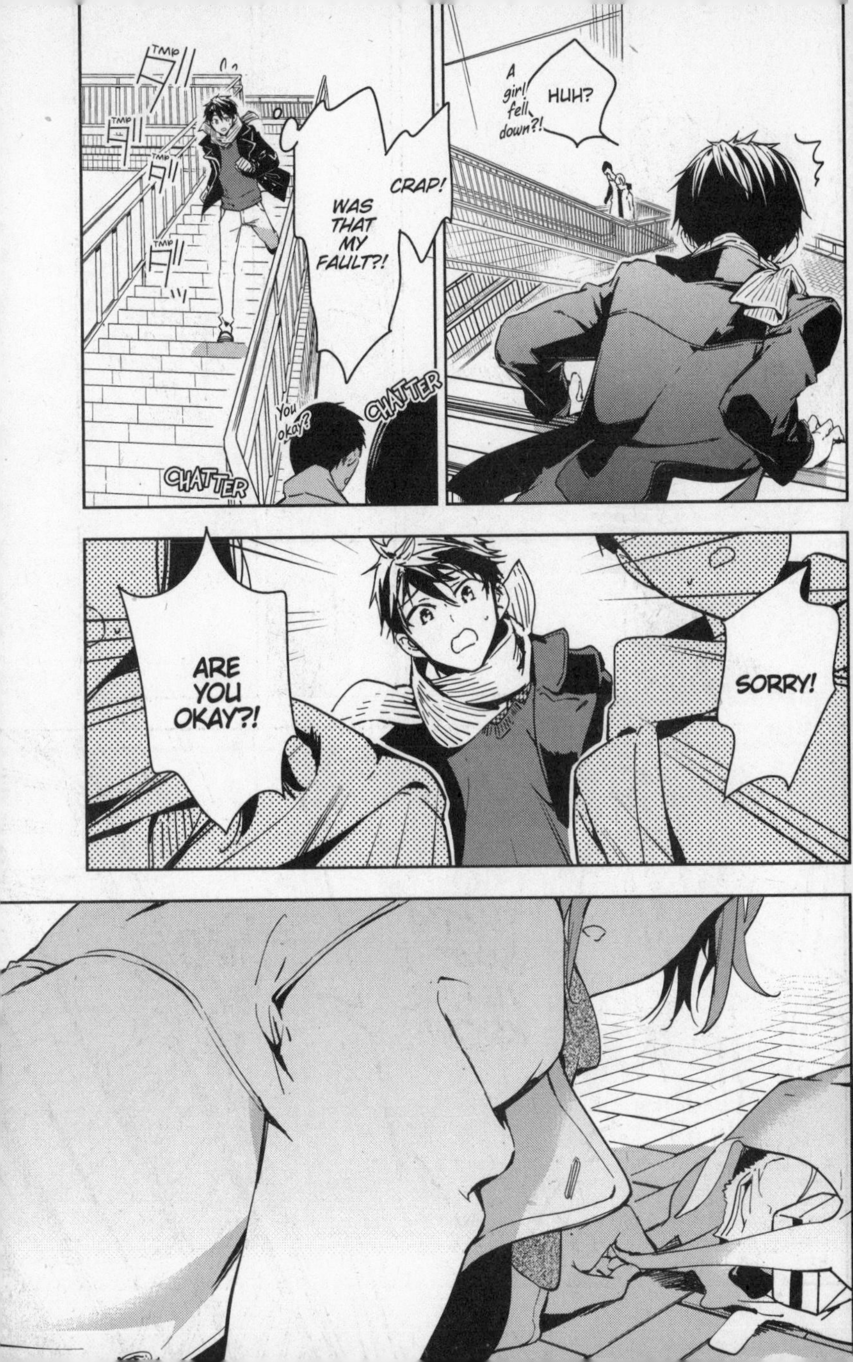
HUH?
A girl! fell down?!
TMP
TMP
TMP
TMP
CRAP!
WAS THAT MY FAULT?!
CHATTER
You okay?
CHATTER
SORRY!
ARE YOU OKAY?!

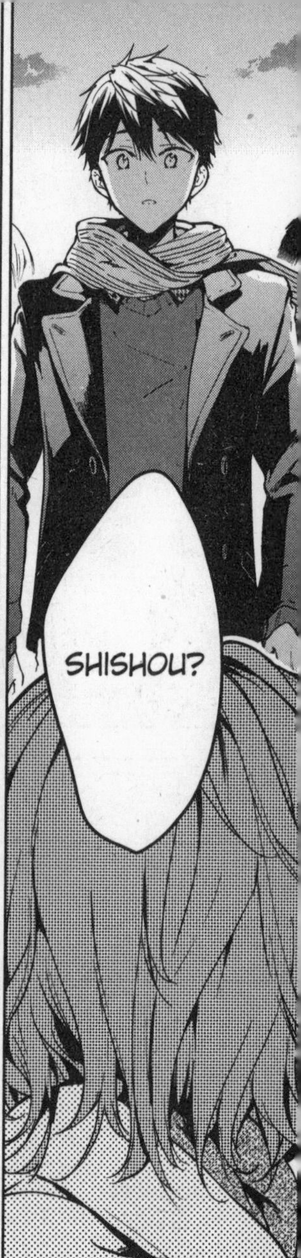
SHISHOU?

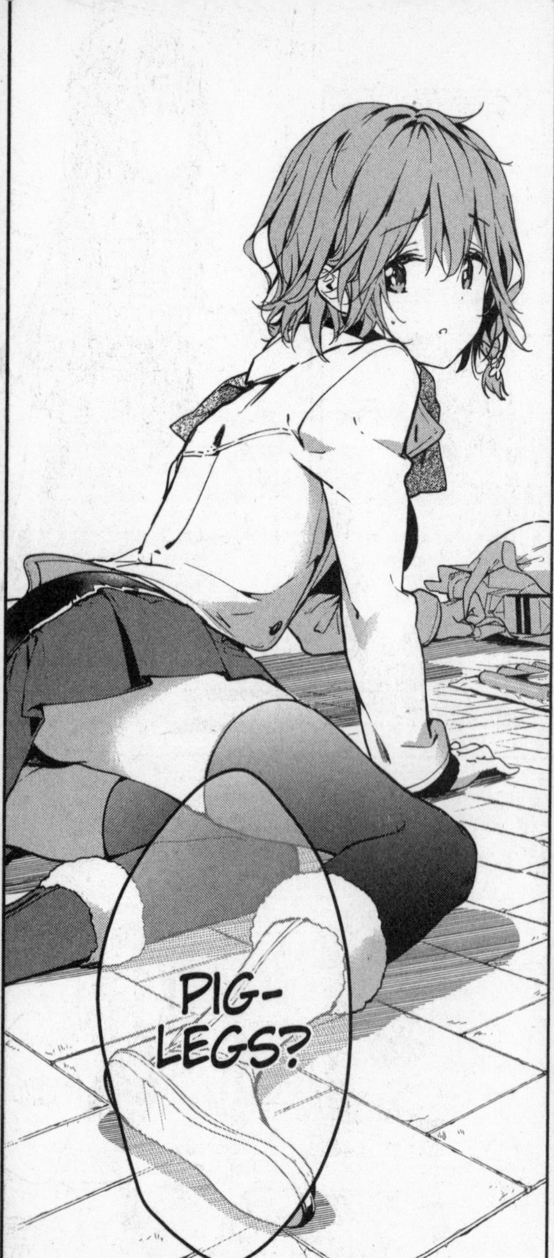
PIG-
LEGS?

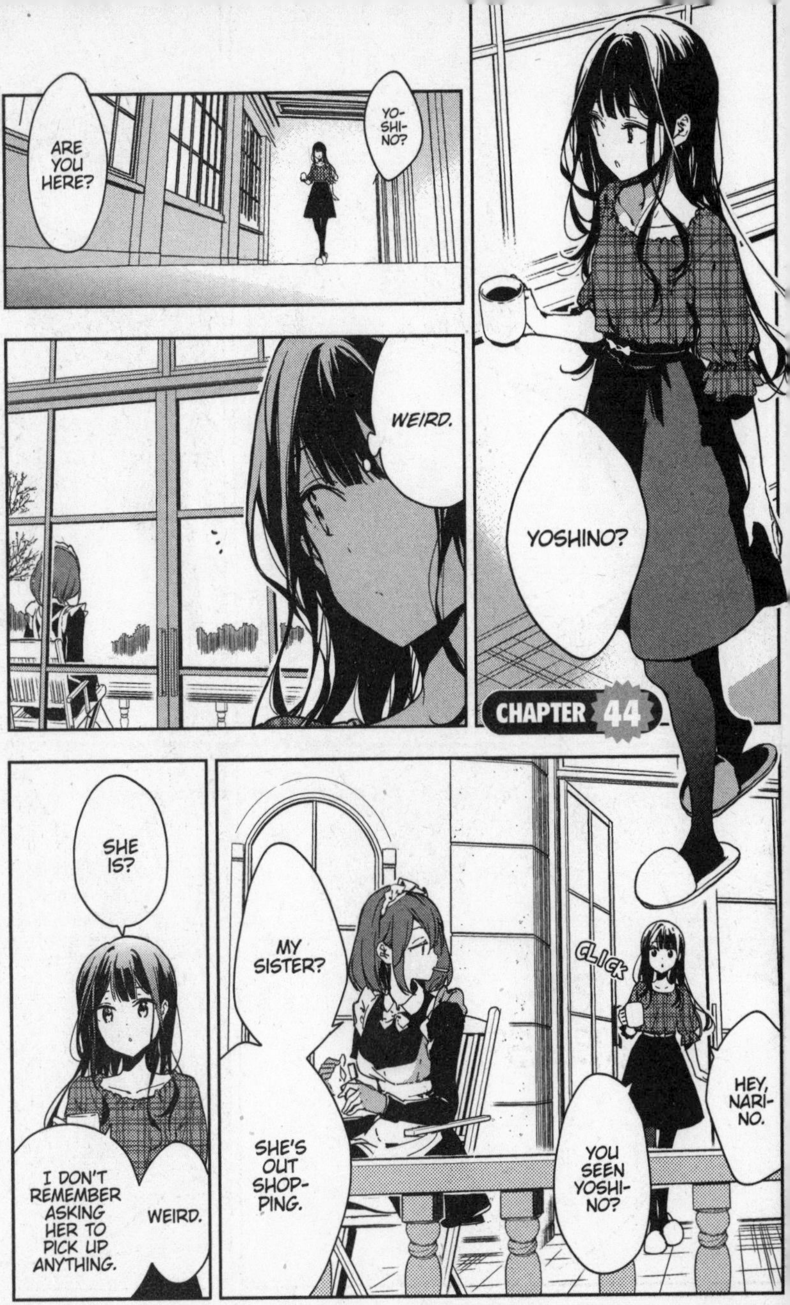
YOSHINO?
CHAPTER 44
YO-SHI-NO?
ARE YOU HERE?
WEIRD.
HEY, NARI-NO.
YOU SEEN YOSHI-NO?
CLICK
MY SISTER?
SHE'S OUT SHOP-PING.
SHE IS?
I DON'T REMEMBER ASKING HER TO PICK UP ANYTHING.
WEIRD.

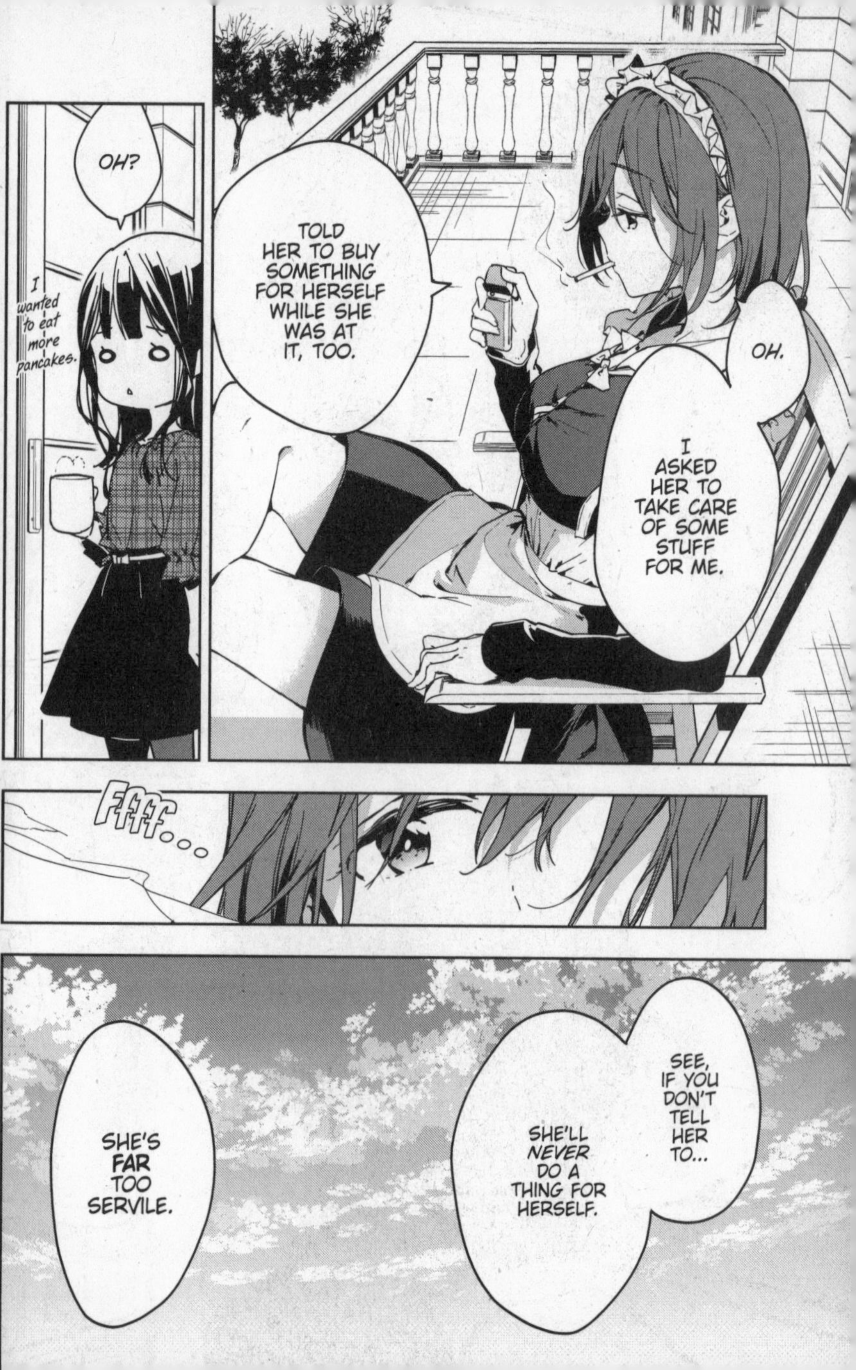
OH.
I ASKED HER TO TAKE CARE OF SOME STUFF FOR ME.
TOLD HER TO BUY SOMETHING FOR HERSELF WHILE SHE WAS AT IT, TOO.
OH?
I wanted to eat more pancakes.
Ffff...
SEE, IF YOU DON'T TELL HER TO...
SHE'LL *NEVER* DO A THING FOR HERSELF.
SHE'S **FAR** TOO SERVILE.

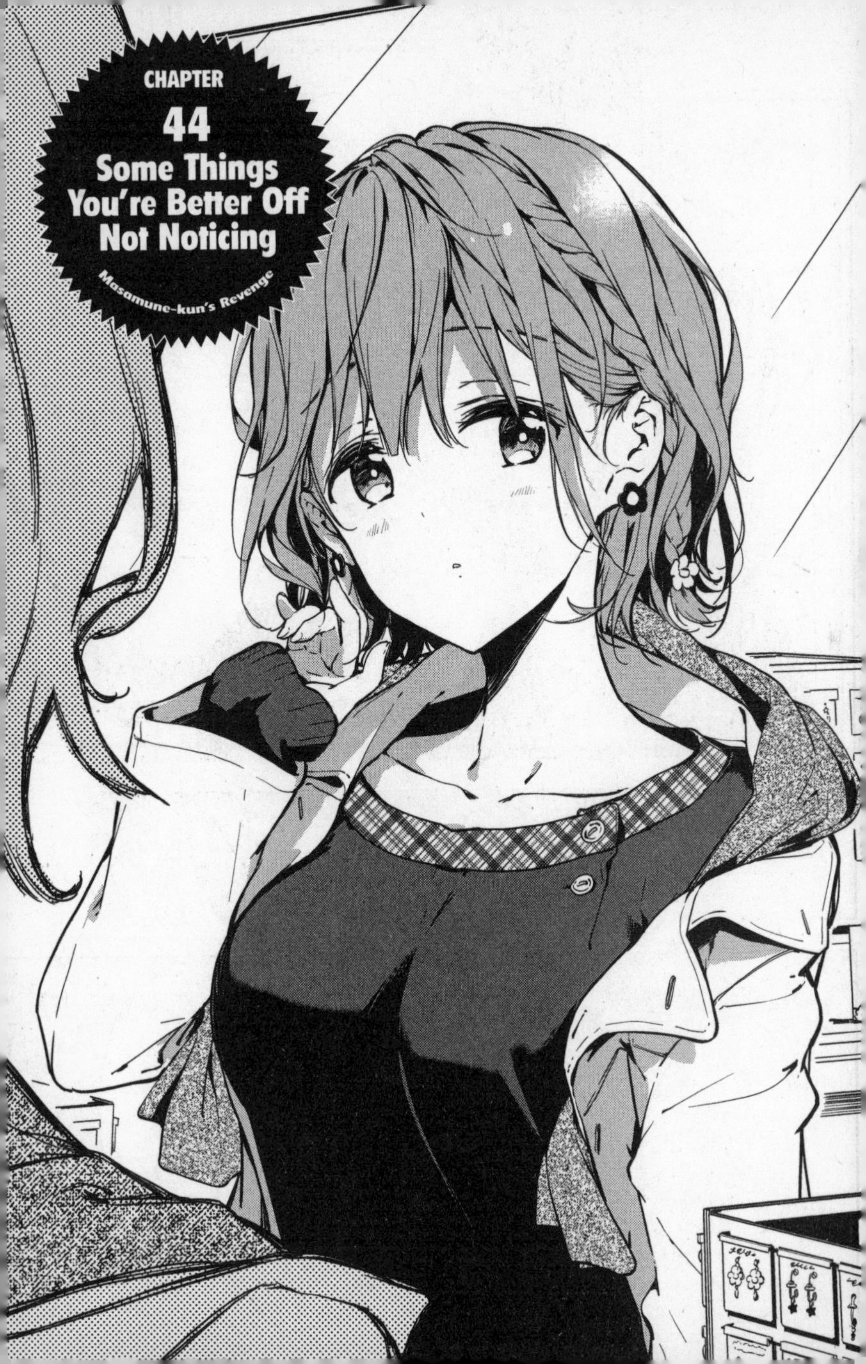
CHAPTER
44
Some Things You're Better Off Not Noticing
Masamune-kun's Revenge

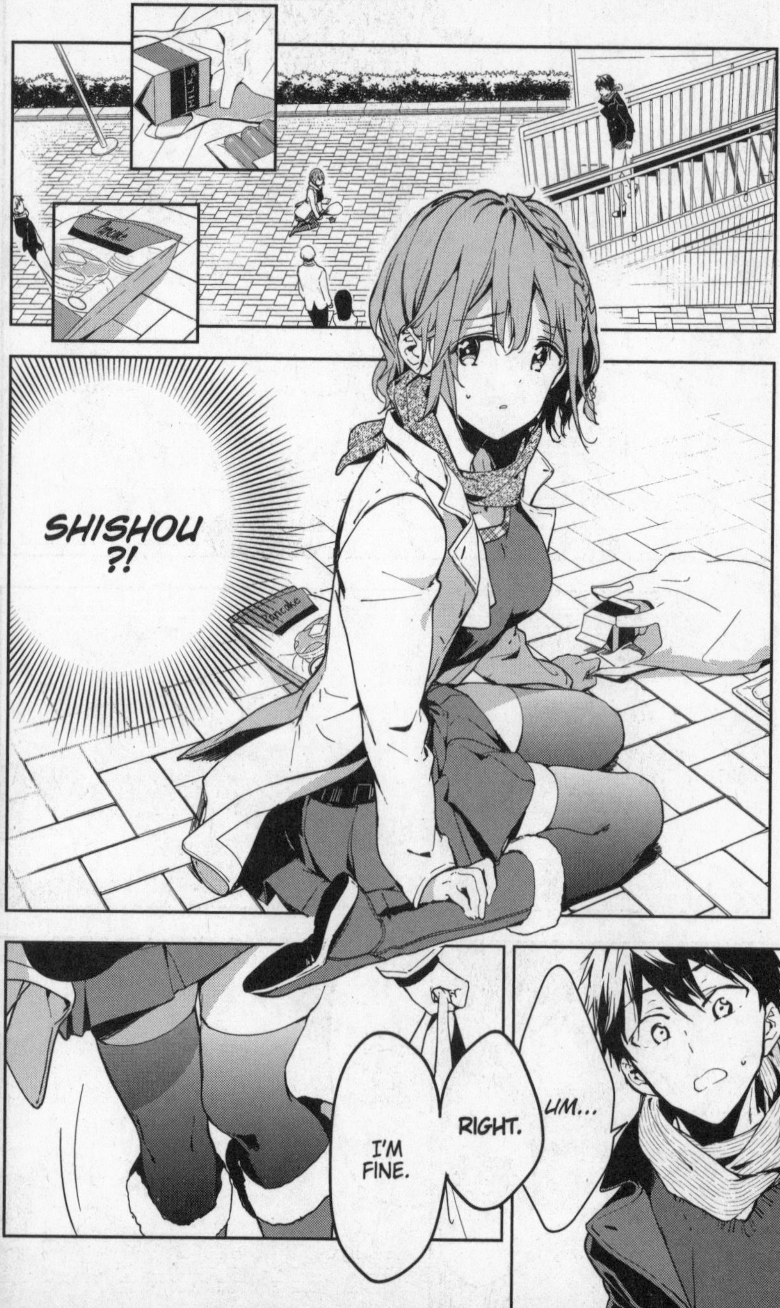
SHISHOU ?!
UM...
RIGHT.
I'M FINE.

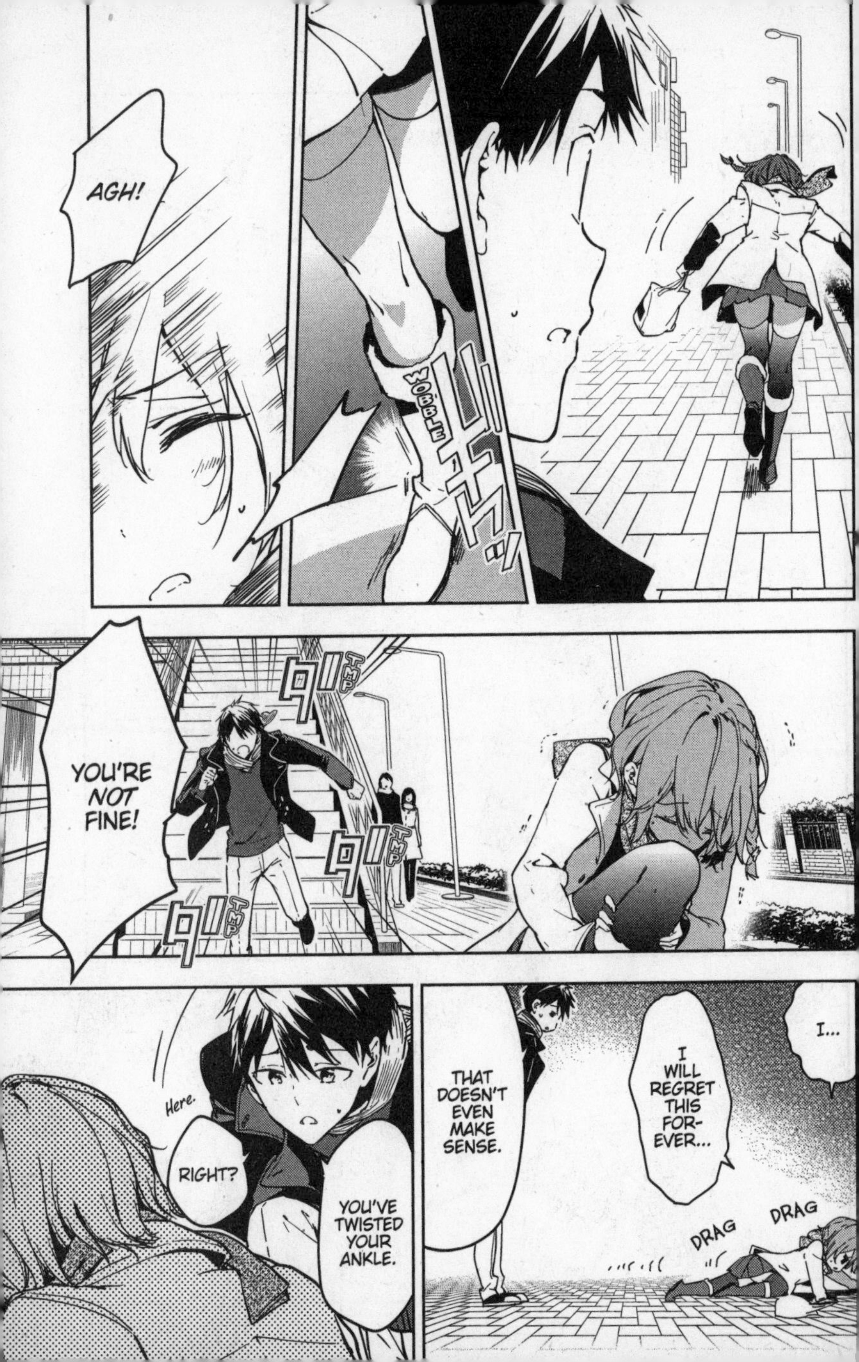

WOBBLE
AGH!
TMP
TMP
TMP
YOU'RE NOT FINE!
I...
I WILL REGRET THIS FOR-EVER...
THAT DOESN'T EVEN MAKE SENSE.
DRAG
DRAG
YOU'VE TWISTED YOUR ANKLE.
RIGHT?
Here.

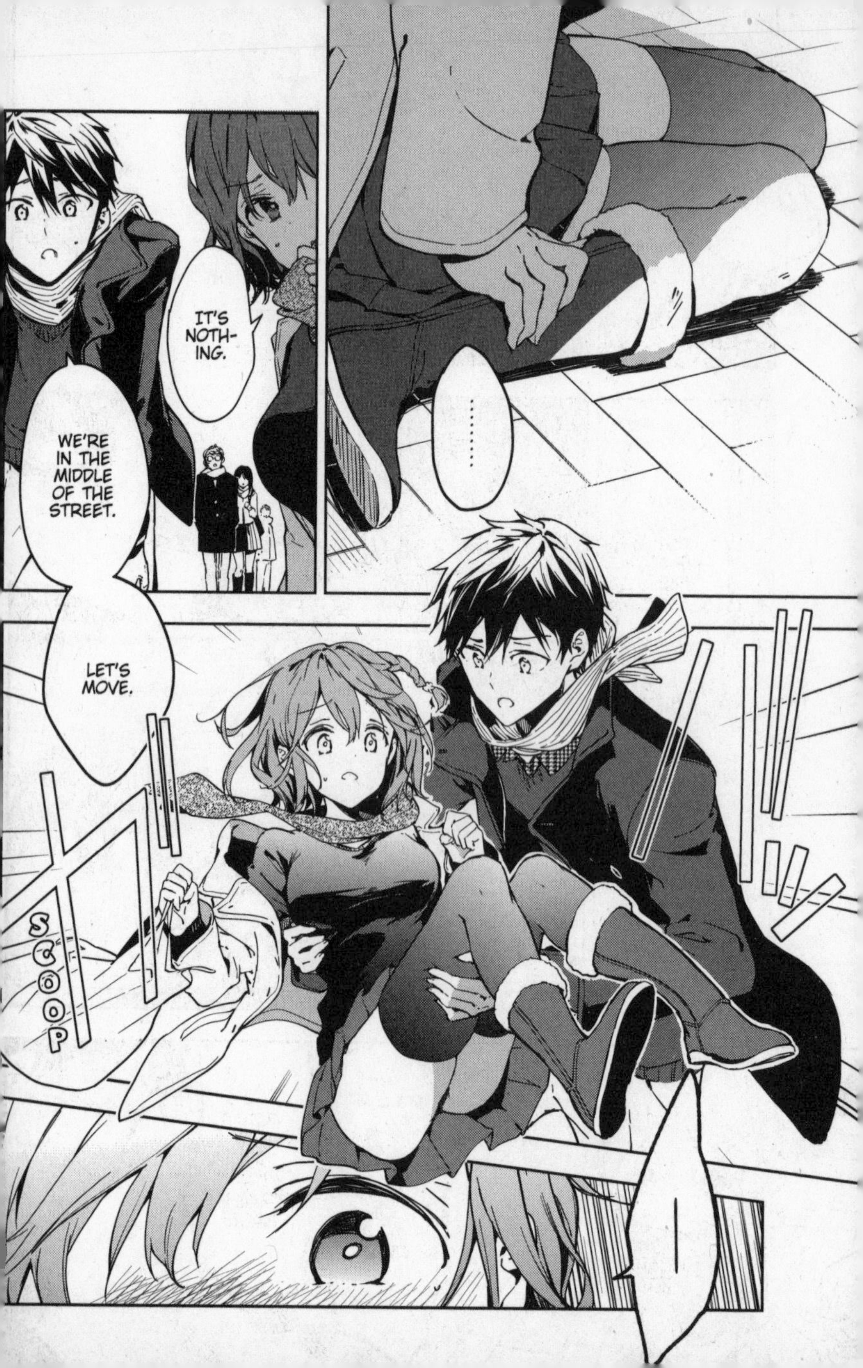
......
IT'S NOTHING.
WE'RE IN THE MIDDLE OF THE STREET.
LET'S MOVE.
SCOOP
!

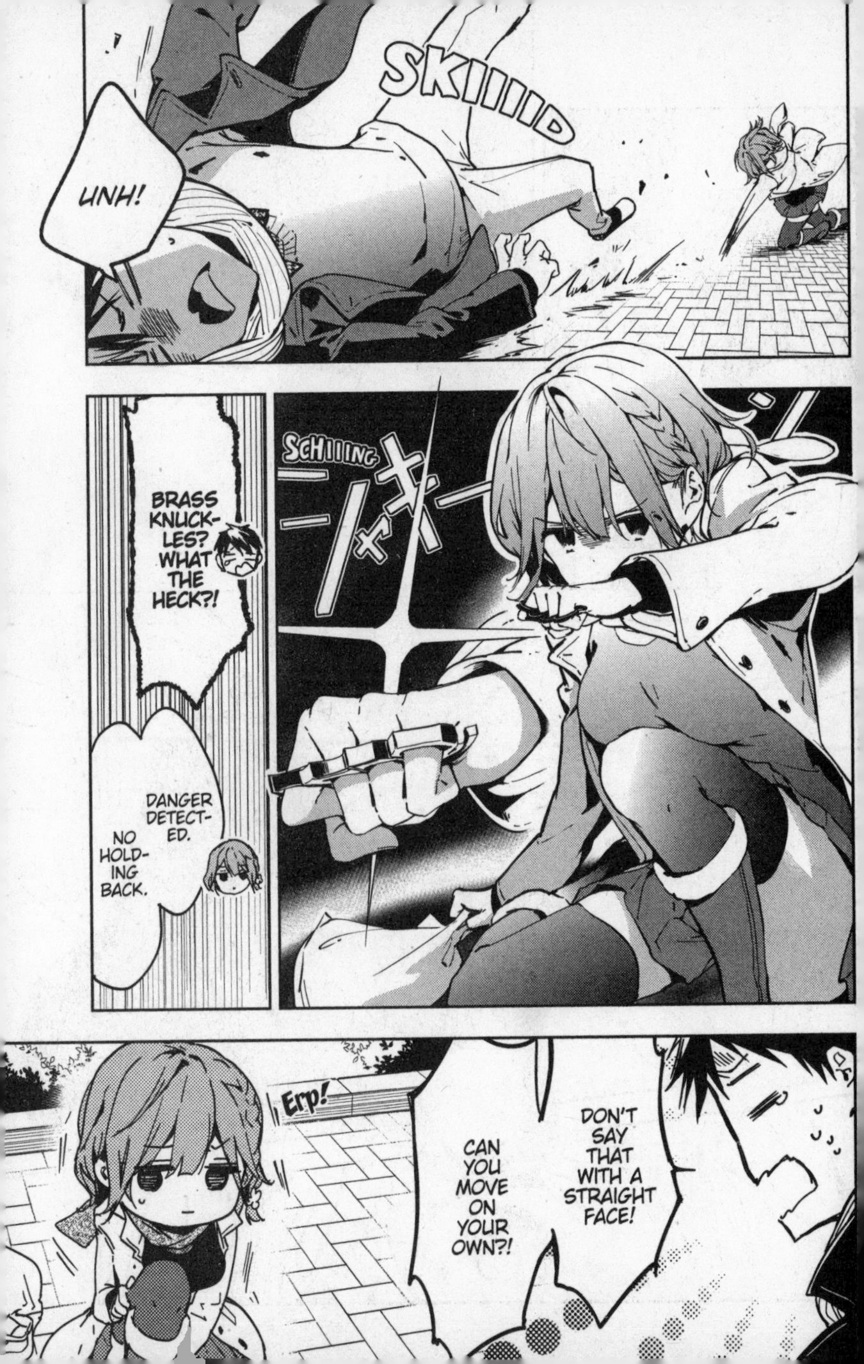
SKIIIID
UNH!
SCHIIING
BRASS KNUCKLES? WHAT THE HECK?!
DANGER DETECTED. NO HOLDING BACK.
DON'T SAY THAT WITH A STRAIGHT FACE!
CAN YOU MOVE ON YOUR OWN?!
Erp!

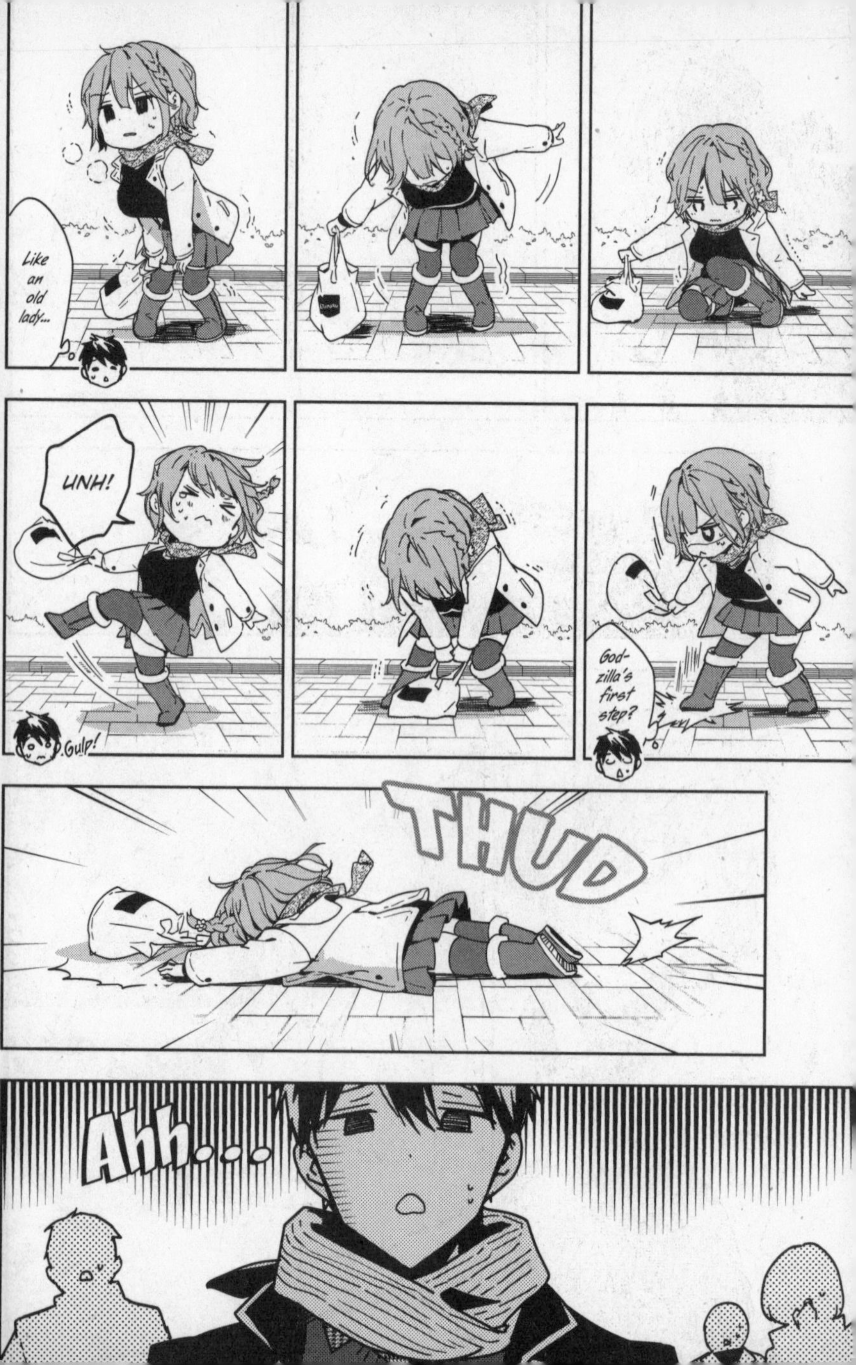
Like an old lady...
God-zilla's first step?
UNH!
Gulp!
THUD
Ahh...

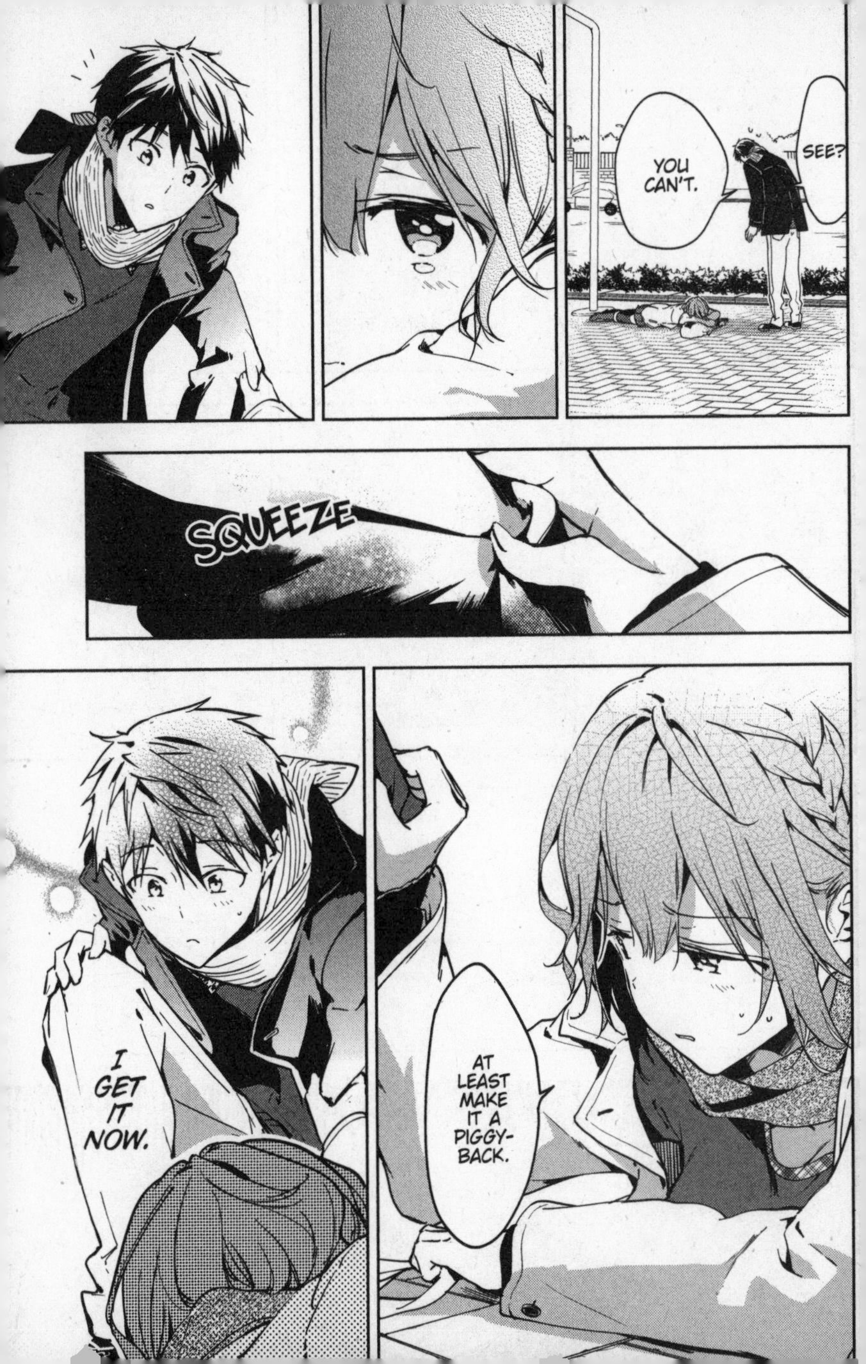
SEE?
YOU CAN'T.
SQUEEZE
AT LEAST MAKE IT A PIGGY-BACK.
I GET IT NOW.

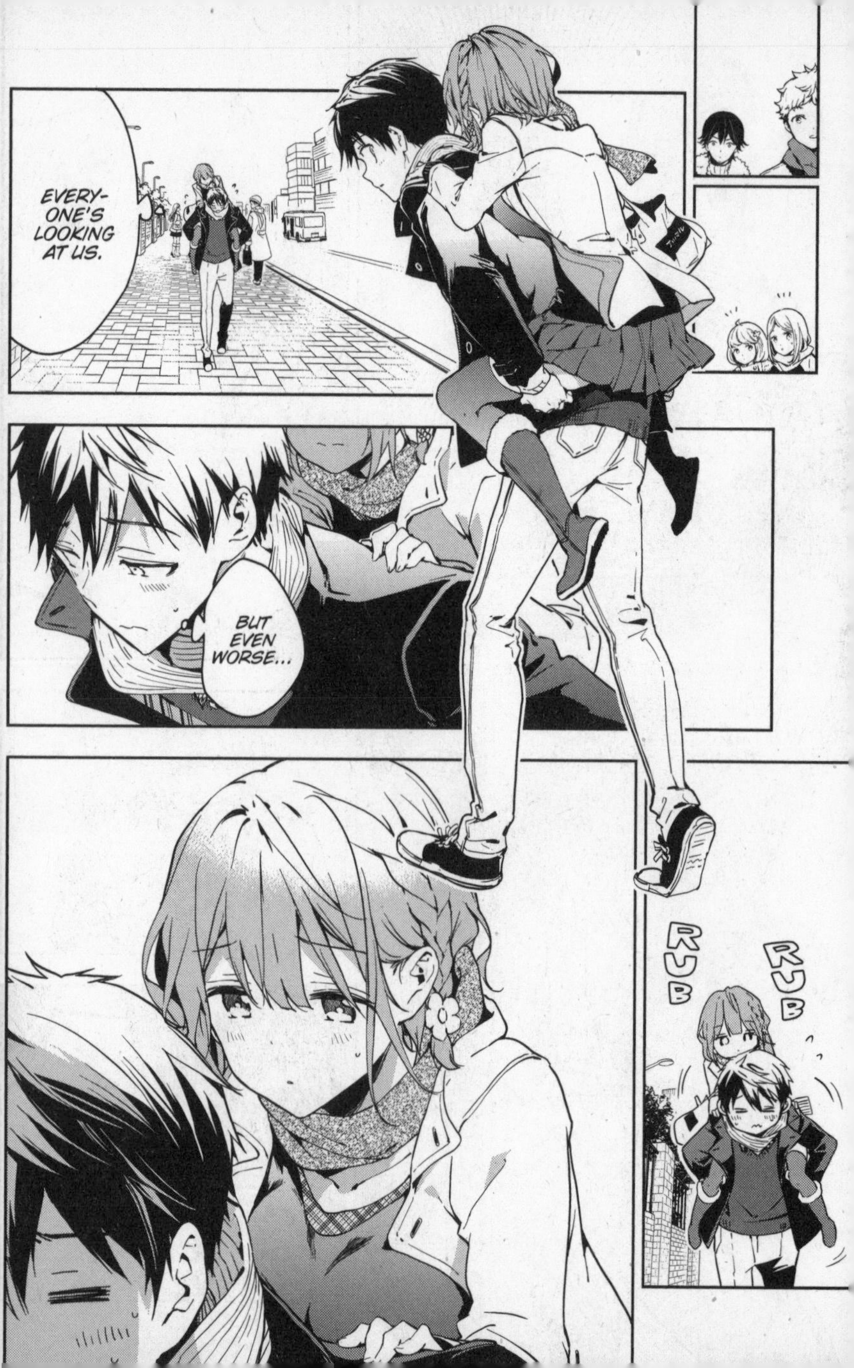
EVERY-ONE'S LOOKING AT US.
BUT EVEN WORSE...
RUB
RUB

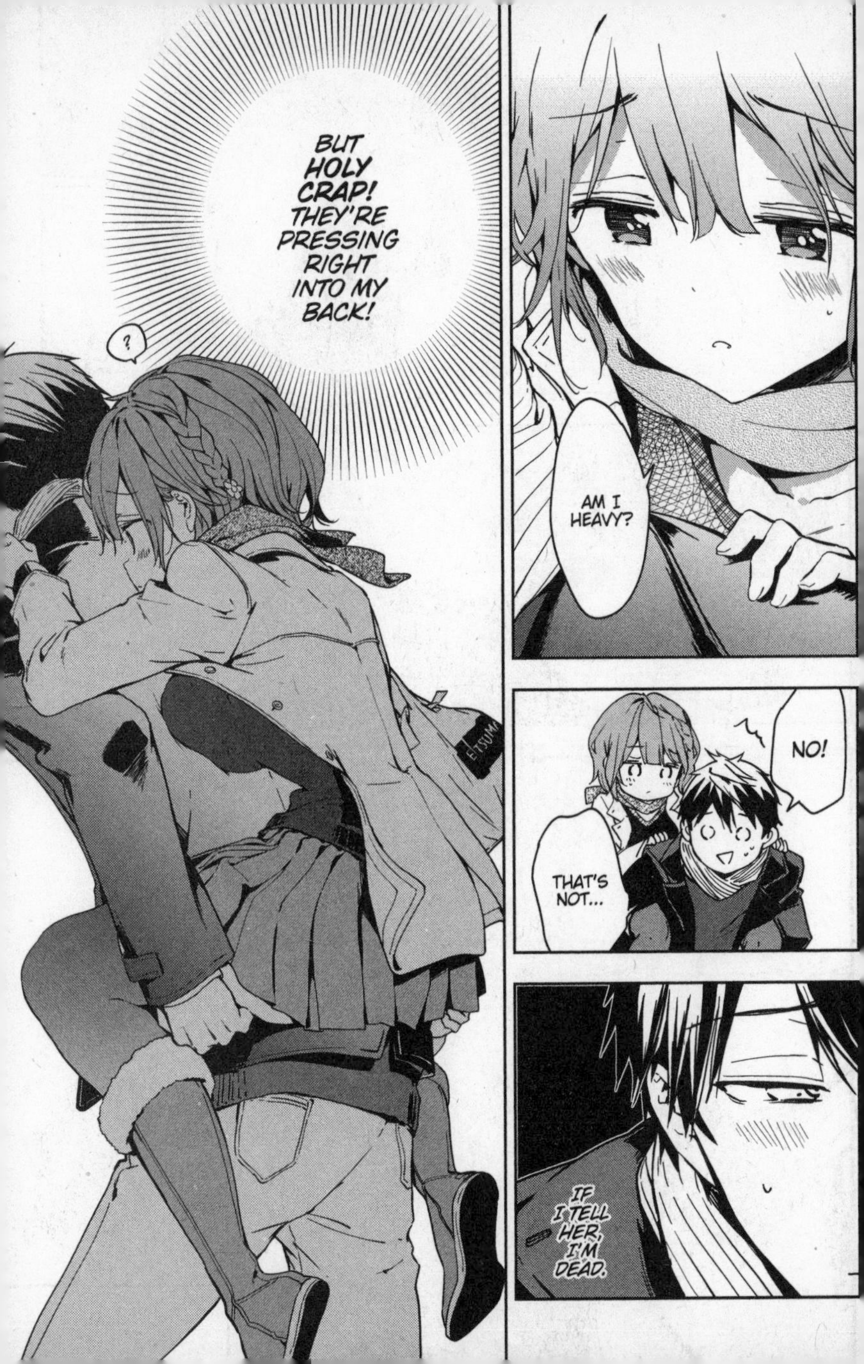
AM I HEAVY?
NO!
THAT'S NOT...
IF I TELL HER, I'M DEAD.
BUT HOLY CRAP! THEY'RE PRESSING RIGHT INTO MY BACK!
?

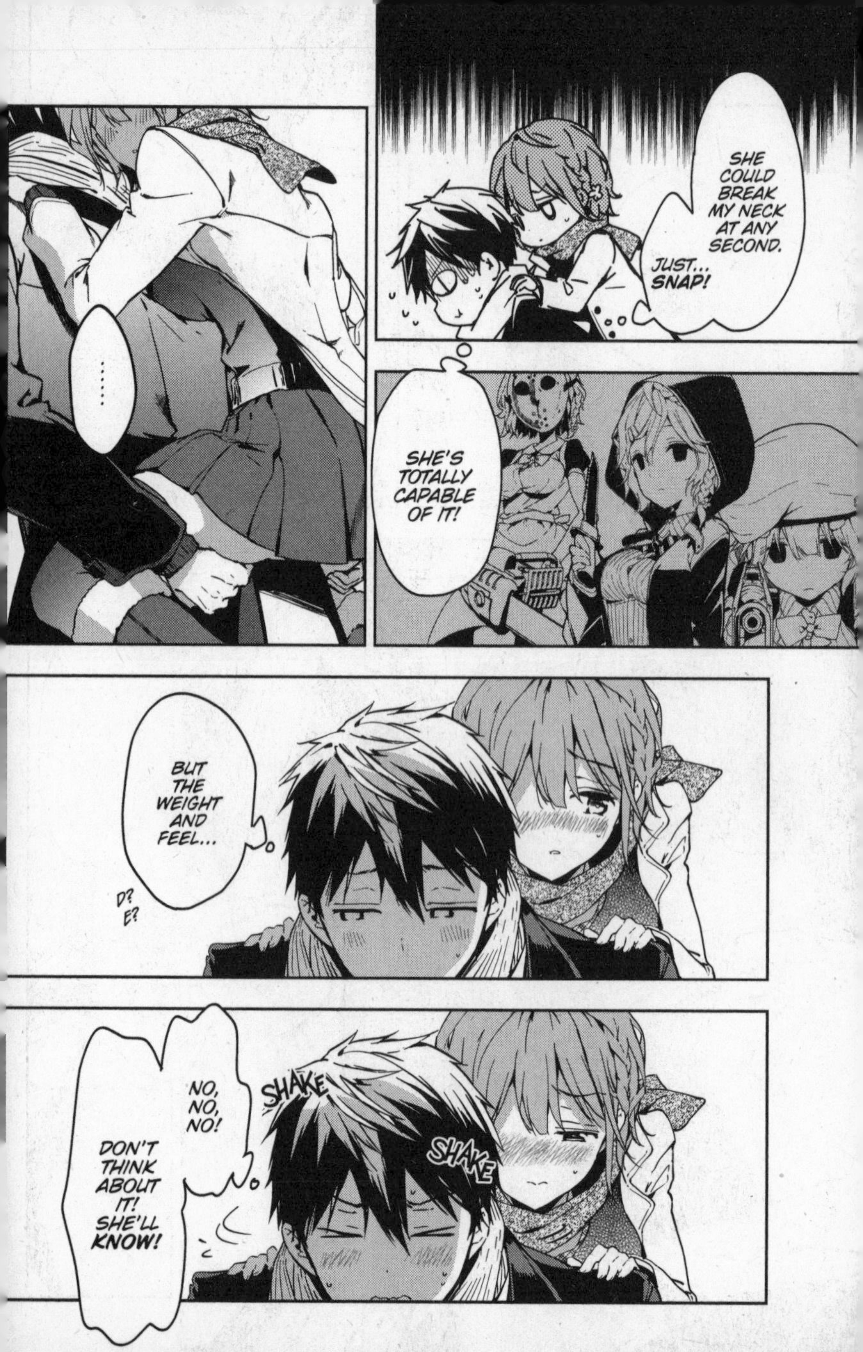
SHE COULD BREAK MY NECK AT ANY SECOND.
JUST... SNAP!
SHE'S TOTALLY CAPABLE OF IT!
......
BUT THE WEIGHT AND FEEL...
D? E?
SHAKE
SHAKE
NO, NO, NO!
DON'T THINK ABOUT IT! SHE'LL KNOW!

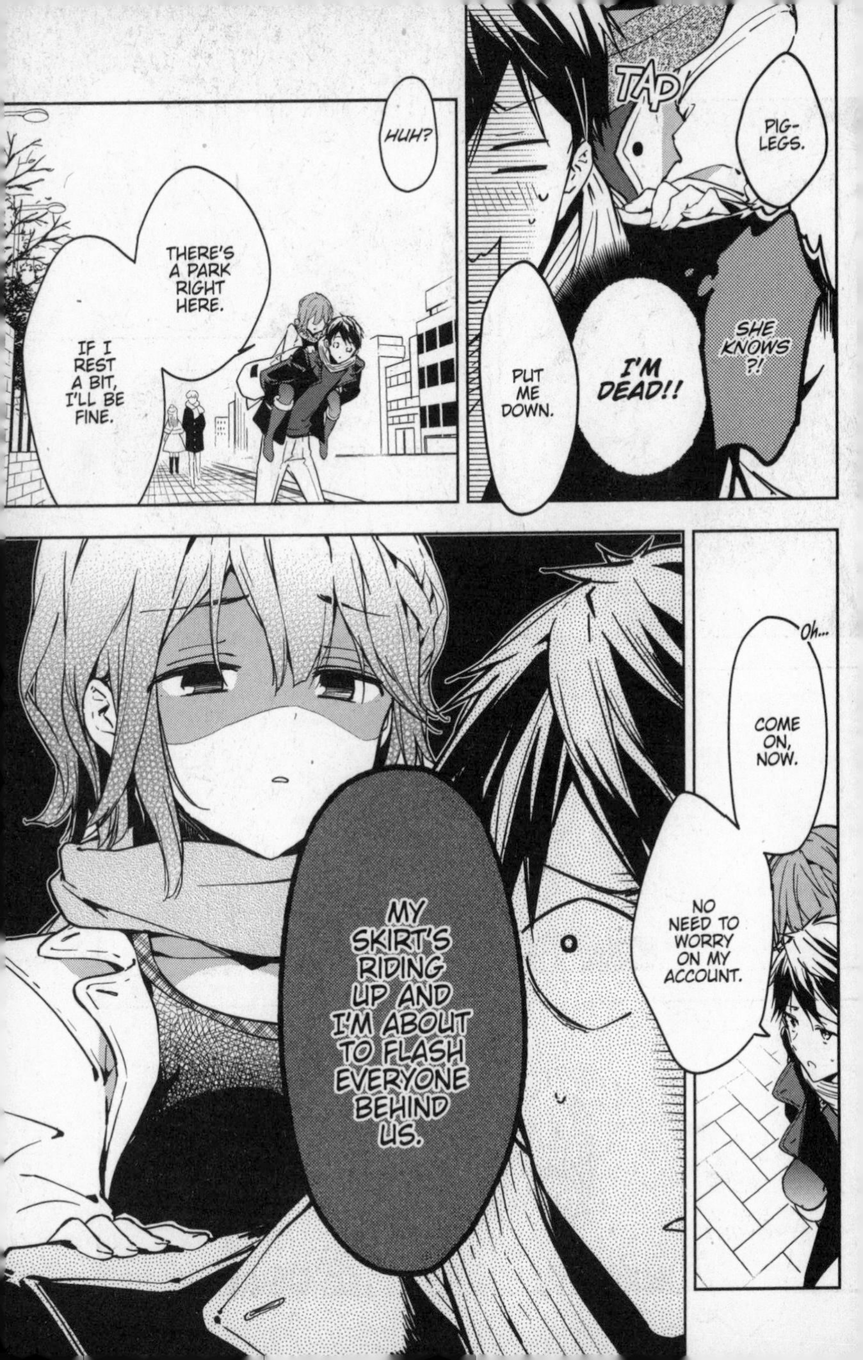
TAP
PIG-LEGS.
SHE KNOWS?!
I'M DEAD!!
PUT ME DOWN.
HUH?
THERE'S A PARK RIGHT HERE.
IF I REST A BIT, I'LL BE FINE.
Oh...
COME ON, NOW.
NO NEED TO WORRY ON MY ACCOUNT.
MY SKIRT'S RIDING UP AND I'M ABOUT TO FLASH EVERYONE BEHIND US.

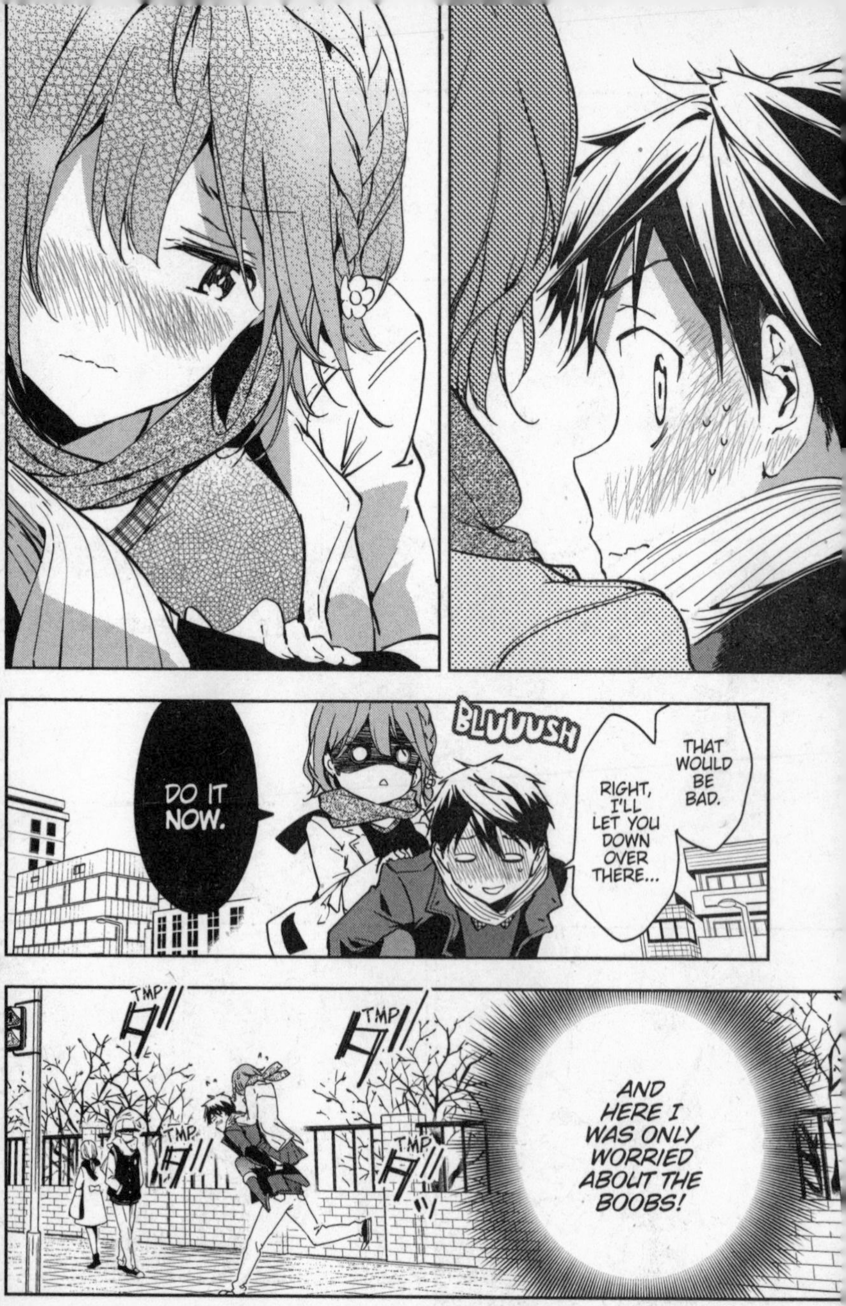
THAT WOULD BE BAD.
RIGHT, I'LL LET YOU DOWN OVER THERE...
BLUUUSH
DO IT NOW.
AND HERE I WAS ONLY WORRIED ABOUT THE BOOBS!
TMP
TMP
TMP
TMP

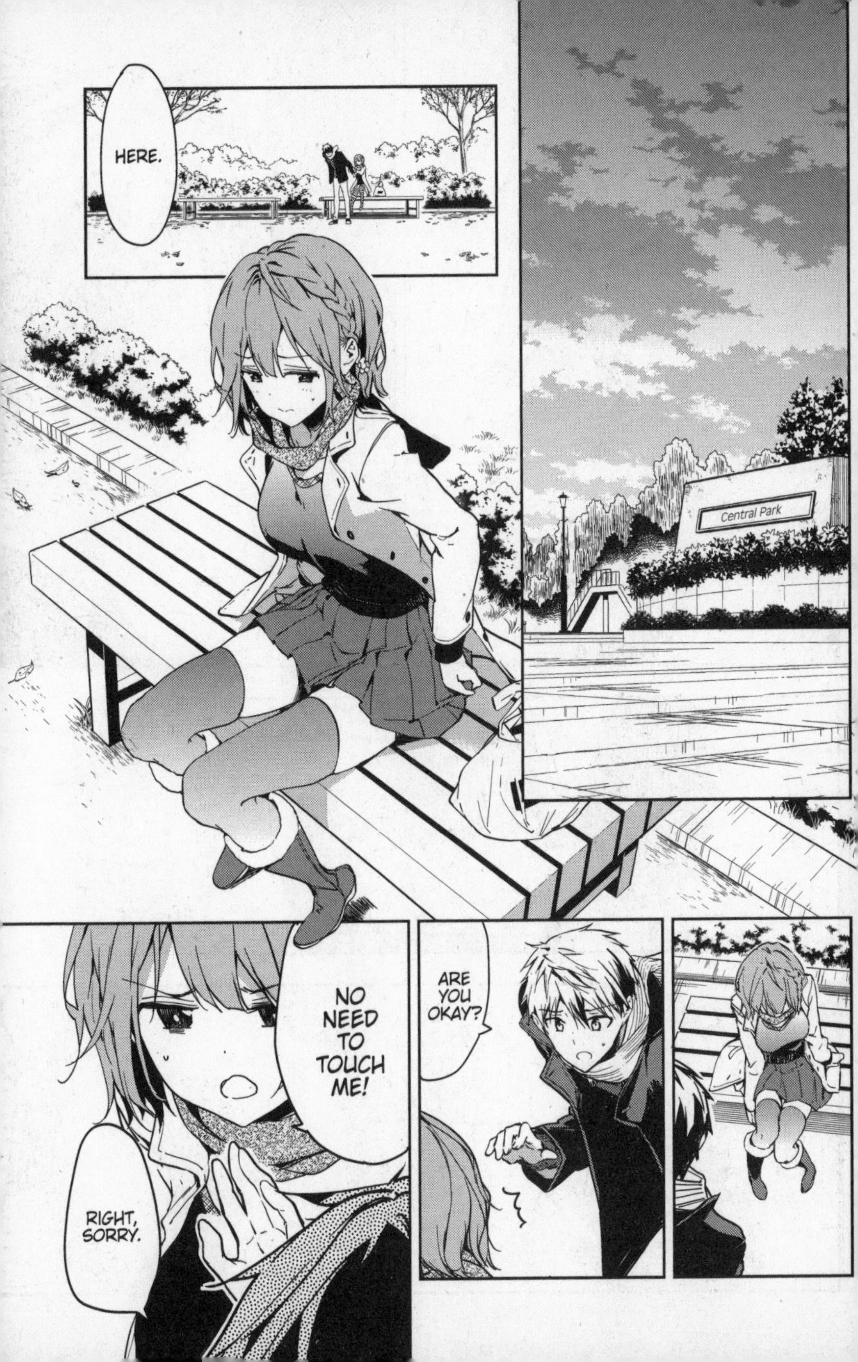
Central Park
HERE.
ARE YOU OKAY?
NO NEED TO TOUCH ME!
RIGHT, SORRY.

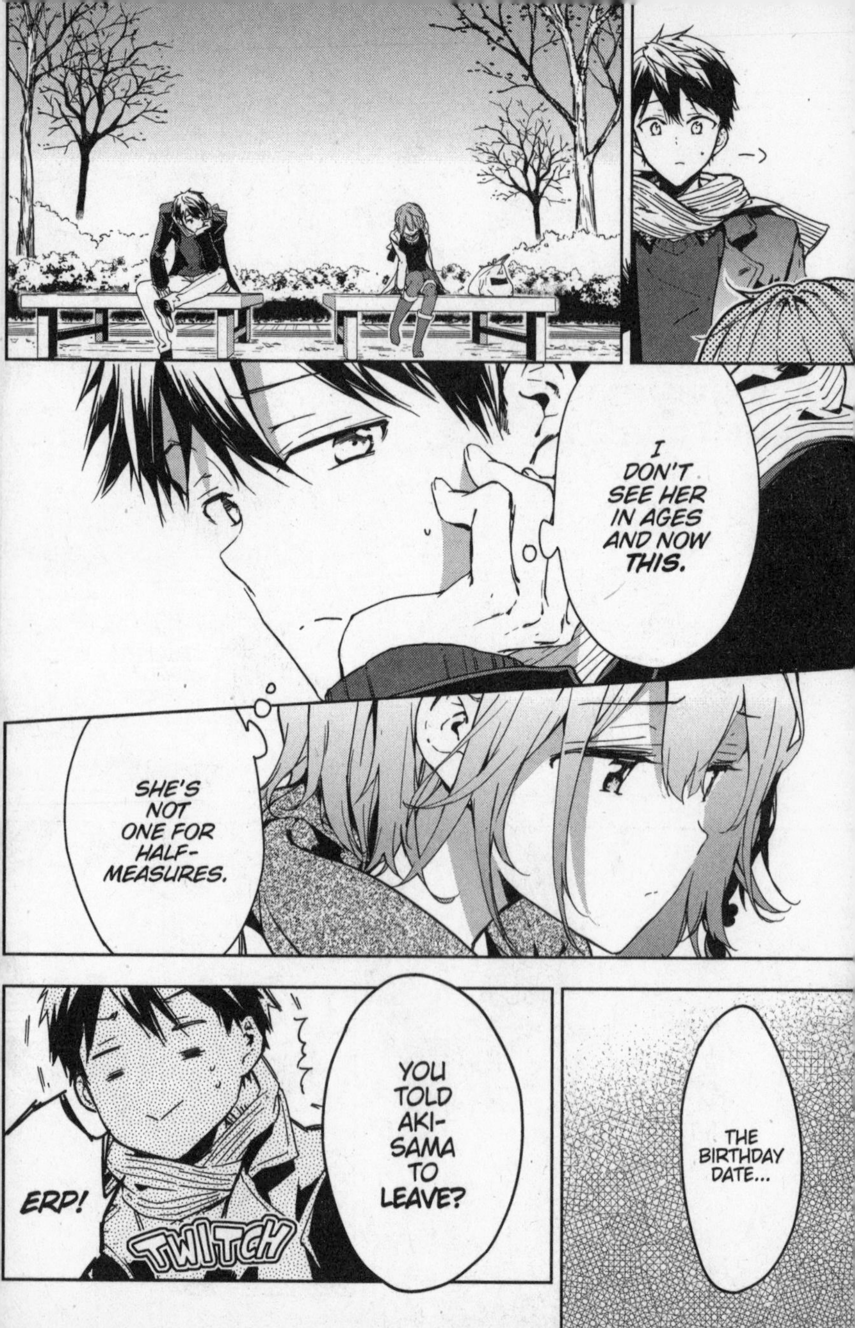
I DON'T SEE HER IN AGES AND NOW THIS.
SHE'S NOT ONE FOR HALF-MEASURES.
THE BIRTHDAY DATE...
YOU TOLD AKI-SAMA TO LEAVE?
ERP!
TWITCH

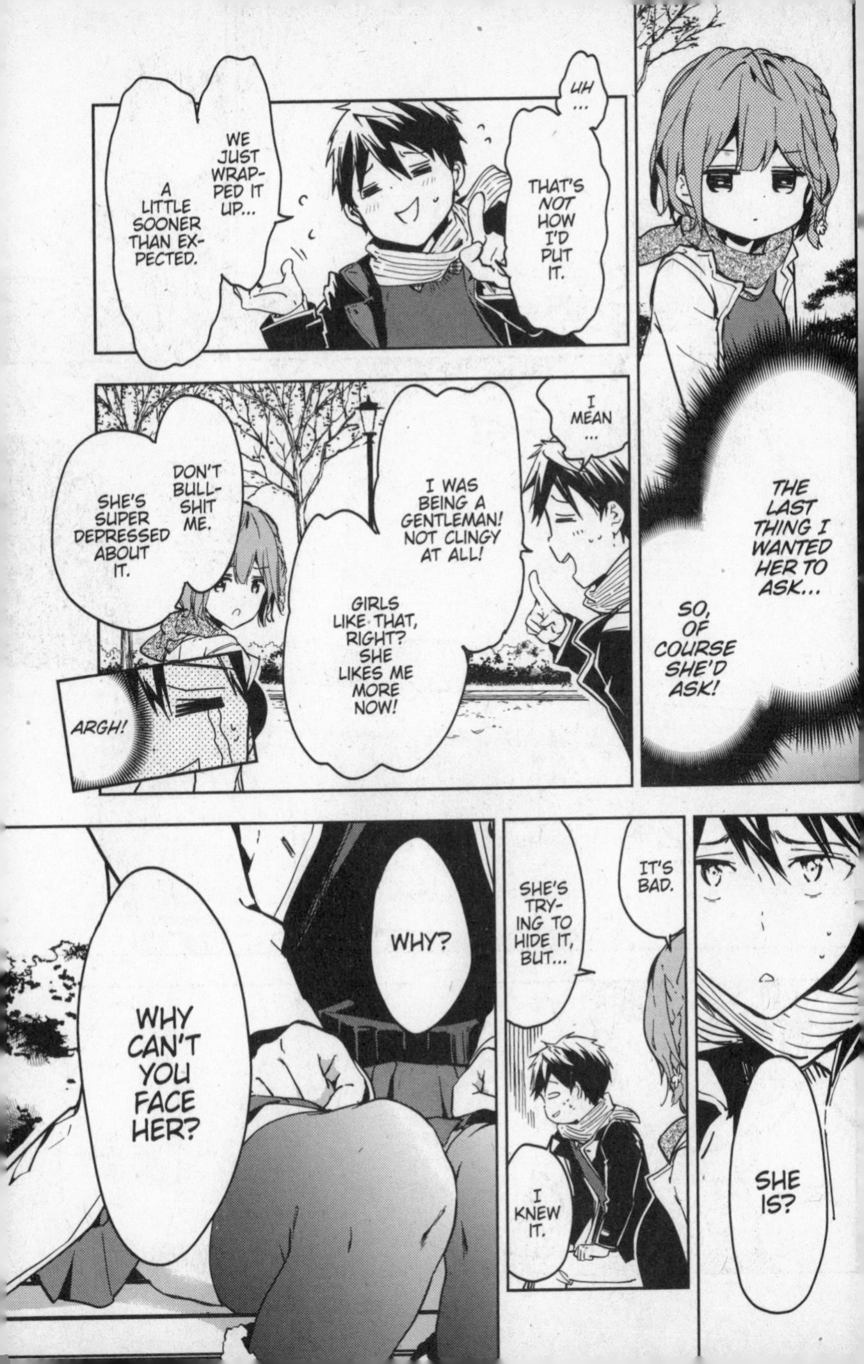
THE LAST THING I WANTED HER TO ASK...
SO, OF COURSE SHE'D ASK!
UH...
THAT'S *NOT* HOW I'D PUT IT.
WE JUST WRAPPED IT UP...
A LITTLE SOONER THAN EXPECTED.
I MEAN...
I WAS BEING A GENTLEMAN! NOT CLINGY AT ALL!
GIRLS LIKE THAT, RIGHT? SHE LIKES ME MORE NOW!
DON'T BULLSHIT ME.
SHE'S SUPER DEPRESSED ABOUT IT.
ARGH!
SHE IS?
IT'S BAD.
SHE'S TRYING TO HIDE IT, BUT...
I KNEW IT.
WHY?
WHY CAN'T YOU FACE HER?

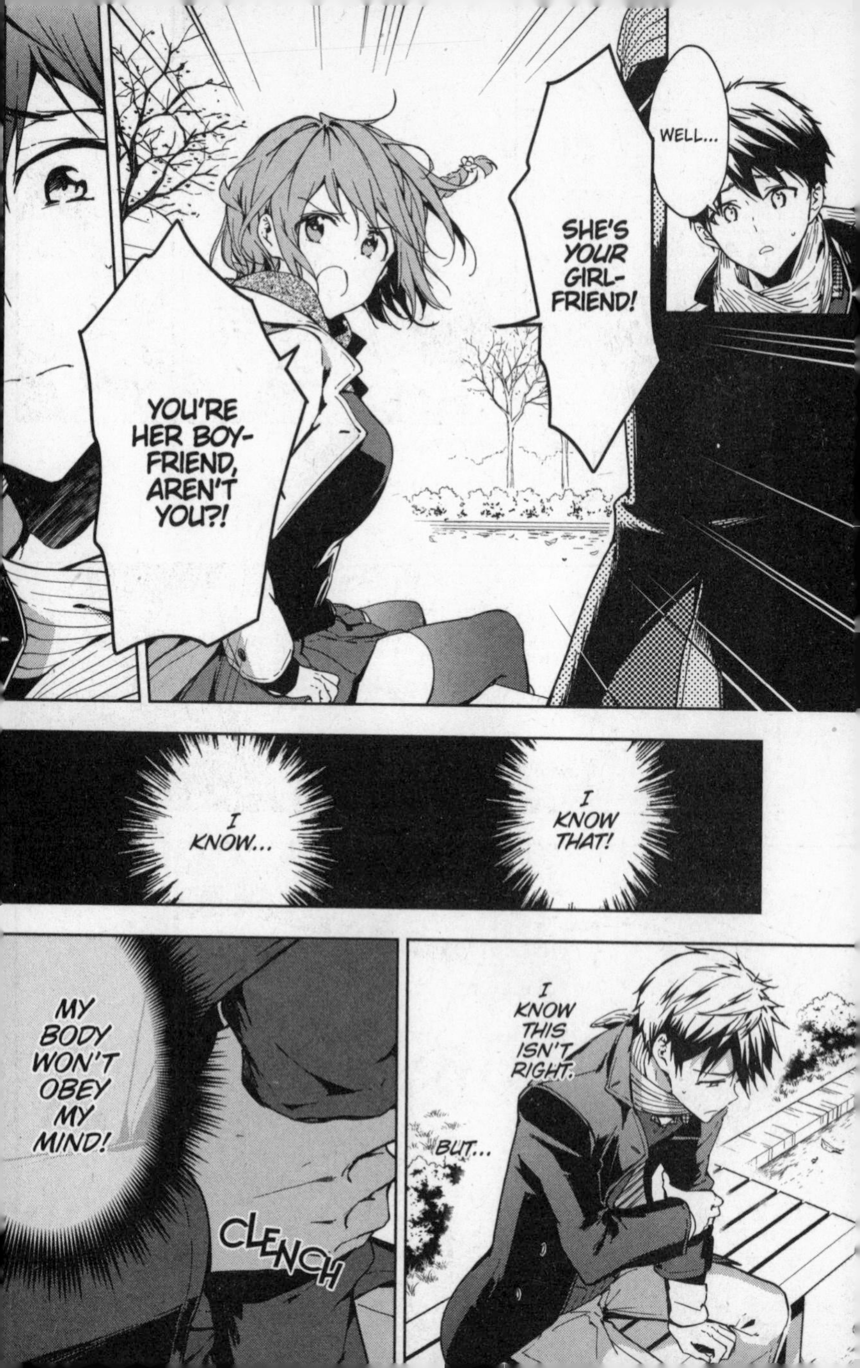
WELL...
SHE'S YOUR GIRL-FRIEND!
YOU'RE HER BOY-FRIEND, AREN'T YOU?!
I KNOW THAT!
I KNOW...
I KNOW THIS ISN'T RIGHT.
BUT...
MY BODY WON'T OBEY MY MIND!
CLENCH

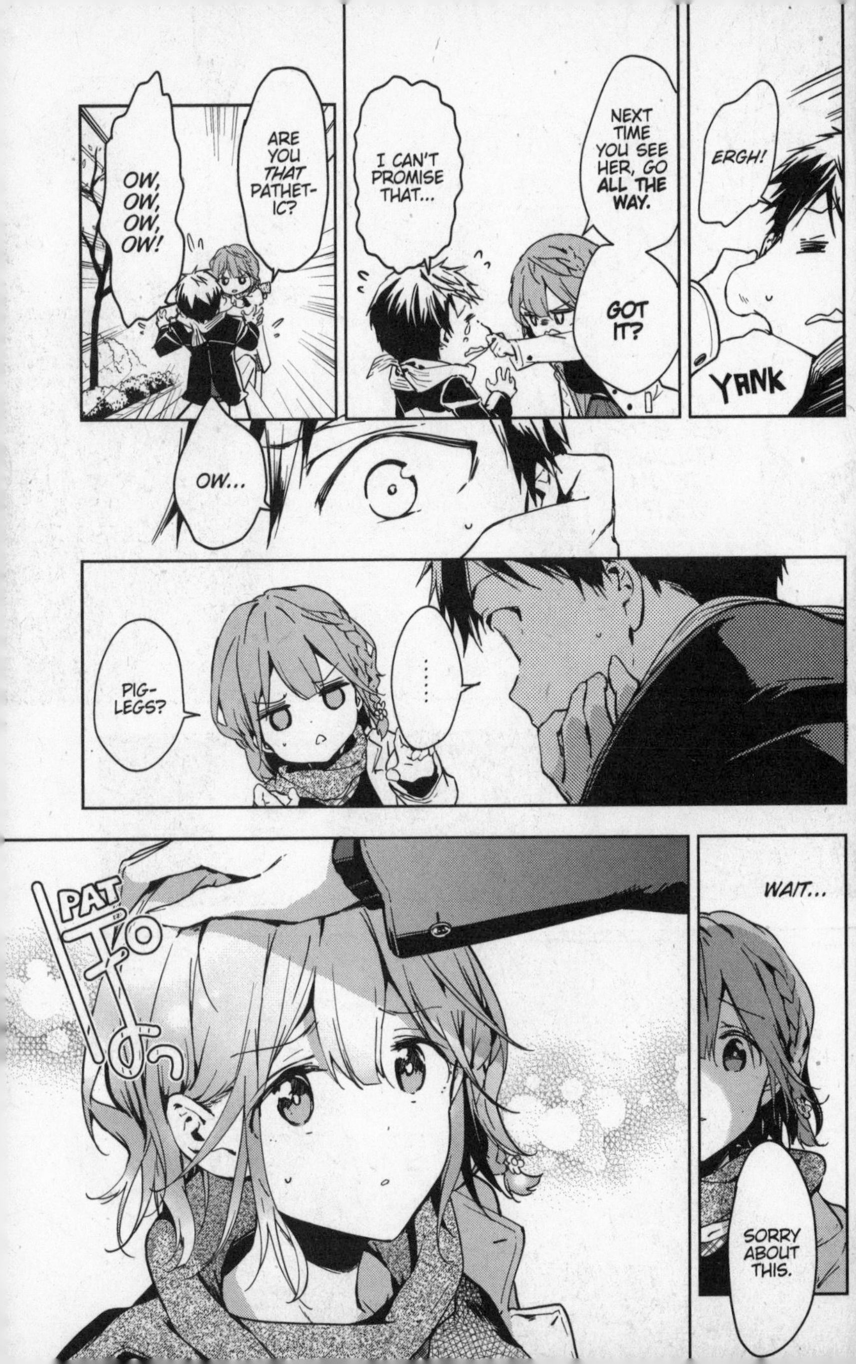
ERGH!
YANK
NEXT TIME YOU SEE HER, GO ALL THE WAY.
GOT IT?
I CAN'T PROMISE THAT...
ARE YOU *THAT* PATHETIC?
OW, OW, OW, OW!
OW...
......
PIG-LEGS?
WAIT...
SORRY ABOUT THIS.
PAT

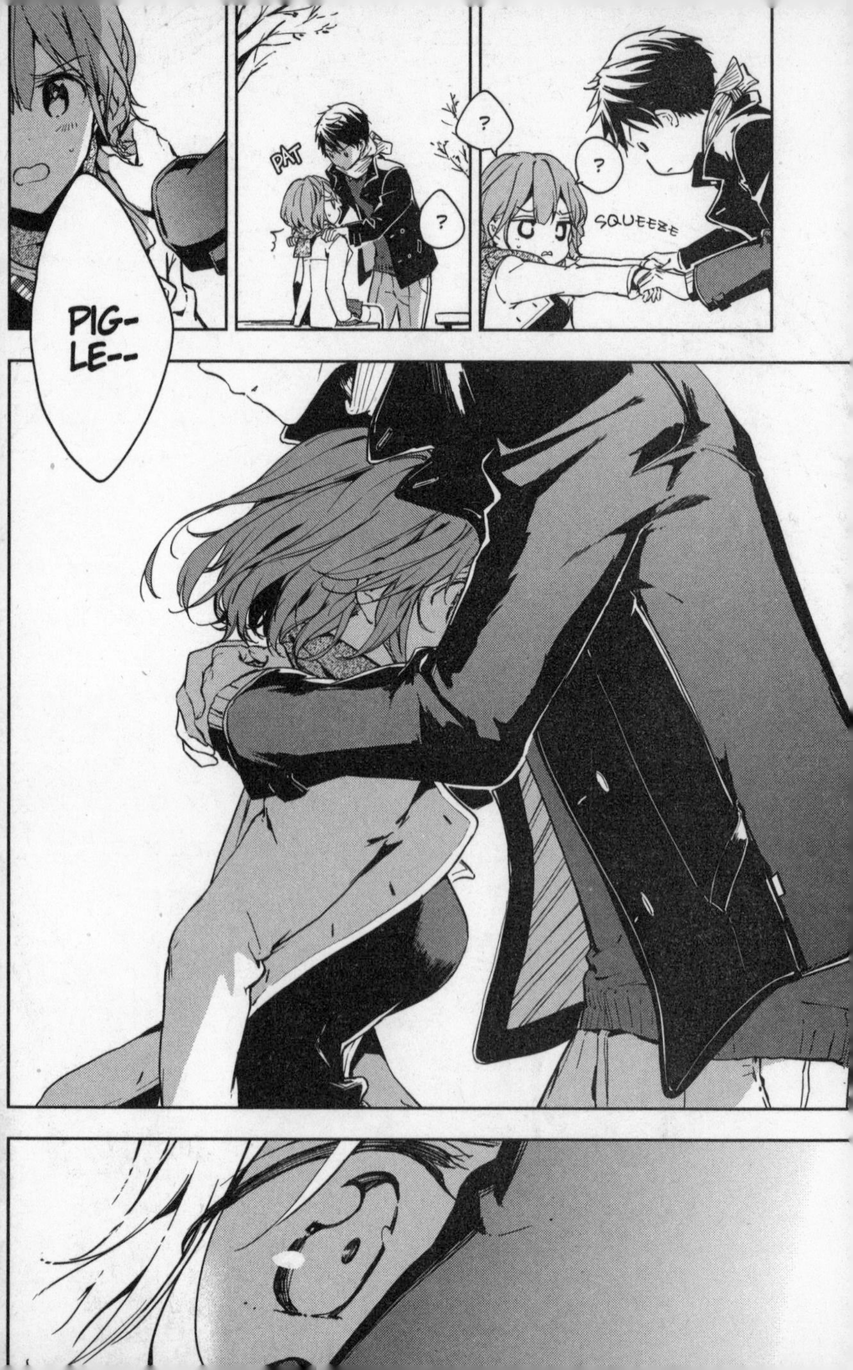
?
?
SQUEEZE
PAT
?
PIG-
LE--

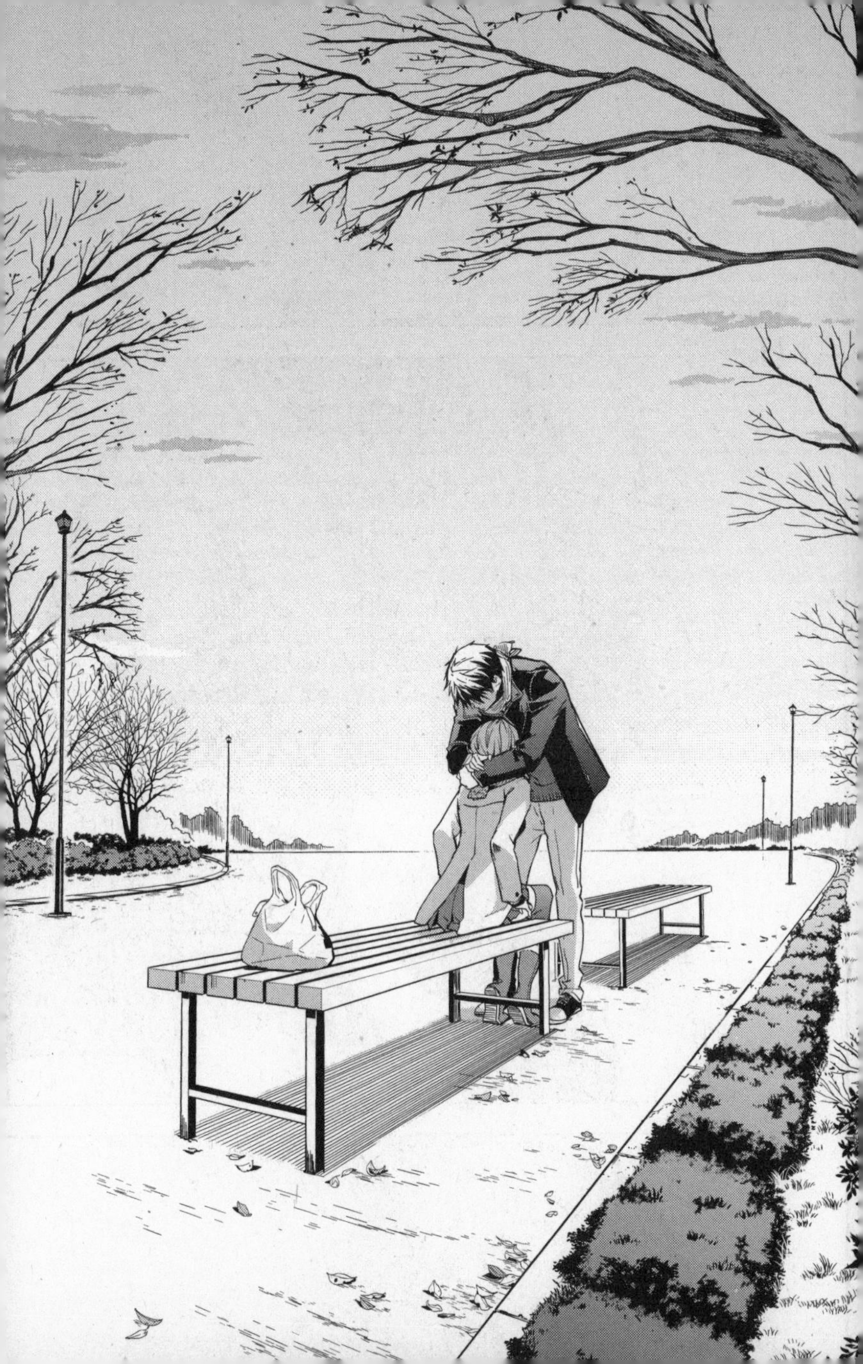

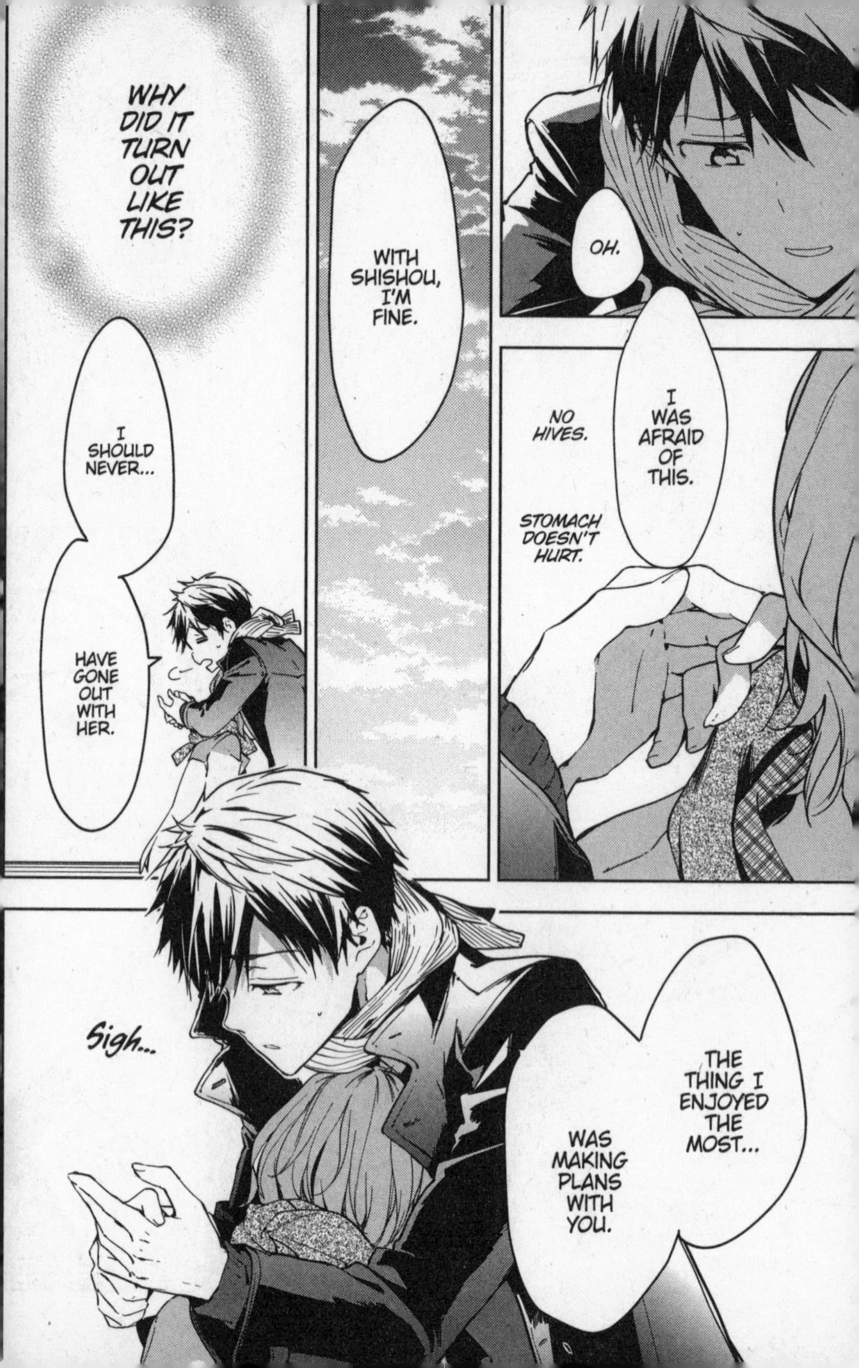
OH.
I WAS AFRAID OF THIS.
NO HIVES.
STOMACH DOESN'T HURT.
WITH SHISHOU, I'M FINE.
WHY DID IT TURN OUT LIKE THIS?
I SHOULD NEVER...
HAVE GONE OUT WITH HER.
THE THING I ENJOYED THE MOST...
WAS MAKING PLANS WITH YOU.
Sigh...

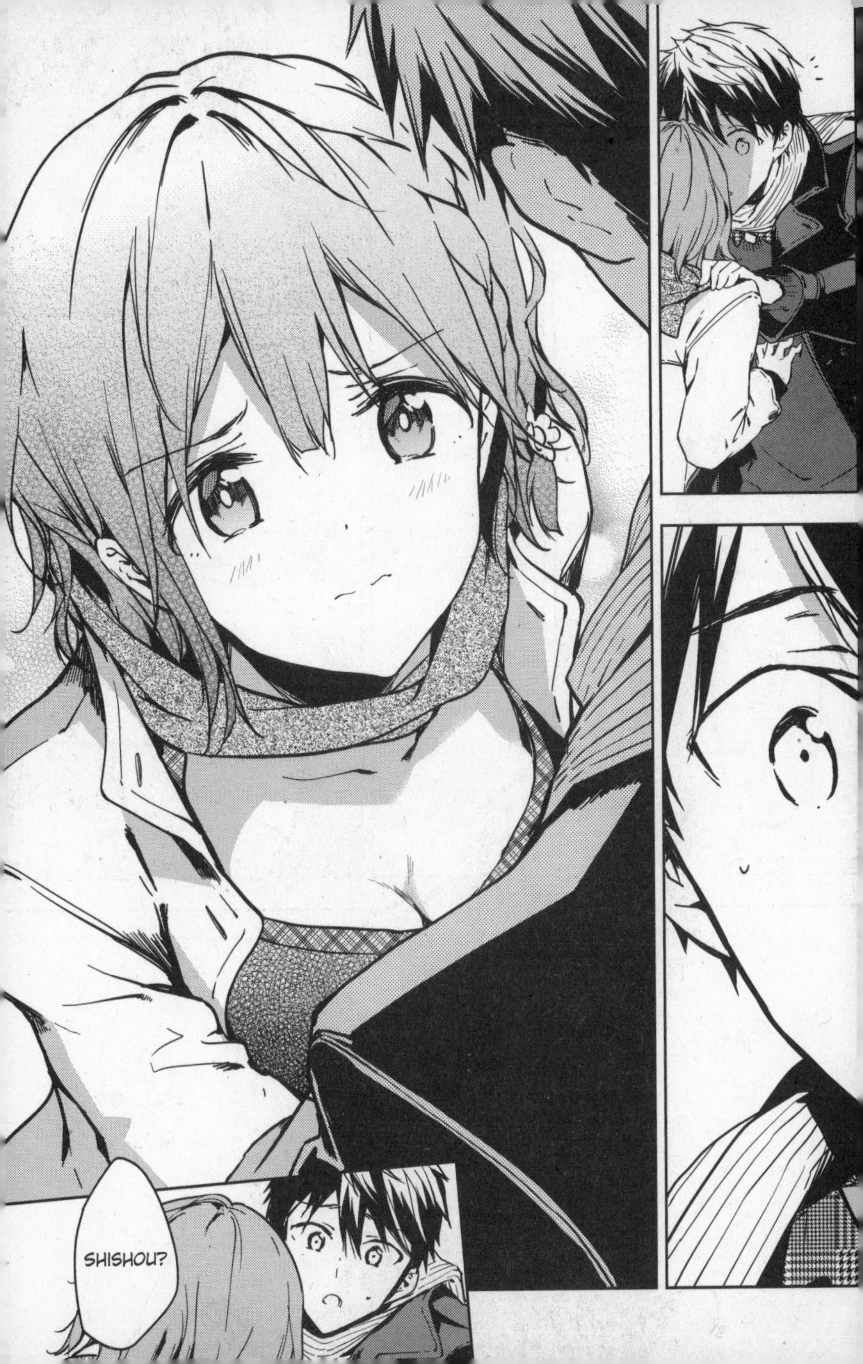
SHISHOU?

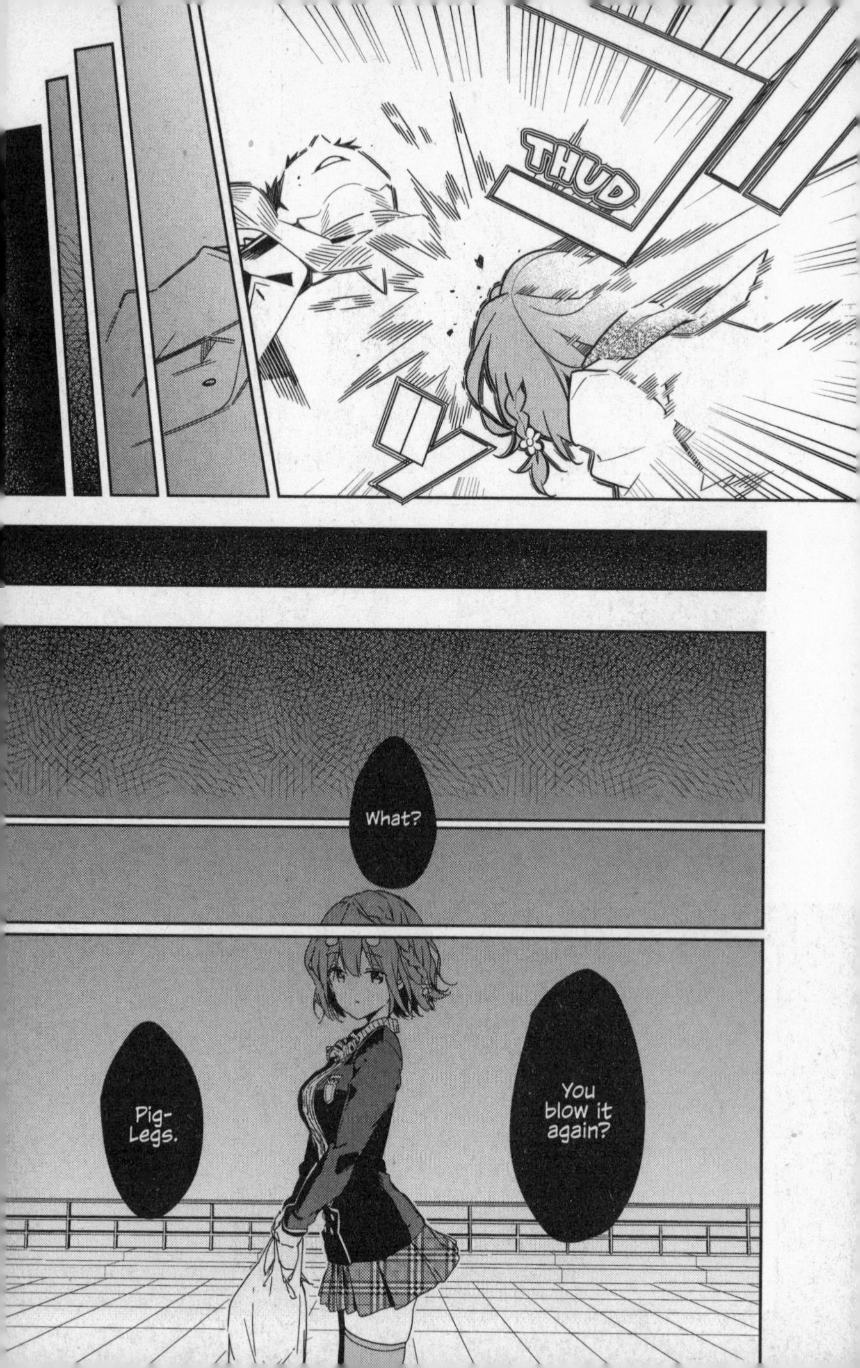
THUD
What?
You blow it again?
Pig-Legs.

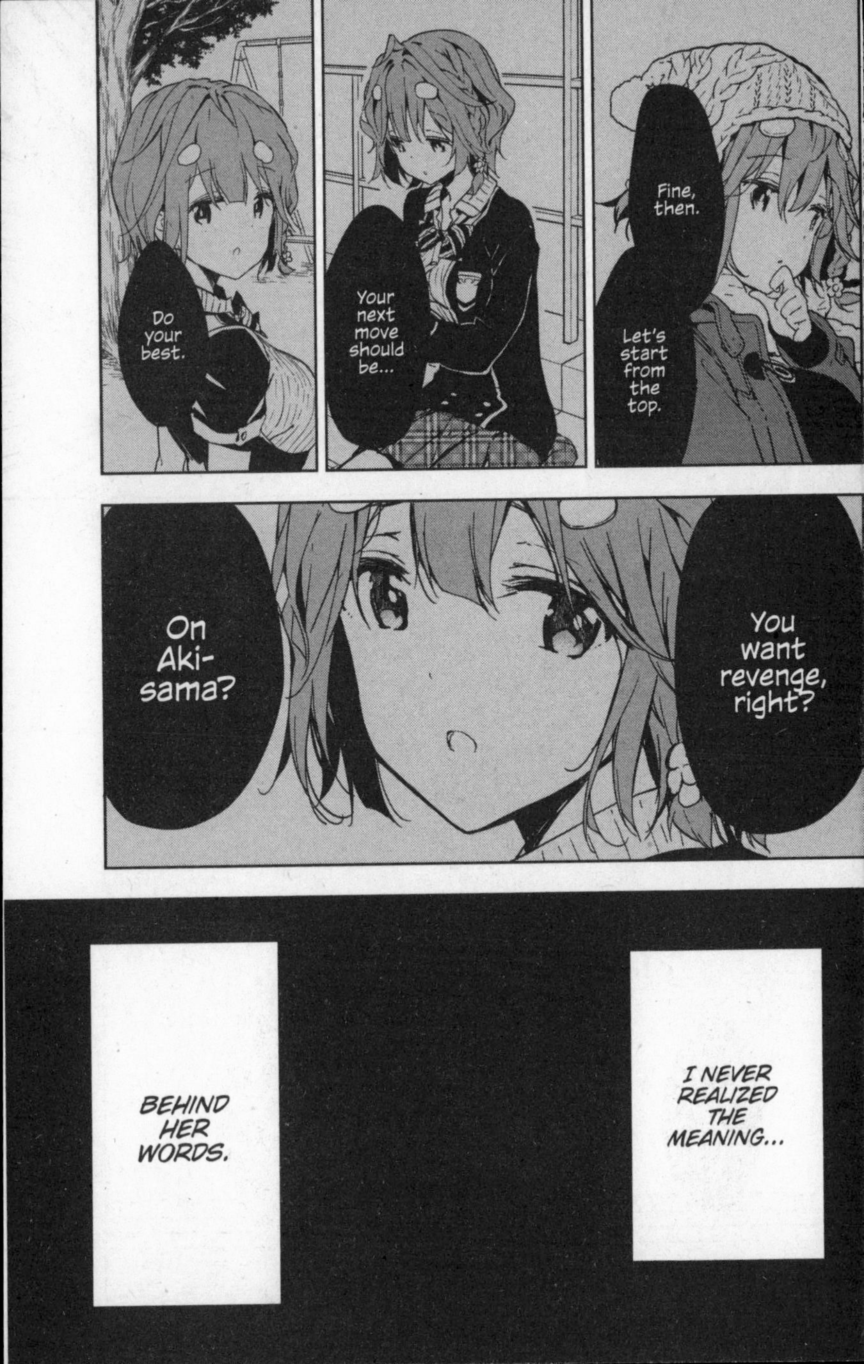
Fine, then.
Let's start from the top.
Your next move should be...
Do your best.
You want revenge, right?
On Aki-sama?
I NEVER REALIZED THE MEANING...
BEHIND HER WORDS.

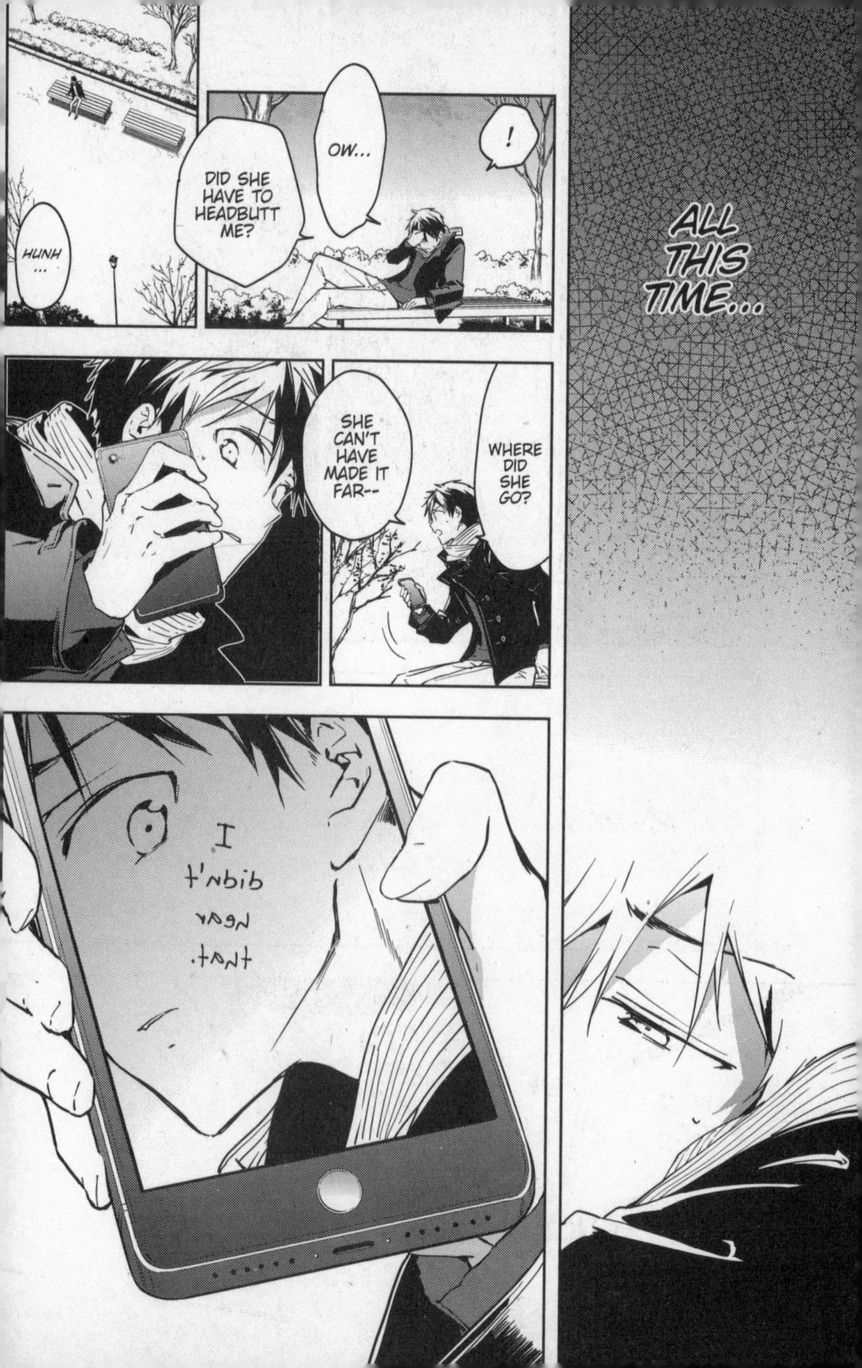
!
OW...
DID SHE HAVE TO HEADBUTT ME?
HUNH ...
WHERE DID SHE GO?
SHE CAN'T HAVE MADE IT FAR--
I didn't hear that.
ALL THIS TIME...

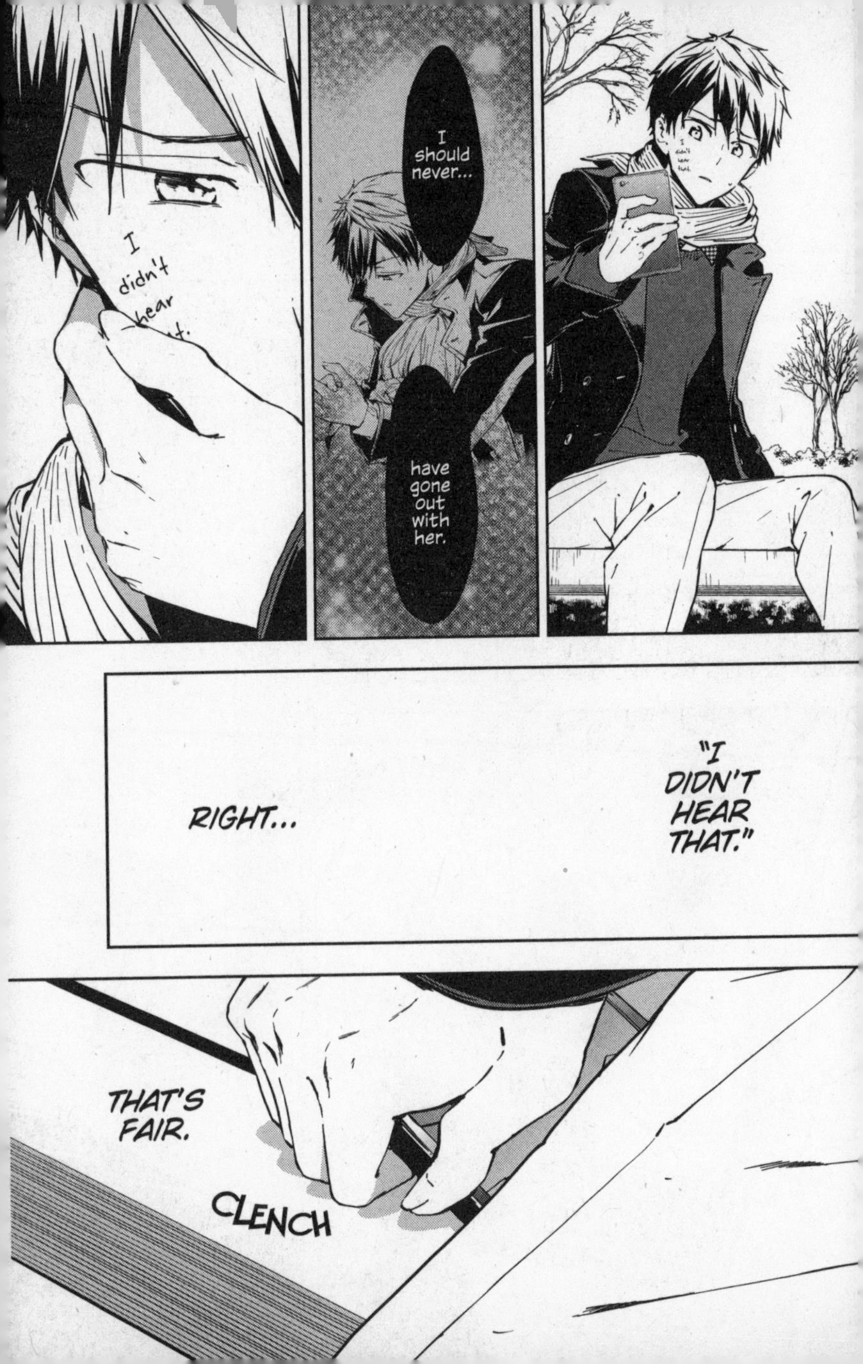
I didn't hear that.
I should never...
have gone out with her.
I didn't hear
"I DIDN'T HEAR THAT."
RIGHT...
THAT'S FAIR.
CLENCH

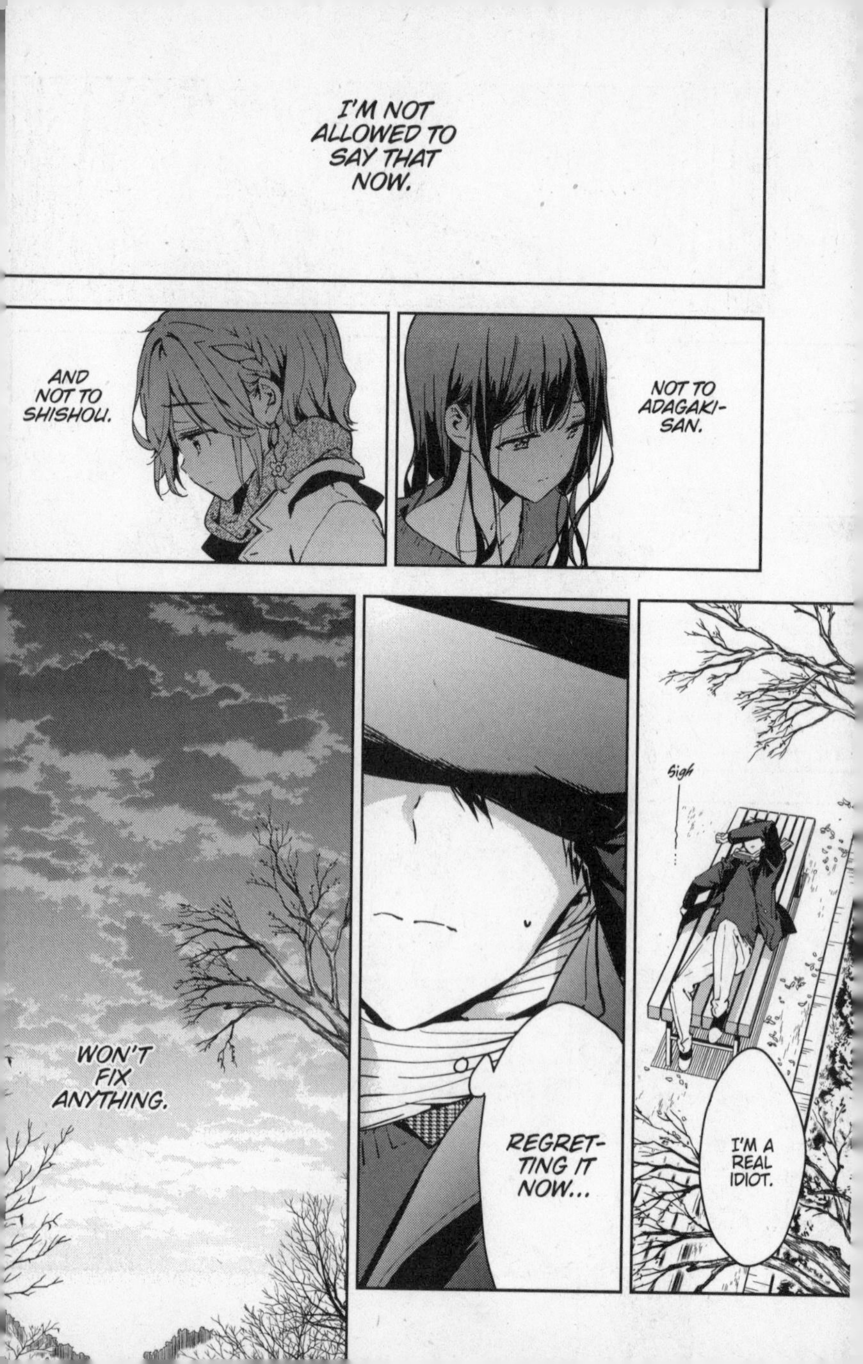
I'M NOT ALLOWED TO SAY THAT NOW.
NOT TO ADAGAKI-SAN.
AND NOT TO SHISHOU.
Sigh
I'M A REAL IDIOT.
REGRETTING IT NOW...
WON'T FIX ANYTHING.

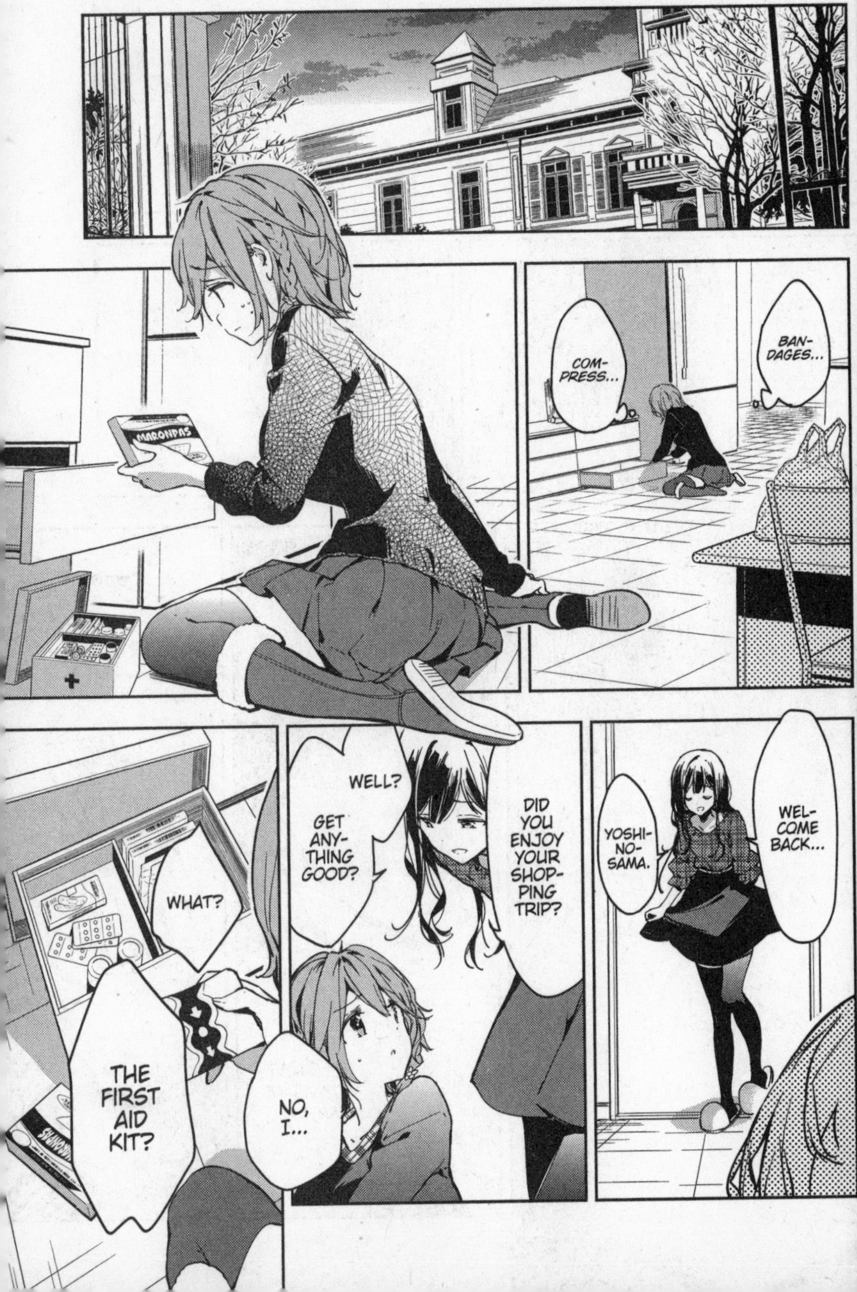
BAN-DAGES...
COM-PRESS...
MARONPAS
WEL-COME BACK...
YOSHI-NO-SAMA.
DID YOU ENJOY YOUR SHOP-PING TRIP?
WELL?
GET ANY-THING GOOD?
WHAT?
THE FIRST AID KIT?
NO, I...

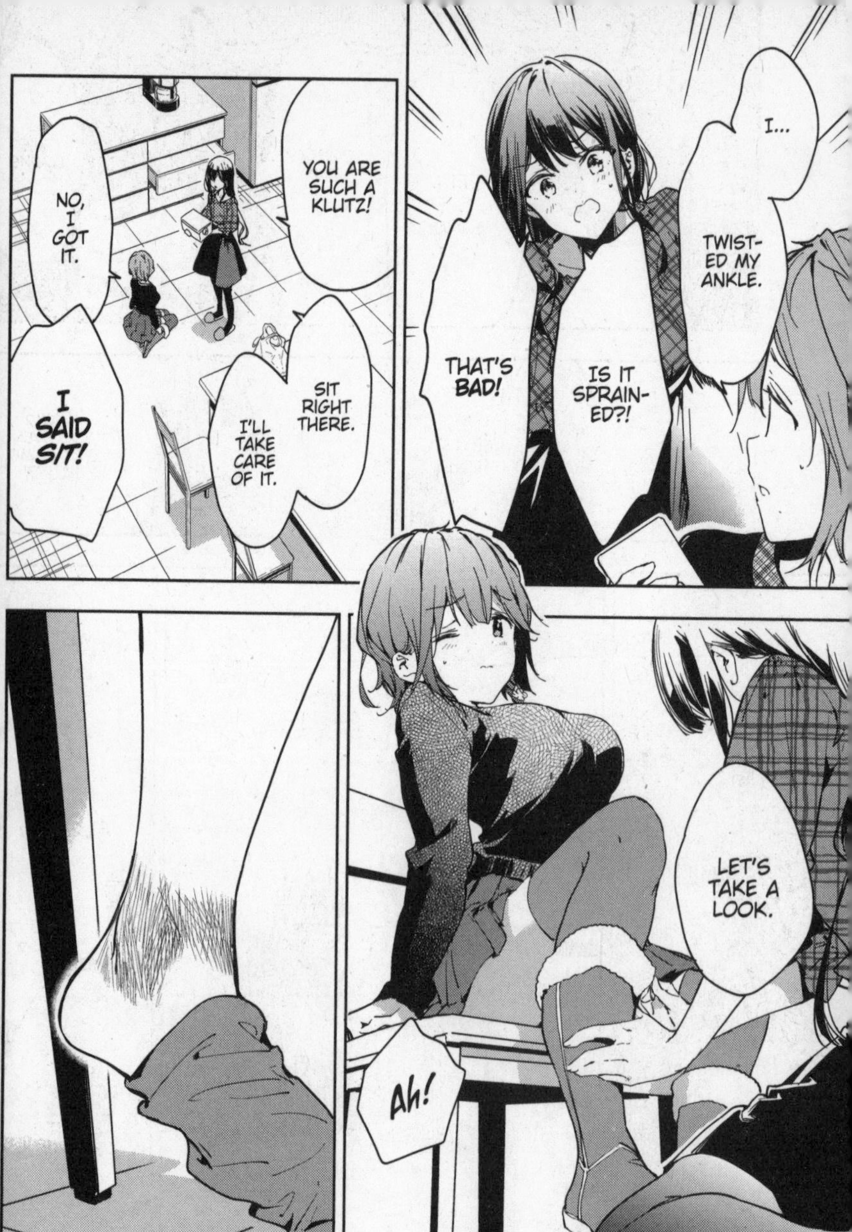
I...
TWIST-ED MY ANKLE.
IS IT SPRAIN-ED?!
THAT'S BAD!
YOU ARE SUCH A KLUTZ!
NO, I GOT IT.
SIT RIGHT THERE.
I'LL TAKE CARE OF IT.
I SAID SIT!
LET'S TAKE A LOOK.
Ah!

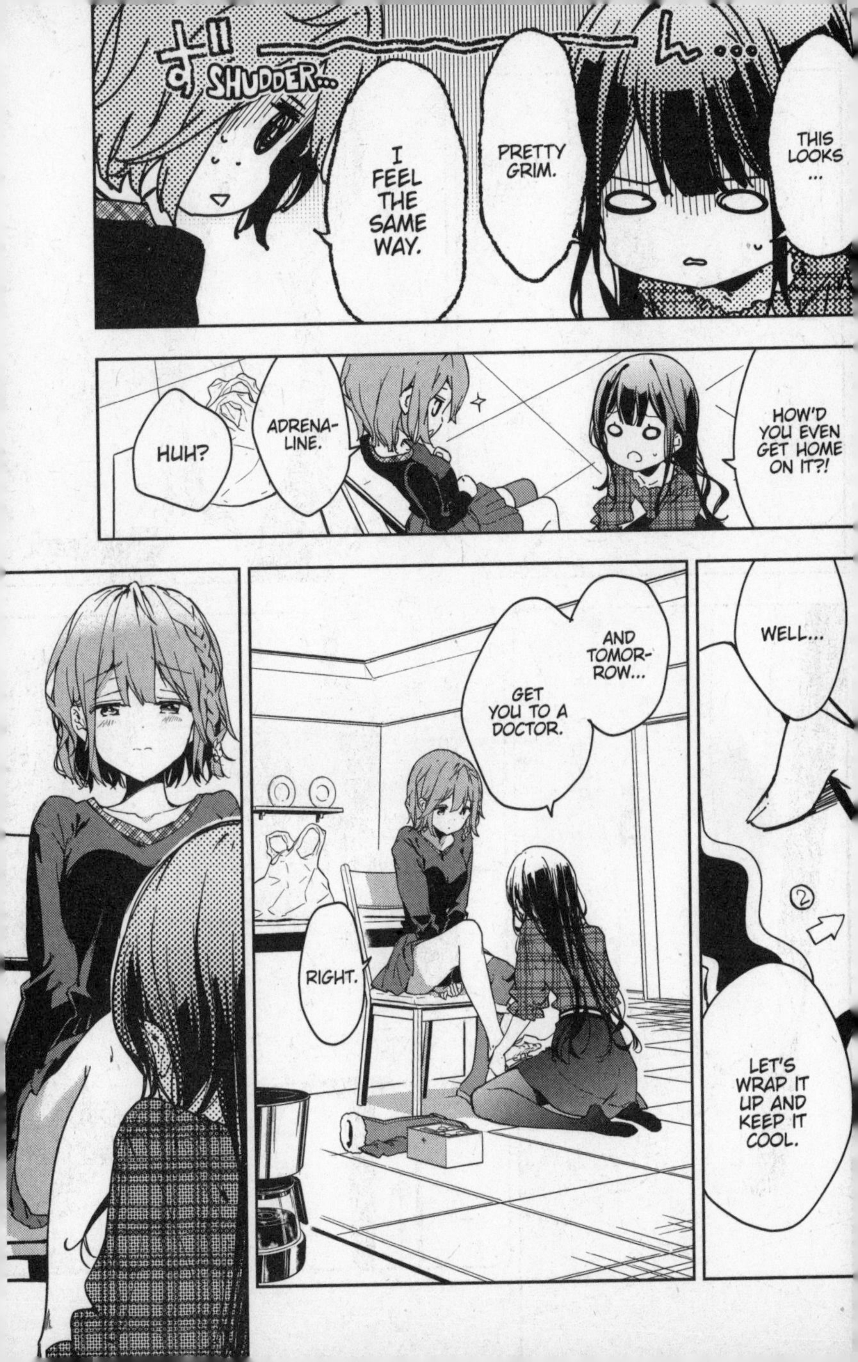
THIS LOOKS ...
PRETTY GRIM.
I FEEL THE SAME WAY.
SHUDDER...
HOW'D YOU EVEN GET HOME ON IT?!
ADRENA-LINE.
HUH?
WELL...
LET'S WRAP IT UP AND KEEP IT COOL.
AND TOMOR-ROW...
GET YOU TO A DOCTOR.
RIGHT.

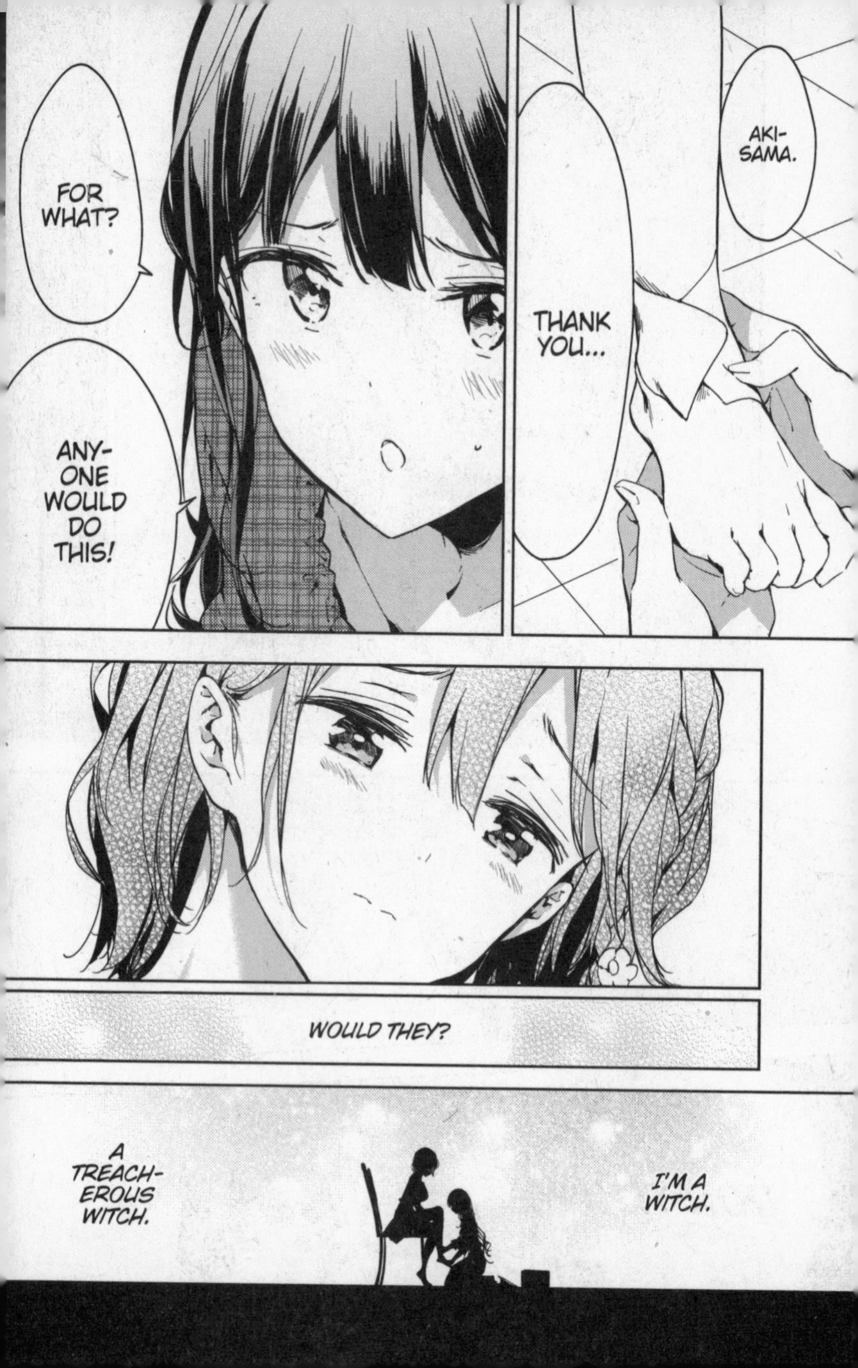
AKI-SAMA.
THANK YOU...
FOR WHAT?
ANY-ONE WOULD DO THIS!
WOULD THEY?
I'M A WITCH.
A TREACH-EROUS WITCH.

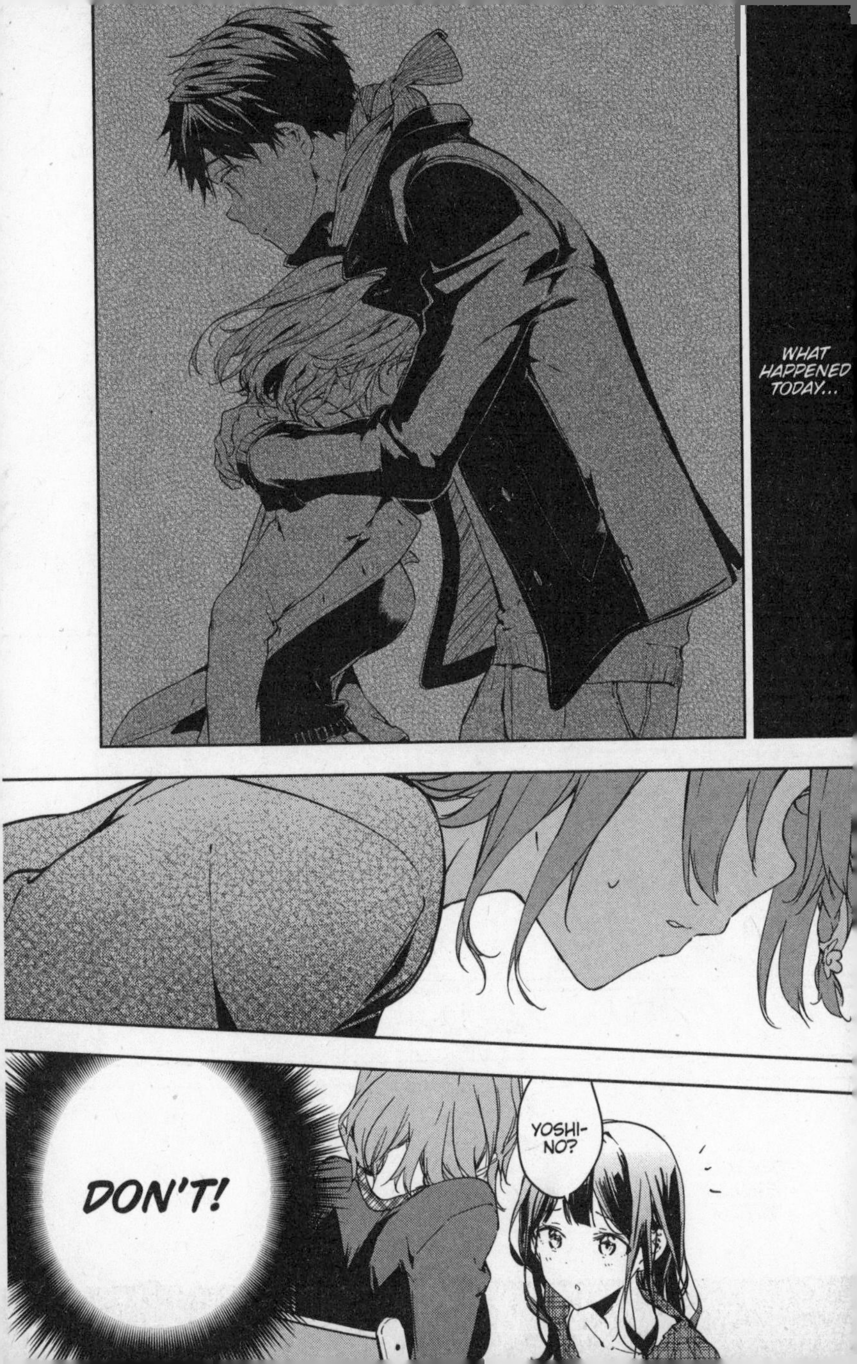
WHAT HAPPENED TODAY...
YOSHI-NO?
DON'T!

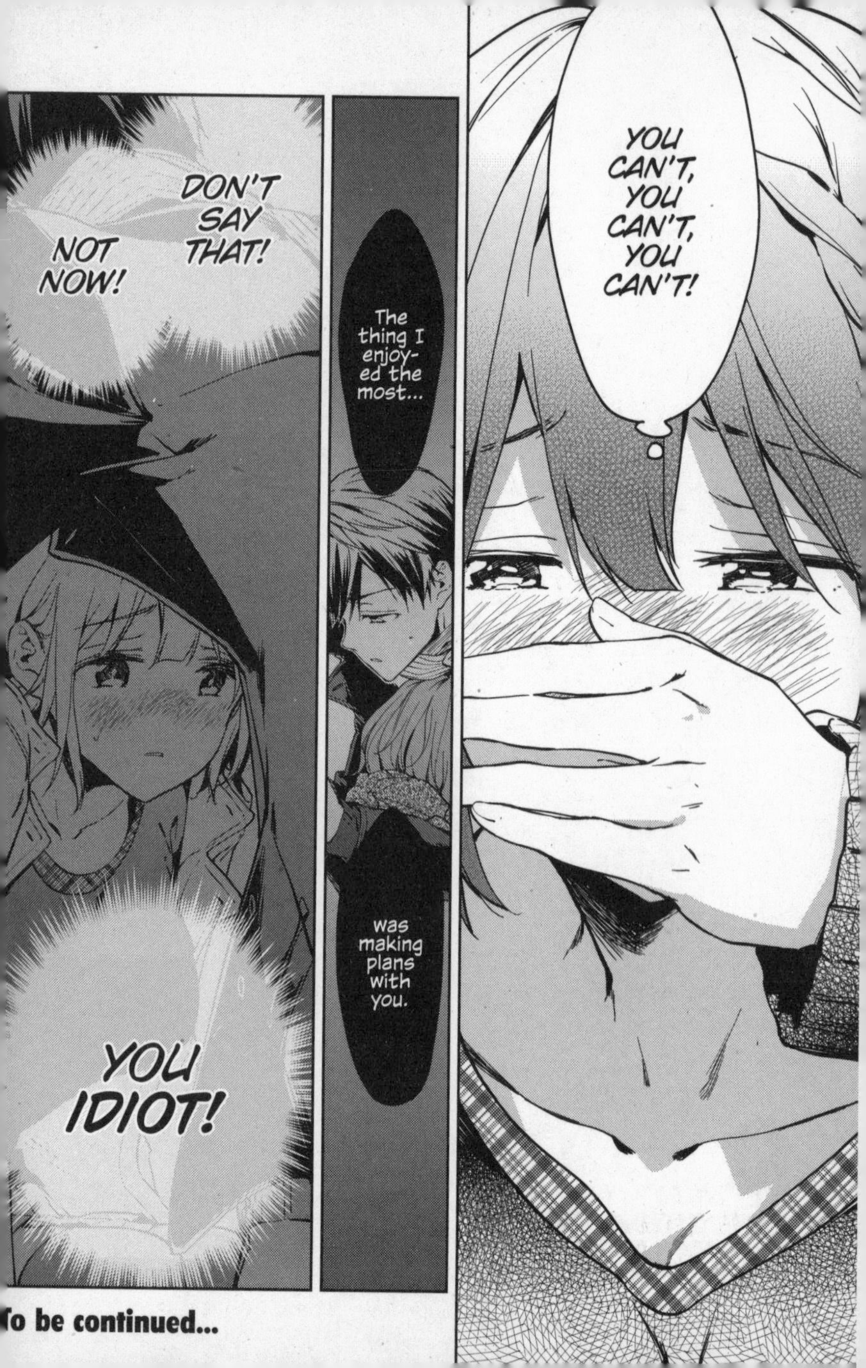
YOU CAN'T, YOU CAN'T, YOU CAN'T!
The thing I enjoy-ed the most...
was making plans with you.
DON'T SAY THAT!
NOT NOW!
YOU IDIOT!

To be continued...